GRADE 5

Student Guide

THIRD EDITION

KENDALL/HUNT PUBLISHING COMPANY
4050 Westmark Drive   Dubuque, Iowa 52002

A TIMS® Curriculum
University of Illinois at Chicago

MATH TRAILBLAZERS®

Dedication

This book is dedicated to
the children and teachers who
let us see the magic in their classrooms
and to our families who wholeheartedly
supported us while we searched for
ways to make it happen.

The TIMS Project

 UIC The University of Illinois
at Chicago

The original edition was based on work supported by the National Science Foundation under grant No. MDR 9050226 and the University of Illinois at Chicago. Any opinions, findings, and conclusions or recommendations expressed in this publication are those of the authors and do not necessarily reflect the views of the granting agencies.

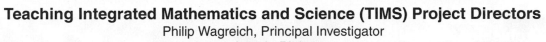
Acknowledgments

Teaching Integrated Mathematics and Science (TIMS) Project Directors
Philip Wagreich, Principal Investigator
Joan L. Bieler
Howard Goldberg (emeritus)
Catherine Randall Kelso

Principal Investigators

First Edition	Philip Wagreich	
	Howard Goldberg	

Directors

Third Edition	Joan L. Bieler	
Second Edition	Catherine Randall Kelso	

Senior Curriculum Developers

First Edition	Janet Simpson Beissinger	Carol Inzerillo
	Joan L. Bieler	Andy Isaacs
	Astrida Cirulis	Catherine Randall Kelso
	Marty Gartzman	Leona Peters
	Howard Goldberg	Philip Wagreich

Curriculum Developers

Third Edition	Janet Simpson Beissinger	Philip Wagreich
	Lindy M. Chambers-Boucher	
Second Edition	Lindy M. Chambers-Boucher	Jennifer Mundt Leimberer
	Elizabeth Colligan	Georganne E. Marsh
	Marty Gartzman	Leona Peters
	Carol Inzerillo	Philip Wagreich
	Catherine Randall Kelso	
First Edition	Janice C. Banasiak	Jenny Knight
	Lynne Beauprez	Sandy Niemiera
	Andy Carter	Janice Ozima
	Lindy M. Chambers-Boucher	Polly Tangora
	Kathryn Chval	Paul Trafton
	Diane Czerwinski	

Illustrator

	Kris Dresen	

Editorial and Production Staff

Third Edition	Kathleen R. Anderson	Anne Roby
	Lindy M. Chambers-Boucher	
Second Edition	Kathleen R. Anderson	Georganne E. Marsh
	Ai-Ai C. Cojuangco	Cosmina Menghes
	Andrada Costoiu	Anne Roby
	Erika Larson	
First Edition	Glenda L. Genio-Terrado	Sarah Nelson
	Mini Joseph	Biruté Petrauskas
	Lynelle Morgenthaler	

Acknowledgments

TIMS Professional Developers

Barbara Crum
Catherine Ditto
Pamela Guyton

Cheryl Kneubuhler
Lisa Mackey
Linda Miceli

TIMS Director of Media Services

Henrique Cirne-Lima

TIMS Research Staff

Stacy Brown
Reality Canty

Catherine Ditto
Catherine Randall Kelso

TIMS Administrative Staff

Eve Ali Boles
Kathleen R. Anderson
Nida Khan

Enrique Puente
Alice VanSlyke

Research Consultant

First Edition   Andy Isaacs

Mathematics Education Consultant

First Edition   Paul Trafton

National Advisory Committee

First Edition

Carl Berger
Tom Berger
Hugh Burkhardt
Donald Chambers
Naomi Fisher
Glenda Lappan

Mary Lindquist
Eugene Maier
Lourdes Monteagudo
Elizabeth Phillips
Thomas Post

TIMS Project Staff

Table of Contents

Additional student pages may be found in the *Discovery Assignment Book*, *Adventure Book*, or the *Unit Resource Guide*.

Table of Contents

Additional student pages may be found in the *Discovery Assignment Book, Adventure Book,* or the *Unit Resource Guide.*

Table of Contents

Additional student pages may be found in the *Discovery Assignment Book, Adventure Book,* or the *Unit Resource Guide.*

Dear Parents,

Math Trailblazers® is based on the ideas that mathematics is best learned through solving many different kinds of problems and that all children deserve a challenging mathematics curriculum. The program provides a careful balance of concepts and skills. Traditional arithmetic skills and procedures are covered through their repeated use in problems and through distributed practice. *Math Trailblazers,* however, offers much more. Students using this program will become proficient problem solvers, will know when and how to apply the mathematics they have learned, and will be able to clearly communicate their mathematical knowledge. Computation, measurement, geometry, data collection and analysis, estimation, graphing, patterns and relationships, mental arithmetic, and simple algebraic ideas are all an integral part of the curriculum. They will see connections between the mathematics learned in school and the mathematics used in everyday life. And, they will enjoy and value the work they do in mathematics.

The *Student Guide* is only one component of *Math Trailblazers.* Additional material and lessons are contained in the *Discovery Assignment Book*, the *Adventure Book,* and in the teacher's *Unit Resource Guides.* If you have questions about the program, we encourage you to speak with your child's teacher.

This curriculum was built around national recommendations for improving mathematics instruction in American schools and the research that supported those recommendations. The first edition was extensively tested with thousands of children in dozens of classrooms over five years of development. In preparing the second and third editions, we have benefited from the comments and suggestions of hundreds of teachers and children who have used the curriculum. *Math Trailblazers* reflects our view of a complete and well-balanced mathematics program that will prepare children for the 21st century—a world in which mathematical skills will be important in most occupations and mathematical reasoning will be essential for acting as an informed citizen in a democratic society. We hope that you enjoy this exciting approach to learning mathematics and that you watch your child's mathematical abilities grow throughout the year.

Philip Wagreich

Philip Wagreich
Professor, Department of Mathematics, Statistics, and Computer Science
Director, Institute for Mathematics and Science Education
Teaching Integrated Mathematics and Science (TIMS) Project
University of Illinois at Chicago

Unit 1

Populations and Samples

	Student Guide	Discovery Assignment Book	Adventure Book	Unit Resource Guide*
Lesson 1				
Eyelets	●			●
Lesson 2				
Review: Representing Data				●
Lesson 3				
Analyzing Data	●			
Lesson 4				
A Matter of Survival			●	
Lesson 5				
Searching the Forest	●			●
Lesson 6				
Practice Problems	●			

Unit Resource Guide pages are from the teacher materials.

Eyelets

Slip-ons and Sneakers

"I'm not sure those sneakers go with that outfit, Blanca," Mrs. Campos said. "Why don't you wear your slip-ons? I think that would look pretty."

"I hate those slip-ons, Mama," answered Blanca. "Nobody wears shoes like that anymore. Don't you want me to look stylish for my first day of fifth grade?"

"Of course I want you to look nice," Mrs. Campos answered. "That's no problem—you're a beautiful girl. But those sneakers . . ."

"Trust me, Mom," interrupted Blanca. "This look is cool."

Later, at school, Blanca met her friend Irma. "¡Hola! Irma. Guess what? My mom wanted me to wear slip-ons for the first day of school. She said sneakers don't go with my outfit."

"Oh, no!" said Irma. "How'd you convince her to let you wear them?"

"I told her to trust me, and she did—for today," said Blanca. "But I'm afraid she'll make me wear those ugly shoes sooner or later. How can I convince her that nobody wears slip-ons anymore?"

"I don't know. You could bring your mom here and just have her look around. There's not a slip-on in sight."

"That's it! I'll do a survey of the shoes everybody's wearing. It will show her that not one kid wears slip-ons anymore," said Blanca.

"Just like those surveys we did last year," said Irma. "Can I help?"

"Sure. Let's get started."

Blanca and Irma did their survey. They studied the kinds of shoes the students in their class wore the first day of school. This is what they found:

Kind of Shoe	Number of Pairs of Shoes
High-top Sneakers	9
Low-top Sneakers	8
Lace Boots	4
Sandals	3
Slip-ons	0

 **Discuss**

1. **A.** Do you think Blanca's data will help her convince her mother that slip-ons are not fashionable?

   B. Would a graph help?

2. What is the most common kind of shoe in Blanca's class?

3. If you surveyed your class, how do you think the data would compare with Blanca's?

4. What kind of shoes are stylish in your school?

Variables are things that change or vary in an experiment or survey. Blanca and Irma's survey has two main variables: "Kind of Shoe" and "Number of Pairs of Shoes." The kinds of shoes vary from high-top sneakers to lace boots to sandals.

All the kinds of shoes listed in the first column of the data table are values of the variable Kind of Shoe. The number of pairs of shoes varied from 0 to 9 pairs. We can say that 0, 3, 4, 8, 9 are values of the variable "number of pairs of shoes." So, the possible outcomes for each variable are called **values.**

5. What else could you study about the way people look and the way they dress? Make a list of variables you could study. List two or three values for each variable. Make a table like the one shown.

Variables and Possible Values

Variables	Values
Kind of Shoe	High-top Sneakers, Lace Boots, Slip-ons
Number of Pairs of Shoes	0, 3, 5
Shirt Color	White, Red, Plaid
Height	56 inches, 58 inches

Numerical variables are variables with values that are numbers. Number of pairs of shoes and height are numerical variables. **Categorical variables** have values that are not numbers. Kind of shoe and shirt color are examples of categorical variables.

6. On the data table you made for Question 5, write an *N* beside the numerical variables. Write a *C* beside the categorical variables.

Eyelets

In this lab, you will answer a certain question about how the students in your class dress for school. As you do the lab, you will learn a method that you can use to find answers to other questions—questions about how people dress or questions that have nothing to do with clothing. We call this method the TIMS Laboratory Method. This method is very much like the method scientists use in their investigations.

Usually, an investigation begins with a question. For this investigation, we ask the question: *How many eyelets are on students' shoes in your class?*

To answer this question scientifically, we need to identify the important variables. The two main variables in the lab are:

- the total number of eyelets on a pair of shoes (*E*)
- the number of pairs of shoes (*P*).

Your class will conduct a survey to answer the question.

Draw

A picture is a good way to show what an experiment is about and what the important variables are. In most experiments that use the TIMS Laboratory Method you draw a picture. Here is a sample picture for this experiment:

7. Draw your own picture of the experiment. Be sure to label the variables.

E = number of eyelets on two shoes

P = number of pairs of shoes with that number of eyelets

Collect

Experiments involve counting or measuring. The information you collect during a survey or experiment is called **data.** Organizing and checking data are important parts of a scientist's work. A good tool for handling data is a data table. Here is a data table for *Eyelets:*

8. Gather data from students in your class. Your teacher will make a class data table. Your teacher may also ask you to make your own data table.

| E
Number of Eyelets | P
Number of Pairs of Shoes |
|---|---|
| | |
| | |
| | |
| | |

Scientists look for patterns in data. Graphing your data can help you see patterns that are hard to notice in the data table. The third step in the TIMS Laboratory Method is graphing.

9. Make a bar graph of your class data. Graph the Number of Eyelets (E) on the horizontal axis (⟷). Graph the Number of Pairs of Shoes (P) on the vertical axis (⇕) .

The last step in the TIMS Laboratory Method is analyzing the whole experiment. This means understanding what happened and using your understanding to make predictions. Questions for new investigations may also come up during this step. Most labs have questions to help you better understand the important ideas. Your teacher may ask you to answer these questions alone or in small groups. Be ready to explain how you found your answers.

Use the class graph and data table to answer the following questions.

10. **A.** How many pairs of shoes have 20 eyelets?

    B. How many pairs of shoes have 8 eyelets?

    C. How many pairs of shoes have 0 eyelets?

11. **A.** What number of eyelets is most common in your class? (This number is called the **mode.**)

    B. How can you find the mode by looking at your graph?

12. **A.** List all the values for Number of Eyelets that have bars above them.

    B. What do you notice about these numbers? Explain.

13. Alexis told her class that she had 14 eyelets on her pair of shoes. Do you think she is correct? Why or why not?

14. Describe the shape of your graph.

   A. How many bars are on your graph?

   B. Are the bars all about the same height or are some bars much taller than others?

   C. Are the tallest bars at the beginning, middle, or end of the graph?

15. Describe the *Eyelets* graph for a professional basketball team. (Would the tallest bars be at the beginning, middle, or end of the graph? Would there be many bars or just one or two?)

16. Describe the *Eyelets* graph for data collected at the beach. (Would the tallest bars be at the beginning, middle, or end of the graph? Would there be many bars or just one or two?)

17. What is the total number of eyelets in your class?

18. Estimate how many eyelets are on all the shoes of all the fifth-grade students in your school. Explain how you made your estimate.

19. How would the graph be different if you gathered data from all the fifth graders in your school?

The TIMS Laboratory Method

You will use the TIMS Laboratory Method many times this year. In this lab, you used the TIMS Laboratory Method to study the number of eyelets on the shoes of the students in your class. There were four steps:

- **Draw.** The investigation started with a question. The question was made clearer by identifying variables that could be counted or measured. A picture showed what the experiment was about.
- **Collect.** You used data tables to organize the data.
- **Graph.** A graph showed patterns in the data more clearly than the table.
- **Explore.** You answered questions about the lab and thought about what might make things turn out differently.

Three Schools

Here are *Eyelets* graphs from three schools: Augusta Academy, Toussaint School, and G.W. Carver Elementary School. Augusta Academy is a school in New Jersey where all the students wear uniforms; Toussaint School is in Haiti in the Caribbean; G.W. Carver School is in the American Midwest. The graphs are not labeled, so you cannot tell which graph comes from which school.

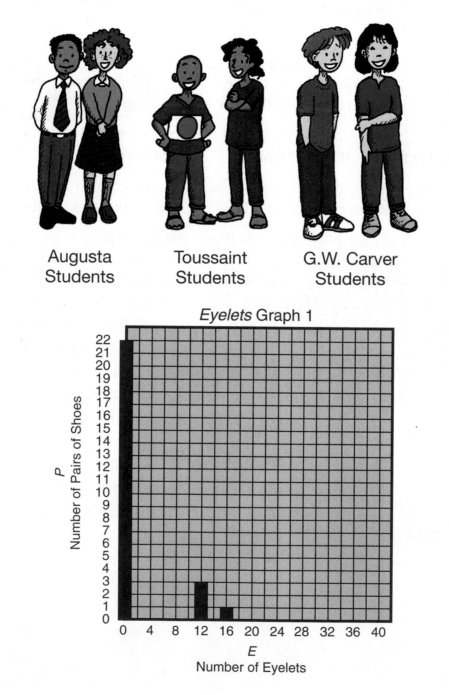

Augusta Students   Toussaint Students   G.W. Carver Students

Eyelets Graph 1

P Number of Pairs of Shoes (vertical axis, 0–22)

E Number of Eyelets (horizontal axis, 0 4 8 12 16 20 24 28 32 36 40)

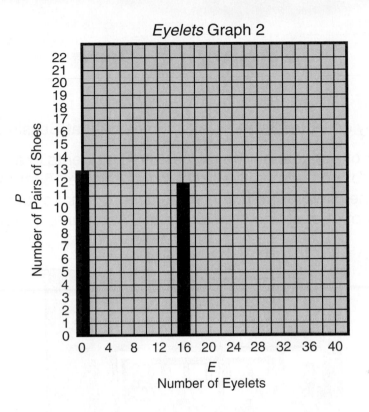

Eyelets Graph 2

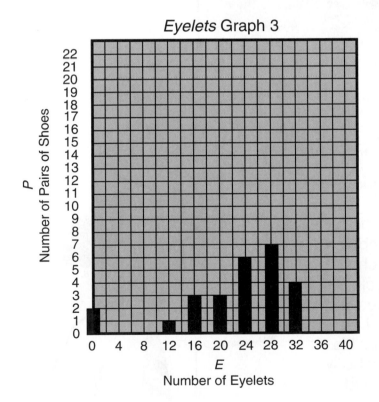

Eyelets Graph 3

1. Tell which graph you think goes with each school. Explain why you think so. (*Hint:* Tell why the bars on each graph are where they are.)

2. What is the mode for each graph? (The mode is the most common number of eyelets.)

3. Which graph is most like your class's graph? Which school do you think is most like your school? Explain.

4. What would an eyelets graph look like if you collected data in a kindergarten at your school? Describe the graph using words, a sketch, or both.

Eyelets

Analyzing Data

Which Graph Is Which?

Professor Peabody collected three sets of survey data at Bessie Coleman School.

- the number of pockets on the clothes of 15 students in a classroom
- the number of pockets on the clothes of the same 15 students as they played on the playground (Each student wore a jacket outside.)
- the number of pockets on the clothes of 31 students in a different classroom

For each set of data, Professor Peabody drew a picture, recorded the data in a table, and made a graph. Just as Professor Peabody finished graphing the data, he remembered that he had to get back to his lab to check on another experiment. When he got back, he discovered that he had left his pictures and data tables at Bessie Coleman school. All Professor Peabody had at his lab were his graphs. However, when Professor Peabody looked at his graphs, he saw that he had forgotten to write titles on them.

Here are Professor Peabody's graphs:

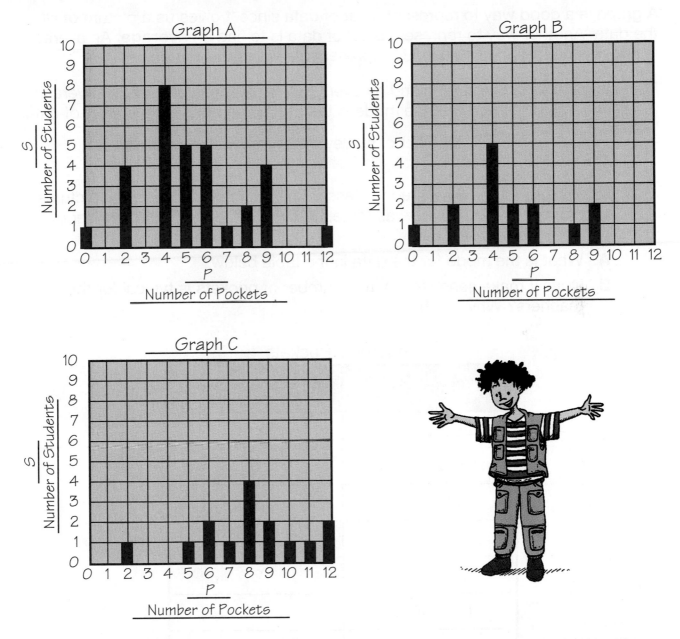

1. Write a title for each graph. Choose titles that will match each graph with the correct survey.

2. Describe each graph in words.

3. Write a note to Professor Peabody. Explain to him how you were able to match the graphs with the three surveys. You must convince him that you titled the graphs correctly.

Reviewing Averages

A graph is a good way to represent a set of data since it gives us a picture of *all* the data. Another way to represent a set of data is to find an **average.** An average is one number that can be used to represent a set of data.

There is more than one way to find an average. The **mode** is one kind of average. In Lesson 1, you learned that the mode is the most common value in a set of data.

4. Find the mode for each set of survey data represented by a graph in Question 1.

5. Professor Peabody returned to Bessie Coleman School to get his pictures and data tables. While he was there, he collected data on the number of pockets the teachers had.

   A. What is the mode for the data in the table below?

   B. Does it make sense to say this number of pockets is typical for the teachers? Why or why not?

Teachers' Pockets

Teacher	Number of Pockets
Mrs. Dewey	1
Mr. Martinez	6
Mrs. Lee	0
Mr. Green	6
Mrs. Scott	2
Mrs. Grace	3
Mrs. Sharma	4

The **median** is another kind of average. You have used the median to average data in labs or other activities. It is the number that is exactly in the middle of the data. For example, to find the median of the number of teachers' pockets, you can list the numbers in order from smallest to largest like this.

$$0, \quad 1, \quad 2, \textcircled{3,} \quad 4, \quad 6, \quad 6$$

Since 3 is exactly in the middle of the data, 3 pockets is the median.

6. Which average, the median or the mode, do you think represents the Teachers' Pockets data better? Tell why.

Here is another example. Professor Peabody found the height of six teachers. He found the median as shown.

Teachers' Heights

Teacher	Height in Inches
Mrs. Dewey	66
Mr. Martinez	70
Mrs. Lee	60
Mr. Green	72
Mrs. Scott	62
Mrs. Sharma	61

60 inches, 61 inches, 62 inches, 66 inches, 70 inches, 72 inches

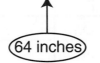

64 inches

The median height is 64 inches, since it is exactly in the middle of the data. (It is halfway between 62 inches and 66 inches.)

The **mean** is a third kind of average. When people talk about averages in everyday life, they usually are talking about the mean. We will review the mean in a later unit.

7. **A.** Find the median of the data in Graph B. (*Hint:* How many students are represented in the graph? What number of pockets is exactly in the middle of the data?)

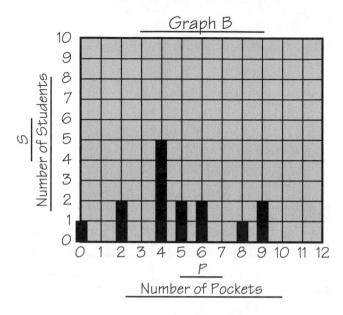

Graph B

Number of Students

Number of Pockets

B. Are the median and the mode the same for this set of data?

8. Fruit Gem Snacks come in three sizes. Arti and Jessie wanted to know how many fruit gems come in each size bag. They counted the number of fruit gems in three bags of each size and recorded the data in this table. Find the median number of fruit gems in each size bag.

Size	Number of Fruit Gems			
	Bag 1	Bag 2	Bag 3	Median
Small	10	12	11	
Medium	18	18	16	
Big Snack	25	27	24	

9. Lin, Jacob, Grace, and Luis are in four different fifth-grade classrooms. Each class gives spelling quizzes with 10 words. Their spelling scores are listed below:

Lin: 10, 4, 9, 10, 8
Jacob: 8, 9, 8, 6, 5, 6
Grace: 7, 8, 8, 9, 8, 10
Luis: 8, 8, 8, 8, 8

A. Find the median spelling score for each student.

B. Who do you think is the best speller? Explain your thinking.

Mr. Moreno's fifth-grade class collected three sets of data:

- the heights of the students in Mr. Moreno's fifth-grade class
- the heights of a class of kindergarten students
- the heights of 23 students in the school cafeteria at lunch time (Students in kindergarten through fifth grade eat lunch together.)

1. They made a graph for each set of data. These graphs are shown here. Write a title for each graph. Explain how you chose each title.

A.

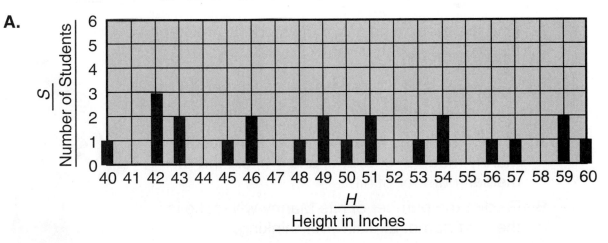

B.

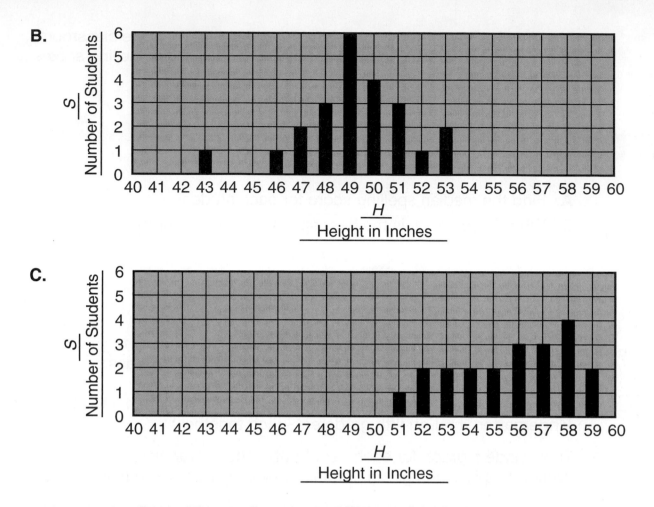

C.

2. **A.** Find the median height of the students in Graph C.

   B. Find the mode.

3. Lee Yah spent $2.10, $3.50, $2.75, $2.50, and $3.00 for lunches one week. Find her median cost.

4. **A.** In the first six baseball games of the season, Manny made 2, 3, 0, 2, 3, and 1 hits. Find the median number of hits.

   B. Predict the number of hits Manny will make in the next game. Explain your thinking.

5. Blanca counted the eyelets on her shoes at home. On four pairs of shoes, she counted 0, 32, 24, and 20 eyelets.

   A. Find the median number of eyelets.

   B. Do you think this value represents this set of data well? Why or why not?

Searching the Forest

Populating the Forest

You are going to "populate a forest" for another group. This means you are going to put a mixture of colored tiles into a bag for another group to study.

- Agree with your group on a "recipe" for your bag. Your recipe must follow these three rules:

    A. There must be exactly 50 tiles in the bag.

    B. The number of tiles of each color must be a multiple of 10.

    C. There must be at least two different colors in the bag.

- Write down your recipe. Use a table like this one:

C Color	*N* Number

- Every person in your group must sign the paper with the recipe. This will show that everyone agrees that the recipe is correct.
- Count out the proper number of tiles of each color, and put the tiles in the bag. Label the bag with the initials of the people in your group.
- Seal your recipe in an envelope. Write your initials on the envelope.
- Give your envelope and the bag of tiles to your teacher.

This recipe needs a dash of blue.

Experiment: Searching the Forest

You should have a bag that another group has "populated" with colored tiles. Your job is to predict the number of each color in the bag. But you cannot dump all the tiles out and count them! You are like a scientist exploring a big, deep forest. You can only look at a little bit of the forest at a time.

You are only allowed to take samples of the tiles. Each sample must have exactly ten tiles in it. After each sample, return the tiles to the bag and shake it up before you take the next sample.

1. Draw a picture of the experiment. Label the variables in your picture.

2. **A.** What are the two main variables in your experiment?
   B. Tell whether each of the main variables is categorical or numerical.

3. Why is it a good idea to shake up the bag before taking each sample?

4. Take at least three samples from the "forest." Each sample should have ten tiles in it. Remember to return all the tiles to the bag and shake after each sample. Keep track of your data in a table as shown.

C Color	N Number Pulled			
	Sample 1	Sample 2	Sample 3	Median

5. When you are finished filling in your data table, find the median number of each color.

6. Make a bar graph of your data on a sheet of graph paper.

7. **A.** What color (or colors) was most common in your samples?

   B. On average, how many of the most common color did you pull? (Use the median.)

8. **A.** What color was least common in your samples?

   B. On average, how many of the least common color did you pull? (Use the median.)

9. Predict the total number of each color in the bag. Write your predictions in a table like this one. (Remember that there are 50 tiles in all and the number of each color must be a multiple of 10.)

Color	Prediction	Actual

10. After you have made your predictions, count the number of each color that are actually in the bag. Write the actual number of each color in your table. Also, check the recipe in the envelope for your bag.

11. Did you make good predictions? Explain what happened.

Fractions and Probability

Here is Lin's data:

Color	Prediction	Actual
Red	20	20
Green	10	10
Blue	20	20

12. **A.** What fraction of Lin's tiles are red?

   B. What fraction are green?

   C. What fraction are blue?

13. If Lin puts all her tiles back in the bag, mixes them up, and then picks one tile from her bag, what color or colors will she most likely pick?

Since 20 out of the 50 tiles are red, there are 20 chances out of 50 that she will pick a red tile. If Lin picks one tile out of the bag, the **probability** that she will pick a red tile is $\frac{20}{50}$.

14. **A.** What is the probability that Lin will pick a green tile?

   B. What is the probability that she will pick a blue tile?

15. Suppose you return all your tiles to your bag, mix them up, and pick one tile:

   A. What is the most likely color you will choose? (Note: There may be more than one.)

   B. What is the probability that you will pick that color? Write the probability as a fraction.

   C. What is the least likely color?

   D. What is the probability that you will pick that color?

Radio Favorites

Michael asked some fifth-grade students at his school about the type of music played on their favorite radio stations. This is what he found:

Type of Music	Number of Students
classical	2
alternative rock	4
oldies	4
country and western	6
rock	5
rap	4

1. How many students did Michael survey?

2. **A.** Is Type of Music a numerical or categorical variable? How can you tell?

   B. Is Number of Students a numerical or categorical variable? How can you tell?

3. What was the most popular type of music?

4. You may want to organize your answers to this question in a table.

   A. What fraction of the sample liked each type of music?

   B. There are 100 fifth-grade students altogether in Michael's school. Estimate how many fifth graders like each type of music.

5. Describe a survey you would like to carry out. Tell what variables you would study and what values of those variables you would expect. (For example, the variables Michael studied were type of music and the number of students. The values of type of music were classical, alternative rock, oldies, etc.)

Candy Grab

You will need a sheet of graph paper to complete this part of the homework.

Alexis pulled candies from a brown bag. This is her data:

C Color	N Number Pulled			
	Sample 1	Sample 2	Sample 3	Median
red	6	8	5	
green	2	1	2	
blue	2	1	3	

6. What is the median number for each color?

7. Make a bar graph of Alexis's data.

8. If Alexis takes another sample, which color would be most common? Why do you think so?

9. Alexis's bag has 50 candies. The number of each color is a multiple of 10. How many candies of each color do you think are in the bag?

Use your answer to Question 9 to answer Question 10.

10. Suppose Alexis pulls just one candy from the bag.
    A. What is the probability that the candy is red?
    B. What is the probability that the candy is green?
    C. What is the probability that the candy is blue?

Practice Problems

Choose an appropriate method to solve each of the following problems. For some questions you may need to find an exact answer. For others you may only need an estimate. Use appropriate tools such as calculators, paper and pencil, mental math, or estimation.

1. A company has 1000 jump ropes that need to be put in packages of 5 jump ropes each. How many packages are needed?

2. Three friends want to evenly split the cost of a pizza. If the pizza costs $5, then about how much should each person pay?

3. A disc factory has 10,000 CDs to ship to stores. The factory shipped 30 boxes that hold 200 CDs each and 5 boxes that hold 100 CDs each. How many CDs are left to be shipped?

4. Five classes went to the museum. There are 24 students in each class. Two classes went on Tuesday. The remaining classes went on Wednesday.

   A. How many students went on Tuesday?

   B. How many students went on Wednesday?

   C. How many students went to the museum in all?

5. Three boxes of bananas, three boxes of oranges, and three boxes of apples were sent to a school lunchroom. All the boxes weighed the same, and altogether the fruit weighed 270 pounds. How many pounds of each kind of fruit were sent to the lunchroom?

6. In five days, a fruit stand had sales of $158, $139, $225, $195, and $125. The total expenses for the five days were $500. About how much profit did the fruit stand make? (Profit is the amount of money earned after all expenses are paid.)

7. Jerry bowled three games. His scores were 120, 87, and 123. Find his median score.

Unit 2

Big Numbers

	Student Guide	Discovery Assignment Book	Adventure Book	Unit Resource Guide*
Lesson 1				
Reading and Writing Big Numbers	●	●		
Lesson 2				
Facts I Know	●	●		●
Lesson 3				
The Base-Ten Number System				●
Lesson 4				
The Chinese Abacus	●			●
Lesson 5				
Multiplication	●			●
Lesson 6				
Estimating Products	●			
Lesson 7				
Sand Reckoning			●	
Lesson 8				
Exponents and Large Numbers	●			
Lesson 9				
Stack Up				●
Lesson 10				
Portfolios	●			

Unit Resource Guide pages are from the teacher materials.

Reading and Writing Big Numbers

Students in a fifth-grade Social Studies class are learning about populations. Their teacher wrote some of the populations on the board for them to read and write.

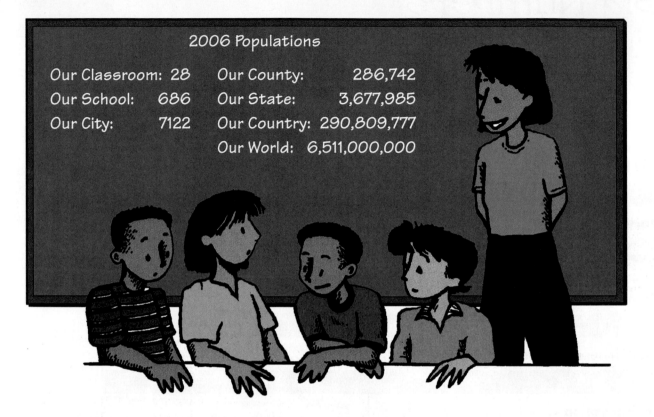

2006 Populations

Our Classroom:	28	Our County:	286,742
Our School:	686	Our State:	3,677,985
Our City:	7122	Our Country:	290,809,777
		Our World:	6,511,000,000

Some students had difficulty reading and writing the big numbers. The teacher gave these students a play to read. The play was about students who worked together to solve a problem about big numbers.

The characters in the play are:
N.S. (Not Sure)
P.S. (Problem Solver)
L.L. (Loves Lists)
R.R. (Remembers Rules)
Teacher

Teacher: Think about the meaning of each word on the list at the right as you review reading and writing numbers in the millions and billions. Then give examples of the terms.

N.S.: Wow! That number is mind-boggling! Is it in the millions or in the billions? Reading and writing big numbers is not so easy. I've seen most of these words on the list before, but when I try to think about numbers in the millions, I get confused about what some of the words mean.

It is estimated that there are close to 6,511,000,000 people in the world. Use this number to give an example of each of the following terms:

- digit
- place
- place value
- period
- expanded form
- word form
- standard form

P.S.: Remember the problem-solving strategy, Make It Simpler. Let's start with a small number and figure out what the words mean for the small number. If we look at how the small number is organized, it might help us read and write larger numbers. Let's use 365, the number of days in a year.

R.R.: There must be some rules to help us. I'll look in our math book.

L.L.: Let's list some things we know, and we can add other things as we go along. What do we know about digits? I'll write our study notes on the chalkboard.

Study Notes:
- There are ten **digits** in our number system:

  0 1 2 3 4 5 6 7 8 9

R.R.: I found this rule: The value of each **digit** in a number is determined by its position or **place.** This is called its **place value.** Add that to the study notes.

> Study Notes:
> • There are ten **digits** in our number system:
>
>   0 1 2 3 4 5 6 7 8 9
>
> • The value of each **digit** is determined by its position or **place.**

N.S.: Okay, back to 365. The 3 is three hundred because, because. . . . If I draw a place value chart on the chalkboard, it's easier to explain.

Ones		
Hundreds	**Tens**	**Ones**
3	6	5

When 3 is in this position or place, it really means 3 hundreds or 300. The 6 really means 6 tens or 60 and the 5 means 5 ones or 5.

R.R.: The value of each digit in 365 is *300 + 60 + 5.* This way of writing a number is called **expanded form.**

L.L.: Should I add that to our notes?

P.S.: I don't think so, but now I remember—**standard form** is just the regular way to write a number using digits, 365.

N.S.: Now I remember another term on that list! **Word form** just means that the digits are written in words, three hundred sixty-five.

P.S.: There's another problem-solving strategy that can help us. Find a Pattern. That way you don't have to remember so many rules. There is a pattern in reading and writing larger numbers, and it has something to do with knowing the **periods.**

R.R.: There's a rule about that: Read the number in each period and say the name of each period. A **period** is a group of three places in a large number. If you can read three-digit numbers, and you know the names of the periods, reading big numbers is easy. We need this rule on our study notes.

> Study Notes:
> • There are ten **digits** in our number system:
>
>   0 1 2 3 4 5 6 7 8 9
>
> • The value of each **digit** is determined by its position or **place.**
>
> • Read the number in each **period** and say the name of each **period.**

N.S.: I guess I need to get a better picture of the periods in my head.

P.S.: Okay. Let's go back to the place value chart.

L.L.: It was my tenth birthday a week ago. My family always figures out our age in days, so right now I can say my age in days, 3657. Three **thousand,** six hundred fifty-seven days. Hey, is that the **word form** or the **standard form?**

Trillions			Billions			Millions			Thousands			Ones		
HUNDRED	TEN	ONE	HUNDRED	TEN	ONE	HUNDRED	TEN	ONE	HUNDRED	TEN	ONE	HUNDRED	TEN	ONE
											3	6	5	7

P.S.: We can't read your mind. Only you know which one you pictured in your head. I think those terms are used for writing numbers, not for talking.

N.S.: Thinking about reading the three digits in each **period** makes it easy to write the expanded form. 3000 + 600 + 50 + 7. Each period has a hundred, ten, and ones' place in it, and it is named by its place value. Let's try reading some more numbers. The population of our county is two hundred eighty-six **thousand,** seven hundred forty-two. The population of our state is three **million,** six hundred seventy-seven **thousand,** nine hundred eighty-five.

R.R.: One more thing. We usually place commas between the numbers in each period to help keep track of the periods. In some countries they use spaces instead of commas. The population of the world is usually written 6,511,000,000 in the United States. It is written 6 511 000 000 in some other countries.

P.S.: Now let's get back to the world population and try to apply each of the words . . .

Teacher: Time's up! You can finish the review at home, and we'll discuss any of your questions tomorrow.

N.S.: I guess our group will be taking the world population home with us tonight!

Discuss

Reading, Writing, and Ordering Big Numbers

2006 Populations Table 1

State	Nickname	Population
Alabama	Heart of Dixie	4,500,752
Alaska	Last Frontier	648,818
Arizona	Grand Canyon State	5,580,811
Arkansas	Natural State	2,725,714
California	Golden State	35,484,453
Colorado	Centennial State	4,550,688
Connecticut	Constitution State	3,483,372
Delaware	First State	817,491
Florida	Sunshine State	17,019,068

Using the 2006 Populations Table 1:

1. What is the reported population in Alabama?

2. What is the reported population in Florida?

3. A. Which state populations have an 8 in the ten thousands' place?

   B. The populations of which states have a 5 in the hundred thousands' place?

(*Hint:* There may be more than one answer for each question.)

4. A. In which state do the students in the play live?

   B. How many people live in that state?

---

5. What is the estimated world population?

6. List the populations of Arizona, Colorado, and Connecticut in order from smallest to largest.

7. **A.** Write the reported population of Alabama in expanded form.

   B. Write the reported population of Florida in expanded form.

8. **A.** Write the reported population of Connecticut in word form.

   B. Write the reported population of Delaware in word form.

9. Which state has a reported population closest to 1 million?

10. Complete the number lines on the *Population Lines* Activity Page in the *Discovery Assignment Book.* Show the position of each state's population in the 2006 Populations Table 1 on the appropriate number line. Alaska has been written as an example on the correct number line.

11. Use the *Population Lines* Activity Page to help you:

    A. Round the population of Arizona to the nearest million.

    B. Round the population of Alabama to the nearest million.

    C. Round the population of Delaware to the nearest hundred thousand.

12. **A.** Round the population of Arkansas to the nearest million.

    B. Round the population of Arkansas to the nearest hundred thousand.

13. **A.** Round the population of Florida to the nearest ten million.

    B. Round the population of Florida to the nearest million.

Spin and Read Number Game

Players

This game is for groups of three students. Two students play and one student serves as a judge.

The purpose of the game is to practice reading large numbers.

Materials

- one deck of playing cards (use ace as "1" and the king as "0" and remove the queens, jacks, and tens) or four sets of *Digit Cards 0–9*
- *Spin and Read Number Game Spinners* Activity Page
- one clear plastic spinner or paper clip and pencil
- *Place Value Chart* Activity Page
- one calculator

Rules

Shuffle the cards together to make one deck of 40 cards. Spin to determine the number of cards to pick up. (Use Spinner 1 on the Activity Page the first few times you play the game, then use Spinner 2 for a greater challenge.) The first player spins and lays down that many cards from the deck face-up on the table. That player then reads the number. If it is read correctly, the player records the number on the *Place Value Chart* and returns the cards to the deck. If it is not read correctly, the other player gets the opportunity. If neither reads it correctly, the cards go back into the deck and the deck is reshuffled. It is the judge's responsibility to determine whether the number was read correctly. If there is a dispute, it is resolved by a discussion of the number. Each game consists of four rounds, with each player beginning two rounds.

At the end of the game, players use their calculators to total the numbers they recorded. The calculator may go into scientific notation. The player with the larger total wins. Play rotates, and a new student serves as the judge.

2006 Populations Table 2

State	Nickname	Population
Georgia	Peach State	8,684,715
Hawaii	Aloha State	1,257,608
Idaho	Gem State	1,366,332
Illinois	Prairie State	12,653,544
Indiana	Hoosier State	6,195,643
Iowa	Hawkeye State	2,944,062
Kansas	Sunflower State	2,723,507
Kentucky	Bluegrass State	4,117,827
Louisiana	Pelican State	4,496,334

1. Read each of the numbers aloud. List the numbers in order from the largest to the smallest.

2. Use expanded form to write the numbers that have a 5, 6, or 8 in the 10,000s' place.

3. Use word form to write the numbers for the four states that have reported populations closest to 2 million.

4. Round the population of Kansas to the nearest hundred thousand.

5. Round the population of Illinois to the nearest thousand.

6. The population of Georgia as reported in a 1995 atlas was 6,508,419 people. About how many more people were there in Georgia in 2006 than in 1995? If Georgia continues to grow at this rate, when might the population of Georgia go over twelve million? Estimate the year.

Note:

These populations were reported in the *2006 Rand McNally Road Atlas*. If you have access to a more current edition, you can determine how much each state has increased or decreased in population.

Facts I Know

Multiplication Facts and Triangle Flash Cards

1. Work with a partner. Use the directions below and your *Triangle Flash Cards: 5s* and *10s* to practice the multiplication facts.

   A. One partner covers the corner containing the highest number. (This number is lightly shaded on each triangle.) This number is the answer to a multiplication problem, called the **product.** The second person multiplies the two uncovered numbers which are called the **factors.**

   $5 \times 4 = ?$

   $4 \times 5 = ?$

   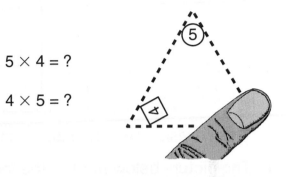

   B. Place each flash card in one of three piles: those facts you know and can answer quickly, those you can figure out with a strategy, and those you need to learn.

   C. Begin your *Multiplication Facts I Know* chart. Circle those facts you know well and can answer quickly.

   For example, Felicia looked through the pile of facts she knew well and answered quickly. Felicia knew that $5 \times 4 = 20$ and $4 \times 5 = 20$. She circled two 20s on the chart. Look for the two other 20s on the chart. Why didn't Felicia circle these as well?

   D. Discuss how you can figure out facts you don't recall right away. Share your strategies with your partner.

   E. Practice the last two piles at home for homework—the facts you can figure out with a strategy and those you need to learn. Make a list of those facts you need to practice.

Multiplication Facts I Know

×	0	1	2	3	4	5	6	7	8	9	10
0	0	0	0	0	0	0	0	0	0	0	0
1	0	1	2	3	4	5	6	7	8	9	10
2	0	2	4	6	8	10	12	14	16	18	20
3	0	3	6	9	12	15	18	21	24	27	30
4	0	4	8	12	16	(20)	24	28	32	36	40
5	0	5	10	15	(20)	25	30	35	40	45	50
6	0	6	12	18	24	30	36	42	48	54	60
7	0	7	14	21	28	35	42	49	56	63	70
8	0	8	16	24	32	40	48	56	64	72	80
9	0	9	18	27	36	45	54	63	72	81	90
10	0	10	20	30	40	50	60	70	80	90	100

Fact Families

2. The picture below models the following problem: *if a rectangle has a total of 20 squares organized in 4 rows, how many squares are in each row?*

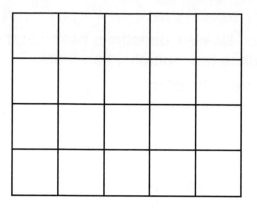

What division sentence describes this problem?

3. The picture below models the following problem: *if a rectangle has a total of 20 squares organized in 5 rows, how many squares are in each row?*

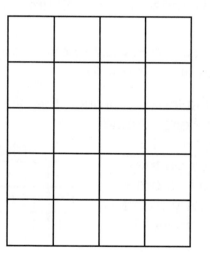

What division sentence describes this problem?

4. What do you notice about the rectangles in Questions 2 and 3? (If you need to, draw both of these rectangles on a piece of *Dot Paper*. Cut them out and lay one on top of the other.)

5. What two multiplication sentences describe the two rectangles in Questions 2 and 3?

The four facts: $4 \times 5 = 20$
$5 \times 4 = 20$
$20 \div 4 = 5$
and $20 \div 5 = 4$ are related facts. We say they are in the same **fact family.**

6. Solve each pair of related facts. Name two other facts in the same fact family.

   A. $5 \times 2 = ?$ and $2 \times 5 = ?$ **B.** $10 \times 3 = ?$ and $3 \times 10 = ?$

   C. $10 \times 5 = ?$ and $50 \div 10 = ?$ **D.** $6 \times 5 = ?$ and $30 \div 5 = ?$

7. Write the complete number sentence for each related fact.

   A. $8 \times 5 =$ _____

   _____ $\div 5 =$ _____

   _____ $\div 8 =$ _____

   $5 \times$ _____ $=$ _____

   B. $7 \times 10 =$ _____

   _____ $\div$ _____ $= 7$

   _____ $\div 7 =$ _____

   $10 \times$ _____ $=$ _____

   C. $90 \div$ _____ $= 9$

   _____ $\times 10 =$ _____

   _____ $\div 9 =$ _____

   _____ $\times 9 =$ _____

   D. $5 \times$ ___ $= 45$

   $45 \div$ _____ $=$ _____

   _____ $\times 9 =$ _____

   $45 \div$ _____ $=$ _____

8. What is 5×5? Name a related fact for 5×5. Is there more than one?

9. What is 10×10? Name a related fact for 10×10. Is there more than one?

10. The numbers 25 and 100 are square numbers. How are the fact families for the square numbers different from other fact families?

11. Solve the given fact. Then name other facts in the same fact family.

    A. $10 \times 6 = ?$ **B.** $20 \div 10 = ?$ **C.** $7 \times 5 = ?$ **D.** $80 \div 8 = ?$

    E. $15 \div 3 = ?$ **F.** $4 \times 10 = ?$ **G.** $3 \times 5 = ?$ **H.** $10 \div 2 = ?$

Division Facts and Triangle Flash Cards

12. With a partner, use the directions below and your *Triangle Flash Cards: 5s* and *10s* to practice the division facts.

    A. One partner covers the number in the square. This number will be the answer to a division problem, called the **quotient.** The number in the circle is the **divisor.** The second person solves a division fact with the two uncovered numbers as shown.

    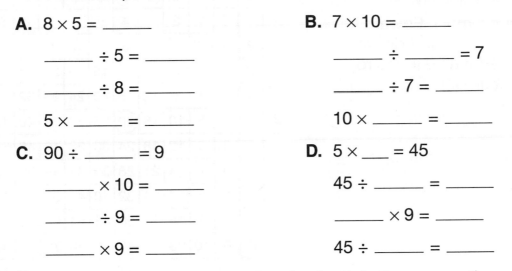

    $20 \div 5 = ?$

B. Place each flash card in one of three piles: those facts you know well and can answer quickly, those you can figure out with a strategy, and those you need to learn.

C. Begin your *Division Facts I Know* chart. Circle the facts you know well and can answer quickly.

For example, Edward knew $20 \div 5 = 4$. So Edward circled the 20 in the row for a divisor of 5.

Division Facts I Know

×	0	1	2	3	4	5	6	7	8	9	10
0	0	0	0	0	0	0	0	0	0	0	0
1	0	1	2	3	4	5	6	7	8	9	10
2	0	2	4	6	8	10	12	14	16	18	20
3	0	3	6	9	12	15	18	21	24	27	30
4	0	4	8	12	16	20	24	28	32	36	40
5	0	5	10	15	(20)	25	30	35	40	45	50
6	0	6	12	18	24	30	36	42	48	54	60
7	0	7	14	21	28	35	42	49	56	63	70
8	0	8	16	24	32	40	48	56	64	72	80
9	0	9	18	27	36	45	54	63	72	81	90
10	0	10	20	30	40	50	60	70	80	90	100

Divisor (along the left axis)

D. Sort the cards again. This time your partner covers the number in the circle. The number in the square is now the divisor. Solve a division fact with the two uncovered numbers.

E. Update your *Division Facts I Know* chart. Circle the facts you know well and can answer quickly.

$20 \div 4 = ?$

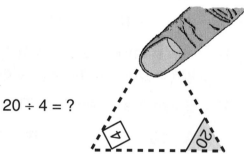

F. Discuss how you can figure out facts you don't recall right away. Share your strategies with your partner.

G. Practice the last two piles at home for homework—the facts you can figure out with a strategy and those you need to learn. Make a list of these facts.

13. Compare your *Multiplication Facts I Know* chart to your *Division Facts I Know* chart. Look for facts in the same fact family. Do you know any complete fact families? Which family or families? Explain.

You will continue to use *Triangle Flash Cards* to study other groups of facts. You will be reminded to update your *Multiplication* and *Division Facts I Know* charts. If you know one or two of the facts in a fact family, use those facts to help you learn the others.

The Chinese Abacus

Building the Abacus

What saves trees, never needs a battery or a source of light, and is used for calculating by millions of people? An abacus.

Some form of this tool was used by the ancient Greeks and Romans. It is still used today in many countries, including China, Korea, Japan, and Russia.

Below is a picture of a Chinese abacus. We will explore how using the Chinese abacus is similar to computing in our own number system.

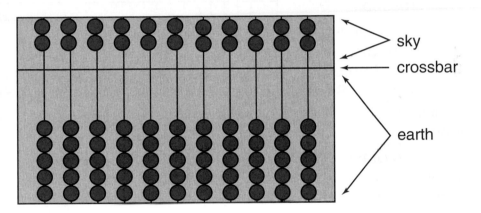

sky

crossbar

earth

The top section of the abacus is called the sky. The bottom section is called the earth.

Materials

You will need the following materials to build your own Chinese abacus.

- piece of cardboard, about 14 cm by 24 cm
- centimeter ruler
- 77 pieces of ditali macaroni or pony beads
- 11 pieces of kite string or thin twine, each about 16 cm long
- 3 pieces of $\frac{1}{2}$ inch masking tape, each 24 cm long
- scissors

Directions

Follow these steps to make your own Chinese abacus.

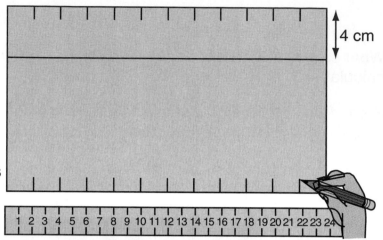

A. Draw a horizontal line 4 cm from the top edge of your piece of cardboard as shown in the picture at the right. The line should run all the way across the board. Later you will place tape over this line. The tape will be your crossbar.

B. Make tick marks at 2 cm intervals along the top and bottom edges of the cardboard. This is shown in the picture above. Start measuring from the left or right edge. Snip a slit at each tick mark. The slits should not be very deep (about 1 centimeter long).

C. Slip each of the 11 pieces of string into a slit. The strings will form the columns. Then place a strip of masking tape over the line you made in step one to form the crossbar. The tape should keep the string in place. See the picture below.

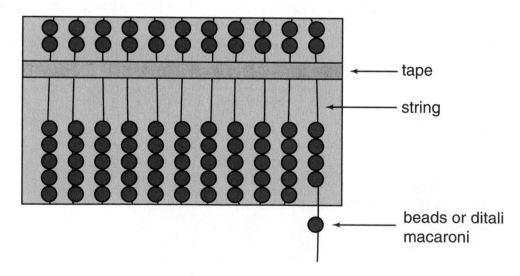

tape

string

beads or ditali macaroni

D. Release the strings from their slits in the sky section. Slip 2 pieces of ditali macaroni or 2 beads onto each string. Then place each string back into its slit.

E. Release the strings from their slits in the earth section. Slip 5 pieces of macaroni or 5 beads onto each string. Then place each string back into its slit.

F. Tape the string ends to the back of the abacus, and you are ready to show some numbers.

Numbers on the Abacus

Like our number system, the Chinese abacus has place value columns. The column on the right is the 1s column, the next column is the 10s column, then the 100s column, and so on. This is similar to our own system. The beads in the earth section in the ones column stand for 1 when they are pushed to the crossbar. Each of the sky beads in the ones column, however, stands for 5 times 1, or 5. Likewise, each of the earth beads in the tens column stands for 10. Each of the sky beads in the tens column stands for 5 times 10, or 50. The number 678 is shown on the abacus in the picture below.

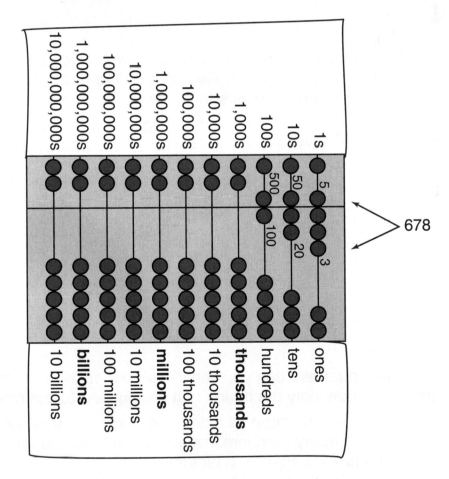

Position one of the *Column Place Value Guides* along the top edge of the abacus and the other below as shown in the picture.

The Chinese Abacus

Lay the abacus flat on the desk. Hold the abacus with your left hand and use your right hand to position the beads. Use your thumb for the earth beads and your forefinger for the sky beads. This is the official method of operating an abacus, even for left-handed people. Clear the abacus by pushing all of the beads away from the crossbar. To show a number, push the bead(s) to the crossbar.

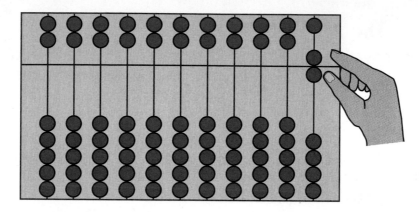

Representing Numbers Using Three Beads

1. **A.** Use three beads to make as many numbers as you can in the ones column. Here is an example. Record it on the *Abacus Pictures* Activity Page. Label your picture as shown here.

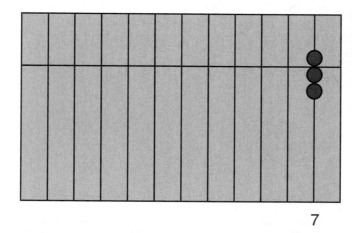

7

How many numbers can you show? Record each number on *Abacus Pictures*. (Show only the beads that are pushed to the crossbar.)

B. Use three beads to make as many numbers as you can in the tens column. How many numbers can you show? Record each number on *Abacus Pictures*. Label each picture.

C. Use three beads to make as many numbers as you can in the hundreds column. How many numbers can you show? Record each number on *Abacus Pictures*. Label each picture.

D. Describe any patterns you see for the numbers you made for each of the columns. Will this pattern continue to the millions and billions?

2. **A.** Use four beads to make as many numbers as you can in the ones column. Record and label your work on the *Abacus Pictures* Activity Page.

   B. How many numbers can you make with four beads in the tens column? Record and label your work.

   C. How many numbers can you make with four beads in the hundreds column? Record and label your work.

   D. Describe any patterns you see for the numbers you made for each of the columns. Compare these patterns with those you found in Question 1D.

Representing Numbers in More than One Way

Felicia showed the number 75 two different ways using the abacus.

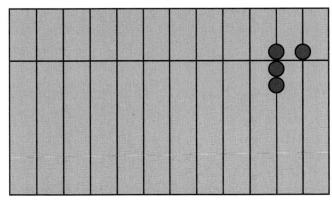

50 + 20 + 5 = 75

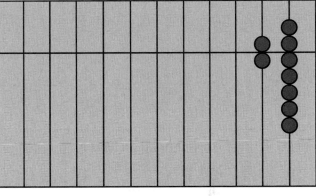

50 + 10 + 5 + 5 + 5 = 75

3. Find three ways to make each of the following numbers. Record each way on *Abacus Pictures*. Compare your pictures with those of your classmates to see if they found different ways. Be sure to label each picture.

   A. 15   **B.** 150   **C.** 1500

4. Find two ways to make the following numbers. Record and label both ways on *Abacus Pictures*. Compare your pictures with those of your classmates.

   A. 84   **B.** 4121

5. For each number in Questions 3 and 4, circle the picture that shows the fewest number of beads.

6. Use your abacus to show each of these 2006 population numbers from these cities:

   A. Tanana, Alaska: 300
   B. Archdale, North Carolina: 9241
   C. Farmington, Missouri: 14,335
   D. Fairmont, West Virginia: 18,984

7. Use your abacus to show each of these 2006 population numbers from these states:

   A. New Mexico: 1,874,614
   B. New York: 19,190,115
   C. North Carolina: 8,407,248
   D. North Dakota: 633,837

   Remember to practice using the right-hand thumb and forefinger technique if you want to become speedy.

Adding and Subtracting on the Abacus

8. Use your abacus to compute the answers to the following addition and subtraction problems.

   A. 8 + 2   **B.** 9 – 5   **C.** 16 – 4   **D.** 17 + 6   **E.** 28 – 9
   F. 34 + 8   **G.** 73 + 23   **H.** 82 – 26   **I.** 42 + 38   **J.** 60 – 37

9. Mosquito populations are often affected by the amount of rainfall and changes in weather patterns. At the beginning of the season, the Mosquito Control Center sampled the population. They estimated the number of mosquitos in the area they studied to be 7,085,298,000. The table shows the increases and decreases that occurred during the season. On the abacus, show the new population after each change in population. Copy and complete this table.

Mosquito Population

Change in Population	New Population
Increase of 20,000	
Decrease of 9000	
Increase of 500,000	
Increase of 1,000,000	
Increase of 7000	
Decrease of 30,000	
Increase of 1,000,000,000	
Decrease of 50,000,000	

Showing Numbers on the Abacus

You will need two copies of the *Abacus Pictures* Activity Page to complete this assignment.

1. Show the following numbers on your abacus using the fewest beads. Then record and label your work on copies of the *Abacus Pictures* Activity Page.

   A. 6   **B.** 600   **C.** 6000   **D.** 60,000

   E. 17   **F.** 170   **G.** 1700   **H.** 17,000

   I. 54   **J.** 540   **K.** 5400   **L.** 54,000

   M. 589   **N.** 735   **O.** 2550   **P.** 38,964

Moon Problems

The earth's closest neighbor in space is our moon. It is the earth's only natural satellite.

Solve the following problems about the earth and the moon. You can use any of these tools to solve Questions 2–5: paper and pencil, calculator, or your abacus.

2. The earth has a diameter of about 7926 miles. The moon's diameter is about 2160 miles. What is the difference between the diameter of the moon and the diameter of the earth?

3. Although from space the earth may look like a perfect ball, it really is not. The circumference of the earth at the equator is nearly 24,901 miles. The distance around the earth at the meridian (an imaginary line circling the earth through both poles) is nearly 24,860 miles. Find the difference between these numbers.

4. The average distance from the earth to the moon is about 238,800 miles. Estimate the number of miles in a round trip. Explain your thinking.

5. The average distance from the earth to the moon is about 238,800 miles. However, it can be as far away as 252,710 miles and as close as 221,463 miles. Estimate the difference between the farthest distance and the nearest distance. How did you make your estimate?

Use your abacus or paper and pencil to solve Questions 6–13.

6.
$$367 + 213$$

7.
$$309 - 176$$

8.
$$1348 + 471$$

9.
$$2078 - 563$$

10.
$$2472 - 1895$$

11.
$$6882 + 6754$$

12.
$$62,395 - 48,778$$

13.
$$23,334 + 95,767$$

Multiplication

Reach for the Stars

Mr. Moreno's class is about to begin a unit on the solar system. Irma, Alexis, and Nila thought it would be fun to decorate the classroom. Mr. Moreno allowed them to stay after school to work on this project.

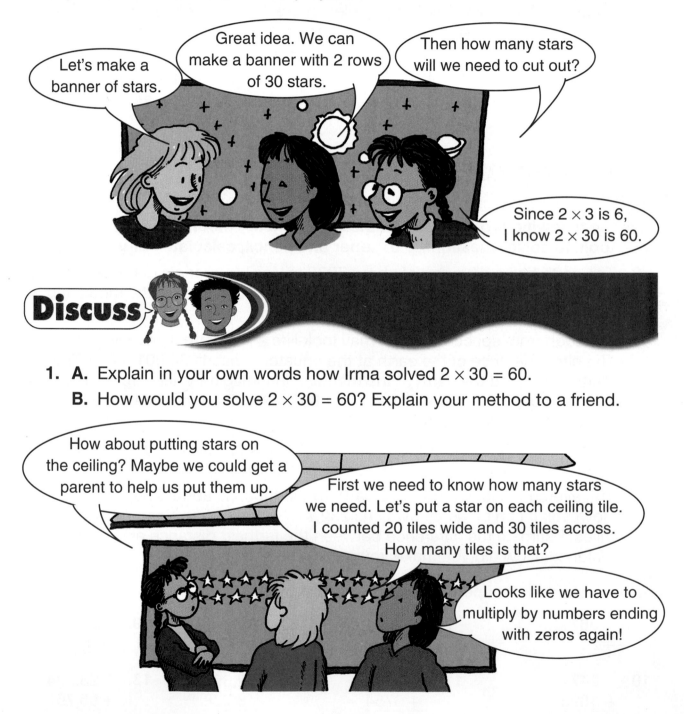

Discuss

1. **A.** Explain in your own words how Irma solved $2 \times 30 = 60$.

   B. How would you solve $2 \times 30 = 60$? Explain your method to a friend.

2. Irma learned to look for patterns when multiplying numbers that end in zeros. Find the following products. Use a calculator if needed. Describe the patterns you see.

   A. $2 \times 3 =$

   B. $2 \times 30 =$

   C. $20 \times 3 =$

   D. $20 \times 30 =$

   E. $200 \times 300 =$

   F. $200 \times 30 =$

   G. $20 \times 300 =$

3. How many stars do the students need to cut out to put a star on each ceiling tile?

4. Discuss other ways to compute 20×30.

5. Find the following pairs of products in your head. Check your work on a calculator if needed.

   A. $\begin{array}{r} 80 \\ \times\,2 \\ \hline \end{array}$ $\begin{array}{r} 80 \\ \times\,20 \\ \hline \end{array}$

   B. $\begin{array}{r} 20 \\ \times\,4 \\ \hline \end{array}$ $\begin{array}{r} 20 \\ \times\,40 \\ \hline \end{array}$

   C. $\begin{array}{r} 50 \\ \times\,7 \\ \hline \end{array}$ $\begin{array}{r} 50 \\ \times\,70 \\ \hline \end{array}$

   D. $\begin{array}{r} 90 \\ \times\,7 \\ \hline \end{array}$ $\begin{array}{r} 90 \\ \times\,70 \\ \hline \end{array}$

   E. $\begin{array}{r} 70 \\ \times\,1 \\ \hline \end{array}$ $\begin{array}{r} 70 \\ \times\,10 \\ \hline \end{array}$

   F. $\begin{array}{r} 30 \\ \times\,6 \\ \hline \end{array}$ $\begin{array}{r} 30 \\ \times\,60 \\ \hline \end{array}$

   G. $90 \times 20 =$
   $90 \times 2 =$

   H. $40 \times 50 =$
   $4 \times 50 =$

   I. $60 \times 40 =$
   $6 \times 40 =$

6. Irma, Alexis, and Nila get a package of construction paper. The package contains 20 sheets each of red, blue, yellow, green, and black paper.

   A. How many sheets of construction paper are in the package?

   B. There are 20 packages of construction paper in a box. How many sheets of construction paper are in a box?

   C. If Bessie Coleman School orders 50 boxes of construction paper, how many sheets of construction paper will the school receive?

Find the following products with your calculator. Look for patterns.

7. $4 \times 7 =$
    $40 \times 7 =$
    $4 \times 70 =$
    $40 \times 70 =$
    $400 \times 70 =$
    $40 \times 700 =$
    $400 \times 700 =$

8. $6 \times 7 =$
    $60 \times 7 =$
    $6 \times 70 =$
    $60 \times 70 =$
    $600 \times 70 =$
    $60 \times 700 =$
    $600 \times 700 =$

9. $8 \times 5 =$
    $80 \times 5 =$
    $8 \times 50 =$
    $80 \times 50 =$
    $800 \times 50 =$
    $80 \times 500 =$
    $800 \times 500 =$

10. Nila says she can multiply 40×40 in her head easily. What method do you think Nila is using? What is 40×40?

11. Nila saw that for every zero in the factors, there is a zero in the product. Do you agree? Explain.

12. Alexis says multiplying 60×500 is tricky. What is 60×500? Why is it tricky?

Find the value of *n* in Questions 13–16.

13. $n \times 40 = 200$

14. $n \times 50 = 2000$

15. $n \times 10 = 2000$

16. $n \times 80 = 4000$

The Solar System

Mr. Moreno's class learned that our solar system includes eight planets: Mercury, Venus, Earth, Mars, Jupiter, Saturn, Uranus, and Neptune.

Earth makes a complete rotation about its axis in about 24 hours. (One rotation of the earth is like one rotation of a basketball on a finger.)

One Earth rotation is what we call a day. To find the number of hours in a week, we multiply 7 days × 24 hours. One way to model this multiplication is to use the base-ten pieces.

Remember, the **base-ten pieces** can be used to model our number system: The **bit** can represent 1:

Since 10 bits make a **skinny,** a skinny can represent 10:

Since 10 skinnies make a **flat,** a flat can represent 100:

Since 10 flats make a **pack,** a pack can represent 1000:

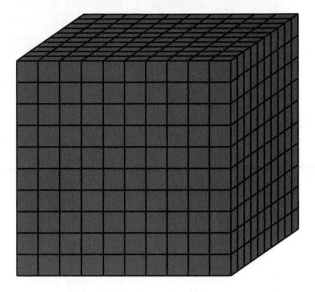

To model 7×24, we take 7 groups of 24:

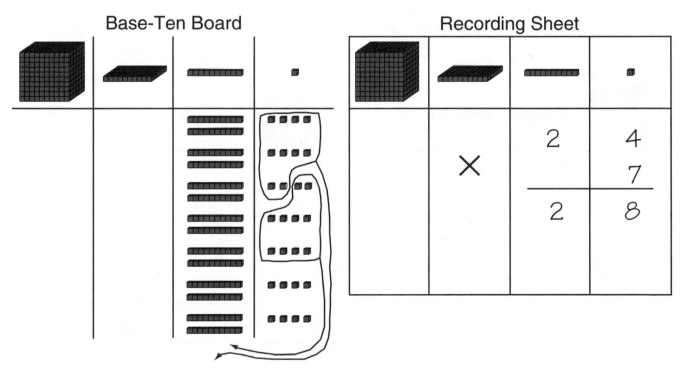

The 7 groups of 4 bits is 28 bits or 2 skinnies and 8 bits. This is the same as saying 2 tens and 8 ones.

Multiplication

The 7 groups of 2 skinnies gives 14 skinnies. When we add the 2 skinnies we traded for 20 bits, we have 16 skinnies or 1 flat and 6 skinnies.

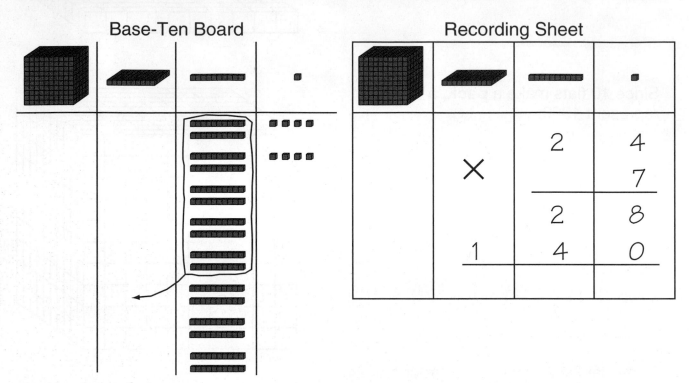

Together there is 1 flat, 6 skinnies, and 8 bits or 1 hundred, 6 tens, and 8 ones.

Model Questions 17–20 using the base-ten pieces, or sketch the problems using base-ten shorthand. Then solve the problem.

17. 43
    × 4

18. 314
    × 3

19. 502
    × 5

20. 1023
    × 3

The table *Our Solar System* gives some information about our solar system. Use it to help you solve the problems on the next few pages. (*Note:* One rotation of any planet is a day on the planet. The fourth column of the table gives the number of Earth hours it takes each planet to make one rotation. One Earth year is equal to the number of Earth days it takes the earth to make one revolution about the sun. The third column in the table gives the number of Earth days it takes each planet to revolve around the sun.)

Our Solar System

Planet	Average distance from the sun in miles (approx.)	Revolution around the sun in Earth days (approx.)	Rotation in Earth hours (approx.)	Diameter at equator (miles) (approx.)
Mercury	36,000,000	88	59	3031
Venus	67,000,000	225	5832	7519
Earth	94,000,000	365	24	7926
Mars	141,000,000	687	25	4221
Jupiter	483,000,000	4332	9	88,734
Saturn	885,000,000	10,760	11	71,000
Uranus	1,779,000,000	30,684	17	32,000
Neptune	2,788,000,000	60,188	16	30,540

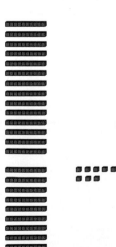

A day on Uranus is shorter than a day on Earth. It takes Uranus about 17 Earth hours to make a complete rotation.

How many Earth hours are in 14 days on Uranus?

Since there are 14 days, multiply
17 Earth hours × 14 rotations or 14 × 17.
To model 14 × 17, we can show 14 groups of 17:

There are enough bits to make 9 new skinnies with 8 bits left over.

From the 23 skinnies, 20 make 2 flats with 3 skinnies left. Thus, 17 × 14 = 238.

There are many ways to multiply using paper-and-pencil methods. Here are two ways:

All-partials Method	Compact Method

$$
\begin{array}{r}
17 \\
\times\,14 \\
\hline
28 \\
40 \\
70 \\
100 \\
\hline
238
\end{array}
\qquad\qquad
\begin{array}{r}
\overset{2}{} \\
17 \\
\times\,14 \\
\hline
68 \\
170 \\
\hline
238
\end{array}
$$

21. Which method do you like to use when you multiply? Explain to another person the steps you take to multiply 17 × 14 using your favorite paper-and-pencil method.

22. It takes Venus 225 Earth days to make a complete revolution about the sun. This means a year on Venus is the same as 225 days on Earth. How long is 7 years on Venus? Solve this problem two ways. First, use base-ten shorthand. Then do the problem using a paper-and-pencil method.

23. If you live on Earth, you have a birthday every 365 days. A year on Mars is equal to 687 Earth days. How many Earth days would pass before your third birthday on Mars?

24. The average Earth month is about 30 days. About how many hours is 30 days on Neptune?

Find the products using mental computation.

1.	40 × 70	2.	60 × 60	3.	500 × 60	4.	800 × 30	5.	300 × 30

6.	100 × 100	7.	600 × 40	8.	400 × 200	9.	2000 × 800	10.	6000 × 700

11. Explain how to multiply two numbers that end in zeros.

Find the value of n in Questions 12–19.

12. $200 \times n = 1400$ **13.** $3000 \times 40 = n$

14. $60 \times n = 42{,}000$ **15.** $90 \times 90 = n$

16. $n \times 800 = 64{,}000$ **17.** $50 \times n = 100$

18. $n \times 50 = 250{,}000$ **19.** $n \times 100 = 10{,}000$

20. The problem below was computed using the all-partials method.

$$
\begin{array}{r}
32 \\
\times\, 76 \\
\hline
12 \\
180 \\
140 \\
2100 \\
\hline
2432
\end{array}
$$

 A. What numbers were multiplied to get the partial product 12?

 B. What numbers were multiplied to get the partial product 180?

 C. What numbers were multiplied to get the partial product 140?

 D. What numbers were multiplied to get the partial product 2100?

21. A. What multiplication problem are the base-ten pieces modeling?

 B. Find the solution to the multiplication problem.

Find the products using any method.

22. 743	**23.** 209	**24.** 83	**25.** 26
×5	×6	×47	×38

26. Approximately how many Earth hours are there in 14 Martian days?

27. If you were an earthling who is 8 years old today, about how many days would you have lived?

28. About how many Earth hours are in 6 days on Mercury?

29. Approximately how many Earth hours are in 23 Uranus days?

30. About how much farther is Neptune from the sun than Uranus? (Use data for their average distances from the sun.)

31. About how much farther is Neptune from the sun than Saturn?

32. Which orbit, the orbit of Mars or the orbit of Venus, is closer to the earth's orbit? How do you know?

33. Which planet has a diameter about 10 times greater than the earth's diameter?

34. Which is longer, a day on Venus or a year on Venus? Explain your reasoning.

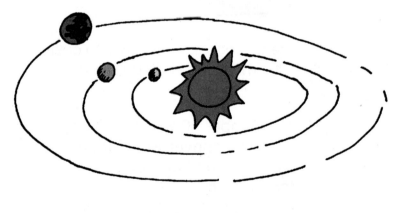

35. 167	**36.** 986	**37.** 22	**38.** 72
×7	×5	×16	×34

Estimating Products

Alexis and her brother Nick both want to buy posters of the solar system. Each poster costs $17.65. Alexis estimates that the two posters will cost about $36.00. In order to estimate, Alexis chose 18 as a convenient number. The number 18 is close to $17.65 and is easier to work with. Alexis multiplied 2×18 in her head to get the estimate $36.00.

Nick said, "The two posters are going to cost under $40.00. I estimated $17.65 is about $20.00. Then twice $20.00 is $40.00. I know $40.00 is too much, but it is close."

Nick chose the number 20 when estimating because it was convenient for him. Alexis chose 18 as a convenient number because she could double 18 in her head easily. Remember, a number that is convenient for one person might not be convenient for another.

We find estimates when we need to have a good idea about how big or small a number is, but we do not need to know exactly. Sometimes it is impossible to know an exact answer. We use estimates in many different situations.

For example:
You can estimate how far you live from school.
You can estimate how many people are watching a concert.
You can estimate how much you will pay for a full cart of groceries.

When we **estimate,** we find a number or answer that is reasonably close to the actual number. It may be bigger or smaller than the actual number, depending on the problem. To make an estimate we sometimes need to do some number operations in our heads. To make these computations easy to do, we often choose **convenient numbers** to make our estimates. Convenient numbers are really estimates as well.

Estimate to solve the following problems. Be ready to explain how you chose numbers convenient for you.

1. Sarah counted 9 chocolate chips in one chocolate chip cookie. If there are about the same number of chips in each cookie, how many chocolate chips are there in 3 dozen cookies?

2. There are 571 students at Fair Oaks Elementary School. There are a total of 8 elementary schools in the school district. All have about the same number of students. About how many students are in the school district?

3. The Smith family spent an average of $76.00 per month on electricity last year. About how much money did they spend on electricity last year?

4. The average electric bill for Walden Junior High School is $1647.00 per month. About how much money is spent on electricity per year?

5. It costs $11,234 per year to educate one student at Glen Oaks High School. There are 2743 students currently enrolled. About how much does it cost to educate all the high school students?

Choose convenient numbers to help you make quick estimates in Questions 1–11. Do not use a calculator.

1. Mr. Moreno's class is taking a field trip to the planetarium. The cost of admission is $4.35 a student. If 27 students attend, about how much money is needed for admission?

2. The planetarium is celebrating its 9th anniversary. The planetarium is open 357 days a year. About how many days has the planetarium been open?

3. On average, 2376 people visit the planetarium every day. About how many people visit the planetarium every year?

4. The planetarium is planning a new hands-on exhibit for children. The cost of the exhibit is $235,450. They received a gift of $45,000. About how much money do they still need?

5. One type of large jet airplane can travel at 534 mph. It can carry enough fuel for about 8 hours of flight. The airplane uses 3,361 gallons of fuel per hour.

   A. About how many miles can the airplane travel without refueling?

   B. It costs about $7,098 an hour to operate the airplane. It takes about 12 hours to fly from Los Angeles to Beijing, China. About how much does the trip cost?

   C. It takes about 19 hours to fly from New York to Melbourne, Australia. About how far is it from New York to Melbourne? How many stop-overs are necessary?

   D. About how much fuel does the airplane use on the 19 hour flight from New York to Melbourne?

6. Chicago's O'Hare Airport is one of the busiest airports in the United States. In 1992, a total of 64,441,087 passengers traveled through O'Hare. A total of 26,483,717 passengers traveled through Miami International Airport. About how many more passengers traveled through O'Hare than Miami?

7. A large airline had a total of 85,955,000 passengers one year. If the number of passengers per year stays the same, about how many people total will this airline serve in 5 years?

Use the Solar System Chart in Lesson 5 to answer the following questions.

8. Is Uranus's year about 3 times longer than Saturn's year? Explain how you know.

9. If I were a three-year-old Neptunian, about how many Earth days would I have lived?

10. The diameter of the sun is 864,000 miles. About how many Jupiters would need to be lined up to approximate the diameter of the sun?

11. Pluto was once considered to be a planet. At its closest, Pluto is about 2,663,000,000 miles from the earth. About how many round trips would it take to log 1 trillion miles traveling from Earth to Pluto and back?

Estimate the products. First choose numbers that are convenient.

12. 229,476
× 27

13. 356,234,045
× 9023

14. 1,029,576,123
× 4329

15. 1349
× 267

16. 421,467
× 38

17. 12,976
× 343

18. 2,794,271
× 679

19. 111,111
× 1111

20. 343,217
× 999

Exponents and Large Numbers

Exponents

In the Adventure Book *Sand Reckoning,* Archimedes estimated that the number of grains of sand it would take to fill the universe was the number 10^{63}.

10^{63} means we multiply 10 by itself 63 times.
10^2 means $10 \times 10 = 100$.
10^3 means $10 \times 10 \times 10 = 1000$.
10^6 means $10 \times 10 \times 10 \times 10 \times 10 \times 10 = 1{,}000{,}000$.

When we write 10^6, the number 10 is called the **base.** The number 6 is the **exponent** or **power.** We say "ten to the sixth power" or just "ten to the sixth." We call 10^6 the sixth power of 10.

Other numbers can be written using exponents.

For example,
$\quad 2^3$ means $2 \times 2 \times 2 = 8$
$\quad 5^2$ means $5 \times 5 = 25$
$\quad 3^4$ means $3 \times 3 \times 3 \times 3 = 81$
$\quad 7^1$ means 7

When we write 2^3, the 2 is the base and 3 is the power or exponent.

1. **A.** Name the base and the exponent in 5^2.
   B. Name the base and the power in 3^4.

2. Find n.
   A. $4^3 = n$ **B.** $2^5 = n$ **C.** $6^1 = n$

3. Find n.
   A. $10^1 = n$ **B.** $10^2 = n$ **C.** $10^3 = n$ **D.** $10^4 = n$
   E. $10^5 = n$ **F.** $10^6 = n$ **G.** $10^7 = n$ **H.** $10^8 = n$

4. Describe any patterns you see in the numbers in Question 3.

5. Use the patterns from Questions 3 and 4 to find n for the numbers below.
   A. $10^9 = n$ **B.** $10^{11} = n$

6. Describe in words what 10^{63} looks like written in standard form.

Reading Large Numbers on a Calculator
Using Scientific Notation

The distance from the earth to the sun is 90,000,000 miles (rounded to the nearest ten million miles). We can use exponents to write this number in a shorter form.

$$90{,}000{,}000 = 9 \times 10{,}000{,}000 = 9 \times 10^7$$

The 9×10^7 is a number written in **scientific notation.** A number written in scientific notation has 2 factors. The first factor is a number greater than or equal to 1 and less than 10 (9 in this example). The second factor is a power of 10 (10^7 in this example). The number 90,000,000 is written in **standard form.**

7. The 9×10^7 means to multiply $9 \times 10 \times 10 \times 10 \times 10 \times 10 \times 10 \times 10$. Try it on your calculator. How many zeros follow the 9?

Scientists often report the distance to the sun rounded to the nearest million miles, or 93,000,000 miles. Written in scientific notation, 93 million is 9.3×10^7. Note that this number also has two factors. We use a decimal to write the first factor as a number greater than or equal to one and less than ten (9.3). The second factor is a power of 10 (10^7).

$$93{,}000{,}000 = 9.3 \times 10{,}000{,}000 = 9.3 \times 10^7$$

8. To change 9.3×10^7 to standard form, multiply $9.3 \times 10 \times 10 \times 10 \times 10 \times 10 \times 10 \times 10$. Try this on your calculator. How many digits follow the 9?

To change 9.3×10^7 to standard form, we can move the decimal point over 7 spaces to the right. This is the same as multiplying by 10, 7 times.

9.3⌣⌣⌣⌣⌣⌣⌣

Since there are no digits after the 3, zeros must be inserted as place holders to give 93,000,000.

93000000.⌣⌣⌣⌣⌣⌣⌣

To change 6×10^5 to standard form, move the decimal point 5 places to the right. Since there are no digits after the 6, zeros must be inserted as place holders to give 600,000.

600000.⌣⌣⌣⌣⌣

The following numbers are written in scientific notation. Write the numbers in standard form.

9. 6×10^2 **10.** 7×10^4 **11.** 4×10^3

12. 7.8×10^4 **13.** 7.08×10^9 **14.** 1×10^3

15. **A.** Multiply 20,000,000 × 30,000,000 without your calculator.

    B. How many zeros follow the 6?

    C. Multiply 20,000,000 × 30,000,000 on your calculator.

Calculators automatically put large numbers into scientific notation.

Some calculators show scientific notation like this:

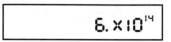

Some calculators show 6×10^{14} something like this:

These calculators display the power of 10 in the right corner. They do not show the 10.

16. **A.** Multiply 400,000 × 30,000,000 without your calculator.

    B. How many digits follow the 1?

    C. Multiply 400,000 × 30,000,000 with your calculator.

Do the following problems using a calculator. Write the answers in scientific notation and in standard form.

17. 20,000 × 80,000,000   18. 2000 × 50,000,000

19. 600,000 × 1,200,000   20. 7,000,000 × 70,000,000

21. 110,000 × 110,000   22. 2,500,000 × 300,000

23. Earth is about 93 million miles from the sun. Neptune is about 30 times farther from the sun than Earth.

    A. Write the number 93 million in standard form.

    B. About how far is Neptune from the sun?

24. Scientists have found that there are other star systems beyond our own. The very nearest star system is Alpha Centauri. Alpha Centauri is about 7000 times farther from us than Pluto. Pluto is about 3,573,000 miles from Earth.

    A. Write the number 3,573,000 in words.

    B. About how far are we from Alpha Centauri? Explain your thinking.

Find *n* in Questions 1–9.

1. $2^4 = n$

2. $5^3 = n$

3. $9^2 = n$

4. $3^3 = n$

5. $4^2 = n$

6. $6^3 = n$

7. $10^{10} = n$

8. $12^1 = n$

9. $20^2 = n$

The numbers in Questions 10–15 are written in scientific notation. Write them in standard form.

10. 4×10^6

11. 2×10^2

12. 9×10^4

13. 3.2×10^5

14. 9.3×10^8

15. 4.1×10^2

Do the following problems using a calculator or paper and pencil. Write the answers in scientific notation or in standard form.

16. $40{,}000 \times 600{,}000$

17. $150{,}000 \times 150{,}000$

18. $120{,}000 \times 4{,}000{,}000$

19. 5000×8000

20. Ellen and her father estimated that there were 110,000 leaves in their yard.

   A. There are 12 houses on Ellen's block. If each house has about the same number of leaves, how many leaves are on Ellen's block?

   B. There are about 300 blocks in Ellen's town. Estimate the number of leaves in the town.

   C. There are 28 students in Ellen's class. Estimate the number of leaves the entire class must rake if every student has to rake about 110,000 leaves in their own yards. Explain your thinking.

Portfolios

Mr. Moreno and his students are getting ready for their open house. They are trying to organize the work that they want to show their parents.

"I have so many papers in my desk and collection folder that I'm not sure what to choose," complained John.

"I can't find the lab I want to show my Dad. My desk is a mess. I have the picture and the data, but I can't find the graph or my questions," said Jessie.

"Why don't you keep your best work together in a portfolio, as artists do?" suggested Mr. Moreno. "A **portfolio** is a collection of your work. It shows your parents what you do in class, and they will be able to see the improvements you make in math this school year."

"That's a great idea," said Jessie. "How do we start?"

1. What are some ways that you can organize your work in a portfolio?

2. What are some ways that a portfolio can be used?

John and Jessie decide to make a Table of Contents for their portfolios. That way, they will be able to see quickly what is inside their portfolios.

Jessie's Table of Contents is shown below.

Jessie's Portfolio
Table of Contents

Item	Description	Date
Eyelets	I counted eyelets on shoes.	September 1
Searching the Forest	I predicted populations from samples.	September 8
Stack Up	I estimated the number of pennies that stack to the moon.	September 29

3. Choose pieces from your collection folder to place into your portfolio.

Examples of items you might choose are:

- *Searching the Forest* from Unit 1.
- The problem *Stack Up* from Unit 2.
- *Eyelets* lab.
- Items your teacher recommends.

4. Start a Table of Contents. The Table of Contents should include the name of each piece of work, a short description of the work, and the date it was finished. Add to the Table of Contents as you add to your portfolio.

5. Examine the items in your portfolio. Write a short paragraph explaining how you could improve one of the items in your portfolio.

Fractions and Ratios

	Student Guide	Discovery Assignment Book	Adventure Book	Unit Resource Guide*
Lesson 1				
Wholes and Parts	●	●		●
Lesson 2				
Fraction Sentences	●			
Lesson 3				
Equivalent Fractions	●	●		
Lesson 4				
Comparing Fractions	●			
Lesson 5				
Using Ratios	●			●
Lesson 6				
Distance vs. Time	●			●
Lesson 7				
Speedy Problems	●			

Unit Resource Guide pages are from the teacher materials.

Wholes and Parts

Irma told her friends that she ate half of a cake yesterday. They all had a different idea about what that meant.

1. If each student shown here is thinking of $\frac{1}{2}$ of a cake, why are all the pieces of cake different sizes?

Numerators and Denominators

The numerator and denominator of a fraction work together to tell the size of the number represented by the fraction.

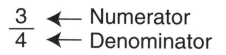

$$\frac{3}{4}$$ ← Numerator
← Denominator

The **denominator** of a fraction tells us to divide the whole into that many equal parts. The 4 in the fraction shown above tells us to divide the whole into four equal parts (fourths).

The **numerator** tells us the number of parts to consider, so the 3 tells us we are interested in three of the parts.

$\frac{3}{4}$ of a cake $\frac{3}{4}$ of the students are
wearing glasses. $\frac{3}{4}$ of a hexagon

2. When you read a fraction:
   A. What information does the denominator give you?
   B. What information does the numerator give you?

3. If the fraction $\frac{1}{4}$ represents $\frac{1}{4}$ of a cake, what other information is necessary to know the size of this piece of cake?

Pattern Block Fractions

In this unit you will use pattern blocks to model fractions. For different questions, different shapes will represent one whole. As you work, be sure you know which "whole" to use.

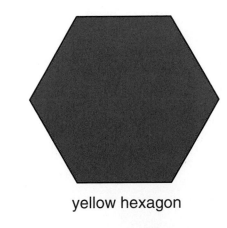

green triangle   yellow hexagon   blue rhombus

red trapezoid   brown trapezoid   purple triangle

---

4. A. Cover a green triangle with purple triangles. How many purple triangles do you need?

B. How many green triangles cover one yellow hexagon?

5. A. Cover a yellow hexagon with purple triangles. How many purple triangles do you need?

B. Cover a brown trapezoid with purple triangles. How many purple triangles make the same shape as a brown trapezoid?

6. A. How many brown trapezoids cover a red trapezoid?

1 whole

B. If the red trapezoid is one whole, which block models $\frac{1}{2}$?

C. If the red trapezoid is one whole, which block models $\frac{1}{6}$?

D. If the red trapezoid is one whole, which block models $\frac{1}{3}$?

E. If the red trapezoid is one whole, which block models 2?

7. If the blue rhombus is one whole, write a number for each of the following blocks:

1 whole

A. one purple triangle
B. two purple triangles
C. one green triangle
D. three purple triangles
E. four purple triangles
F. five purple triangles
G. one red trapezoid
H. one yellow hexagon

8. A. If the purple triangle is $\frac{1}{2}$, what is one whole?
   B. If the purple triangle is $\frac{1}{3}$, what is one whole?
   C. If the purple triangle is $\frac{1}{6}$, what is one whole?
   D. If the purple triangle is $\frac{1}{12}$, what is one whole?

9. For this question, the blue rhombus is $\frac{1}{2}$.

one-half

A. Draw one whole.
B. Draw $\frac{3}{4}$.
C. Draw $\frac{1}{8}$.
D. Draw $\frac{3}{8}$.

10. The trapezoid made of purple triangles shown here is one whole. Write a fraction for each of the following blocks:

    A. one purple triangle

    B. seven purple triangles

    C. one brown trapezoid

11. The trapezoid to the right is one whole. Write two fractions for each of the following:

    A. one green triangle

    B. one blue rhombus

    C. one red trapezoid

    D. five purple triangles

one whole

12. We can use decimals to represent the blocks in Questions 10–11. For example:

one purple triangle $= \frac{1}{10}$ (one-tenth) or 0.1

seven purple triangles $= \frac{7}{10}$ (seven-tenths) or 0.7

one brown trapezoid $= \frac{3}{10}$ (three-tenths) or 0.3

13. Show the following fractions using pattern blocks. The yellow hexagon is one whole. Record each fraction on a *Pattern Block Record Sheet* by shading in the correct portion of the yellow hexagon. Be sure to write the fraction by your drawing. Follow the example for $\frac{5}{12}$.

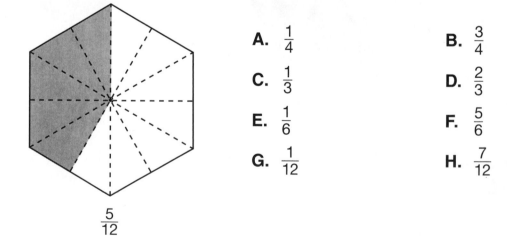

$\frac{5}{12}$

    A. $\frac{1}{4}$ **B.** $\frac{3}{4}$

    C. $\frac{1}{3}$ **D.** $\frac{2}{3}$

    E. $\frac{1}{6}$ **F.** $\frac{5}{6}$

    G. $\frac{1}{12}$ **H.** $\frac{7}{12}$

Fraction Sentences

Mr. Moreno gave his class this challenge: Show one whole using three colors of blocks. Then write a number sentence for your figure. For this lesson, the yellow hexagon is one whole.

David and Brandon work together. Here is their figure.

Here is David's number sentence: $1 = \frac{3}{12} + \frac{1}{4} + \frac{1}{2}$

Here is Brandon's number sentence: $1 = \frac{1}{12} + \frac{1}{12} + \frac{1}{12} + \frac{1}{4} + \frac{1}{2}$

1. Show one whole a different way using three colors of blocks. Write a number sentence for your figure.

2. Lin shows $\frac{1}{2}$ using two colors. First, she shows $\frac{1}{2}$ with a red trapezoid. Then she trades blocks until she has the figure she wants.

   She represents her figure with this number sentence: $\frac{1}{2} = \frac{1}{6} + \frac{1}{6} + \frac{1}{12} + \frac{1}{12}$

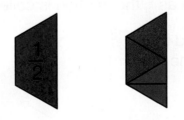

   A. Write another number sentence for Lin's figure.
   B. Show $\frac{1}{2}$ a different way using two colors. Write a number sentence for your figure.

For Questions 3–8, show the fraction. Then write a number sentence for your figure. Remember, the yellow hexagon is one whole.

3. Show $\frac{1}{2}$ using brown and two other colors.

4. Show $\frac{3}{4}$ using brown and two other colors. (*Hint:* Show $\frac{3}{4}$ with three browns first. Then, either cover the brown pieces or trade pieces.)

5. Show $\frac{5}{6}$ using purple, green, and blue.

6. Show $\frac{2}{3}$ without using blue.

7. **A.** Show one whole using one color. (Use any color but yellow.)

   B. Show one whole using a different color.

   C. What can you say about the numerator and denominator of a fraction that is equal to 1?

8. Show $\frac{5}{3}$ using two colors.

Fractions Greater Than One

Ana shows $\frac{5}{3}$ using one color and writes these number sentences:

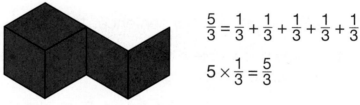

$$\frac{5}{3} = \frac{1}{3} + \frac{1}{3} + \frac{1}{3} + \frac{1}{3} + \frac{1}{3}$$

$$5 \times \frac{1}{3} = \frac{5}{3}$$

When the numerator is greater than or equal to the denominator, the fraction is called an **improper fraction**. Both $\frac{5}{3}$ and $\frac{3}{3}$ are improper fractions. When the numerator is less than the denominator, such as $\frac{2}{3}$, the fraction is called a **proper fraction**.

Manny shows $\frac{5}{3}$ using yellow and blue and writes these number sentences:

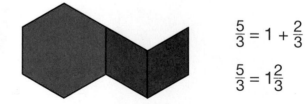

$$\frac{5}{3} = 1 + \frac{2}{3}$$

$$\frac{5}{3} = 1\frac{2}{3}$$

Numbers that are made up of a whole number and a fraction are called **mixed numbers**. $1\frac{2}{3}$ is a mixed number.

9. **A.** Show $\frac{7}{4}$ using only brown blocks. Write an addition sentence and a multiplication sentence for your figure.

   B. Show $\frac{7}{4}$ using yellow and brown blocks. Write an addition sentence for your figure.

   C. Write $\frac{7}{4}$ as a mixed number.

10. **A.** Show $\frac{5}{2}$ using only red blocks. Write an addition sentence and a multiplication sentence for your figure.

   B. Show $\frac{5}{2}$ using the fewest number of blocks possible. Write an addition sentence for your figure.

   C. Write a mixed number for $\frac{5}{2}$.

11. **A.** Show $2\frac{1}{3}$ using only blue blocks. Write a number sentence for your figure.

   B. Show $2\frac{1}{3}$ using the fewest number of blocks possible. Write an addition sentence for your figure.

   C. Write $2\frac{1}{3}$ as an improper fraction.

12. Write a mixed number and an improper fraction for the following figures:

   A.

   B.

13. Write each improper fraction as a mixed number. Use pattern blocks to help you.

   A. $\frac{9}{4}$ **B.** $\frac{17}{12}$ **C.** $\frac{11}{3}$ **D.** $\frac{11}{6}$

14. Write each mixed number as an improper fraction. You can use pattern blocks.

   A. $1\frac{1}{12}$ **B.** $3\frac{1}{2}$ **C.** $2\frac{2}{3}$ **D.** $2\frac{3}{4}$

15. Explain to a friend how you can change an improper fraction to a mixed number without using pattern blocks. Use an example in your explanation.

16. Explain to a friend how you can change a mixed number to an improper fraction without using pattern blocks. Use an example in your explanation.

17. Write each mixed number as an improper fraction.

   A. $1\frac{3}{8}$ **B.** $3\frac{3}{4}$ **C.** $3\frac{4}{5}$ **D.** $4\frac{5}{6}$

18. Write each improper fraction as a mixed number.

   A. $\frac{13}{4}$ **B.** $\frac{9}{2}$ **C.** $\frac{14}{3}$ **D.** $\frac{12}{5}$

Homework

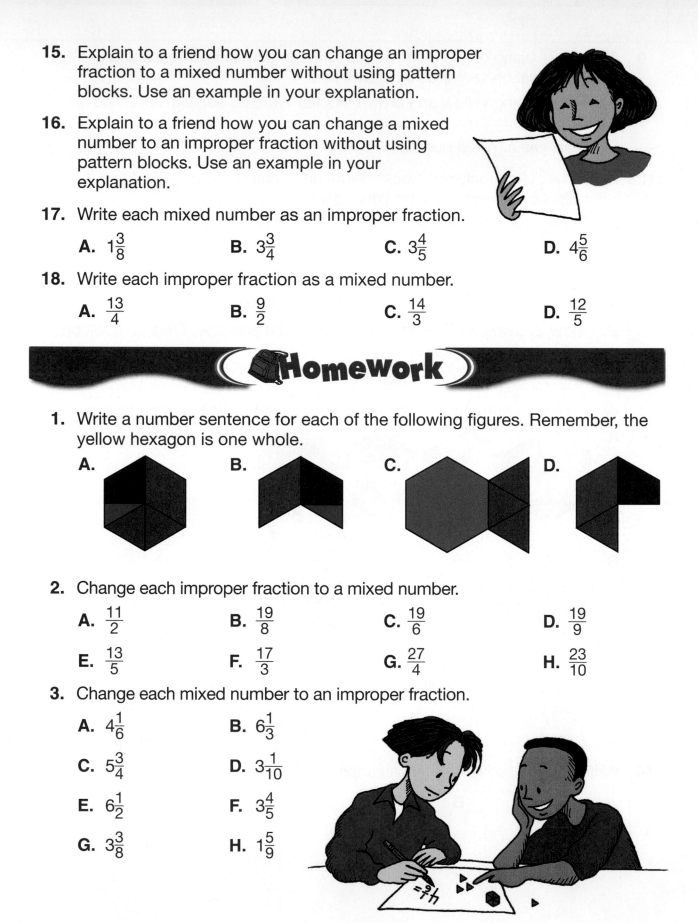

1. Write a number sentence for each of the following figures. Remember, the yellow hexagon is one whole.

   A.   **B.**   **C.**   **D.**

2. Change each improper fraction to a mixed number.

   A. $\frac{11}{2}$ **B.** $\frac{19}{8}$ **C.** $\frac{19}{6}$ **D.** $\frac{19}{9}$

   E. $\frac{13}{5}$ **F.** $\frac{17}{3}$ **G.** $\frac{27}{4}$ **H.** $\frac{23}{10}$

3. Change each mixed number to an improper fraction.

   A. $4\frac{1}{6}$ **B.** $6\frac{1}{3}$

   C. $5\frac{3}{4}$ **D.** $3\frac{1}{10}$

   E. $6\frac{1}{2}$ **F.** $3\frac{4}{5}$

   G. $3\frac{3}{8}$ **H.** $1\frac{5}{9}$

Equivalent Fractions

Equivalent Fractions and Pattern Blocks

Fractions that have the same value are called **equivalent fractions.** For example, $\frac{3}{4}$ is equivalent to $\frac{9}{12}$. We can show this using pattern blocks. The yellow hexagon is one whole.

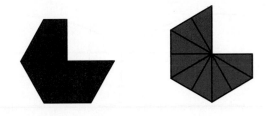

1. Jackie uses pattern blocks to show that $\frac{1}{3}$ is equivalent to $\frac{4}{12}$. She writes a number sentence for this pair of equivalent fractions.

   A. Find another fraction equivalent to $\frac{1}{3}$ that can be shown with pattern blocks.

   B. Write a number sentence for this pair of equivalent fractions. Follow Jackie's example.

2. For each of the following fractions, find all the equivalent fractions that can be shown with pattern blocks. Write a number sentence for each pair of equivalent fractions.

   A. $\frac{1}{6}$ **B.** $\frac{3}{12}$

   C. $\frac{4}{3}$ **D.** $\frac{2}{1}$

   E. $\frac{1}{2}$

3. **A.** Look at your list of sentences for $\frac{1}{2}$. What patterns do you see? How can you tell if a fraction is equal to $\frac{1}{2}$?

   B. Does the number sentence $\frac{1}{2} = \frac{5}{10}$ fit the pattern?

   C. Does $\frac{1}{2} = \frac{50}{100}$ fit the pattern?

   D. Michael and Manny share a pizza. Michael says that he ate $\frac{1}{2}$ of the pizza. Manny says that he ate $\frac{4}{8}$ of the pizza. Did they share the pizza fairly? How do you know?

Equivalent Fractions and Fractohoppers

Fractohoppers are imaginary creatures that live on number lines. Every time a fractohopper hops, it hops the same distance. For example, a $\frac{1}{2}$ hopper takes two equal hops to travel from zero to one.

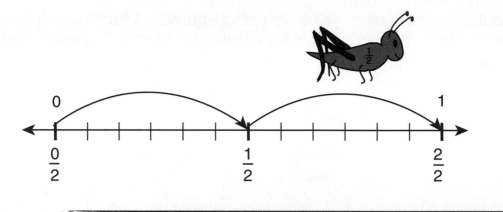

Discuss

4. A $\frac{1}{3}$ hopper takes three equal hops to go from zero to one. Where does a $\frac{1}{3}$ hopper land after two hops?

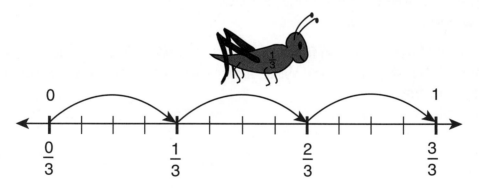

5. To show how a $\frac{1}{6}$ hopper hops, the number line must be divided into sixths. Where does a $\frac{1}{6}$ hopper land if it hops five times?

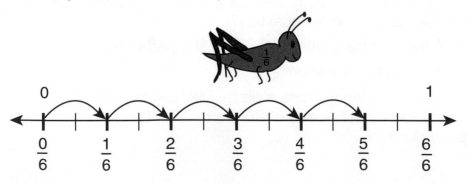

6. Jackie wrote two number sentences for the movements of the $\frac{1}{6}$ hopper in Question 5.

$$\frac{1}{6} + \frac{1}{6} + \frac{1}{6} + \frac{1}{6} + \frac{1}{6} = \frac{5}{6} \qquad 5 \times \frac{1}{6} = \frac{5}{6}$$

Write two number sentences for the movements of the $\frac{1}{3}$ hopper in Question 4.

7. This number line shows how a $\frac{2}{6}$ hopper travels from zero to one.

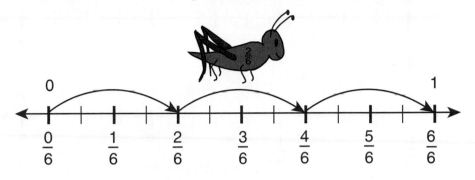

A. How many hops does it take?

B. Fractohoppers can have more than one name. Use the number lines below to find another name for a two-sixths hopper.

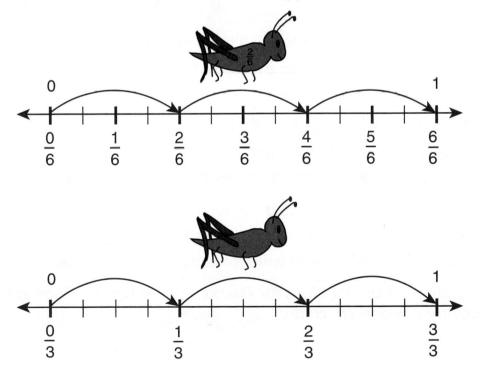

Use the number lines to answer Questions 8–9.

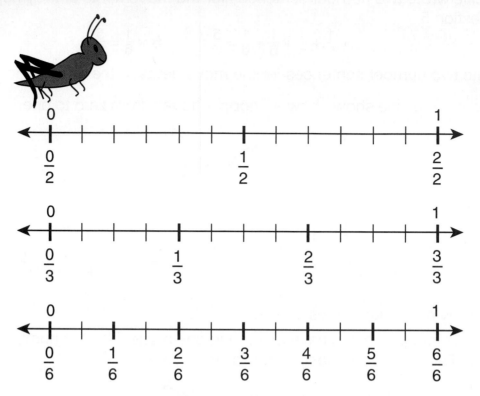

8. **A.** Where does a $\frac{1}{6}$ hopper land if it hops three times?

   B. What is another name for this point on the number line?

   C. Write a number sentence to show that this pair of fractions is equivalent.

9. **A.** Where does a $\frac{1}{6}$ hopper land if it hops two times?

   B. What is another name for this point on the number line?

   C. Write a number sentence to show these fractions are equivalent.

10. **A.** Where does a $\frac{1}{2}$ hopper land if it hops 2 times?

   B. Where does a $\frac{1}{3}$ hopper land if it hops 3 times?

   C. Use the number lines to write three fractions equivalent to 1.

11. Complete the *Number Lines for Fractohoppers* Activity Page in the *Discovery Assignment Book.*

Using Number Lines to Find Equivalent Fractions

Use your number lines on the *Number Lines for Fractohoppers* Activity Page to solve the following problems.

12. Use the number lines to find a value for *n* that will make the number sentence true. Write the complete number sentence.

A. $\frac{2}{5} = \frac{n}{10}$ **B.** $\frac{10}{12} = \frac{n}{6}$ **C.** $\frac{1}{4} = \frac{n}{12}$

D. $\frac{1}{4} = \frac{2}{n}$ **E.** $\frac{8}{10} = \frac{4}{n}$ **F.** $\frac{1}{3} = \frac{n}{12}$

13. Fractions that name the same point on a number line are equivalent fractions.

A. Name all the fractions on the number lines that are equivalent to $\frac{3}{4}$. Write number sentences to show your answers.

B. What patterns do you see? How can you tell if a fraction is equal to $\frac{3}{4}$?

14. We can write: $\frac{3}{4} = \frac{3 \times 2}{4 \times 2} = \frac{6}{8}$ and $\frac{3}{4} = \frac{3 \times 3}{4 \times 3} = \frac{9}{12}$. Is $\frac{15}{20}$ equivalent to $\frac{3}{4}$? How do you know?

15. A. Find all the fractions on the number lines that are equivalent to $\frac{8}{12}$. Write number sentences to show your answers.

B. What patterns do you see?

16. We can write: $\frac{8}{12} = \frac{8 \div 4}{12 \div 4} = \frac{2}{3}$. Is $\frac{4}{6}$ equivalent to $\frac{8}{12}$? How do you know?

17. Name all the fractions on the number lines that are equivalent to 1.

18. How can you find equivalent fractions without using the number lines?

19. Use your method to complete the following number sentences.

A. $\frac{1}{4} = \frac{n}{20}$ **B.** $\frac{2}{5} = \frac{n}{20}$ **C.** $\frac{4}{3} = \frac{n}{9}$

D. $\frac{8}{16} = \frac{n}{4}$ **E.** $\frac{3}{15} = \frac{1}{n}$ **F.** $\frac{1}{4} = \frac{n}{100}$

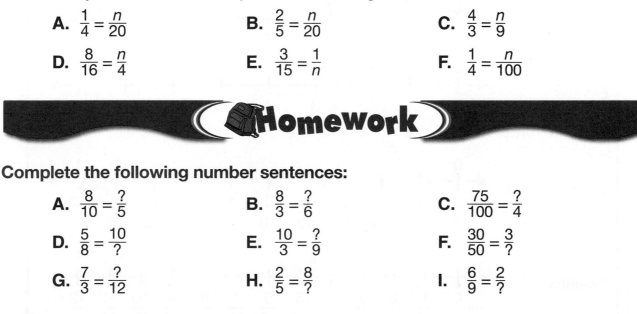

Homework

Complete the following number sentences:

A. $\frac{8}{10} = \frac{?}{5}$ **B.** $\frac{8}{3} = \frac{?}{6}$ **C.** $\frac{75}{100} = \frac{?}{4}$

D. $\frac{5}{8} = \frac{10}{?}$ **E.** $\frac{10}{3} = \frac{?}{9}$ **F.** $\frac{30}{50} = \frac{3}{?}$

G. $\frac{7}{3} = \frac{?}{12}$ **H.** $\frac{2}{5} = \frac{8}{?}$ **I.** $\frac{6}{9} = \frac{2}{?}$

Comparing Fractions

Number Lines for Fractohoppers

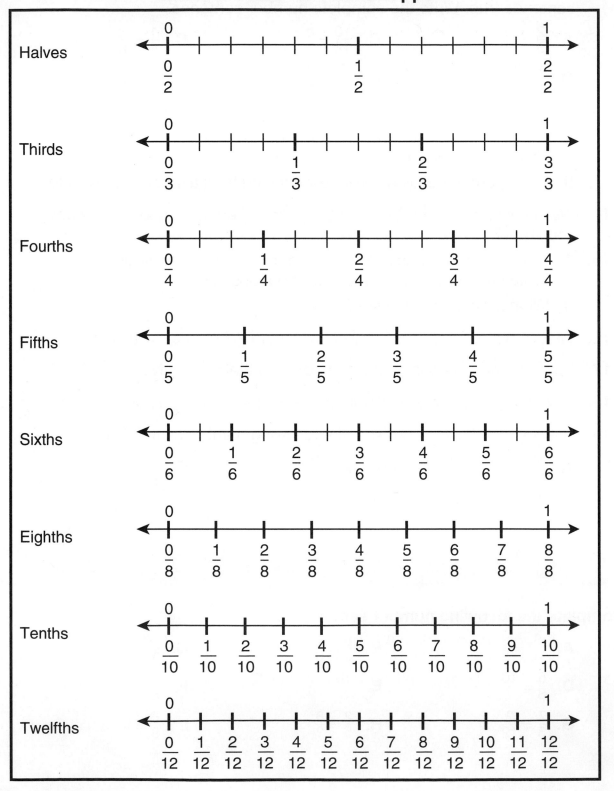

Study the following data table. Look for patterns within each column.

Fractions near or equal to 0	Fractions near or equal to $\frac{1}{2}$	Fractions near or equal to 1	Fractions much greater than 1
$\frac{0}{8}, \frac{2}{12}, \frac{1}{8}$	$\frac{3}{8}, \frac{4}{8}, \frac{2}{4}, \frac{7}{12}, \frac{4}{10}$	$\frac{5}{6}, \frac{8}{8}, \frac{9}{8}$	$\frac{16}{8}, \frac{19}{10}$

Use the table above or the Number Lines for Fractohoppers chart on the previous page to help you complete the following questions.

1. Make a table like the one above. Sort the following fractions in your table.
   $\frac{11}{12}, \frac{0}{12}, \frac{5}{12}, \frac{25}{12}, \frac{1}{12}, \frac{10}{12}.$

2. **A.** How are the fractions near 0 alike?

   B. How are the fractions near $\frac{1}{2}$ alike?

   C. How are the fractions near 1 alike?

   D. How can you tell if a fraction is greater than 1?

3. Add these fractions to your table: $\frac{2}{4}, \frac{1}{10}, \frac{24}{6}, \frac{1}{11}, \frac{6}{10}, \frac{5}{8}, \frac{2}{10}, \frac{7}{8},$ and $\frac{17}{10}.$

4. Add these fractions to your table: $\frac{14}{15}, \frac{11}{20}, \frac{1}{9}, \frac{103}{100}, \frac{40}{20}, \frac{20}{40}, \frac{3}{20},$ and $\frac{60}{100}.$

5. Write each of the following sets of fractions in order from smallest to largest. Use the symbol for "less than" (<) in your answer. Follow the example:

   Example: $\frac{2}{12}, \frac{19}{10}, \frac{4}{8}, \frac{5}{6}$ Answer: $\frac{2}{12} < \frac{4}{8} < \frac{5}{6} < \frac{19}{10}$

   A. $\frac{5}{12}, \frac{1}{10}, \frac{5}{6}, \frac{9}{8}$ **B.** $\frac{4}{5}, \frac{3}{6}, \frac{5}{4}, \frac{0}{2}$

   C. $\frac{12}{10}, \frac{10}{12}, \frac{7}{12}, \frac{1}{6}$ **D.** $\frac{20}{10}, \frac{1}{20}, \frac{7}{8}, \frac{3}{5}$

6. Write each of the following sets of fractions in order from smallest to largest. Use the symbol for "less than" (<) in your answer. Follow the example:

   Example: $\frac{2}{8}, \frac{7}{8}, \frac{5}{8}, \frac{1}{8}$ Answer: $\frac{1}{8} < \frac{2}{8} < \frac{5}{8} < \frac{7}{8}$

   A. $\frac{4}{5}, \frac{1}{5}, \frac{6}{5}, \frac{3}{5}$ **B.** $\frac{11}{12}, \frac{2}{12}, \frac{8}{12}, \frac{7}{12}$

   C. If two or more fractions have the same denominator, how can you tell which of the fractions is larger?

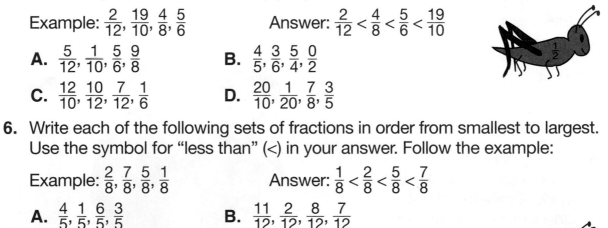

7. Write each of the following sets of fractions in order from smallest to largest.

A. $\frac{1}{3}, \frac{1}{4}, \frac{1}{2}, \frac{1}{10}$

B. $\frac{3}{5}, \frac{3}{10}, \frac{3}{8}, \frac{3}{2}$

C. If two or more fractions have the same numerator, how can you tell which of the fractions is larger?

8. Write each of the following sets of fractions in order from smallest to largest.

A. $\frac{7}{12}, \frac{3}{8}, \frac{1}{12}, \frac{10}{10}$

B. $\frac{2}{9}, \frac{12}{11}, \frac{8}{14}, \frac{4}{8}$

C. $\frac{7}{8}, \frac{7}{4}, \frac{7}{11}, \frac{7}{9}$

D. $\frac{9}{6}, \frac{3}{6}, \frac{1}{6}, \frac{5}{6}$

E. $\frac{2}{12}, \frac{20}{10}, \frac{4}{6}, \frac{2}{4}$

F. $\frac{7}{10}, \frac{10}{9}, \frac{1}{10}, \frac{4}{9}$

Write the following sets of fractions in order from smallest to largest. Use the strategies that you have learned. Tell which strategy you used to answer each question.

1. $\frac{2}{12}, \frac{2}{3}, \frac{2}{5}, \frac{2}{10}$

2. $\frac{7}{8}, \frac{1}{12}, \frac{3}{6}, \frac{13}{5}$

3. $\frac{3}{10}, \frac{7}{10}, \frac{2}{10}, \frac{5}{10}$

4. $\frac{11}{12}, \frac{4}{9}, \frac{0}{3}, \frac{1}{3}$

5. $\frac{5}{9}, \frac{5}{4}, \frac{5}{12}, \frac{5}{6}$

6. Manny walks $\frac{1}{2}$ mile to school each day. David walks $\frac{2}{3}$ mile to school, and Brandon walks $\frac{1}{4}$ mile.

   A. Who has the shortest walk? Explain how you know.

   B. Who has the longest walk? Explain how you know.

    Comparing Fractions

Using Ratios

The Fun Fair

Each year, the fifth-grade students at Bessie Coleman School organize a Fun Fair for the school. They plan games and sell refreshments. This year, Frank and Edward are in charge of the bake sale. Here is their price list:

Edward made the following table to help them find the cost of the muffins:

Edward's Table

Number of Muffins	Cost
1	30¢
2	60¢
3	90¢
4	$1.20

Edward said, "If we make a table like this one for everything we sell, we will be able to find the prices of things quickly. We can multiply or use patterns to fill in the tables."

Frank thought for a few minutes and then he got a piece of graph paper and began to draw a graph. "You're right, a table will work, but we will have to figure out the whole table. Look at this graph. The points for one, two, and three muffins are in a line."

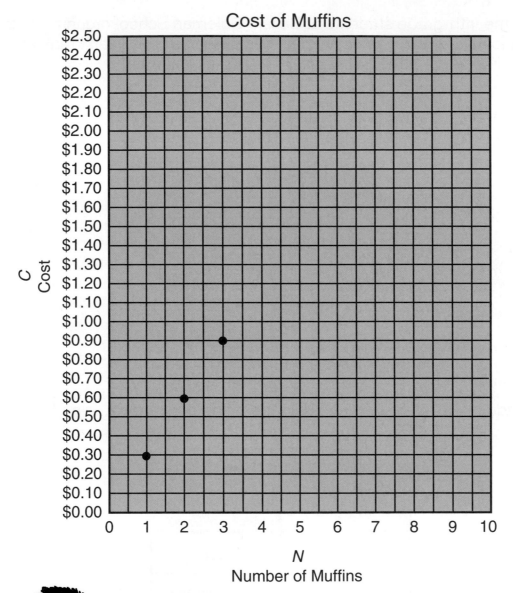

Cost of Muffins

C Cost

N Number of Muffins

Using Ratios

"If we use a ruler to draw the line, we can use the line to find the cost of different numbers of muffins. See, the line shows that 4 muffins will cost $1.20. That matches the table."

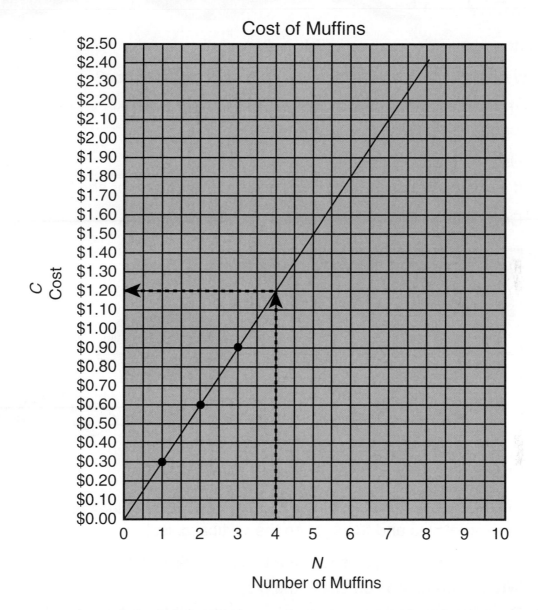

Cost of Muffins

N
Number of Muffins

Edward studied his table and Frank's graph. "You can see the same patterns in both the table and graph. For every muffin you add to the table, the cost goes up 30¢. Each time you add a muffin to the graph, you move one to the right and the line goes up another 30¢. That's because the cost of one muffin is 30¢."

1. What patterns do you see in Edward's table?

2. How could you complete the table by using multiplication?

3. What patterns do you think Edward sees in both the table and graph? Describe the patterns in your own words.

4. **A.** Use the graph to find the cost of seven muffins.

   B. If a customer has $1.50, how many muffins can he or she buy?

5. **A.** Copy and complete the table for the cost of cookies.

Number of Cookies	Cost
2	25¢
6	
	$1.00

   B. Make a graph of the data. Graph the number of cookies on the horizontal axis and the cost on the vertical axis.

6. **A.** What patterns do you see in the table in Question 5?

   B. What patterns do you see in the graph?

   C. Describe any patterns you see in both the table and graph.

7. **A.** Use your graph in Question 5B to find the cost of 1 dozen (12) cookies.

   B. What is the cost of three cookies?

Ratios

Edward and Frank used ratios to help them with the prices for the bake sale. A **ratio** is a way to compare two numbers or quantities. When they were finding out prices of muffins they used the ratio "1 muffin costs 30 cents." They found equal ratios: "2 muffins cost 60 cents" and "3 muffins cost 90 cents."

8. Use your table or graph in Question 5 to name two ratios equal to the ratio "2 cookies for 25¢."

The decorating committee plans to decorate the gym with crepe paper, ribbon, and balloons.

The committee measured the length and width of the gym in yards. They measured the height of the booths in feet. When they went to the store, they found that ribbon is sold by the yard. Crepe paper is sold by the foot. One way to convert feet to yards and yards to feet is by using a graph. The students made a graph that compares feet to yards and yards to feet. It is on the following page.

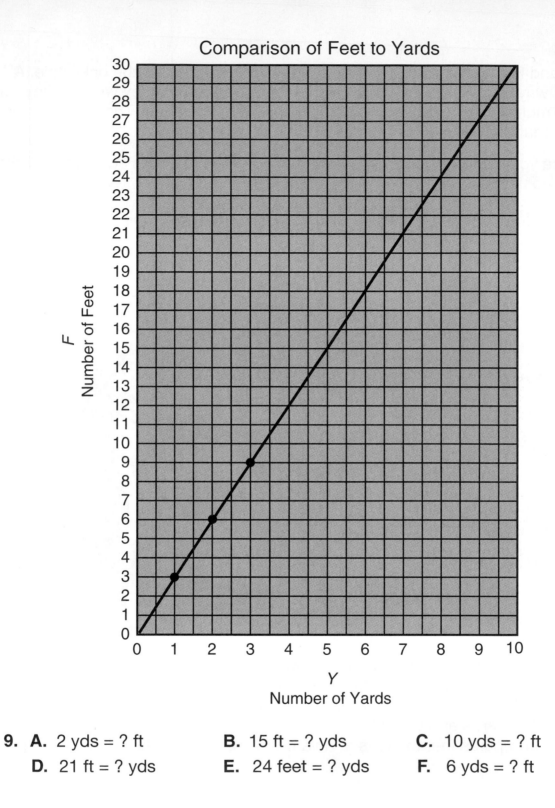

Comparison of Feet to Yards

9. A. 2 yds = ? ft **B.** 15 ft = ? yds **C.** 10 yds = ? ft
D. 21 ft = ? yds **E.** 24 feet = ? yds **F.** 6 yds = ? ft

Ratios can be written as fractions. To compare feet and yards, we can write the ratio $\frac{3\,ft}{1\,yd}$. We can write number sentences using fractions that show ratios are equal. When the fractions are equal, the ratios are equal:

$$\frac{3\,ft}{1\,yd} = \frac{6\,ft}{2\,yds} \text{ and } \frac{3\,ft}{1\,yd} = \frac{15\,ft}{5\,yds}$$

10. Complete the following number sentence: $\frac{3\,ft}{1\,yd} = \frac{21\,ft}{?\,yds}$.

You can also compare feet to yards by looking at the ratio of yards to feet. For example:

$$\frac{1\,yd}{3\,ft} = \frac{2\,yds}{6\,ft} = \frac{5\,yds}{15\,ft}$$

11. Using fractions, write two other ratios that are equal to $\frac{3\,ft}{1\,yd}$.

12. Edward and Frank decided to sell 1 cookie for 15¢.

   A. Are the following two ratios equal? Why or why not?

$$\frac{25¢}{2\text{ cookies}} \text{ and } \frac{15¢}{1\text{ cookie}}$$

   B. Add a point to the graph you made for Question 5 which shows that 1 cookie costs 15¢. Is this point on your line? Why or why not?

13. Using fractions, write two ratios that are equal to $\frac{30¢}{1\text{ muffin}}$.

14. Using fractions, write two ratios equal to $\frac{25¢}{2\text{ cookies}}$.

Homework

You will need enough graph paper to make two graphs.

1. **A.** The fifth graders decided to make data tables to help the first graders use coins to pay for games and food at the fun fair. Copy and complete the tables on your paper. Fill in at least 5 rows in each table.

Number of Nickels	Number of Dimes
2	1

Number of Quarters	Number of Dimes
2	5
4	

B. Make a graph that compares the value of dimes to the value of nickels. (Put the number of nickels on the horizontal axis and the number of dimes on the vertical axis.)

C. Use fractions to write three ratios equal to $\frac{1 \text{ dime}}{2 \text{ nickels}}$.

D. Make a graph that compares the value of dimes to the value of quarters. (Put quarters on the horizontal axis.)

E. Use fractions to write three ratios equal to $\frac{5 \text{ dimes}}{2 \text{ quarters}}$.

2. There are four quarts in a gallon.

A. Make a table with at least 5 rows that can be used to convert quarts to gallons.

B. Write three ratios equal to $\frac{4 \text{ quarts}}{1 \text{ gallon}}$.

3. The poster for the bake sale says that one dozen rolls cost $2.40.

A. How much will three dozen rolls cost?

B. How much will six rolls cost? Explain how you found your answer.

4. The poster for the bake sale says that brownies cost 50¢ each or 3 for $1.00.

   A. Write a fraction that shows the cost of one brownie as a ratio of cost to the number of brownies.

   B. Write a fraction that shows the cost of three brownies as a ratio of cost to the number of brownies.

   C. Are the ratios in Parts A and B equal? Why or why not?

Use the graph below to answer the following questions.

5. A. What is the cost for three people to see a movie?

   B. What is the cost for six people to see a movie?

   C. A customer paid the ticket seller $35.00. How many tickets did he or she buy?

   D. Choose a point on the graph, and write a ratio that shows the cost to the number of people.

   E. Write two other ratios equal to the ratio you wrote in Part D.

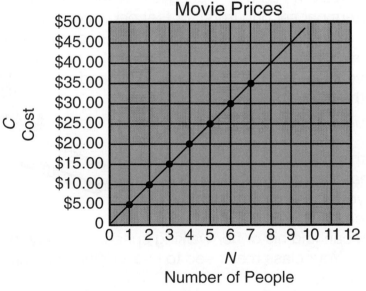

Distance vs. Time

 **Discuss**

1. If you walk at a steady pace for one hour, how far can you walk?

2. If you walk at a steady pace, how long does it take you to walk a mile?

3. How fast do you walk—about 1 mile per hour, 5 miles per hour, or 10 miles per hour?

4. What can you measure that will help you answer these questions?

To find out how fast someone or something is moving, we measure speed. To measure speed, consider both time and distance. **Speed** is the ratio of distance to time. So, speed can be written as a fraction:

$$\text{Speed} = \frac{\text{Distance moved}}{\text{Time taken}}$$

Since speed involves both distance and time, the unit of measure involves both as well. Speed is measured in miles per hour (mph), meters per second (m/s), or feet per second (ft/s), and so on. For example, if a car travels 55 miles in one hour, the speed of the car is $\frac{55 \text{ miles}}{1 \text{ hour}}$ or 55 mph. If a toy car travels 6 meters in 2 seconds, the speed of the toy car is $\frac{6 \text{ meters}}{2 \text{ seconds}}$ which is equivalent to $\frac{3 \text{ meters}}{1 \text{ second}}$ or 3 m/s.

In this experiment, you will measure the time it takes one of your classmates to walk three different distances. Then you can find his or her walking speed. One way to do the experiment is described here. Your class may need to use a different setup.

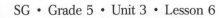

Materials

You will need the following materials for your group:

chalk or tape
yardstick (or meterstick with inches)
three stopwatches
Three-trial Data Table

Lab Setup

- Use a yardstick or meterstick to measure a straight track that is 12 yards long. Use chalk or tape to mark the beginning and end of the track. Also, mark points that are 6 yards and 9 yards from the starting line. (Remember, a meterstick is about 39 inches long, which is about 3 inches longer than a yard.)

- Three members of the group will be timers. Another member will be the walker. One timer should stand near the 6-yard mark, one timer should stand near the 9-yard mark, and one timer should stand near the 12-yard mark.

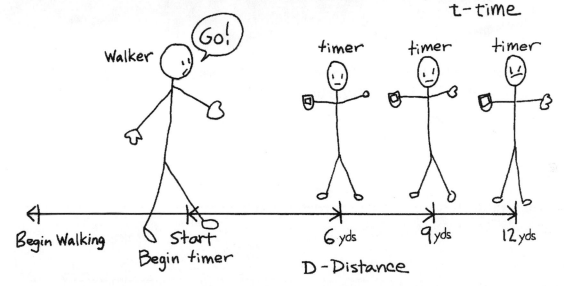

- The walker should begin walking at a steady pace several feet behind the starting line. When the walker crosses the starting line, he or she should say, "Go." At that moment, all three timers begin their stopwatches. When the walker's front foot touches or crosses each mark, the timer at that marker stops his or her stopwatch. (Practice once or twice with your group before you begin recording your data.)

Draw

5. If your group uses a setup different from the one shown in the picture, draw a picture of your setup. Be sure to label the variables with symbols.

6. **A.** What variables will you measure in this experiment?

   B. What variables are held fixed? **Fixed variables** are variables that stay the same during the whole experiment so that the only thing that affects the "time taken" is the distance walked.

Collect

7. **A.** Use a data table similar to the one shown below to record your data. Repeat the procedure three times, and record the results of all three trials.

   B. Find the average time for each distance to the nearest second. Use the median as your average.

Distance vs. Time

D Distance (in yards)	T Time (in seconds)			
	Trial 1	Trial 2	Trial 3	Average

8. Make a point graph of your data. Scientists usually graph time (*T*) on the horizontal axis and distance (*D*) on the vertical axis.

9. What were the measurements for time and distance when the walker crossed the starting line? (When *D* = 0 yds, *T* = ? sec.) Add this point to your graph.

10. If your points lie close to a line, use a ruler to draw a best-fit line. The **best-fit line** is the line that comes closest to the most number of points.

Explore

11. Use your graph to find the time taken to walk 8 yards.

12. Find the distance walked after 10 seconds.
    A. Give your answer in yards.
    B. Give your answer in feet.

13. A. Choose a point on the line. Use it to write the walker's speed as a ratio of distance traveled to time taken written as a fraction.
    B. Write two more ratios equal to the ratio in Part A.

14. A. How many yards did the walker travel in one second?
    B. Give the walker's speed in yards per second (yd/s).

15. A. How many feet does the walker travel in one second?
    B. Give the walker's speed in feet per second (ft/s).

16. A. If the walker continues at the same pace for one hour, about how far will he or she walk? Explain how you found your answer.
    B. About how many miles can he or she walk in one hour? (1 mile = 5280 ft) Check your answer. Is it reasonable?

17. If the walker continues at the same pace, about how long will it take him or her to walk one mile?

18. Do you think the walker can walk at the same speed you calculated in Questions 16 and 17 for one hour or longer? Why or why not?

Homework

Felicia biked for one hour on a bike path. She biked at the same speed for the entire time. The following graph shows her speed.

1. How far did Felicia travel after 15 minutes?

2. How long did it take Felicia to bike 10 miles?

3. **A.** Choose a point on the graph. Use it to write Felicia's speed as a ratio of distance traveled to time taken. (Include units.)

   B. Write two more ratios equal to the ratio in Part A.

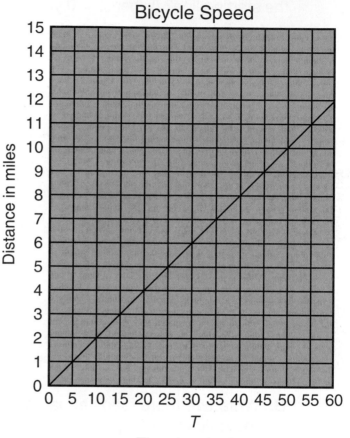

Bicycle Speed

D — Distance in miles

T

Time in minutes

4. If Felicia biked at the same speed for $1\frac{1}{2}$ hours, how far would she travel? Explain how you know.

5. The bike path is 16 miles long. If Felicia biked the entire path at the same speed, how long did she travel? Explain how you know.

6. **A.** How far did Felicia travel in one hour?

   B. Give Felicia's speed in miles per hour.

Speedy Problems

Use appropriate tools to solve the following problems.

1. A salesperson has to drive 500 miles. For the first three hours, she drove at 65 miles per hour. For the next two hours, she drove at 55 miles per hour. How many more miles does she have left to drive?

2. John bicycles for 2 hours at a speed of 15 miles per hour. How many hours will it take Shannon to cover the same distance at a speed of 10 miles per hour?

3. A truck driver drives 1000 miles. The truck uses a gallon of diesel fuel for every 15 miles. About how many gallons of fuel are needed?

4. One Earth Day, four workers planted 500 white pine seedlings. Each worker could plant 25 trees an hour. How many hours did it take to plant all 500 trees?

5. A teacher wants to interview each of his students. He needs 15 minutes for each interview. How long, in hours and minutes, will it take him to interview all 25 students in his class?

6. Alexis, Ana, and Felicia each ate fractions of pie for dessert. Alexis ate $\frac{2}{5}$ of a pie. Ana ate $\frac{2}{3}$ of a pie. Felicia ate $\frac{1}{6}$ of a pie.

   A. If all the pies were the same size, who ate the most pie? Explain.

   B. Who ate the least pie? Tell how you know.

7. Lin, Manny, and Arti each bought the same size box of pencils. One month later, $\frac{3}{8}$ of Lin's pencils are missing; $\frac{1}{8}$ of Manny's pencils are missing; $\frac{5}{8}$ of Arti's pencils are missing.

   A. Who lost the most pencils?

   B. Who lost the least number of pencils?

Unit 4

Division and Data

	Student Guide	Discovery Assignment Book	Adventure Book	Unit Resource Guide*
Lesson 1				
Grid Area	●	●		
Lesson 2				
Modeling Division	●			
Lesson 3				
Paper-and-Pencil Division	●			●
Lesson 4				
How Close Is Close Enough?	●	●		●
Lesson 5				
Mean or Median?	●			
Lesson 6				
Spreading Out	●			
Lesson 7				
George Washington Carver: Man of Measure		●	●	
Lesson 8				
Review Problems	●			
Lesson 9				
Midterm Test				●

Unit Resource Guide pages are from the teacher materials.

Grid Area

Area is a measurement of size. We measure the area of a floor to find the amount of carpet needed to cover the floor. We can also use area to measure the amount of paper needed to wrap a present.

Area is the amount of surface that is needed to cover something. To measure the area of a shape, we tell the number of squares needed to cover the shape.

A **square centimeter** is the area of a square that is 1 centimeter long on each side. This is 1 square centimeter.

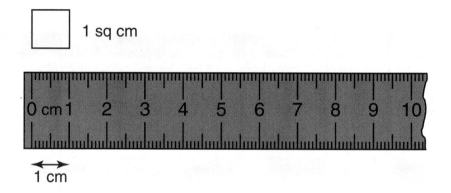

1 sq cm

1 cm

1. Manny found the area of Figures A and B in square centimeters. He said they both have an area of 11 square centimeters. Is Manny correct?

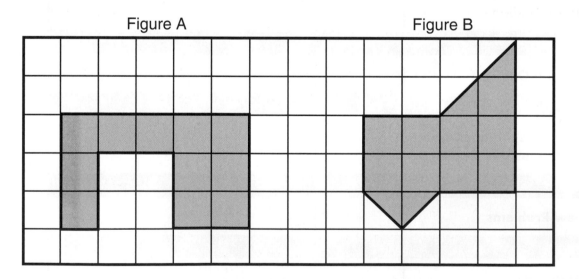

Figure A   Figure B

2. A. Study the shaded rectangle in Figure C. How is it different from the shapes in Question 1 and the shapes you measured earlier in this lesson?

B. What strategies could be used to find the area of the shaded rectangle?

Figure C

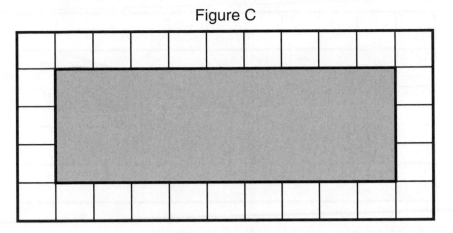

To find the area of a rectangle, we can multiply the length times the width. We call one side of a rectangle the **length** and an adjacent side the **width.**

3. What two numbers do you multiply together in Figure C to get the area?

4. A. Discuss strategies for finding the area of Figure D. Devise a plan to find the area, and then try your plan. Compare your work with that of your classmates.

B. Did you use multiplication in your plan? If so, explain how.

C. What other operations did you use to find the total shaded area of Figure D?

Figure D

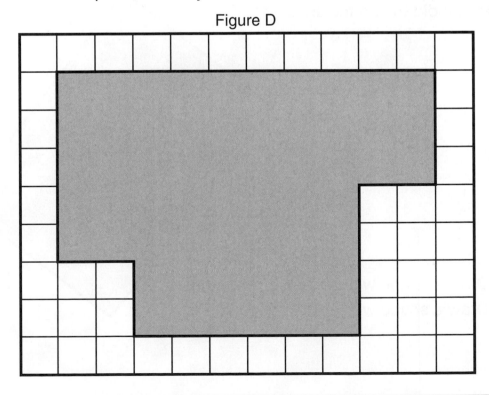

5. Look at the shaded triangle in Figure E. To find the area of this right triangle, we use the area of the rectangle that "surrounds" it.

Figure E

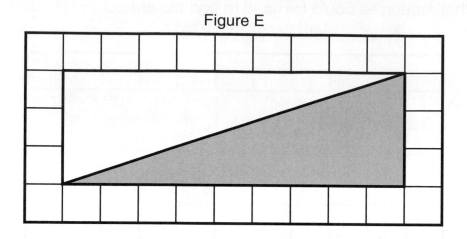

A. What fraction of the rectangle is shaded?

B. Can you use multiplication to find the area of the shaded triangle in Figure E? Explain.

C. Did you use an operation other than multiplication to find the area? If so, which operation?

6. What tool do you need to find the area of Figure F? What unit of measure will you use?

7. Find the area of the rectangle in Figure F. Write a number sentence that shows what you did to find the area.

Figure F

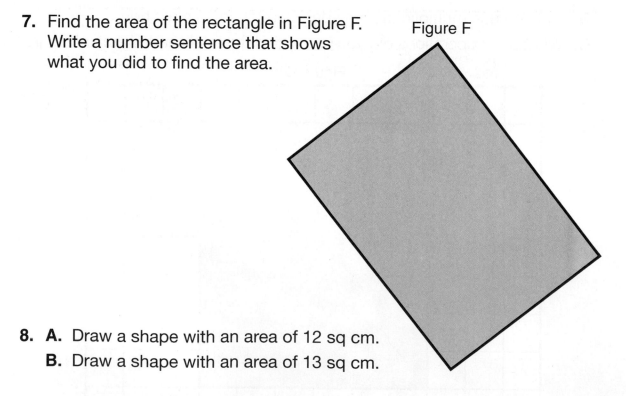

8. A. Draw a shape with an area of 12 sq cm.

B. Draw a shape with an area of 13 sq cm.

You will need three or four sheets of *Centimeter Grid Paper* to complete the homework.

1. Find the area of the following shapes. Record the area of each shape. Explain what strategies you used. Use number sentences in your explanations when appropriate. Don't forget to give the correct units.

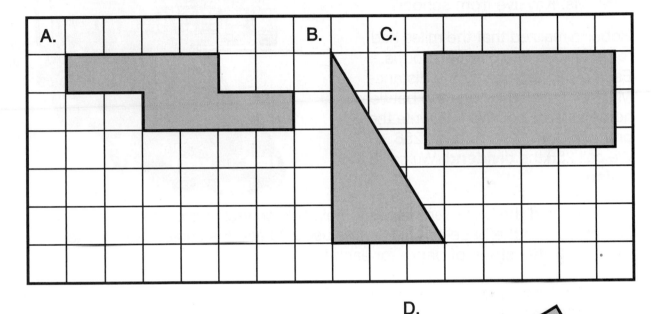

D.

Use *Centimeter Grid Paper* to complete the following problems.

2. Draw a shape with an area of 21 sq cm.

3. Draw a shape with curved sides that has an area of about 14 sq cm.

4. Draw a rectangle with the area of 21 sq cm. Write a multiplication sentence to show how to find the area.

5. Draw a triangle with the area of 6 sq cm. Explain how you did this.

6. Draw a shape with more than 4 sides that has an area of 16 sq cm.

Modeling Division

Interpreting Division

Ms. Kay is a teacher at Bessie Coleman School. She traveled 256 miles driving between home and school for four days. How far does Ms. Kay live from school?

Roberto realized that the miles had to be divided into 8 equal groups. Each group represents the distance Ms. Kay traveled on one trip between home and school. We can write the problem as 8 ⟌ 256 or as 256 ÷ 8. We call 256 the **dividend.** We call 8 the **divisor.**

Roberto used the base-ten pieces to help him solve the problem. To model 256 miles with the base-ten pieces, he used 2 flats, 5 skinnies, and 6 bits. He used 8 little strips of paper for each trip.

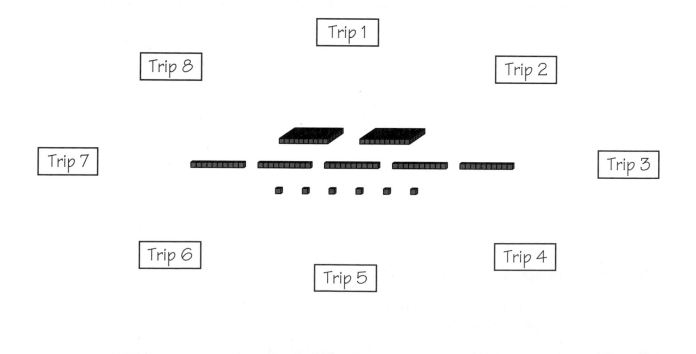

Roberto began to distribute the base-ten pieces. He saw that he could not give every trip a flat. So he broke up the 2 flats into 20 skinnies. Roberto then had 25 skinnies. He gave each trip 3 skinnies. He had one skinny and six bits left over.

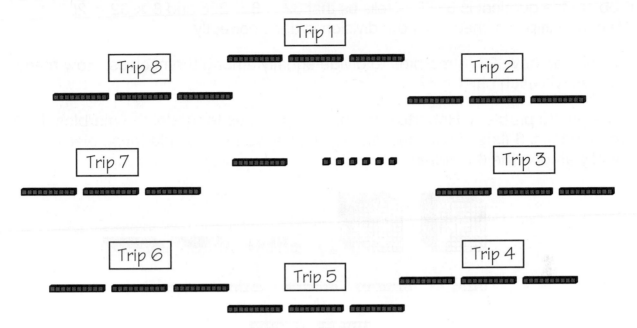

Roberto then broke up his remaining skinny into 10 bits so he had 16 bits. He gave each trip 2 bits. Each trip then had 32 miles.

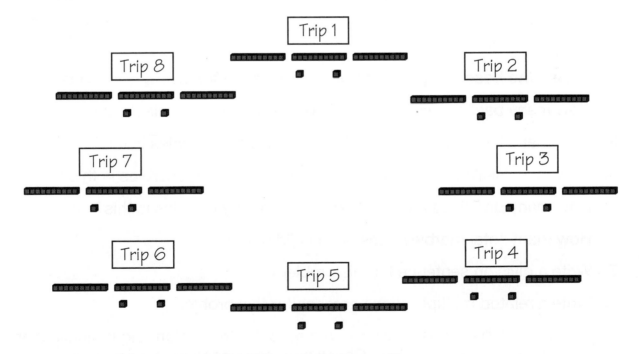

Roberto said, "Ms. Kay lives 32 miles from school."

One way of looking at division is to think of dividing something into equal pieces or groups. Here, Roberto divided the 256 miles into 8 equal groups. We can write 256 ÷ 8 = 32. The answer to a division problem is called the **quotient.** In this problem the quotient is 32. This tells us that 32 × 8 = 256 and 8 × 32 = 256. We can multiply to check that our division is done correctly.

Six children have 2376 marbles to divide equally among themselves. How many marbles will each child get?

To begin the problem, Roberto used base-ten pieces to model the marbles. He took 2 packs, 3 flats, 7 skinnies, and 6 bits. He wants to divide these pieces equally among the 6 children.

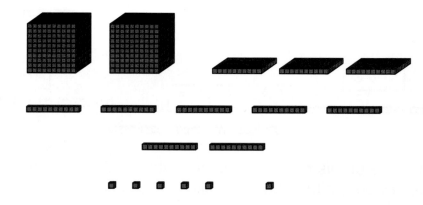

1. Estimate the number of marbles each child will get. Explain how you got your estimate.

You may use the base-ten pieces to help answer the following questions.

2. How many packs does each child get? How many marbles is this?

3. How many flats does each child get? How many marbles is this?

4. How many skinnies does each child get? How many marbles is this?

5. How many bits does each child get? How many marbles is this?

6. How many total marbles does each child get?

7. Write a division sentence for this problem.

8. Write a related multiplication sentence for this problem.

9. Try these problems using base-ten pieces. Write division and multiplication sentences for each problem. Check your sentences on a calculator.

    A. 6 ⟌ 756   **B.** 3 ⟌ 4209   **C.** 9 ⟌ 6003

Roberto remarked that some division problems are easy to do mentally, just like multiplication problems.

Try these division problems. Check them on a calculator.

10. **A.** $6 \div 2$ **B.** $9 \div 3$ **C.** $12 \div 3$ **D.** $40 \div 5$
  $60 \div 2$ $90 \div 3$ $120 \div 3$ $400 \div 5$
  $600 \div 2$ $900 \div 3$ $1200 \div 3$ $4000 \div 5$
  $6000 \div 2$ $9000 \div 3$ $12,000 \div 3$ $40,000 \div 5$
  $60,000 \div 2$ $90,000 \div 3$ $120,000 \div 3$ $400,000 \div 5$

11. **A.** $60 \div 30$ **B.** $90 \div 10$ **C.** $240 \div 60$ **D.** $450 \div 50$
  $600 \div 30$ $900 \div 10$ $2400 \div 60$ $4500 \div 50$
  $600 \div 300$ $900 \div 100$ $2400 \div 600$ $4500 \div 500$
  $6000 \div 30$ $9000 \div 10$ $24,000 \div 60$ $45,000 \div 50$
  $6000 \div 300$ $9000 \div 100$ $24,000 \div 600$ $45,000 \div 500$

Interpreting Remainders

Before school began at Wentworth Elementary School, there were 165 students enrolled in the fifth grade. If there are six fifth-grade classrooms, how many students are in each class? (There are about the same number of students in each class.)

Roberto modeled this problem with the base-ten shorthand. He used 1 flat, 6 skinnies, and 5 bits to represent the students. He needed to break up these pieces into 6 equal groups.

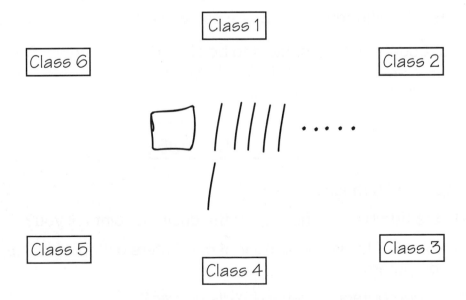

12. About how many students do you think are in each class? Explain your reasoning.

Modeling Division

Roberto divided the base-ten pieces evenly. He found there are 2 skinnies and 7 bits in each group with 3 bits left over. The bits left over are called the **remainder.**

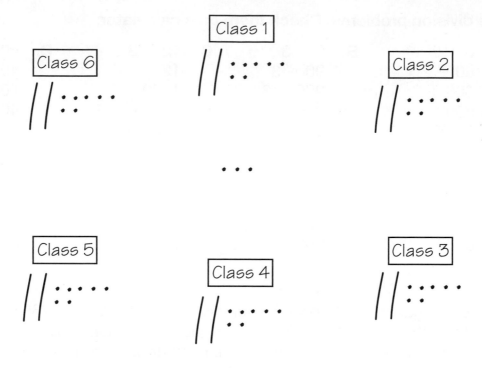

13. How many students are in each class?

14. What do the remaining 3 bits mean?

15. How will the 165 students be divided among the 6 classes?

We say 165 ÷ 6 is 27 with remainder 3. We can write 27 R3. 165 = 6 × 27 + 3.

A school district bought 670 computers to be shared by 7 schools. Roberto computed 670 ÷ 7 on his calculator to find the number of computers each school received. His calculator window showed:

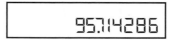

16. What does the 95 mean?

17. What do the numbers to the right of the decimal point tell you?

18. Multiply 95 × 7. This is the number of computers distributed if each school gets 95 computers.

19. How many computers are left to be distributed?

20. Fill in the missing number: 95 × 7 + ? = 670.

   Modeling Division

For Questions 1–4:
- **Use base-ten shorthand to sketch the problem and find the solution.**
- **Write a division sentence for the problem.**
- **Write a multiplication sentence for the problem.**

1. $144 \div 3$

2. $364 \div 7$

3. $603 \div 3$

4. $1856 \div 8$

Compute the following quotients.

5. **A.** $6 \div 2$ **B.** $14 \div 7$ **C.** $27 \div 9$ **D.** $48 \div 6$
   $60 \div 2$ $140 \div 7$ $270 \div 9$ $480 \div 6$
   $600 \div 2$ $1400 \div 7$ $2700 \div 9$ $4800 \div 6$
   $6000 \div 2$ $14,000 \div 7$ $27,000 \div 9$ $48,000 \div 6$

6. **A.** $5 \div 5$ **B.** $28 \div 7$ **C.** $42 \div 6$ **D.** $25 \div 5$
   $50 \div 50$ $280 \div 70$ $420 \div 60$ $250 \div 50$
   $500 \div 50$ $2800 \div 70$ $4200 \div 60$ $2500 \div 50$
   $5000 \div 50$ $28,000 \div 70$ $42,000 \div 60$ $25,000 \div 50$
   $50,000 \div 50$ $280,000 \div 700$ $420,000 \div 6000$ $250,000 \div 5000$

7. Fill in the missing numbers:

   A. Since $57 \times 8 = 456$, then $456 \div 8 = ?$

   B. Since $9 \times 412 = 3708$, then $3708 \div 9 = ?$

   C. Since $1014 \times ? = 6084$, then $6084 \div 6 = 1014$

Use base-ten shorthand to find the solutions to Questions 8 and 9.
Estimate first to see if your answer is reasonable. Explain any remainders.

8. A high school has 5 computer labs. The school bought 148 computers. If each computer lab is to get about the same number of computers, how many new computers will each lab get?

9. A CD rack holds 276 CDs. There are 6 sections, which all hold the same number of CDs. How many CDs does each section hold?

---

10. Blanca computed 473 ÷ 4 on her calculator. The calculator display showed:

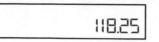

$$118.25$$

    A. What does the 118 mean?

    B. What does the .25 mean?

    C. Fill in the number that makes the statement true: 118 × 4 + ? = 473.

    D. What is the remainder?

$$\begin{array}{r} 118 \text{ R }? \\ 4\overline{)\ 473} \end{array}$$

11. Fill in the missing numbers.

    A. $360 \div 9 = n$ **B.** $120 \div n = 40$ **C.** $360 \div n = 90$

    D. $n \div 5 = 30$ **E.** $n \div 6 = 30$ **F.** $4900 \div n = 70$

    G. $400 \div n = 5$ **H.** $160 \div n = 4$ **I.** $3276 \div 4 = n$

Estimate the answers to Questions 12–15.

12. A fifth-grade math textbook has 427 pages. If the 8 chapters are all about the same length, about how many pages are in each chapter?

13. A school spent $2400 on graphing calculators. Each calculator costs $80. How many calculators did the school buy?

14. A school can purchase regular calculators for $11.25 each. If they buy 245 calculators, about how much money will they spend?

15. The volleyball club spent $320.72 for t-shirts. They bought 38 t-shirts. About how much did each t-shirt cost?

Paper-and-Pencil Division

The Good-For-You Bakery baked 425 banana walnut muffins. They packaged them in packages of 6. How many packages of banana walnut muffins did they make?

Nila says she knows a paper-and-pencil method for doing division. She calls this the **forgiving division method.** Nila thought about the base-ten pieces as she did the problem. The base-ten pieces can represent the muffins.

Nila wrote the problem like this:

$$6 \overline{)425}$$

"To use the forgiving method, I make an estimate about the number of packages I think they made. My first estimate is 20."

$$
\begin{array}{r|l}
6 \overline{)425} & \\
\underline{-120} & 20 \\
305 &
\end{array}
$$

"Since $20 \times 6 = 120$, this means I have taken care of 120 muffins. There are 305 still to be packaged. This time I'll choose a larger number: 40. Since $40 \times 6 = 240$, this means I have packaged 240 more muffins. There are 65 muffins left to package."

$$
\begin{array}{r|l}
6 \overline{)425} & \\
\underline{-120} & 20 \\
305 & \\
\underline{-240} & 40 \\
65 &
\end{array}
$$

"Now I know 10 × 6 = 60, so I can make 10 more packages with 5 muffins remaining."

```
            70 R5
      6 | 425
        −120    | 20
         305
        −240    | 40
          65
        − 60    | 10
           5    | 70
```

"So, altogether, 70 packages of muffins can be made with 5 muffins left."

We can write:

$$6 × 70 + 5 = 425$$

A box of marbles contains 5386 marbles. The marbles are to be shared equally among 8 children. How many marbles does each child get?

Nila wrote the problem like this:

```
      8 | 5386
```

"To use the forgiving method, I make an estimate about the number of marbles each child will get. My first guess is 300. That's like giving 3 flats to each child, so I write:

```
      8 | 5386
        −2400  | 300
         2986
```

"Since 8 × 300 = 2400, this means I have taken care of 2400 of the marbles. I still have 2986 left to distribute. The 300 means each child has already gotten 300 marbles. Now I guess at how many more marbles I can give each child. I'll use 300 again, since 2400 will take care of a lot of the 2986 remaining. Now I have 586 left."

```
      8 | 5386
        −2400  | 300
         2986
        −2400  | 300
          586
```

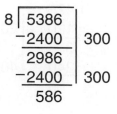

"I can't use 300 again because it is way too big. I'll try 20. Since 20 × 8 = 160, I have 426 left. I'll try something bigger next."

```
8 │ 5386   │
   -2400   │ 300
   ─────
    2986
   -2400   │ 300
   ─────
     586
    -160   │  20
   ─────
     426
```

"I'll try 50. 8 × 50 = 400. Now I have 26 left."

```
8 │ 5386   │
   -2400   │ 300
   ─────
    2986
   -2400   │ 300
   ─────
     586
    -160   │  20
   ─────
     426
    -400   │  50
   ─────
      26
```

"Now I'll try 3. Since 8 × 3 = 24, there are 2 marbles left over. Then 5386 divided by 8 is 673 (300 + 300 + 20 + 50 + 3) with remainder 2. Each child gets 673 marbles, with 2 left over."

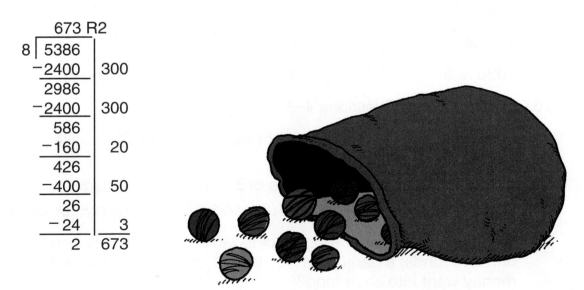

```
       673 R2
8 │ 5386   │
   -2400   │ 300
   ─────
    2986
   -2400   │ 300
   ─────
     586
    -160   │  20
   ─────
     426
    -400   │  50
   ─────
      26
     -24   │   3
   ─────   ─────
       2     673
```

Nila thought about a multiplication sentence for this problem. On her calculator, she found 673 × 8 = 5384. When she added the remainder 2, she got 5386. Another way to write this is to say 673 × 8 + 2 = 5386.

Try these problems, using the forgiving method. Write number sentences for each problem.

A. 4⟌856

B. 7⟌1256

C. 547 ÷ 9

D. 3476 ÷ 4

E. 8⟌901

F. 9017 ÷ 8

G. 562 ÷ 5

H. 5667 ÷ 5

I. 5274 ÷ 2

J. 2⟌527

K. 7⟌8413

L. 792 ÷ 7

1. Twenty-four cookies fit on a pan at the Good-For-You Bakery. If the baker makes 16 pans of cookies, how many cookies does he bake?

2. The Good-For-You Bakery has 6 ovens. They bake 173 pies every day and bake about the same number of pies in each oven. About how many pies are baked in each oven?

3. The bakery makes 4 different kinds of breads: whole wheat, rye, oatmeal, and cinnamon. They bake a total of 509 loaves of bread a day. If they bake about the same number of each type, about how many loaves of each bread do they bake?

Compute the following. Use the forgiving method or another method. Do not use a calculator. Remember to check whether your answer seems reasonable.

4. 4⟌586

5. 3⟌904

6. 819 ÷ 7

7. 1028 ÷ 6

8. 9⟌2349

9. 2049 ÷ 5

10. Choose one of Questions 4–9. Write a story about it.

11. For a fund-raiser, the members of the Wilderness Club baked 789 chocolate chip cookies.

    A. If they sell them in packages of 5, how many packages can they make?

    B. The Wilderness Club sold 102 packages. How many cookies were left?

12. The club earned $157. They decided to split this money equally into different funds: a party, new equipment, and camping fees. How much money went into each fund?

The following problems are about lawns and plants:

13. There are about 1700 grass plants in 2 square feet of a healthy lawn. About how many plants are in 1 square foot?

14. There are 8 single-family homes on Elm Street in Mathville. The families who live there spend a total of about $1040 a year on grass care. If they spend about the same amount, about how much does each family spend?

15. In 1993, the same families on Elm Street spent a total of about $536 on flower gardens. If they spent about the same amount, about how much did each family spend?

16. Believe it or not, 5 grass plants will produce about 1875 miles of roots in their lifetimes. About how many miles of roots will one plant produce?

17. A store sells tulip bulbs. The bulbs come in packages of 8. If they sold 216 bulbs, about how many packages did they sell?

18. 4122 ÷ 8   **19.** 4$\overline{)2601}$ **20.** 6$\overline{)2072}$

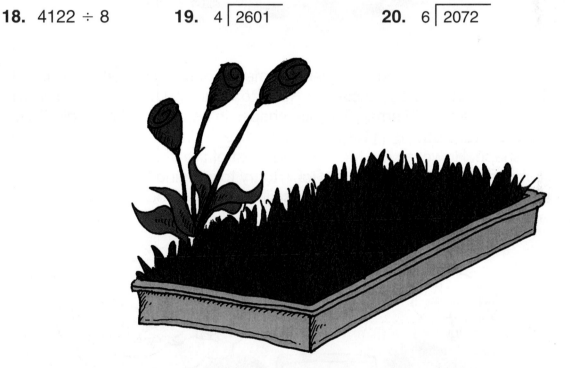

How Close Is Close Enough?

The students in Mr. Moreno's Social Studies class are learning about the dangers of oil spills in the waters of the world. They use a computer program to learn about the effects of the oil spills on sea life as well as their effects on humans.

One computer report lists the area in square kilometers of several past oil spills. While working on the computer, Felicia and Roberto recall how they counted square centimeters to find the area of small, irregular shapes in Lesson 1 of this unit. They remember that several students in their class had different measurements for the area of an irregular shape. However, Mr. Moreno told most of the students that they were close in their measurements. Felicia and Roberto try to imagine the huge size of the oil spills. They wonder how the area of these spills are measured and how accurate the data are.

Mr. Moreno overheard their conversation. He said to the class, "Felicia and Roberto have a good question. How accurate can the measurements of an irregular shape be? How close is close enough?"

He gave each student a copy of an irregular shape that was traced on *Centimeter Grid Paper*. He asked each student to find the area of the shape in square centimeters. Felicia, Roberto, and the three other students in their group estimate the area of Shape A. Felicia's and Roberto's work is shown below.

Felicia's work on Shape A

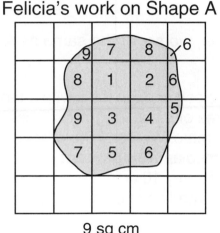

9 sq cm

Roberto's work on Shape A

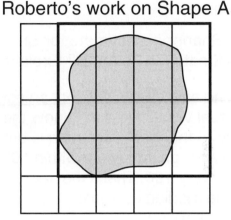

4 × 4 = 16 sq cm

The members in Felicia and Roberto's group compare their estimates. They each record their own measurement in a data table. Five other students measure a different shape, Shape B. Here are the estimates for Shape A and Shape B.

Shape A

Name	Estimate
Lin	10 sq cm
Felicia	9 sq cm
Shannon	7 sq cm
Roberto	16 sq cm
Irma	11 sq cm

Shape B

Name	Estimate
Arti	45 sq cm
Romesh	42 sq cm
Lee Yah	42 sq cm
Nicholas	49 sq cm
Nila	36 sq cm

1. What is the median estimate for Shape A? How do you know?

2. What is the median estimate for Shape B? How do you know?

3. What is the difference between Shannon's estimate and the median estimate for Shape A?

4. What is the difference between Felicia's estimate for Shape A and the median estimate?

5. What is the difference between Lee Yah's estimate and the median estimate for Shape B?

6. What is the difference between Arti's estimate for Shape B and the median estimate?

7. Is Shannon's estimate for Shape A better, worse, or the same as Arti's estimate for Shape B? Explain.

Mr. Moreno said, "Let's say that an estimate is close enough if it's within ten percent of the actual value. We don't know the exact area of these irregular shapes. We'll assume that the median of each is our best estimate. We'll say the other estimates are close enough if they are within 10% of the median. **Ten percent** (10%) means 10 out of every 100. That's the same as 1 out of every 10 or $\frac{1}{10}$. Let's find out what 10% of the median estimate for Shape A is. The median estimate is 10 sq cm, so 10% or $\frac{1}{10}$ of 10 is 1."

Ten percent of 10 is 1, so 10% less than 10 is 9 and 10% more than 10 is 11. Thus, any estimate in the range between 9 and 11 is within 10% of 10.

8. **A.** Look back at the estimates for Shape A. Which estimates are within 10% of the median?

   B. Which estimates are not within 10% of the median?

Mr. Moreno said, "Now let's find 10% of the median estimate for Shape B. The median estimate is 42 sq cm. How can we find 10% of 42?"

Felicia estimates $\frac{1}{10}$ of 42 in her head. She says, "42 ÷ 10 is about 4."

Romesh uses a calculator to find $\frac{1}{10}$ of 42.
He divides 42 by 10. Since the display reads 4.2, he agrees with Felicia that 10% of 42 is about 4.

Any estimate in the range between 38 and 46 is within 10% of 42, since:

$$42 - 4 = 38$$
$$\text{and}$$
$$42 + 4 = 46.$$

9. Look back at the estimates for Shape B. Which estimates are within 10% of the median? Is Arti's?

10. Answer the following questions using the data for Shape C.

    A. What is the median estimate for Shape C?

    B. What is 10% of the median?

    C. What is the range of estimates that are within 10% of the median?

    D. Which estimates are within 10% of the median?

    E. Which estimates are not within 10% of the median?

Shape C

Name	Estimate
Manny	32 sq cm
Blanca	31 sq cm
Michael	32 sq cm
Jackie	42 sq cm
Ana	28 sq cm
Edward	35 sq cm

11. Below is the data table for Shape D. Answer the following questions using this set of data.

    A. What is the median estimate?

    B. Look at the data. Compare the five estimates. Do any of the estimates seem unreasonable? Would you consider throwing out any of the data? If so, which one or ones?

    C. Take out the pieces of data that seem "way off." Now, find the median of the remaining data. Do the high and low estimates affect the median very much? Explain.

Shape D

Name	Estimate
Frank	91 sq cm
Brandon	86 sq cm
David	100 sq cm
Jessie	80 sq cm
John	88 sq cm

1. Frank drew a shape with curved sides on *Centimeter Grid Paper.* Each student in the class estimated its area. The class's median estimate for Frank's shape is 51 sq cm. Is an estimate of 60 sq cm within 10% of the median estimate for the area of Frank's shape? Show how you know.

2. Brandon drew a shape, too. The class's median estimate for his shape is 103 sq cm. Is an estimate of 115 square centimeters within 10% of the median estimate for the area of Brandon's shape? Show how you know.

3. Before completing the *Distance vs. Time* lab in Unit 2, Jessie predicted that she could walk about 20 yards in 10 seconds. After completing the lab, she found that she actually walked 15 yards in 10 seconds. Is her prediction of 20 yards within 10% of the actual distance of 15 yards? Why or why not?

4. Mr. Moreno brought in a jar filled with pennies. Felicia estimated that the jar contained 215 pennies. There were actually 198 pennies in the jar. Is Felicia's estimate within 10% of the actual number of pennies in the jar?

5. On a television game show, contestants win a prize if they guess the price within 10% of the actual price. If a television costs $225, what is the range of winning guesses?

6. On the same game show, a new car is offered as a prize. A contestant estimates the price of the car to be $15,000. The actual price is $14,500. Does the contestant win the prize? How do you know?

7. Brandon's sister Becky is a waitress at a restaurant. She received a 10% tip on a customer's bill. If she received a $2 tip, what was the customer's bill?

8. One of Becky's customers wants to leave a 20% tip. If his bill is $16, how much should he leave? (*Hint:* Find 10% of the bill first.)

Mean or Median?

Another Average: The Mean

Romesh is on the basketball team.

Here are the points he scored for the first five games.

Game	Points
Game #1	4
Game #2	6
Game #3	4
Game #4	23
Game #5	28

My median score is 6 points per game. I can say that is my average score. But, it doesn't really show my last two games when I scored a lot of points.

Remember, the average is one number that represents a typical value in a set of data. The median is the number that is exactly in the middle of the data. The median is often used as the average because it is easy to find. Another kind of average, called the mean, is also used. Sometimes the mean describes the data better.

To find Romesh's mean score, we can use connecting cubes.

1. **A.** For this problem, each connecting cube represents one point. How many connecting cubes do you need to represent all the points Romesh scored?

   B. Make 5 towers, one for each game. Use cubes to show the points Romesh scored during each game. Then divide the connecting cubes into 5 equal towers. Think of this as dividing all the points evenly among the five games.

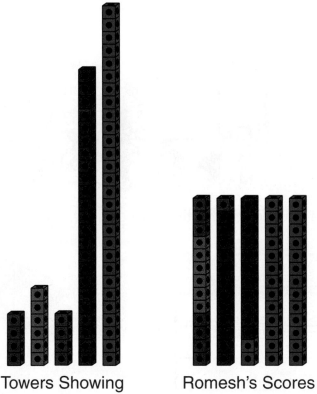

Towers Showing
Romesh's Scores

Romesh's Scores
Evened Out

2. How many connecting cubes are in each tower?

Romesh's mean score is 13 points per game. We can say he averaged 13 points per game.

To find his mean points per game on a calculator, Romesh used the following keystrokes:

| 4 | + | 6 | + | 4 | + | 23 | + | 28 | = | ÷ | 5 | = |

He added his points and then divided by the number of games.

3. Which average—the mean or the median—do you think better describes Romesh's scores?

The mean and the median are two kinds of averages. The **mean** for any data set is an average of numbers. It is found by adding the values of the data and dividing by the number of values.

There are 6 students in Irma's group. Here are the number of books they read in one month.

Student	Number of Books Read
Irma	8
Blanca	2
Arti	6
John	11
Lin	12
Edward	7

Find the mean number of books Irma's group read. Use connecting cubes.

4. How many connecting cubes do you need?

5. How many towers will you make?

6. What is the mean number of books?

It is impossible to give each tower an equal number of cubes. Each tower has at least 7 cubes. This tells us that the average is over 7, but less than 8.

7. Find the mean number of books Irma's group read. Use a calculator.

   A. What numbers did you add?

   B. What number did you divide by?

8. Find the median number of books Irma's group read.

9. How do the mean and the median compare?

10. Shannon and Roberto's Social Studies teacher, Mrs. Smith, gives geography quizzes. Here are Shannon's and Roberto's quiz scores.

Shannon	3	9	9	2	9
Roberto	15	4	4	15	3

  A. Do you think Shannon would want Mrs. Smith to find her average using the mean or the median? Explain.

  B. Do you think Roberto would want Mrs. Smith to find his average using the mean or the median? Explain.

11. During winter break, Romesh and Alexis played a computer game. During the first game, Romesh got to level 5 while Alexis got to level 8. They kept track of how far they got in each game.

Game	Romesh's Level	Alexis's Level
Game 1	5	8
Game 2	10	2
Game 3	7	5
Game 4	3	18
Game 5	11	18
Game 6	14	8
Game 7	12	5
Game 8	10	16

Romesh says he found their averages and decided that he is the better player. Alexis says she found their averages, too. She claims that she is the better player. Can they both be right? Explain.

12. Sometimes, the mean better describes the data. Other times, the median better describes the data. Here are yearly salaries at the Happy Day Manufacturing Company.

Position	Salary
President	$259,000
Vice-President	$123,000
Worker #1	$36,000
Worker #2	$25,000
Worker #3	$18,000
Worker #4	$32,000
Worker #5	$25,000
Worker #6	$22,000
Worker #7	$27,000

The president of the company announced that the average salary was $63,000 a year.

A. Is she correct?

B. Is the mean a good description of the data? Explain.

13. Last summer, Alexis swam the breaststroke in 5 swim meets. Her times are listed below.

> 56.6 seconds   51.3 seconds   44.8 seconds
> 47.5 seconds   45.8 seconds

A. Find her median time.

B. Use a calculator to find the mean.

Mean or Median?

14. Ana's group collected data for the lab *Distance vs. Time*. Jerome walked along a track. The rest of the group reported the time he took to walk 6 yards, 9 yards, and 12 yards. Ana was the timer at 6 yards. On the first trial she didn't know how to use the stopwatch. Here is the first row of their data table:

D Distance in Yards	T Time in Seconds			
	Trial 1	Trial 2	Trial 3	Average
6	10	3	5	

A. Find the mean value of the three trials.

B. Find the median value of the three trials.

C. Which average, the median or the mean, represents the data better? Explain your reasoning.

Order of Operations: Using Parentheses

Mr. Moreno showed the class another way to find averages on a calculator. If your calculator has (and) keys, try this method. The (and) are left and right parentheses. Parentheses are often used to show what operations to do first. For example, to find the mean number of points Romesh scored in the first 5 basketball games, we write $(4 + 6 + 4 + 23 + 28) \div 5$. Parentheses say do the work inside the parentheses first.

An example of a **numerical expression** is $(4 + 6 + 4 + 23 + 28) \div 5$. Numerical expressions have numbers and operations. In numerical expressions, we follow the order of operations. That is, we divide and multiply and then add and subtract. When there are parentheses in an expression, we do the calculations inside the parentheses first.

Since we multiply and divide before adding and subtracting,

$$3 \times 2 + 5 = 11 \qquad 6 \div 2 \times 4 + 3 = 15$$
$$3 + 2 \times 5 = 13 \qquad 8 - 6 \div 3 + 4 = 10$$

15. Find the values of the following expressions.

A. $5 + 8 \div 4$

B. $18 \div 3 + 4 \times 7$

C. $17 - 14 \div 2 - 3$

D. $6 \times 4 \div 3 - 2$

Work in parentheses must be done first. For example,

Example A. $3 + 6 \div 3 = 5$ Example B. $5 \times 4 + 2 = 22$
$(3 + 6) \div 3 = 3$ $5 \times (4 + 2) = 30$

16. First, find the values of the following expressions without a calculator. Then, use a calculator to check your work.

A. $3 \times (12 - 6) =$ **B.** $3 \times 12 - 6 =$

C. $(6 + 3) \times (5 - 2) =$ **D.** $6 + 3 \times 5 - 2 =$

E. $16 \div 4 - 2 =$ **F.** $16 \div (4 - 2) =$

G. $100 \div 10 - 5 =$ **H.** $100 \div (10 - 5) =$

Homework

1. Mr. Moreno's class recorded the daily high and low temperatures in degrees Fahrenheit for 5 days:

Temperature	Monday	Tuesday	Wednesday	Thursday	Friday
High	52°F	38°F	40°F	35°F	48°F
Low	35°F	28°F	30°F	32°F	43°F

    A. Find the mean high for the 5 days.

    B. Find the mean low for the 5 days.

2. Jessie went bowling with her friends. The first game she bowled 125 points. The second game she bowled 110 points. The third game she bowled 130 points. What was her average score that day? Use the mean.

3. Jessie's team bowled 3 games each. Each team member added their scores for their three games. The totals for the players on her team were 365, 352, 289, and 299. What was the average score for the 4 players on Jessie's team?

4. The heights of 5 players on a basketball team are: 195 cm, 202 cm, 207 cm, 201 cm, and 198 cm.

    A. What is the mean height in cm?

    B. Estimate the average height in inches. (*Hint:* 100 cm is about 39 in.)

    C. Express your answer to Question 4B in feet and inches.

5. Blanca's mother drove a total of 330 miles in 6 hours. What was her mean speed in miles per hour?

6. Felicia's piano teacher has 8 students. Each student plays a song in the piano recital. The ages of the students are 7, 48, 10, 10, 11, 11, 6, and 9 years old.

   A. Find the mean age of the students.

   B. Find the median age.

   C. If you can only use one number to represent the ages of the students in the recital, which value would you use—the mean or the median? Explain.

Find the value of the following expressions. Do not use a calculator. Then use a calculator to check your answers.

   7. $6 + 3 \times 2 =$

   8. $12 \div 2 - 3 =$

   9. $7 \times 4 + 3 =$

   10. $10 - 2 \times 3 =$

   11. $32 + 30 \div 10 =$

   12. $5 - 5 \div 5 \times 5 + 5 =$

   13. $50 - 9 \div 3 =$

   14. $18 - 4 \div 2 \times 6 =$

   15. $(50 + 4) \div 9 =$

   16. $17 - 20 \div 10 =$

   17. $12 \div (6 \div 2) =$

   18. $(6 + 3) \times (7 - 4) =$

   19. $12 \div (11 - 6 + 1) =$

   20. $28 \div (11 - 6 + 2) =$

   21. $(17 + 4) \div 3 =$

   22. $17 - (64 \div 8) \times 2 =$

Spreading Out

Mr. Moreno spilled a cup of coffee on his desk. Arti and Jessie ran to get some paper towels to clean up the coffee.

"Don't grab those school towels!" said Arti. "They don't absorb much."

"I'll get the paper towels from over the sink," said Jessie.

"Thanks," said Mr. Moreno. "I was afraid that coffee would run everywhere."

"How much liquid can a paper towel absorb?" asked Jessie.

"We can always test the paper towels to find out," said Arti.

"That's a great idea for an experiment," said Mr. Moreno. "We can test each towel by dropping a few drops of water from an eyedropper onto it."

"What happens when we drop a drop of water on a paper towel?" asked Mr. Moreno.

"It spreads out and makes a spot," answered Arti.

Jessie said, "To see how many drops will cover the towel, we can drop water on a paper towel. Then we can count the number of drops until the whole towel is covered with water."

Arti said, "That might work, but we would probably lose count."

"There is another way to find how many drops the whole paper towel can absorb. We can first find out what happens when you drop just a few drops of water on a towel. If we know the number of drops and can measure the size of the spots, we can calculate the number of drops it will take to cover the whole paper towel. Let's start by making a list of things that we have to think about," said Mr. Moreno.

After some discussion, their list looked like this:

> Things to think about:
>
> What number of drops should we use?
> How should we measure the size of the spots?
> What variables do we have to keep fixed?
> How many trials should we make?

"I think we should try three different numbers of drops so we have enough data to look for patterns," said Jessie. "We should start with numbers (of drops) that have a pattern. Then it will be easier to see how changing the number of drops changes the area of the spots. We should also do three trials as we did in *Distance vs. Time*. Then, if the areas of the spots for all three trials are close, we will know we didn't make any big mistakes."

Identifying Variables

"As you were talking, you identified the two main variables in your experiment," said Mr. Moreno. "The variables are number of drops (N) and area (A). The two main variables in an experiment have special names. The variable with values we know in the beginning of the experiment is called the **manipulated variable.** We often choose the values of the manipulated variable before collecting the data."

Arti and Jessie chose 1 drop, 2 drops, and 4 drops as the values for the number of drops, so that the spots they made would not be too big. They made three spots of water with 1 drop, three spots of water with 2 drops, and three spots with 4 drops of water on paper towels.

"The variable with values obtained by doing the experiment is called the **responding variable,**" said Mr. Moreno. "Your responding variable is the area of the spots. The area of each spot changes, depending upon the number of drops of water you use."

Mr. Moreno added, "There are other variables that can affect the size of the spots. For example, if we use a bigger eyedropper or a different liquid, the size of the spots might be different. These other variables should stay the same during the whole experiment. In this way, the only thing that affects the area of the spots is the number of drops. The other variables that stay the same are called **fixed variables.**"

When the spots had dried a little, Arti and Jessie traced around each spot with a pencil. They used scissors to cut out each spot. They then measured the area of each spot and recorded it in a data table.

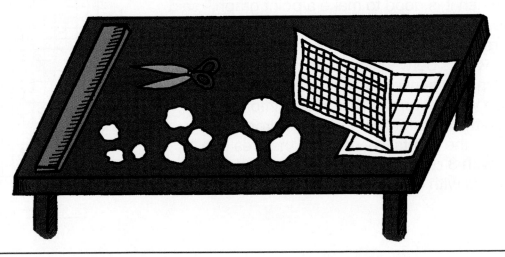

Bar Graph or Point Graph?

Arti and Jessie decided to graph their data. They wanted to see if there were any patterns that could help them find the number of drops of water the paper towel can absorb.

"I think we should make a bar graph," said Arti.

"I think we should make a point graph," said Jessie. "Which kind of graph is best?"

"Let's do both kinds of graphs and find out," said Arti.

Arti made a bar graph, and Jessie made a point graph as shown.

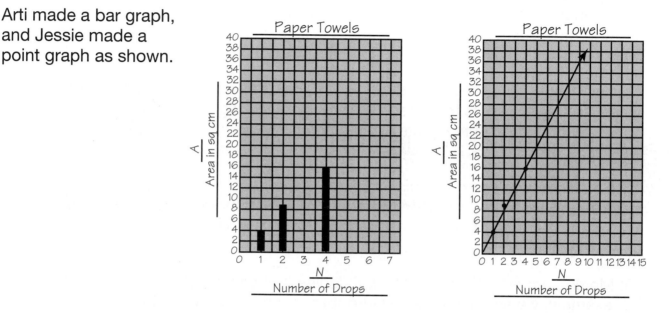

"You were right, Jessie," said Arti. "The point graph is better. We can find the area for any number of drops by using the line. See, I can find the area of a spot with 6 drops like this."

"There are times when it is good to make a bar graph and times when it is good to make a point graph," said Mr. Moreno. "We make a point graph when both variables are numerical and when it makes sense to think about values between the data points. For example, it makes sense to think about the area of a spot made with 3 drops of water. This information lies between the data for 2 drops and 4 drops. By fitting a line to the points, we can find the area of a spot made with 3 drops. We can also find the area of a spot made with 6 drops."

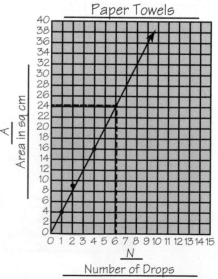

Discuss

1. Describe how Arti and Jessie can measure the area of the spots they made.

2. **A.** What are the two main variables in the lab?
   B. Which variable is the manipulated variable?
   C. Which variable is the responding variable?

3. What variables should be held fixed so that Arti and Jessie can see how changing the number of drops affects the area of the spots?

4. Why is it a good idea to make more than one trial?

Draw

5. Design a lab to find out what happens to the area if you change the number of drops of water used to make the spot. Draw a picture of your plan.
   A. Label the variables in your picture.
   B. Choose values for the number of drops. (You may choose 1, 2, and 4 drops as Arti and Jessie did, or you may choose other values.)

Collect

6. Work with your partner(s) to collect data and record it in a table. Discuss the following before you begin:
   A. How many trials will you need to make? That is, how many times will you make a spot for each number of drops?
   B. How will you organize your data in a data table?
   C. How can you check for mistakes in dropping the water to make the spots?
   D. What unit of measure will you use when finding the area?
   E. How will you check to be sure your data is reasonable?

7. Look at the data you have collected. Will you use the mean or median value to average the data?

8. Make a graph of your data on a sheet of graph paper.

- Graph the number of drops (*N*) on the horizontal axis and the area (*A*) on the vertical axis.

- The vertical axis should be numbered to at least 40 sq cm.

- What is the area of a spot made with zero drops? Add this point to your graph.

9. If the points on your graph suggest a line, use a ruler to draw a best-fit line.

Write the answers to these questions. Use your graph and your data table to help you.

10. A. Use your graph to predict the area of a spot made with three drops of water. Show your work on your graph, and record your prediction.

    B. Make a spot using three drops of water. Find the area.

    C. Was your prediction within 10% of the actual area? Explain why or why not.

11. A. Use your graph to predict the area of a spot made with five drops of water. Show your work on your graph, and record your prediction.

    B. Check your prediction by making a spot with five drops. Find the area of the spot.

    C. Was your prediction within 10% of the actual area? Explain why or why not.

12. A. If you want to make a spot with an area of 40 sq cm, how many drops should you use? Explain how you solved this problem.

    B. Find another way to solve this problem. Explain.

13. **A.** Choose a point on your line. Use it to write the ratio of the area of a spot to the number of drops as a fraction ($\frac{A}{N}$).

   B. Estimate the area covered by 12 drops of water.

   C. Estimate the number of drops of water one sheet of your paper towel will absorb. Explain how you solved this problem. Use the Student Rubric: *Telling* to help you write about your solution.

14. Jessie and Arti used Super Soak paper towels in their experiment. Jerome and Lee Yah used Absorb-Plus paper towels. Their graphs are shown here. Which paper towel can hold more water?

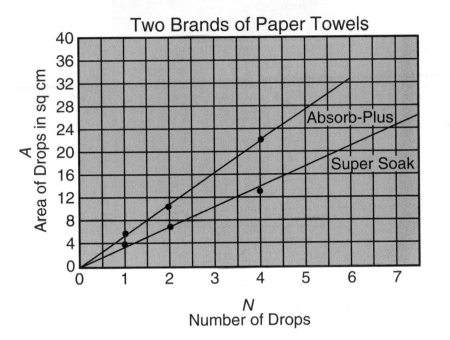

You will need a sheet of graph paper and a ruler to complete this homework.

1. Professor Peabody tested Whizzo brand paper towels. He noticed a very interesting pattern in his data. Then, his pet mouse, Milo, tracked ink across his data table. Look for a pattern in Professor Peabody's data.

N Number of Drops	A Area of Spot in sq cm
1	🐾
2	🐾
🐾	8
8	16

   A. Copy the data table on your paper and fill in the missing values.

   B. Make a point graph of the data. Graph the number of drops on the horizontal axis and the area on the vertical axis. Use a ruler to fit a line to the points.

   C. What would be the area of a spot made with no drops? Add this point to your graph.

2. A. Choose a point on the graph. Use it to write the ratio $\left(\frac{A}{N}\right)$ of the area to the number of drops.

   B. Using fractions, write two ratios equal to the ratio in Question 2A.

3. A. What area would 6 drops make on a Whizzo brand paper towel?

   B. How many drops are needed to make a spot with an area of 28 sq cm? Show your work.

Review Problems

Solve the following problems. Use tools that you feel are appropriate unless other directions are given. Record your solutions. Show any strategies that you used.

1. Lin traveled 7 miles during a hike. There are 5280 feet in 1 mile. How many feet did Lin travel?

2. John plays on a baseball team. He records the number of runs he scores each game. In the first five games of the season he scored 3, 0, 1, 1, and 5 runs.

    A. Find the mean number of runs scored.

    B. Find the median number of runs scored.

    C. Which average, the median or the mean, better represents the number of runs John scored? Explain your choice.

3. One foot is equal to 12 inches.

    A. Make a data table that compares feet to inches. Include at least 3 equal ratios.

    B. Make a graph displaying your data. Put feet on the horizontal axis and inches on the vertical axis.

4. Use paper and pencil to solve these multiplication and division problems. Estimate to be sure your answers are reasonable.

    A. $34 \times 56 =$

    B. $1237 \times 9 =$

    C. $567 \div 3 =$

    D. $7954 \div 7 =$

5. Write the number 3×10^5 in standard form.

6. Jerome's mother is planning to re-tile the bathroom floor. The room measures 8 feet by 8 feet. She is planning to use square tiles that measure 6 inches by 6 inches.

   A. What is the area of the bathroom floor?

   B. How many tiles will she need? (*Hint:* Make a drawing.)

7. David plans to build a rectangular patio with 48 square tiles. Each tile has an area of 1 square foot. He does not want to cut the tiles, so the length and width of the patio must be whole numbers. What are all the possible measurements for the length and width of the patio?

8. Linda dumped out the change in her piggy bank. She arranged the change from her piggy bank into 9 piles of 83 coins each.

   A. About how many coins does Linda have?

   B. If all her coins were nickels, about how much money does she have?

9. What is the value of the 5 in 345,687?

10. Use this pattern block to answer the following questions.

   A. Draw one whole.

   B. Draw one-half.

   C. Draw two-thirds.

   D. Draw five-sixths.

11. Jessie has a bag of tiles. She pulls a sample of tiles from her bag. Her data are shown below. Draw a graph to display her data.

C Color	*N* Number of Tiles Pulled
Red	6
Blue	6
Green	5
Yellow	3

   A. What is the most common color(s) in Jessie's sample?

   B. What is the least common color(s) in Jessie's sample?

   C. How many tiles are in Jessie's sample?

   D. What fraction of the tiles Jessie pulled are blue?

   E. Jessie took her sample from a bag of 200 tiles. Use her sample to predict the total number of tiles of each color. Explain your reasoning.

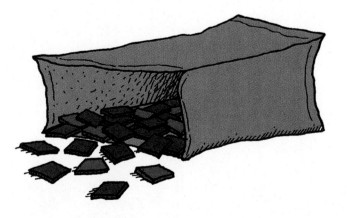

12. Compare the following fractions. Tell which is greater. Write a number sentence to show your answer. Use the symbols < and > in your answer.

   A. $\frac{3}{4}$ or $\frac{6}{5}$

   B. $\frac{4}{9}$ or $\frac{5}{9}$

   C. $\frac{3}{6}$ or $\frac{3}{7}$

13. Estimate the answers to the following problems.

   A. $346{,}000 \times 5$

   B. $251{,}000 \times 7$

   C. $51{,}000 \times 5$

Solve the following problems.

14. **A.** $81 \div 9 =$

   B. $810 \div 9 =$

   C. $810 \div 90 =$

   D. $8100 \div 9 =$

   E. $8100 \div 90 =$

   F. $8100 \div 900 =$

15. Use paper and pencil to divide. Estimate to check if your answer is reasonable.

   A. $5\overline{)756}$　　　**B.** $4\overline{)1596}$　　　**C.** $8\overline{)6407}$

16. **A.** $36 \div (3 \times 3) =$　　　**B.** $36 \div 3 \times 3 =$

   C. $36 \div (4 + 2) =$　　　**D.** $36 \div 4 + 2 =$

Unit 5

Investigating Fractions

	Student Guide	Discovery Assignment Book	Adventure Book	Unit Resource Guide*
Lesson 1				
Geoboard Fractions	●			
Lesson 2				
Parts and Wholes	●			
Lesson 3				
Using Dot Paper Rectangles	●	●		
Lesson 4				
Using Common Denominators	●			
Lesson 5				
A Day at the Races	●			
Lesson 6				
Adding Fractions with Rectangles	●			
Lesson 7				
Adding and Subtracting Fractions	●			●
Lesson 8				
Shannon's Trip to School	●			

Unit Resource Guide pages are from the teacher materials.

Geoboard Fractions

During this unit, you will use geoboards and dot paper to model fractions. Remember, the numerator and the denominator work together to tell the size of the number represented by a fraction. For example, the denominator in the fraction $\frac{3}{4}$ tells us to divide the whole into four equal parts. To model $\frac{3}{4}$, Blanca makes a rectangle on a geoboard and divides it into four equal parts.

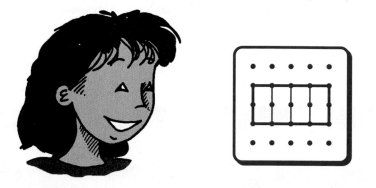

To record her work, Blanca draws the rectangle on dot paper. The numerator tells us the number of parts we are interested in, so Blanca shades in three of the parts.

In this unit, you will solve problems about fractions following a special rule: **The No-Diagonal Rule.**

This rule says that figures may only be divided into parts using vertical or horizontal lines from dot to dot. Diagonals are not allowed.

There are many other ways to divide rectangles on geoboards. But, using this rule, it will be easier to count square units on the geoboard and square centimeters on dot paper.

Sample Problem: This rectangle is one whole. Divide the whole into halves in as many ways as you can. Then, you can model fractions with a denominator of 2.

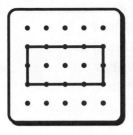

The No-Diagonal Rule means that these answers are allowed:

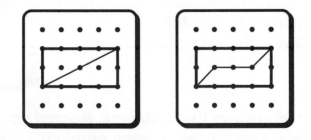

However, these answers are not allowed:

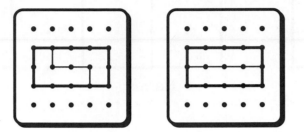

Denominators: Dividing the Whole into Equal Parts

Blanca uses a rectangle that is 2 units by 4 units to represent one whole. She wants to know which fractions she can show with this rectangle. First, she divides the rectangle into halves in as many ways as she can. She records her work on dot paper as shown below.

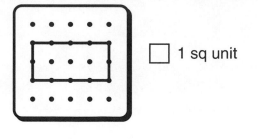

□ 1 sq unit

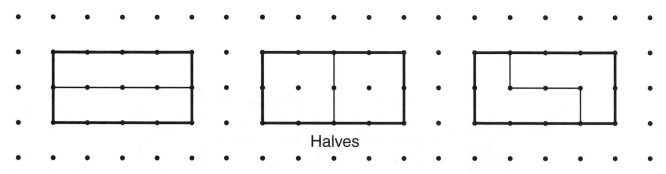

Halves

Then she tries to divide the rectangle into thirds, but decides that it is not possible. "I can divide this rectangle into halves, so I can use it to show fractions with 2 as the denominator. I cannot divide this rectangle into thirds, so I cannot show fractions with 3 in the denominator."

Use a geoboard to help you solve the problems. Record your answers on dot paper. Draw a separate rectangle for each problem. Label your work. If a question asks for something that is *not* possible, say so.

1. For this question, Blanca's rectangle is one whole.
   A. What is the area in square units of the rectangle?
   B. Divide the whole into fourths as many ways as you can.
   C. Divide the whole into eighths.
   D. Divide the whole into fifths.
   E. Divide the whole into sixths.
   F. Using the No-Diagonal Rule, list all the denominators that can be shown dividing the whole.

Numerators: Using Equal Parts of the Whole

For Questions 2–3, organize your work carefully. Here is one way:

- **Work with a partner to model fractions. One partner shows a rectangle on a geoboard divided into equal parts. The other partner records the fraction on dot paper. Use a separate rectangle for each fraction.**
- **Label each fraction. Follow Lin and Nicholas's example in Question 2.**
- **Remember, if a question asks for something that is not possible, say so.**

2. For this question, the rectangle below is one whole. This rectangle is 2 units by 4 units. We call this a 2 × 4 (two by four) rectangle.

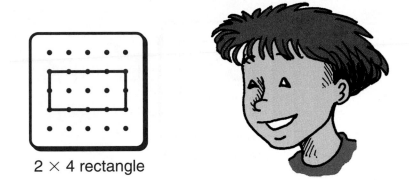

2 × 4 rectangle

Lin makes the rectangle on a geoboard and divides it into fourths. Nicholas models $\frac{1}{4}$ using this rectangle on dot paper.

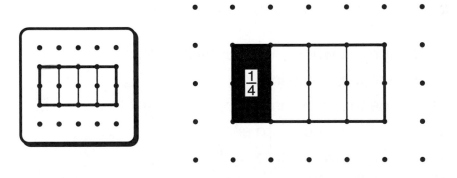

A. Use a 2 × 4 rectangle to model $\frac{3}{4}$. (Remember to label your drawing with the fraction and question number.)

B. Use a 2 × 4 rectangle to model $\frac{4}{4}$.

C. Following the No-Diagonal Rule, can you use a 2 × 4 rectangle to model $\frac{1}{3}$? If so, show how.

D. Can you use a 2 × 4 rectangle to model $\frac{1}{2}$? If so, show how.

E. Can you use a 2 × 4 rectangle to model $\frac{5}{8}$? If so, show how.

---

3. For this question, a 2 × 4 rectangle is one whole. If possible, use it to model the following fractions. Draw a separate rectangle for each fraction.

A. $\frac{1}{2}$ B. $\frac{2}{3}$ C. $\frac{3}{4}$ D. $\frac{6}{8}$ E. $\frac{8}{8}$ F. $\frac{5}{12}$

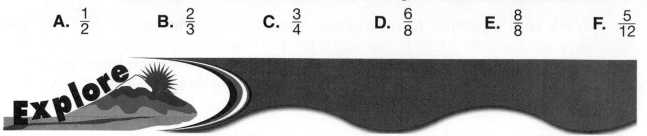

For Questions 4–6, the rectangle below is one whole. It is 3 units by 4 units. Remember, if a question asks for something that is not possible, say so.

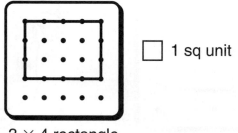

☐ 1 sq unit

3 × 4 rectangle

4. A. Divide the whole into halves in at least three ways. (*Hint:* Each of the halves must have the same area, but they do not have to have the same shape. For example, the rectangle shown here is divided into halves.)

B. Divide the whole into fourths in at least three ways.

C. Divide the whole into eighths.

D. Divide the whole into thirds in at least three ways.

E. Divide the whole into sixths.

F. Divide the whole into twelfths.

G. Divide the whole into fifths.

H. Divide the whole into tenths.

5. A 3 × 4 rectangle is the whole for this question.

A. What is the area in square units of the rectangle?

B. Can fractions with 2 in the denominator be shown using this rectangle?

C. Can fractions with 5 in the denominator be shown using this rectangle?

D. Following the No-Diagonal Rule, list all the denominators that can be shown dividing the whole.

6. For this question, a 3 × 4 rectangle is one whole. If possible, use it to model the following fractions. Use a separate rectangle for each fraction.

   A. $\frac{1}{2}$ B. $\frac{1}{3}$ C. $\frac{3}{4}$ D. $\frac{5}{8}$ E. $\frac{6}{6}$ F. $\frac{5}{12}$

For Questions 7 and 8, a 2 × 3 rectangle is one whole. Label your work clearly.

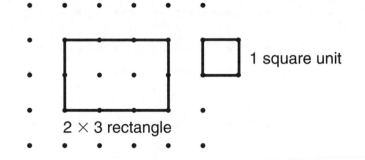

2 × 3 rectangle   1 square unit

7. A. What is the area of the rectangle?

   B. Following the No-Diagonal Rule, which denominators can be shown dividing the whole?

   C. Use dot paper to show the whole divided into these fractions.

8. Use a 2 × 3 rectangle on dot paper to model the following fractions. If a question asks for something that is not possible, say so. Use a separate rectangle for each fraction.

   A. $\frac{1}{2}$ B. $\frac{2}{3}$ C. $\frac{3}{4}$ D. $\frac{5}{6}$ E. $\frac{6}{6}$ F. $\frac{1}{5}$

For Questions 9 and 10, the rectangle below is one whole.

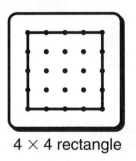

4 × 4 rectangle

9. A. What is the area of the rectangle?

   B. Following the No-Diagonal Rule, which denominators can be shown dividing the whole?

   C. Use dot paper to show the whole divided into these fractions.

10. A 4 × 4 rectangle is one whole. If possible, model the following fractions on dot paper. Use a separate rectangle for each fraction.

   A. $\frac{1}{2}$ B. $\frac{2}{3}$ C. $\frac{3}{4}$ D. $\frac{1}{5}$ E. $\frac{5}{6}$ F. $\frac{3}{8}$ G. $\frac{5}{16}$

Fractions Greater Than One

Blanca draws a 3 cm by 4 cm rectangle on dot paper to model one whole. We call this a 3 × 4 rectangle.

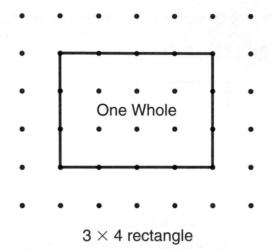

3 × 4 rectangle

She models $\frac{4}{3}$ in two ways. Note that she traces red lines around one whole.

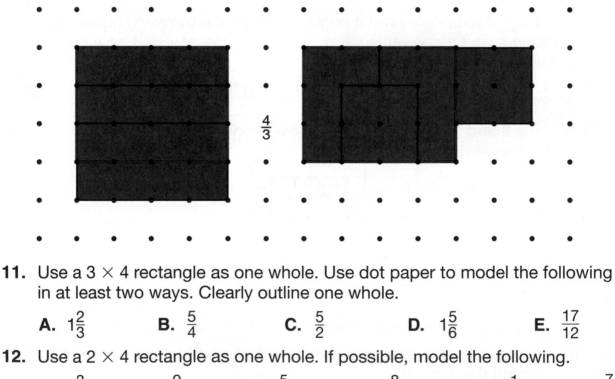

$\frac{4}{3}$

11. Use a 3 × 4 rectangle as one whole. Use dot paper to model the following in at least two ways. Clearly outline one whole.

   A. $1\frac{2}{3}$ **B.** $\frac{5}{4}$ **C.** $\frac{5}{2}$ **D.** $1\frac{5}{6}$ **E.** $\frac{17}{12}$

12. Use a 2 × 4 rectangle as one whole. If possible, model the following.

   A. $1\frac{3}{8}$ **B.** $\frac{9}{4}$ **C.** $\frac{5}{3}$ **D.** $\frac{8}{8}$ **E.** $1\frac{1}{2}$ **F.** $\frac{7}{6}$

You will need 2 or 3 sheets of dot paper to answer these questions. Remember, if it is not possible to model a fraction on dot paper, say so. Label all your drawings with the fraction and question number.

1. **A.** Draw a rectangle that is 2 cm by 5 cm on dot paper. This 2 × 5 rectangle is one whole.

   B. What is the area of the rectangle?

   C. Following the No-Diagonal Rule, which denominators can be shown with this rectangle? Show them.

2. A 2 × 5 rectangle is one whole. If possible, model the following. Use a separate rectangle for each fraction.

   A. $\frac{1}{5}$ **B.** $\frac{1}{2}$ **C.** $\frac{3}{10}$ **D.** $\frac{1}{3}$ **E.** $\frac{3}{4}$ **F.** $\frac{7}{5}$

3. **A.** Draw a 3 × 5 rectangle on dot paper. This rectangle is one whole for this question.

   B. What is the area of the rectangle?

   C. Following the No-Diagonal Rule, which denominators can be shown with this rectangle? Show them.

4. A 3 × 5 rectangle is one whole. If possible, model the following fractions.

   A. $\frac{1}{5}$ **B.** $\frac{1}{2}$ **C.** $\frac{3}{10}$ **D.** $\frac{1}{3}$ **E.** $\frac{3}{4}$ **F.** $1\frac{1}{3}$

5. **A.** Draw a 4 × 5 rectangle on dot paper. This rectangle is one whole.

   B. What is the area of the rectangle?

   C. Following the No-Diagonal Rule, which denominators can be shown with this rectangle? Show them.

6. A 4 × 5 rectangle is one whole. If possible, model the following fractions.

   A. $\frac{1}{5}$ **B.** $\frac{1}{2}$ **C.** $\frac{3}{10}$

   D. $\frac{1}{3}$ **E.** $\frac{3}{4}$ **F.** $\frac{5}{4}$

   G. $1\frac{3}{5}$ **H.** $\frac{13}{10}$ **I.** $\frac{7}{20}$

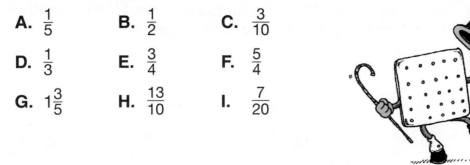

Geoboard Fractions

Parts and Wholes

Mr. Moreno's class uses pattern blocks, geoboards, and rectangles on dot paper to model fractions. For example, David shows $\frac{1}{3}$ of a yellow hexagon, and Lin shows $\frac{1}{3}$ of a 3 × 4 rectangle.

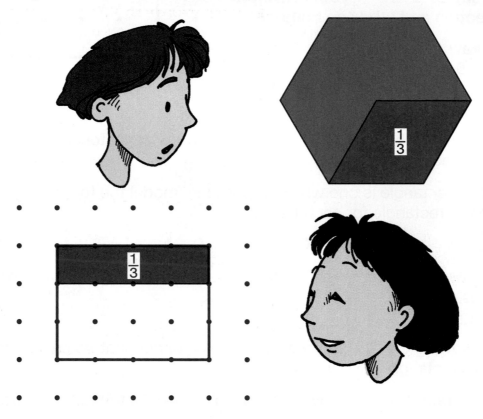

Follow these directions for Questions 1–3.

- **Work with a partner. One partner will model a fraction using pattern blocks. Then the other partner will model the fraction using rectangles on dot paper. Follow David and Lin's example above.**
- **When using pattern blocks, the yellow hexagon is one whole. When using rectangles on dot paper, a 3 × 4 rectangle is one whole. Use a separate rectangle for each fraction.**
- **Remember the No-Diagonal Rule. If you cannot model the fraction using the pattern blocks or a 3 × 4 rectangle, say so.**

1. **A.** $\frac{1}{2}$ **B.** $\frac{1}{6}$ **C.** $\frac{3}{4}$ **D.** $\frac{2}{5}$ **E.** $\frac{3}{12}$

2. **A.** $\frac{6}{6}$ **B.** $\frac{5}{2}$ **C.** $\frac{5}{8}$ **D.** $1\frac{1}{4}$ **E.** $\frac{5}{4}$

3. **A.** $\frac{2}{3}$ **B.** $\frac{4}{6}$ **C.** $\frac{8}{12}$ **D.** $\frac{5}{3}$ **E.** $1\frac{2}{3}$

Parts to Wholes with Pattern Blocks

For Questions 4–6, the whole will be different in each question. If a question asks for something that is not possible, say so. Study this example:

If the brown trapezoid is $\frac{1}{2}$, then the red trapezoid is one whole. The green triangle is $\frac{1}{3}$.

4. If the green triangle is $\frac{1}{3}$, model the following:

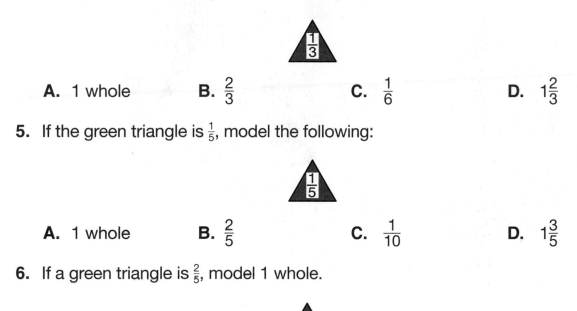

   A. 1 whole   **B.** $\frac{2}{3}$ **C.** $\frac{1}{6}$ **D.** $1\frac{2}{3}$

5. If the green triangle is $\frac{1}{5}$, model the following:

   A. 1 whole   **B.** $\frac{2}{5}$ **C.** $\frac{1}{10}$ **D.** $1\frac{3}{5}$

6. If a green triangle is $\frac{2}{5}$, model 1 whole.

Parts to Wholes with Rectangles

If a 2 × 2 rectangle is $\frac{1}{2}$, then the following rectangles model 1 whole and $\frac{1}{8}$.

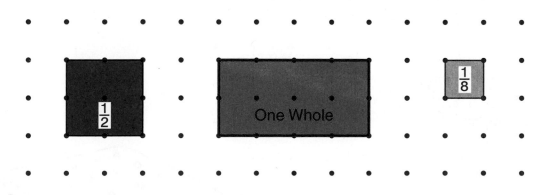

Remember the No-Diagonal Rule. If a question asks for something that is not possible, say so.

7. If a 2 × 1 rectangle is $\frac{1}{3}$, model the following using geoboards or rectangles on dot paper. Use a separate rectangle for each fraction.

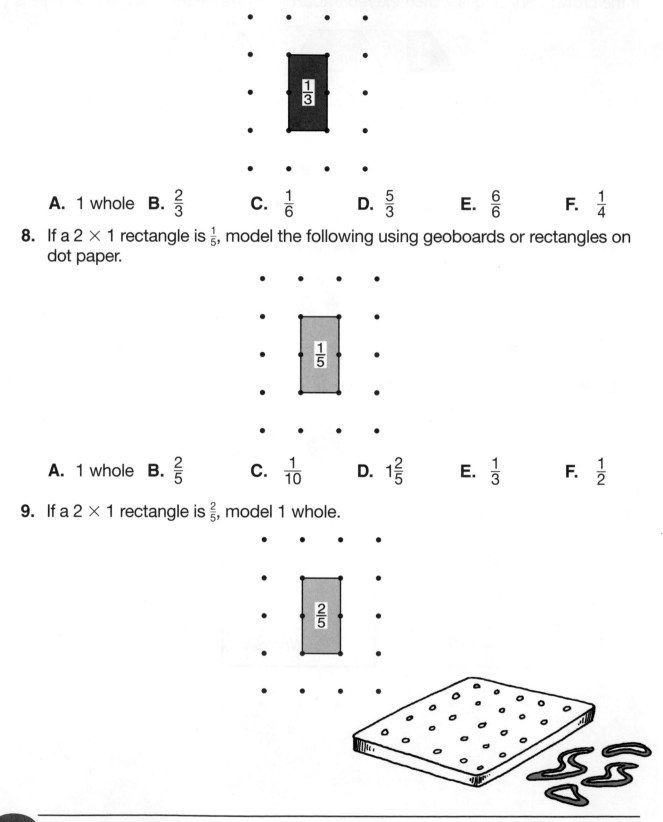

   A. 1 whole **B.** $\frac{2}{3}$ **C.** $\frac{1}{6}$ **D.** $\frac{5}{3}$ **E.** $\frac{6}{6}$ **F.** $\frac{1}{4}$

8. If a 2 × 1 rectangle is $\frac{1}{5}$, model the following using geoboards or rectangles on dot paper.

   A. 1 whole **B.** $\frac{2}{5}$ **C.** $\frac{1}{10}$ **D.** $1\frac{2}{5}$ **E.** $\frac{1}{3}$ **F.** $\frac{1}{2}$

9. If a 2 × 1 rectangle is $\frac{2}{5}$, model 1 whole.

You will need two sheets of dot paper to complete this homework. Organize your work carefully. Here is one way:

- Label each rectangle with the fraction it represents.
- When you have finished all the parts of a question, draw one ring around all the parts.
- Remember to follow the No-Diagonal Rule. If a question asks for something that is impossible, say so.

1. If a 3 cm by 1 cm rectangle is $\frac{1}{3}$, model the following:

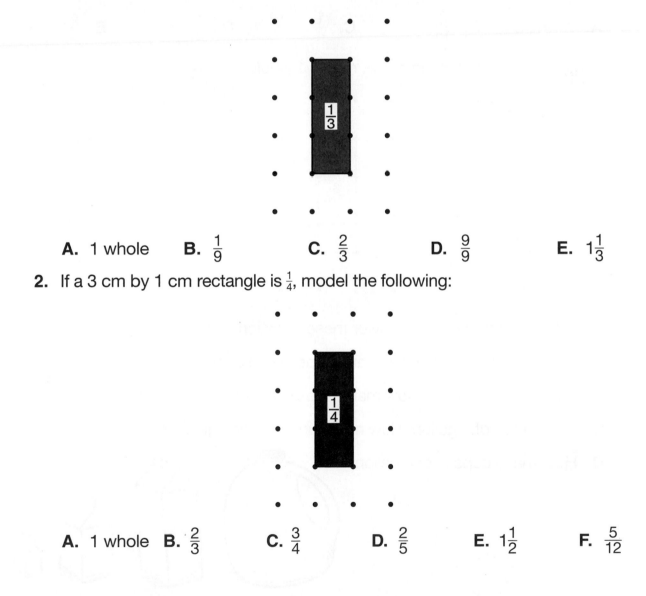

A. 1 whole   **B.** $\frac{1}{9}$ **C.** $\frac{2}{3}$ **D.** $\frac{9}{9}$ **E.** $1\frac{1}{3}$

2. If a 3 cm by 1 cm rectangle is $\frac{1}{4}$, model the following:

A. 1 whole **B.** $\frac{2}{3}$ **C.** $\frac{3}{4}$ **D.** $\frac{2}{5}$ **E.** $1\frac{1}{2}$ **F.** $\frac{5}{12}$

3. If a 3 cm by 1 cm rectangle is $\frac{1}{5}$, model the following:

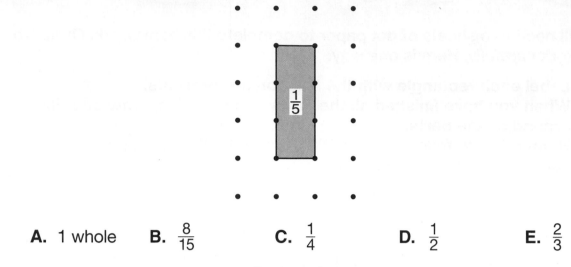

A. 1 whole   **B.** $\frac{8}{15}$ **C.** $\frac{1}{4}$ **D.** $\frac{1}{2}$ **E.** $\frac{2}{3}$

4. If a 3 cm by 1 cm rectangle is $\frac{3}{10}$, model 1 whole.

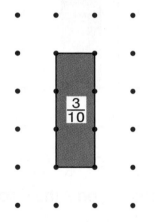

5. Draw pictures to help you answer these questions.

A. A cup is $\frac{1}{4}$ of a quart. How many cups in one quart?

B. A pint is $\frac{1}{2}$ of a quart. How many cups in a pint?

C. A quart is $\frac{1}{4}$ of a gallon. How many quarts in one gallon?

D. How many cups in one gallon?

Using Dot Paper Rectangles

Fraction Cover-All

Players

This game is for any number of players.

Materials

- *Centimeter Dot Paper*
- a set of six cards with the following numbers: $\frac{1}{2}, \frac{1}{4}, \frac{1}{3}, \frac{1}{6}, \frac{1}{12}, \frac{1}{12}$

Rules

1. Your teacher or one student is the leader. The others are the players.
2. Each player draws a 3×4 rectangle on dot paper. The rectangle is one whole.
3. The leader shuffles the cards, takes the top card, and reads the fraction.
4. Each player draws the fraction on his or her rectangle and labels the fraction. The fraction can be any shape, but players must follow the No-Diagonal Rule. The fraction must be made of small squares connected together.
5. The leader returns the card to the deck, shuffles again, chooses a card, and reads another fraction.
6. Play continues until at least one player fills his or her rectangle completely. (If a fraction will not fit on a player's rectangle, but the rectangle is not yet filled, the player does nothing on that turn.)
7. At this point in the game, all the players try to make as many number sentences as they can using the fractions on their rectangles.
   - They may use any operation.
   - They may use whole numbers in the sentences.
   - They may only use fractions and denominators that are on their rectangles.
   - They may only use a fraction as many times as it appears on their rectangles.
8. The winner is the player with the largest number of acceptable number sentences.

Ana played *Fraction Cover-All.* Mr. Moreno read these fractions: $\frac{1}{2}$, $\frac{1}{12}$, $\frac{1}{4}$, $\frac{1}{12}$, and $\frac{1}{12}$. Here are Ana's rectangle and her number sentences. She circled the sentences that were allowed.

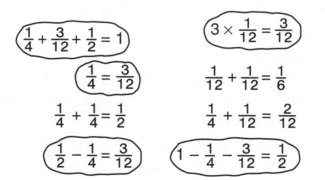

$$\frac{1}{4} + \frac{3}{12} + \frac{1}{2} = 1$$

$$\frac{1}{4} = \frac{3}{12}$$

$$\frac{1}{4} + \frac{1}{4} = \frac{1}{2}$$

$$\frac{1}{2} - \frac{1}{4} = \frac{3}{12}$$

$$3 \times \frac{1}{12} = \frac{3}{12}$$

$$\frac{1}{12} + \frac{1}{12} = \frac{1}{6}$$

$$\frac{1}{4} + \frac{1}{12} = \frac{2}{12}$$

$$1 - \frac{1}{4} - \frac{3}{12} = \frac{1}{2}$$

1. What is wrong with the sentences that are not circled?

2. Write more number sentences for Ana.

For Questions 1–5, the rectangle on the left is one whole. The rectangle on the right has been divided into parts using the No-Diagonal Rule.

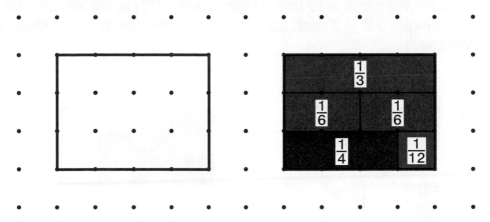

1. Write as many number sentences as you can using the fractions in the rectangle on the right. You may use whole numbers in your sentences, but you may not use fractions which are not shown in the rectangle.

   Here are some examples: $\frac{1}{4} + \frac{1}{12} = \frac{1}{3}$ $\frac{1}{3} - \frac{1}{12} = \frac{1}{4}$ $\frac{1}{3} = 2 \times \frac{1}{6}$

2. **A.** Draw a 3 × 4 rectangle on dot paper. Divide the rectangle into fractions, using the No-Diagonal Rule.

   B. Write as many number sentences as you can using your rectangle. Be sure you can justify each of your sentences using your rectangle.

3. The rectangle below is divided into thirds. Write as many number sentences as you can using this rectangle. Some examples are shown to the right of the rectangle.

4. Draw a 3 × 4 rectangle on dot paper. This rectangle is one whole. Divide it into fourths. Write as many number sentences as you can using this rectangle.

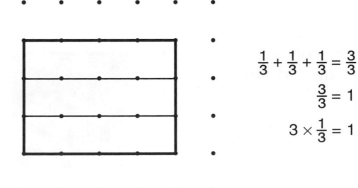

$\frac{1}{3} + \frac{1}{3} + \frac{1}{3} = \frac{3}{3}$

$\frac{3}{3} = 1$

$3 \times \frac{1}{3} = 1$

5. Draw another 3 × 4 rectangle. Divide the whole into sixths. Write as many number sentences as you can using this rectangle.

Using Common Denominators

1. Which is larger, $\frac{3}{4}$ or $\frac{2}{3}$? Justify your answer.

One way to compare fractions is to use rectangles on dot paper. We can show $\frac{3}{4}$ using a 1 × 4 rectangle, a 2 × 2 rectangle, a 2 × 4 rectangle, a 3 × 4 rectangle, or a 4 × 4 rectangle.

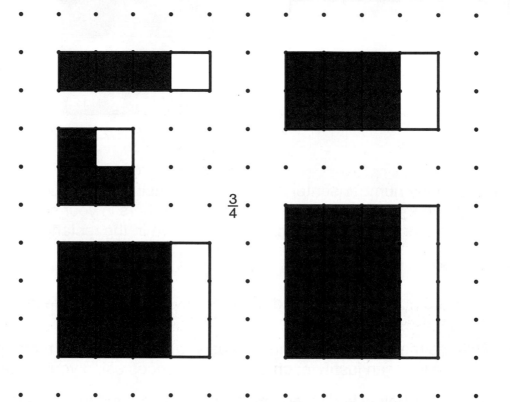

$\frac{3}{4}$

Each of these rectangles is divided into fourths. Since we want to compare $\frac{3}{4}$ to $\frac{2}{3}$, we need to choose a rectangle that can also be divided into thirds. Since the 3 × 4 rectangle can be divided into both thirds and fourths, we use a 3 × 4 rectangle to represent one whole.

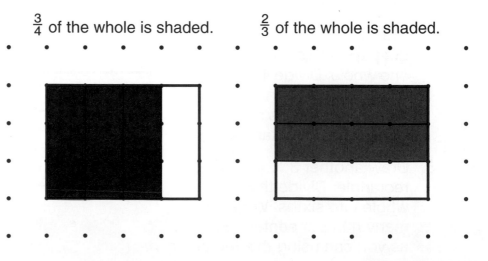

$\frac{3}{4}$ of the whole is shaded. $\frac{2}{3}$ of the whole is shaded.

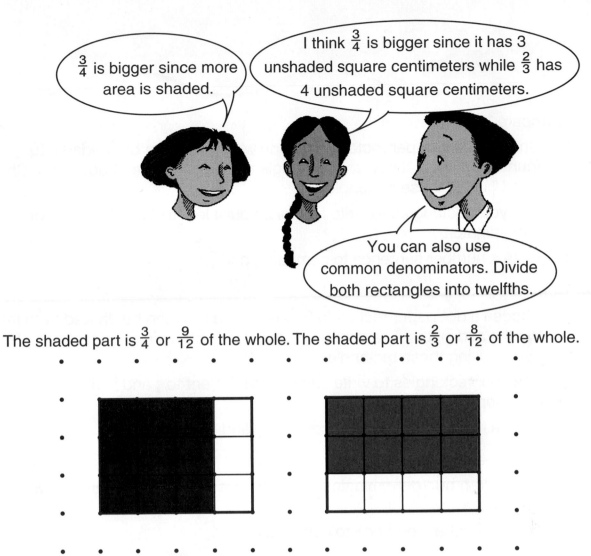

The shaded part is $\frac{3}{4}$ or $\frac{9}{12}$ of the whole. The shaded part is $\frac{2}{3}$ or $\frac{8}{12}$ of the whole.

Since $\frac{9}{12}$ is greater than $\frac{8}{12}$, $\frac{3}{4}$ is greater than $\frac{2}{3}$.

Using Symbols Instead of Fraction Rectangles

Choose a **common denominator** for $\frac{3}{4}$ and $\frac{2}{3}$. Twelfths will work, since 12 can be divided evenly by 4 and 3. Write $\frac{3}{4}$ and $\frac{2}{3}$ with a denominator of 12.

$$\frac{3}{4} = \frac{?}{12} \qquad\qquad \frac{2}{3} = \frac{?}{12}$$

$$\frac{3 \times 3}{4 \times 3} = \frac{9}{12} \qquad\qquad \frac{2 \times 4}{3 \times 4} = \frac{8}{12}$$

$$\text{Since } \frac{9}{12} > \frac{8}{12}, \text{ then } \frac{3}{4} > \frac{2}{3}.$$

2. Compare $\frac{4}{5}$ and $\frac{3}{4}$.

   A. Choose a dot paper rectangle for one whole that can be divided into fourths and fifths. Draw that rectangle twice on a piece of dot paper. Show $\frac{4}{5}$ and $\frac{3}{4}$ using these rectangles.

   B. Use your rectangles to write fractions equivalent to $\frac{4}{5}$ and $\frac{3}{4}$ with a common denominator.

   C. Write a number sentence to compare $\frac{4}{5}$ and $\frac{3}{4}$.

3. Compare $\frac{3}{4}$ and $\frac{5}{6}$.

   A. Choose a dot paper rectangle for one whole that can be divided both into fourths and sixths. Draw that rectangle twice on a piece of dot paper. Show $\frac{3}{4}$ and $\frac{5}{6}$ using these rectangles.

   B. Use your rectangles to write fractions equivalent to $\frac{3}{4}$ and $\frac{5}{6}$ with a common denominator.

   C. Write a number sentence to compare $\frac{3}{4}$ and $\frac{5}{6}$.

4. Compare $\frac{2}{3}$ and $\frac{3}{5}$.

   A. Find a common denominator for $\frac{2}{3}$ and $\frac{3}{5}$. Use that denominator to write fractions equivalent to $\frac{2}{3}$ and $\frac{3}{5}$.

   B. Write a number sentence to compare $\frac{2}{3}$ and $\frac{3}{5}$.

5. Write number sentences to compare the following pairs of fractions. Try different strategies. Be prepared to share your strategies.

   A. $\frac{1}{4}, \frac{7}{10}$ **B.** $\frac{9}{10}, \frac{9}{12}$ **C.** $\frac{7}{10}, \frac{3}{5}$

   D. $\frac{1}{4}, \frac{1}{5}$ **E.** $\frac{7}{8}, \frac{6}{5}$ **F.** $\frac{5}{8}, \frac{11}{12}$

6. Place these fractions in order from smallest to largest: $\frac{11}{10}, \frac{5}{6}, \frac{2}{3}, \frac{1}{12}$. Explain your strategies.

                    Using Common Denominators

Compare each pair of fractions. Write a number sentence to show which fraction is larger. Show the strategies you use. For some pairs of fractions you may need to find a common denominator. Use that denominator to write equivalent fractions. If you want, you can use dot paper to help you solve the problem.

1. $\frac{6}{7}$ and $\frac{2}{7}$

2. $\frac{1}{4}$ and $\frac{3}{10}$

3. $\frac{1}{3}$ and $\frac{1}{2}$

4. $\frac{5}{6}$ and $\frac{7}{8}$

5. $\frac{2}{3}$ and $\frac{5}{9}$

6. $\frac{1}{3}$ and $\frac{3}{8}$

7. $\frac{3}{8}$ and $\frac{3}{10}$

8. $\frac{3}{4}$ and $\frac{1}{3}$

9. $\frac{3}{8}$ and $\frac{5}{12}$

10. $\frac{7}{12}$ and $\frac{3}{4}$

11. Romesh planted a garden. He planted carrots in $\frac{3}{8}$ of his garden and tomatoes in $\frac{5}{12}$ of his garden. Which takes up more space in the garden, the tomatoes or the carrots? Use equivalent fractions to write a number sentence comparing these two spaces.

12. Each year Michael's baseball team and Lee Yah's softball team play the same number of games. Michael's baseball team won $\frac{3}{4}$ of its games. Lee Yah's team won $\frac{7}{12}$ of its games. Which team won more games? Justify your answer.

A Day at the Races

On Olympic Day at Bessie Coleman School, students participated in many events, including the Sack Race and the Backward Race. Roberto and Edward entered the Sack Race. Alexis and Jackie entered the Backward Race.

Contestants in the sack race took turns hopping along the track in a large cloth sack. They hopped for three seconds. Then the racing judge measured the distance each person hopped. Roberto hopped 24 feet and Edward hopped 27 feet.

 **Discuss**

1. **A.** Who moved along the track faster, Edward or Roberto? How do you know?
   B. What variables are involved in the Sack Race?
   C. What variables did students measure?
   D. Which variable was the same for all the participants in the Sack Race?

The Backward Race was different. In this race, contestants tried to run or walk backward in a straight line for six yards. Alexis took 4 seconds to travel the 6 yards from the starting line to the finish line. Jackie crossed the finish line after 2.5 seconds.

2. **A.** Who traveled faster, Jackie or Alexis? How do you know?
   B. What variables are involved in the Backward Race?
   C. What variables did the students measure?
   D. Which variable was the same for all the participants in the Backward Race?

A Day at the Races

3. **A.** What variable is Roberto comparing?

   B. What variable is Jackie comparing?

4. What variables do Jackie and Roberto need to consider to decide who went faster?

Speed and Velocity

To find out how fast someone or something is moving, we measure speed. To compare speeds, you need to consider both time and distance. **Speed** is the ratio of distance traveled to time taken. **Velocity** is speed in a certain direction. For example, Roberto's speed can be written $\frac{24\text{ ft}}{3\text{ sec}}$ which is equal to $\frac{8\text{ ft}}{1\text{ s}}$. This is called a unit ratio and we write $\frac{8\text{ ft}}{\text{s}}$. (We read $\frac{8\text{ ft}}{\text{s}}$ as "eight feet per second.")

You are going to conduct two experiments. In each experiment, you will investigate different ways to compare the speeds of contestants in events like the Backward Race and the Sack Race.

Experiment 1: Six-Yard Race

Work in a group of four or five students. Lay out a straight track that measures 6 yards (18 ft). Each person chooses a different way of traveling down the track: running, walking backward, hopping, crawling, etc. As each person travels down the track, another person uses a stopwatch to find the time it takes to go 6 yards. Record your data in a table.

5. Draw a picture of Experiment 1. Label the variables.

Before collecting the data, discuss the following with your group:

- The distance is the same for each participant. What other variables (or procedures) should stay the same?
- Each participant should try to travel at a constant speed. Where should each person start so that he or she moves at a steady pace for the whole six yards?
- How many trials should you time for each participant?
- If you conduct more than one trial, will you find the median or mean to average the data?
- Decide how your group will organize your data. (*Hint:* You need to record the name and activity for each participant, the time for each trial, and the average time of all the trials.)

6. Collect and record the data in a table. (You may use a *Three-trial Data Table*.)

Use your data from Question 6 to complete a new data table like the one shown below. (You may use a *Five-column Data Table*.) Write each speed as a fraction of distance over time ($\frac{D}{t}$). Note that the units are feet per second ($\frac{ft}{s}$). For example, if Jackie were in your group, her speed would be written $\frac{18\,ft}{2.5\,s}$.

Experiment 1: Six-Yard Race

Name	Activity	D Distance in _____	t Average Time in _____	S in ft/s Speed in Feet per Second

7. What are the measurements for time and distance when each student crosses the starting line?

In the lab *Distance vs. Time* in Unit 3, you graphed data points for the time it took a student to walk at the same speed for different distances. These points lie close to a straight line. In this lab, students move at the same speeds, so we can be pretty sure that data for this lab will lie close to a straight line, too.

8. Make a graph:

   - Title your graph so that you know this graph is for Experiment 1: Six-Yard Race.

   - It is customary to graph time on the horizontal axis. Label the horizontal axis with time in seconds (*t*) and the vertical axis with distance in feet (*D*).

   - For each member of your group, plot a point for his or her distance and time in the race. Connect this point to the point on the graph for *t* = 0 seconds and *D* = 0 ft. Each line on the graph represents the speed for each member of your group. Follow the example for Jackie's and Alexis's data.

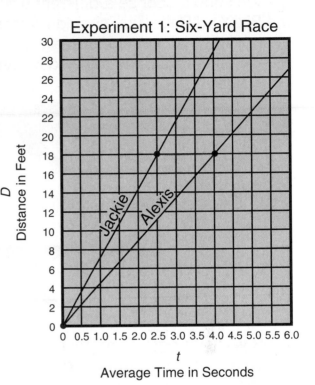

9. **A.** What variables are involved in the experiment?

   B. What variables did you measure?

10. **A.** What two variables are needed to determine the speed of an object?

    B. What variable was the same for all participants in the Six-Yard Race (Experiment 1)?

    C. Do the speeds have a common denominator or a common numerator?

11. **A.** Who traveled at the greatest speed?

    B. Who went the slowest?

12. **A.** Explain how to use the data table to compare speeds.

    B. Explain how to use the graph to compare speeds.

Experiment 2: Three-Second Race

Work with the same group of students. Use the same activities as before, but each person should choose a different way of moving. (For example, if you crawled in the Six-Yard Race, you should not crawl in the Three-Second Race.) For this experiment, each person travels for 3 seconds. Another member of the group measures the distance traveled in feet.

13. Draw a picture of Experiment 2. Label the variables.

Work with your group to develop a procedure for accurately measuring distance and recording the data. Discuss your method with your teacher before you collect your data.

14. Collect the data. Copy the following data table and fill in the information.

Experiment 2: Three-Second Race

Name	Activity	D Average Distance in _____	t Time in _____	S in ft/s Speed in Feet per Second

Graph

15. Graph the data.

   - Title your graph so that you know this graph is for Experiment 2: Three-Second Race.
   - Label the horizontal axis with time in seconds (t) and the vertical axis with distance in feet (D).
   - For each member of your group, plot a point for his or her distance and time in the race. Connect this point to the point on the graph for $t = 0$ seconds and $D = 0$ ft. Each line on the graph shows the speed for each member of your group.

Explore

16. **A.** What variable was the same for all participants in the Three-Second Race?

   B. Do the speeds have a common denominator or a common numerator?

17. **A.** Who traveled at the greatest speed? Explain your answer.

   B. Who went the slowest?

   C. How can you use your graph to decide who traveled fastest?

18. **A.** Copy the following table. Record the distance and time for your activity in Experiment 1: Six-Yard Race. Then record the distance and time of the other person who did the same activity in Experiment 2: Three-Second Race.

Comparing Speeds

Name	Activity	*D* Distance in _____	*t* Average Time in _____	*S* in ft/s Speed in Feet per Second

B. Plot the data points in the table for each person, and connect each point to the point for $t = 0$ seconds and $D = 0$ feet.

C. Who went faster? How do you know?

19. Use your data and graph from Experiment 1: Six-Yard Race to answer the following:

   A. How long did it take you to go 9 feet?

   B. If you could travel at the same speed for 36 feet, how long would it take?

20. Use your data and graph from Experiment 2: Three-Second Race to answer the following:

   A. How far did you travel in 1.5 seconds?

   B. How far would you have gone in 6 seconds at the same speed?

Homework

1. Jessie traveled 22 ft in the Three-Second Race, and David traveled 25 ft in the Three-Second Race. Who traveled at the greater speed?

2. Irma ran and Nicholas jumped in the Six-Yard Race. Irma's speed was $\frac{6 \text{ yds}}{2.3 \text{ s}}$, and Nicholas's speed was $\frac{6 \text{ yds}}{3 \text{ s}}$. Who traveled faster?

3. If Manny ran 2 meters and Michael ran 4 meters, could you tell who was traveling faster? Explain.

4. If Lee Yah traveled for 4 hours and Blanca traveled for 3 hours, could you tell who was traveling faster? Explain.

5. Shannon runs 9 meters in 5 seconds. Felicia runs 6 meters in 4 seconds. Who traveled at the faster speed? Show how you know. (*Hint:* Write each speed as a ratio written as a fraction. Then compare fractions.)

6. A car moves at a constant speed of 20 meters per second. How far will it travel in 5 seconds?

7. Lin can ride 2 blocks in 5 minutes on her bicycle. How long will it take her to ride 6 blocks if she travels at the same speed?

8. Romesh walked 2 miles in a half-hour. Nila walked 4 miles in 40 minutes. Who walked faster? Show how you know.

Adding Fractions with Rectangles

Estimating Sums

Mr. Moreno's class sorted fractions into three groups using benchmarks. Just as Mr. Moreno began to label the groups, the fire alarm sounded, and they had to leave the classroom.

Discuss

1. Copy the circles on your paper and write one of the following labels on each circle:

   - Fractions equal to or close to 0.
   - Fractions equal to or close to 1.
   - Fractions equal to or close to $\frac{1}{2}$.

2. Put these fractions in your circles: $\frac{5}{9}$, $\frac{1}{12}$, $\frac{17}{20}$.

3. Estimate these sums:

   A. $\frac{7}{8} + \frac{5}{6}$ **B.** $\frac{4}{5} + \frac{1}{10}$ **C.** $\frac{11}{12} + \frac{1}{2}$ **D.** $\frac{7}{12} + \frac{2}{4}$

4. Estimate these sums:

   A. $\frac{9}{10} + \frac{1}{20}$ **B.** $\frac{4}{8} + \frac{5}{12}$ **C.** $\frac{8}{9} + \frac{7}{8}$ **D.** $\frac{1}{2} + \frac{1}{10}$

5. **A.** Is $\frac{1}{4}$ closer to 0 or closer to $\frac{1}{2}$?

   B. Is the sum of $\frac{11}{12} + \frac{1}{4}$ greater than one or less than one?

6. **A.** Is $\frac{3}{4}$ closer to $\frac{1}{2}$ or closer to 1?

   B. Is $\frac{3}{4} + \frac{1}{10}$ greater than one or less than one?

7. **A.** Is $\frac{1}{3}$ closer to 0 or closer to $\frac{1}{2}$? (*Hint:* Use the Number Lines for Fractohoppers chart in Unit 3 Lesson 4.)

   B. Is $\frac{1}{3} + \frac{5}{12}$ more than one or less than one?

8. **A.** Is $\frac{2}{3}$ closer to $\frac{1}{2}$ or closer to 1?

   B. Is $\frac{2}{3} + \frac{7}{8}$ more than one or less than one?

Adding Fractions with Rectangles on Dot Paper

Mr. Moreno's class uses rectangles on dot paper as one way to add fractions. They trace dark lines around the perimeter of the rectangles to represent one whole.

9. **A.** Lin and Blanca use rectangles to solve the same addition problem. What problem are they trying to solve?

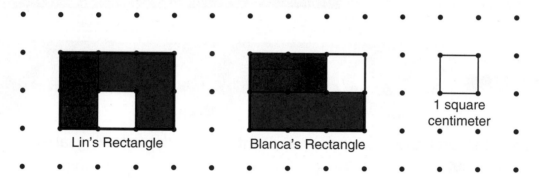

Lin's Rectangle   Blanca's Rectangle   1 square centimeter

   B. Estimate: Will the answer be close to 0? Close to $\frac{1}{2}$? Or, close to 1?

   C. Write a number sentence which shows the answer.

10. **A.** Manny draws this rectangle to solve an addition problem. What problem is Manny trying to solve?

    B. Estimate: Will the answer be close to 0?

    Close to $\frac{1}{2}$? Or, close to 1?

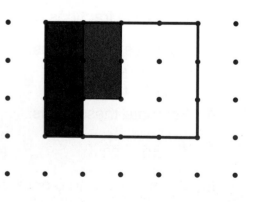

11. Manny changes his rectangle to show twelfths like this. He writes: $\frac{3}{12} + \frac{2}{12} = \frac{5}{12}$. Does the answer match your estimate?

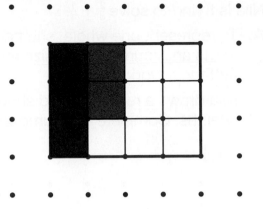

12. A. Here is Edward's problem: $\frac{3}{8} + \frac{7}{8}$. Will the answer be more than one or less than one? Does he need to use one rectangle or two?

B. Edward draws two rectangles together. Draw these rectangles on dot paper. Show $\frac{3}{8} + \frac{7}{8}$ and find the sum.

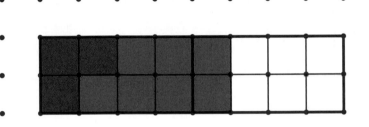

13. A. Nila is trying to solve $\frac{2}{5} + \frac{1}{3}$. Does she need one rectangle or two? Tell how you know.

B. She draws this rectangle and shades $\frac{2}{5}$. How can Nila show $\frac{1}{3}$? Draw Nila's rectangle and show how.

C. Change your rectangle to show fifteenths. Complete this number sentence: $\frac{2}{5} + \frac{1}{3} = \frac{?}{15} + \frac{?}{15} = \frac{?}{15}$

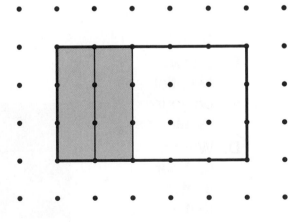

14. Nila is trying to solve $\frac{2}{3} + \frac{1}{4}$.

A. To represent one whole, she needs a rectangle that can be divided into thirds and fourths. What size rectangle can she use? Tell why this rectangle works.

B. Nila draws a rectangle and shades $\frac{2}{3}$ and $\frac{1}{4}$. Then she shows twelfths. Complete this number sentence using Nila's rectangles:

$\frac{2}{3} + \frac{1}{4} = \frac{?}{12} + \frac{?}{12} = \frac{?}{12}$.

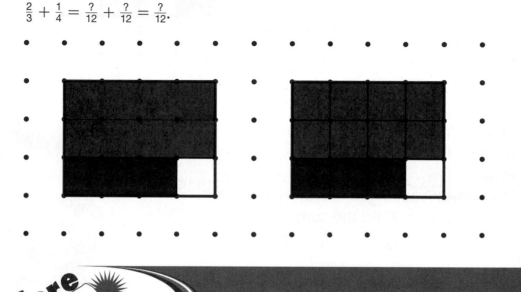

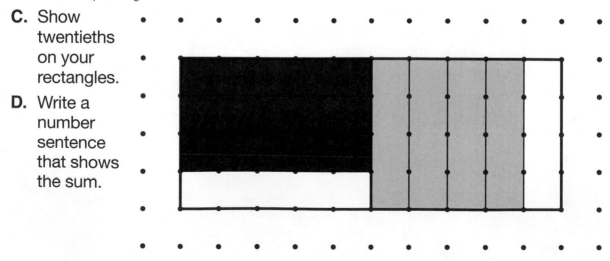

15. Add: $\frac{3}{4} + \frac{4}{5}$.

A. Think: Will your sum be close to 0? Close to $\frac{1}{2}$? Close to 1? Greater than 1? Will you need one rectangle or two?

B. Choose a rectangle for one whole that can be divided into fourths and fifths. Shade $\frac{3}{4}$ and $\frac{4}{5}$.

C. Show twentieths on your rectangles.

D. Write a number sentence that shows the sum.

Draw fraction rectangles to help you solve the following problems. Show all your work. Is your answer reasonable?

16. $\frac{3}{10} + \frac{9}{10} = ?$

(*Hint:* Will the sum be close to 0? Close to $\frac{1}{2}$? Close to 1? Greater than 1?)

17. $\frac{1}{4} + \frac{3}{8} = ?$　　　**18.** $\frac{1}{4} + \frac{7}{10} = ?$　　　**19.** $\frac{5}{6} + \frac{1}{4} = ?$

20. Blanca and Lin bought one sandwich at the deli. Blanca ate $\frac{1}{2}$ of the sandwich, and Lin ate $\frac{3}{8}$ of it. How much of the whole sandwich did the two girls eat?

21. Manny and Frank ordered pizza. Manny ate $\frac{1}{4}$ of the pizza, and Frank ate $\frac{5}{8}$ of the pizza. How much of the whole pizza was eaten?

Solve the following problems. Choose your own strategy. Estimate to see if your answers are reasonable.

22. $\frac{1}{2} + \frac{1}{4}$　　　**23.** $\frac{1}{2} + \frac{3}{4}$　　　**24.** $\frac{1}{12} + \frac{7}{12}$　　　**25.** $\frac{1}{2} + \frac{5}{10}$

Homework

1. Give **estimates** for these sums.

A. $\frac{7}{8} + \frac{9}{10}$　　　**B.** $\frac{2}{5} + \frac{1}{12}$　　　**C.** $\frac{3}{5} + \frac{5}{12}$

Use rectangles on dot paper to solve the following problems. For each problem:

- **Estimate the answer.**
- **Choose a rectangle for one whole.**
- **Decide if you will need one rectangle or two to solve the problem.**
- **Show your work. Write a number sentence for your solution.**
- **Look back and check if your answer is reasonable.**

2. $\frac{5}{12} + \frac{2}{3}$　　　**3.** $\frac{2}{3} + \frac{1}{6}$　　　**4.** $\frac{7}{10} + \frac{1}{2}$　　　**5.** $\frac{3}{4} + \frac{1}{3}$

Solve Questions 6–10. Explain your solutions.

6. After school, Blanca walked $\frac{1}{2}$ mile to the park. She then walked another block, or $\frac{1}{8}$ of a mile, farther to the store. How far did Blanca walk?

7. Shannon and Jackie shared an apple. Shannon ate $\frac{1}{4}$ of the apple. Jackie ate $\frac{1}{3}$ of the apple. How much of the apple was left?

8. Jessie's mom baked an apple pie for dessert. The family ate $\frac{3}{8}$ of the pie the first night. They ate $\frac{1}{4}$ of the pie the next night. How much of the pie was eaten?

9. Jessie's mom used $\frac{1}{2}$ cup of white sugar and $\frac{1}{3}$ cup of brown sugar. How many cups did she use altogether?

10. Shannon ran $\frac{5}{8}$ of a mile. Then she walked $\frac{3}{4}$ mile. Did she go more or less than 1 mile? How do you know?

   Adding Fractions with Rectangles

Adding and Subtracting Fractions

Subtracting Fractions

1. Frank took home $\frac{2}{3}$ of a cake from a party at school. His family ate another $\frac{1}{4}$ of the whole cake after dinner. How much of the whole cake is left?

   A. Estimate the answer to the following subtraction problem: $\frac{2}{3} - \frac{1}{4}$. Is the answer closer to 0 or $\frac{1}{2}$?

   B. Choose a rectangle to represent 1 whole that can be divided into thirds and fourths. Tell why this rectangle works.

   C. Find the difference using rectangles on dot paper.

Shade $\frac{2}{3}$ lightly with a pencil.	Erase $\frac{1}{4}$.	What part of the whole rectangle is shaded?

   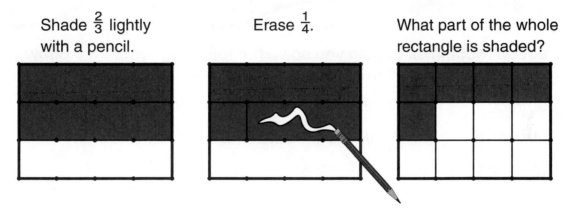

   D. Look back. Is your answer reasonable?

2. A. Estimate the answer to the following subtraction problem: $\frac{3}{4} - \frac{3}{8}$. Is the answer closer to 0 or $\frac{1}{2}$?

B. Find the difference using rectangles on dot paper. Choose a rectangle that can be divided into fourths and eighths.

Shade $\frac{3}{4}$ lightly with a pencil.

Erase $\frac{3}{8}$.

What part of the whole rectangle is shaded?

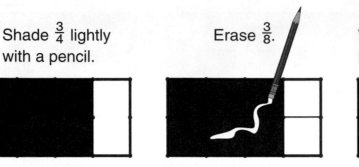

C. Look back. Is your answer reasonable?

Draw fraction rectangles to help you solve the following problems. Show all your work. Estimate to be sure your answers are reasonable.

3. Subtract: $\frac{3}{5} - \frac{1}{4} = ?$ (*Think:* Will the difference be closer to 0 or $\frac{1}{2}$?)

4. Subtract: $\frac{3}{10} - \frac{1}{5} = ?$ (*Think:* Will the difference be closer to 0 or $\frac{1}{2}$?)

5. Subtract: $\frac{4}{5} - \frac{1}{3}$.

6. Subtract: $\frac{11}{12} - \frac{2}{3}$.

7. Manny and Frank ordered sausage on $\frac{1}{4}$ of a pizza and pepperoni on $\frac{1}{2}$ of the pizza. The rest of the pizza had only cheese. How much of the pizza had only cheese?

8. At Brandon's birthday party, the guests ate $\frac{3}{4}$ of his cake. The next day, Brandon's family ate another $\frac{1}{6}$ of the cake. How much of the cake was left?

Using Symbols to Add and Subtract Fractions

You can use symbols when you add or subtract fractions.

9. **A.** Think about the sum of the following addition problem: $\frac{2}{3} + \frac{3}{4}$. Will it be close to one? Greater than one?

B. Twelve is a common denominator for $\frac{2}{3}$ and $\frac{3}{4}$. Why? (Think of dot paper rectangles.)

C. Using 12 as your denominator, write fractions equivalent to $\frac{2}{3}$ and $\frac{3}{4}$.

D. Then add.

$$\frac{3}{4} = \frac{?}{12} \qquad\qquad \frac{2}{3} = \frac{?}{12}$$

$$\frac{3 \times 3}{4 \times 3} = \frac{9}{12} \qquad\qquad \frac{2 \times 4}{3 \times 4} = \frac{8}{12}$$

$$\frac{3}{4} + \frac{2}{3} = \frac{9}{12} + \frac{8}{12} = \frac{17}{12}$$

E. Is the answer reasonable?

10. **A.** Estimate the difference for the following subtraction problem: $\frac{4}{5} - \frac{3}{4}$. Will the difference be closer to 0 or $\frac{1}{2}$?

B. Twenty is a common denominator for $\frac{4}{5}$ and $\frac{3}{4}$. Why?

C. Using 20 as your denominator, write fractions equivalent to $\frac{4}{5}$ and $\frac{3}{4}$.

D. Subtract.

$$\frac{4}{5} = \frac{?}{20} \qquad\qquad \frac{3}{4} = \frac{?}{20}$$

$$\frac{4 \times 4}{5 \times 4} = \frac{16}{20} \qquad\qquad \frac{3 \times 5}{4 \times 5} = \frac{15}{20}$$

$$\frac{4}{5} - \frac{3}{4} = \frac{16}{20} - \frac{15}{20} = \frac{1}{20}$$

E. Look back. Is the answer reasonable?

11. **A.** Add: $\frac{1}{4} + \frac{3}{8}$.

  B. Choose a common denominator for $\frac{1}{4}$ and $\frac{3}{8}$. Eighths will work. Why?

  C. Using 8 as your denominator, write fractions equivalent to $\frac{1}{4}$ and $\frac{3}{8}$.

  D. Add.

12. **A.** Subtract: $\frac{7}{8} - \frac{1}{2}$.

  B. What is a common denominator for $\frac{7}{8}$ and $\frac{1}{2}$?

  C. Using this denominator, write equivalent fractions for $\frac{7}{8}$ and $\frac{1}{2}$.

  D. Subtract.

13. **A.** Add: $\frac{2}{3} + \frac{5}{6}$.

  B. What is a common denominator for $\frac{2}{3}$ and $\frac{5}{6}$?

  C. Using this denominator, write equivalent fractions for $\frac{2}{3}$ and $\frac{5}{6}$.

  D. Add.

  E. Look at your answer. Is there another name for this fraction?

14. **A.** $\frac{2}{5} + \frac{3}{10} = ?$

  B. What is a common denominator for $\frac{2}{5}$ and $\frac{3}{10}$?

  C. Write $\frac{2}{5}$ and $\frac{3}{10}$ with a common denominator.

  D. Add.

15. $\frac{5}{6} - \frac{1}{4} = ?$ 16. $\frac{5}{12} + \frac{3}{4} = ?$

17. $\frac{1}{5} + \frac{1}{3} = ?$ 18. $\frac{5}{8} - \frac{1}{4} = ?$

Homework

Complete the following problems. Show your work. Estimate to be sure your answers are reasonable.

1. $\frac{4}{5} - \frac{1}{4} = ?$

2. **A.** $\frac{11}{12} - \frac{3}{4} = ?$

  B. Look at your answer to Part A. What is another name for this fraction?

3. **A.** $\frac{5}{8} + \frac{1}{2} = ?$

  B. Look at your answer to Part A. What is another name for this fraction?

4. $\frac{2}{3} + \frac{1}{2} = ?$

5. $\frac{4}{5} - \frac{1}{3} = ?$

6. Roberto's older sister jogs every morning. This morning, after running $\frac{7}{10}$ of a kilometer, she met a friend. She stopped to chat. Then she jogged $\frac{1}{4}$ kilometer more.

    A. Did Roberto's sister jog more or less than 1 kilometer?

    B. Find how far she jogged.

7. Brandon saved $\frac{1}{10}$ of his babysitting earnings in his piggy bank.

    A. What fraction of his earnings did he have left to spend?

    B. Brandon spent $\frac{3}{5}$ more of his earnings on baseball cards. Does he have close to nothing left or close to $\frac{1}{2}$ of his earnings left?

    C. What fraction of Brandon's earnings does he have left?

8. Shannon's mother spends $\frac{1}{3}$ of her monthly salary on rent (which includes heat). Groceries for the month and her car payment add up to about $\frac{2}{5}$ of her salary.

    A. Do these bills account for about $\frac{1}{2}$ of her salary, more than $\frac{1}{2}$ of her salary, or all of her salary (1 whole salary)?

    B. What fraction of her salary is spent after paying for rent, groceries, and her car?

Shannon's Trip to School

1. Shannon lives about 1 block from school. The following graph shows Shannon's trip to school one morning.

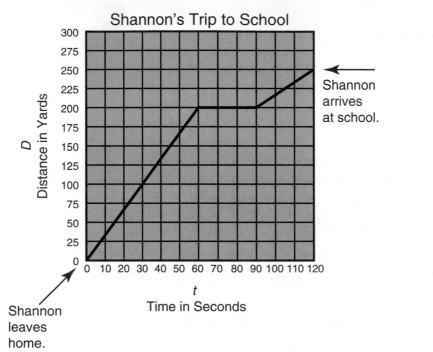

Shannon's Trip to School

Shannon arrives at school.

Shannon leaves home.

t
Time in Seconds

   A. How many yards did Shannon travel?

   B. How long did it take her to get to school? Give your answer in seconds and then in minutes.

   C. How far had she traveled after 1 minute?

   D. How far had she traveled after 90 seconds?

   E. Did Shannon travel at a constant speed all the way to school? Explain how you know.

2. On her way to school Shannon walked, ran, and stopped to talk to a friend.

   A. In what order did she walk, run, and talk to her friend? (What did she do first? What did she do next? What did she do last?)

   B. How long did she run?

   C. How long did she talk to her friend?

3. Find Shannon's speed in yards per second in the first minute. (*Hint:* Find the ratio of distance in yards to time in seconds.)

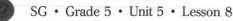

Geometry

	Student Guide	Discovery Assignment Book	Adventure Book	Unit Resource Guide*
Lesson 1				
Angle Measures	●	●		
Lesson 2				
Angles in Triangles and Other Polygons	●	●		
Lesson 3				
Polygon Angles	●	●		
Lesson 4				
Congruent Shapes	●			
Lesson 5				
Quilts and Tessellations	●			
Lesson 6				
Classifying Shapes	●	●		
Lesson 7				
Making Shapes	●			●

Unit Resource Guide pages are from the teacher materials.

Angle Measures

What Is an Angle?

Angles are very important for drawing, building, and finding direction. Angles are made of two different **rays** having the same **endpoint.** The rays are the **sides** of the angle. The endpoint of the rays is the **vertex** of the angle. An angle is named by its vertex point or with 3 letters. We can call the angle here angle E and write ∠E as shorthand. We can also use 3 letters to name an angle. The angle here can be called ∠DEF or ∠FED.

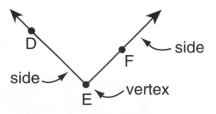

The **degree** of an angle measures the opening between the two sides of the angle. The three angles shown here all measure 20 degrees. We say the measure of ∠A is 20 degrees. We write ∠A = 20°. The little circle (°) stands for the word degree. ∠B = 20° and ∠C = 20° as well. These three are equal angles.

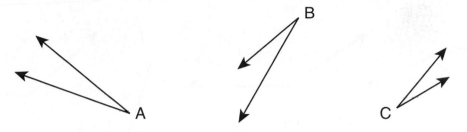

The amount of opening, not the length of the sides, determines the size of the angle. ∠H is a 90° angle. A 90° angle is a **right angle,** or quarter-turn. Since a right angle forms a square corner, a "box" is often drawn at its vertex.

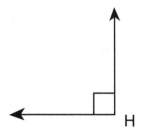

An **acute angle** is an angle whose degree measure is less than 90°. These angles are acute angles:

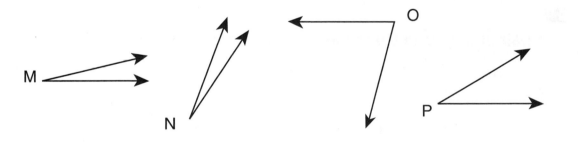

These angles are not acute angles:

Angle Measures

An **obtuse angle** is an angle whose degree measure is more than 90° but less than 180°. These angles are obtuse angles:

These angles are not obtuse angles:

The degree measure of a **straight angle** is 180°. Angle X is a straight angle:

X

For each pair of angles in Questions 1–5, tell which one is the larger angle.

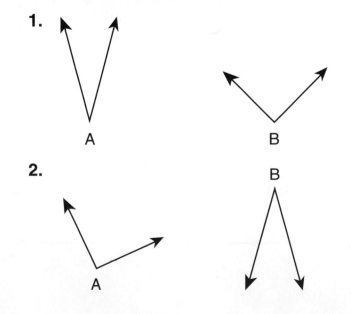

1.

A

B

2.

B

A

3.

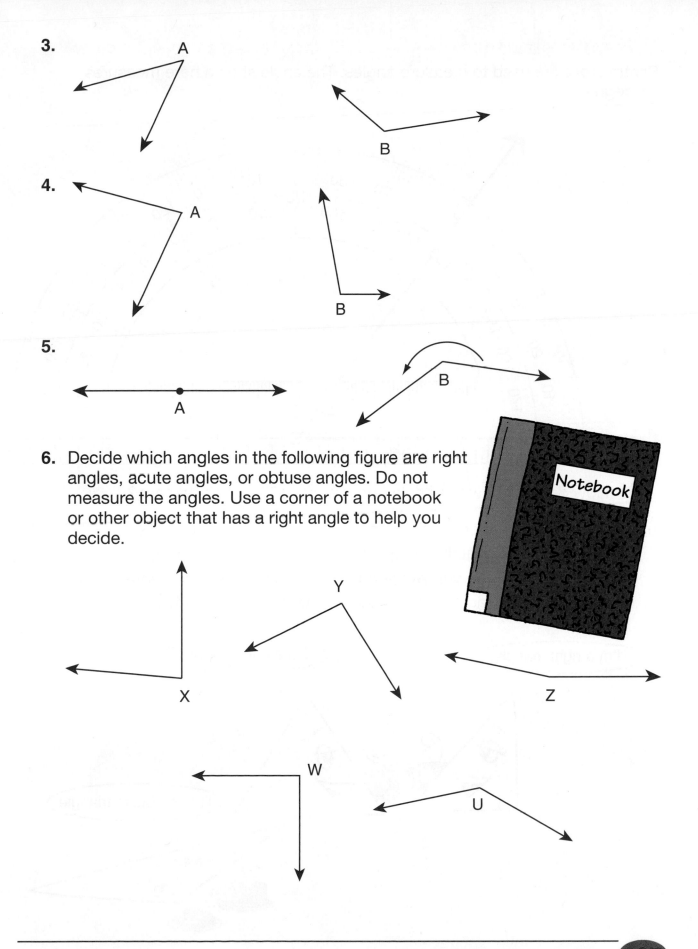

4.

5.

6. Decide which angles in the following figure are right angles, acute angles, or obtuse angles. Do not measure the angles. Use a corner of a notebook or other object that has a right angle to help you decide.

Using a Protractor

Protractors are used to measure angles. The angle shown here measures 53 degrees.

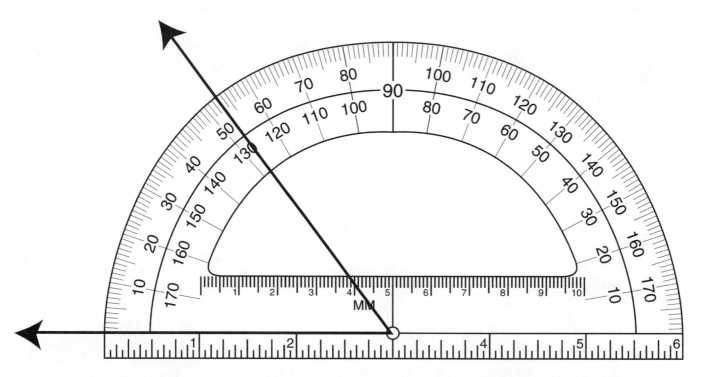

7. How do you know the angle above is not 127 or 133 degrees?

Triangles are often named for their angles.

- A triangle that contains a right angle is called a **right triangle.**
- A triangle that has only acute angles is called an **acute triangle.**
- A triangle that has an obtuse angle is called an **obtuse triangle.**

Here is a right triangle:

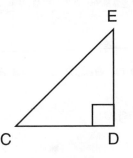

8. Name the right angle in triangle CED.

9. Name the acute angles in triangle CED.

Here is an obtuse triangle:

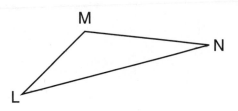

10. Name the obtuse angle in triangle LMN.

11. Name the acute angles in triangle LMN.

12. Using your protractor, draw:
    A. An angle whose degree measure is 40°. Label this angle S.
    B. An angle whose degree measure is 90°. Label this angle T.
    C. An angle whose degree measure is 110°. Label this angle W.
    D. A triangle with a 50° angle. What kind of triangle did you draw (acute, obtuse, or right)?
    E. A triangle with a 121° angle. What kind of triangle did you draw?
    F. A triangle with a 90° angle. What kind of triangle did you draw?

For each pair of angles in Questions 1–4:
- Estimate the degree measure of each of the angles. You may wish to use a right corner.
- Tell which one is the larger angle.

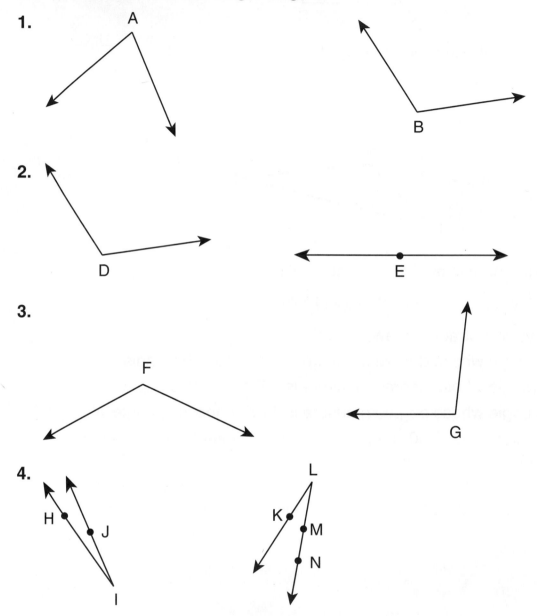

1.

A

B

2.

D

E

3.

F

G

4.

L

H   J

K   M

I   N

5. **A.** ∠I in Question 4 can also be called ∠HIJ. How else could ∠I be named?

   B. Give 3 other names for ∠L in Question 4.

In Questions 6–7, you do not need to measure the angles. Estimate, using a right corner.

6. **A.** Which angles in the figure below appear to be right angles?
   B. Which are obtuse angles?
   C. Which are acute angles?

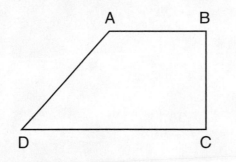

7. **A.** Which angles in the figure below appear to be right angles?
   B. Which are obtuse angles?
   C. Which are acute angles?

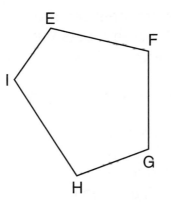

8. Using your protractor, draw:
   A. An angle whose degree measure is 30°. Label this angle M.
   B. An angle whose degree measure is 75°. Label this angle N.
   C. An angle whose degree measure is 145°. Label this angle P.

Angles in Triangles and Other Polygons

Angles in Polygons

A **polygon** is a connected figure whose sides are line segments. Each endpoint of a side meets the endpoint of just one other side, and no sides overlap.

The word *polygon* comes from the prefix *poly* (many) and suffix *gon* (angles). So, a polygon has many angles (or, you could say, many sides). To help us communicate, we often name polygons with letters. When we say the name, we go around the shape. For example, this is triangle JKL. A triangle is a polygon with 3 sides (or we can say 3 angles).

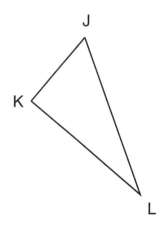

This is quadrilateral MNOP. A **quadrilateral** is a polygon with 4 sides.

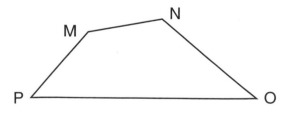

Triangle ABC is pictured here.

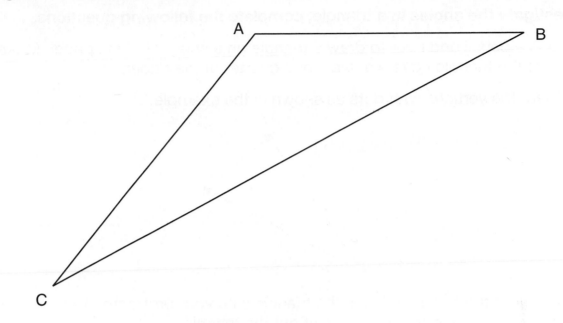

1. Which angles in the triangle are acute?

2. Which angles in the triangle are obtuse?

3. Which angles in the triangle are right angles?

4. Is triangle ABC obtuse, right, or acute?

5. Use a protractor to measure $\angle A$.

6. What is the measure of $\angle B$?

7. What is the measure of $\angle C$?

8. Name three different angles below. Determine whether they are right, obtuse, or acute. Then measure the angles.

Adding the Angles of a Triangle

To investigate the angles in a triangle, complete the following questions.

9. Use a pencil and ruler to draw a triangle on a sheet of blank paper. Make sure the triangle covers at least one quarter of the paper.

10. Mark the vertices with dots as shown in the example.

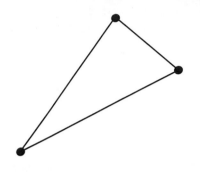

11. Measure the three angles of the triangle with your protractor. Write the angle measures **inside** the triangle. Cut out the triangle.

12. Tear off the three angles as shown in the example.

13. On a different piece of blank paper draw a straight line. Mark a point on the line.

14. Place the three angles on the piece of paper with the drawn line. Place the angles above the line, like the pieces of a puzzle, with all the vertices touching the dot on the line.

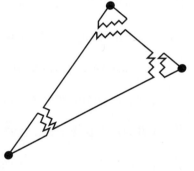

15. What do you notice?

16. What is the sum of the three angles of your triangle?

When the corners of any triangle are torn off and placed together, they form a **straight angle.** For example, your triangle might have looked like this:

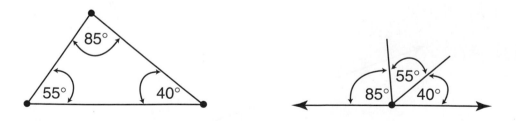

17. How many degrees are in a straight angle?

18. What is the sum of the angles of any triangle?

The students in Mr. Moreno's class did this activity. Alexis found the sum of the angles of her triangle to be 180°. The sum of the angles of Romesh's triangle equaled 179°, and Ana's equaled 182°.

19. The sum of the interior angles of a triangle always sum to 180°. Why do you think Romesh's and Ana's angle measurements did not add up to 180°?

20. With a partner holding the book steady, measure the angles of this triangle. Find the sum of the angles. Did your measurements sum close to 180°?

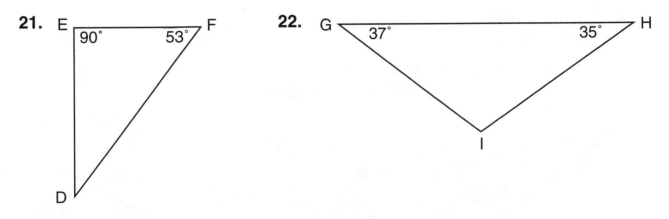

Find the missing degree measure in Questions 21 and 22. Do not measure the angles.

21.

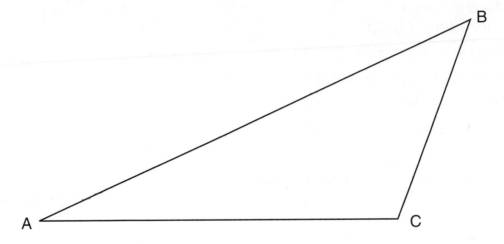

22.

23. Could an obtuse triangle have a right angle? Explain.

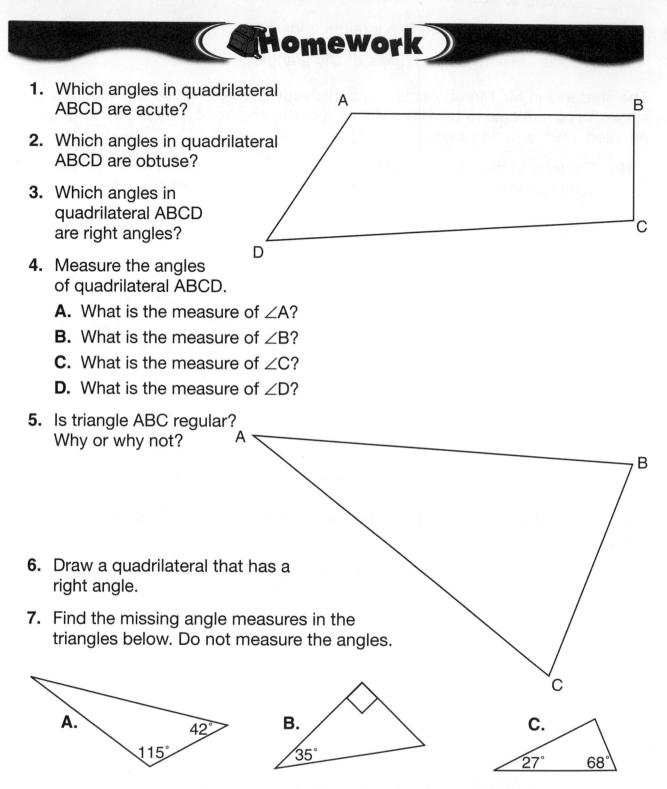

1. Which angles in quadrilateral ABCD are acute?

2. Which angles in quadrilateral ABCD are obtuse?

3. Which angles in quadrilateral ABCD are right angles?

4. Measure the angles of quadrilateral ABCD.

   A. What is the measure of ∠A?

   B. What is the measure of ∠B?

   C. What is the measure of ∠C?

   D. What is the measure of ∠D?

5. Is triangle ABC regular? Why or why not?

6. Draw a quadrilateral that has a right angle.

7. Find the missing angle measures in the triangles below. Do not measure the angles.

   A. 42° 115°

   B. 35°

   C. 27° 68°

8. Use a ruler or the edge of your protractor to draw a quadrilateral. Label it RSTU. Measure all the angles.

9. A pentagon is a polygon with 5 sides. Use a ruler or the edge of your protractor to draw pentagon JKLMN. Measure all the angles.

Polygon Angles

In the last lesson, you learned that the sum of the angles of a triangle is always 180 degrees. A quadrilateral can be divided into two triangles by drawing a diagonal. One way to draw a diagonal in quadrilateral ABCD is shown here:

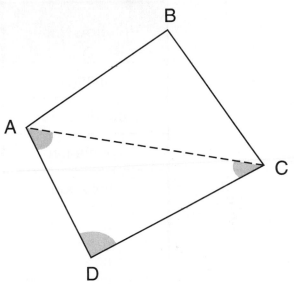

1. Two triangles were formed. One triangle is ABC. Name the other triangle.

2. What is the sum of the shaded angles?

3. What is the sum of the nonshaded angles?

4. What is the sum of the angles of quadrilateral ABCD?

Dividing a polygon into nonoverlapping triangles is called **triangulating** the polygon. To triangulate a polygon, draw diagonals that do not cross each other. There are always two ways to triangulate a quadrilateral.

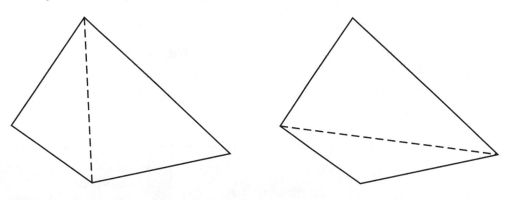

5. Draw a pentagon (a polygon with five sides).

6. Triangulate the pentagon. Make sure the diagonals do not cross.

7. How many triangles are always formed by triangulating a pentagon?

8. Find the sum of the angle measures of the pentagon by looking at the triangles.

The names of the polygons in the table below are of Latin or Greek origin. Many English words use the same prefixes. For example, a **tri**angle is a polygon with three sides or angles. A **tri**cycle is a vehicle with three wheels. A **tri**logy is a story in three parts. The 11-sided polygon does not have a name that is commonly used. This is also true for most polygons that have greater than 12 sides.

Polygon Name	Number of Sides/Angles
triangle	3
quadrilateral	4
pentagon	5
hexagon	6
septagon	7
octagon	8
nonagon	9
decagon	10
dodecagon	12

9. Use the *Polygon Angles Data Table* Activity Page in the *Discovery Assignment Book*. Fill in the rows for the triangle, quadrilateral, and pentagon. Leave the last column blank. Your *Polygon Angles Data Table* should look like this:

Polygon	Number of Sides	Number of Angles	Number of Triangles	Sum of Angles (degrees)	Measure of One Angle of a Regular Polygon (degrees)
triangle	3	3	1	180	
quadrilateral	4	4	2	360	

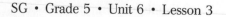

10. Fill in the *Polygon Angles Data Table* through dodecagon (a 12-sided polygon) by triangulating the polygons. Do not fill in the last column yet. Look for patterns.

When mathematicians talk about an *N*-gon, they mean a polygon that has *N* sides, where *N* is a whole number.

11. How many angles does an *N*-gon have? Record this in the table.

12. Look at the patterns. Predict how many triangles are formed when an *N*-gon is triangulated. Record this in the table.

13. By looking at the pattern, predict the sum of the angles of an *N*-gon. Record this in the table.

A polygon is **regular** if all sides are the same length *and* all angles have the same degree measure.

regular quadrilateral

regular triangle

14. A square is a special quadrilateral.
    A. What is the sum of the angles in a square?
    B. Since all the angles of a square are equal, what is the measure of each angle? How do you know?

An equilateral triangle is regular because all its sides are the same length and all its angles are equal.

15. What is the measure of any angle of an equilateral triangle?

16. Fill in the remaining column in the *Polygon Angles Data Table*.

Use your completed *Polygon Angles Data Table* to help you complete these problems.

1. Three of the angles of a quadrilateral have angle measures of 59°, 136°, and 89°. What is the measure of the remaining angle?

2. Four of the angles of a pentagon have angle measures of 74°, 120°, 138°, and 143°. What is the measure of the remaining angle?

3. Two angles of a hexagon have equal measure. The other angles have measures of 83°, 97°, 126°, and 98°. How many degrees are each of the two remaining angles?

4. **A.** Draw an octagon.

   B. Find two different ways of triangulating the octagon. Use different colored pencils or pens to help you.

   C. How many triangles are formed when an octagon is triangulated?

   D. What is the sum of the angles of an octagon?

5. **A.** What is the sum of the angles in degrees of a regular 15-gon (a polygon with 15 sides)?

   B. What is the measure of one angle of a regular 15-gon?

6. **A.** What is the sum of the angles in degrees of a regular 20-gon?

   B. What is the measure of one angle of a regular 20-gon?

Congruent Shapes

Congruent shapes are shapes that can be placed one on top of the other so that all angles and all sides match exactly. **Congruent** shapes are the same size and the same shape. The pairs of figures in A and B are congruent. You can check to see if two shapes are congruent. First, trace one of the shapes. Then place the tracing on top of the other shape.

A. **B.**

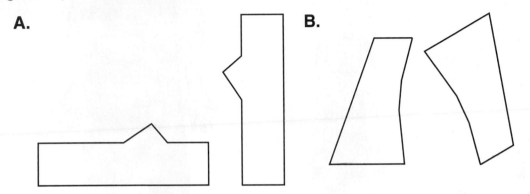

The pairs of figures in C and D are **not** congruent.

C. **D.**

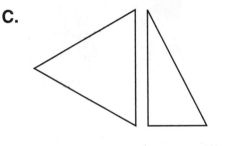
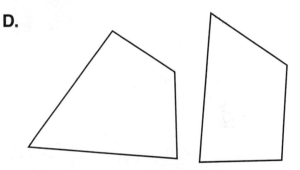

The pairs of shapes in E and F are not congruent either. These shapes are similar. Shapes that are the same shape but not necessarily the same size are called **similar.**

E. **F.**

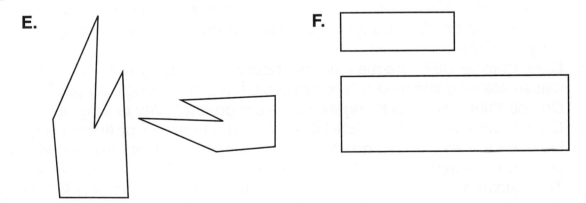

We encounter similar shapes when we enlarge photographs. These are two different copies of the same picture. One is larger than the other. The picture on the right is an enlargement of the picture on the left. It is a picture of the same girl in the same pose. The girl's shape is the same in both pictures.

1. Draw triangle ABC. Side AB = 5 cm, the measure of angle A is 90°, and Side AC is 3 cm. Do you think everyone will draw the same triangle? Why or why not?
2. Draw triangle DEF. The measure of angle E is 45°. Do you think your classmate who sits next to you will draw the same triangle as you? Do you think your two triangles will be congruent? Why or why not?
3. Draw quadrilateral GHIJ. Side HI is 4 cm. The measure of Angle I is 60°. Do you think everyone's quadrilaterals will be congruent? Why or why not?
4. Draw quadrilateral KLMN. Make Sides KL, LM, and MN all the same length. The measure of Angle L is 120°, and the measure of Angle M is 90°. Do you think everyone's quadrilaterals will be congruent? Why or why not?

For each of the following problems, decide whether the two shapes are congruent, similar, or neither. Explain how you decided. You may need to trace one shape in each pair and see if the tracing can lie exactly on top of the other shape.

1.

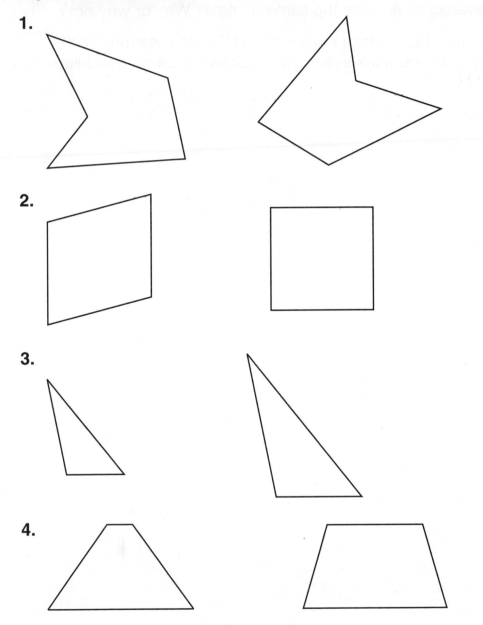

2.

3.

4.

5. Draw triangle PQR. Side PQ = 6 cm, the measure of ∠P is 90°, side PR = 4 cm. Do you think everyone will draw the same triangle? Why or why not?

6. Draw rectangle WXYZ. Make Side XY = 5 cm. Make Side YZ = 7 cm. Do you think everyone will draw the same rectangle? Why or why not?

7. Draw triangle STU. Make Sides ST and TU the same length. Make ∠T = 75°. Do you think everyone will draw the same triangle? Why or why not?

8. Draw quadrilateral ABCD. Make Angles B and C both measure 110°. Side BC is 6 cm. Do you think everyone will draw the same quadrilateral? Why or why not?

Quilts and Tessellations

Quilts are a part of our American heritage. Quilts are used as blankets, but many quilts are also works of art. Why talk about quilts in a math class? As you can see in the picture, quilts often include many interesting geometric shapes and patterns. What patterns do you see in this quilt called Jacob's Ladder?

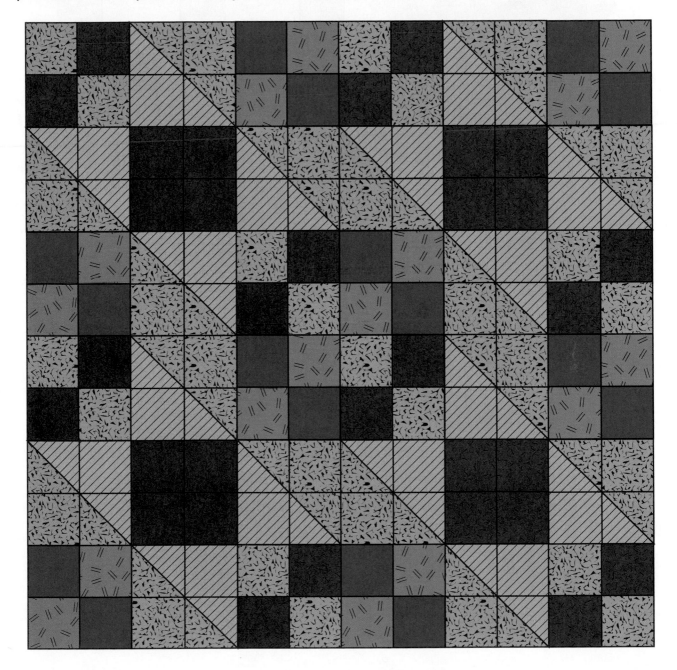

1. Here are four different patterns that are used to make quilts. Use your pattern blocks to make one of these patterns. Repeat the pattern several times.

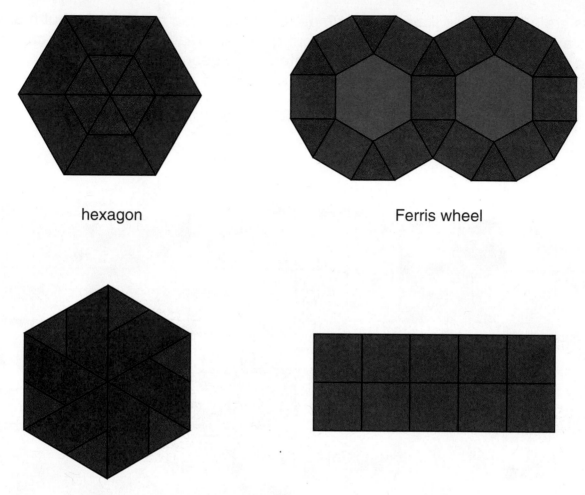

hexagon

Ferris wheel

whirligig wheel

patchwork

2. Copy the pattern on *Triangle Grid Paper* or blank paper and color it. Choose any colors you wish to create an interesting design.

The patterns that you made are called tessellations. **Tessellations** are patterns made from one or more shapes that do not overlap and leave no gaps.

Quilts and Tessellations

The following picture shows a tessellation made entirely of hexagons.

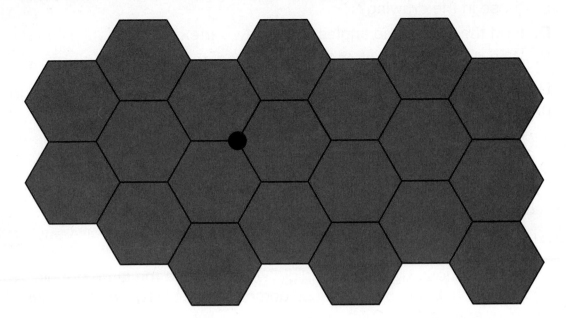

3. A large dot has been placed where three hexagons come together. We call this a **vertex** of the tessellation. Why do the three hexagons fit exactly, leaving no gaps? (*Hint:* Think about the angles at the vertex.)

4. **A.** Copy the hexagon tessellation with your pattern blocks. Then sketch part of it on *Triangle Grid Paper* or blank paper.

   B. Mark another vertex. Are the angles at your new vertex the same as those in the drawing above?

   C. Find the sum of the angles at the new vertex.

5. **A.** Look at the close-up of the Ferris wheel pattern. Notice a large dot has been placed where a hexagon, square, triangle, and square come together. Why do the pieces fit together exactly? (*Hint:* Think about the angles at the vertex.)

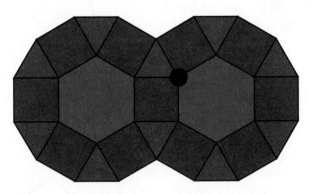

   B. Copy the Ferris wheel pattern with your pattern blocks. Then sketch it.

C. Draw another vertex. Are the angles at your new vertex the same as those in the drawing?

D. Find the sum of the angles at the new vertex.

E. Why do the angles at each vertex fit together and leave no gaps?

6. Use pattern blocks to make your own tessellation. Record it on the grid paper. Color it to make an interesting design.

7. A. Draw a vertex on your tessellation.

B. Find the sum of the angles at your vertex.

1. Look at the close-up of the whirligig wheel. Notice the large dot where two triangles and two rhombuses come together. Why do the pieces fit together exactly?

2. Can a tessellation be made using only regular pentagons? Why or why not? A regular pentagon is pictured here. You may wish to trace it.

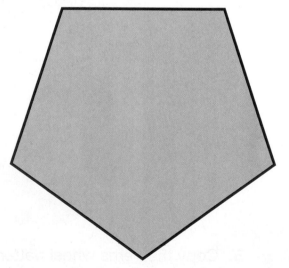

3. Quilts can contain many more geometric shapes than those seen in pattern blocks. The quilt design shown above is used to make the quilt called North Carolina Star. Describe the geometric shapes you see.

Classifying Shapes

Classification is an important part of science. Biologists classify, or sort, animals and plants according to similarities in their physical traits and how they grow. Below is a classification tree for a small group of animals. Study the tree to see if you can determine how it is organized.

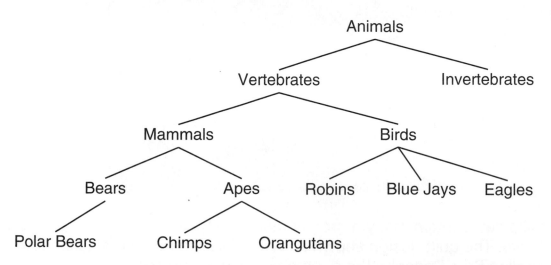

Each kind of living thing has a scientific definition. A simple definition of a **vertebrate** is an animal with a hard internal skeleton including a backbone (vertebral column) and a brain enclosed in a skull. A **mammal** is defined as a vertebrate that usually has hair and nurses its young. This means that all mammals are vertebrates. That is why there is a branch leading from vertebrates to mammals in the classification tree.

1. Lizards, snakes, and turtles are all reptiles. Try to make up a definition of a reptile. Look in the dictionary or ask your teacher for a correct definition. How close was your definition to the scientific definition?

2. Look up the definition of a bat in a dictionary. Is a bat a mammal or a reptile? Where would you place bats in the classification tree above?

3. Copy the classification tree above. Use what you know or can find out about animals to add the following animals to the tree.

   A. Horses   **B.** Reptiles

   C. Worms   **D.** Bald Eagles

Classification in Geometry

Classification is also a part of geometry. Sorting shapes into categories based upon similarities and differences helps us to understand and talk about them.

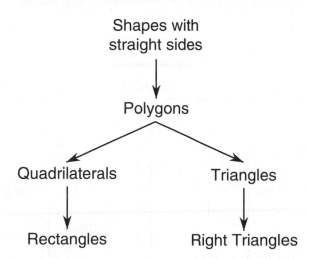

Shapes with straight sides

↓

Polygons

Quadrilaterals — Triangles

↓ ↓

Rectangles — Right Triangles

4. A definition of a **rectangle** is a quadrilateral with four right angles. A definition of a **square** is a quadrilateral with four equal sides and four right angles.

   A. Is every square a quadrilateral? Why?

   B. Is every square a rectangle? Why?

   C. Can a square be a pentagon? Why?

5. Give a definition of a right triangle.

6. Copy the classification tree above. Add these shapes to the classification tree: square, pentagon, obtuse triangle.

7. A **rhombus** is a quadrilateral that has four equal sides. Can a quadrilateral be both a rhombus and a rectangle? Does this kind of shape have a name?

Professor Peabody's Zoo

Professor Peabody was asked to design a zoo. He decided to organize the zoo in a way that made sense to him. Here is the map Professor Peabody made of his zoo. You can see that Gorillas are in the Ape area, and Apes are in the Mammal section.

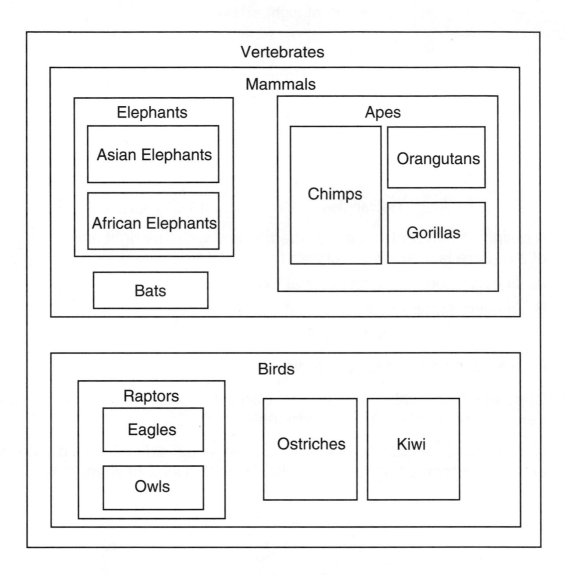

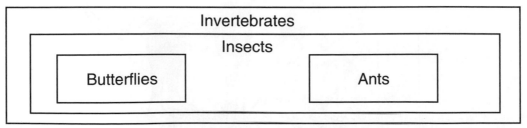

8. Study Professor Peabody's map. Explain how he organized his zoo.

9. If you wanted to add a section for horses, where would you put it? What about hawks?

10. If Professor Peabody wanted to have a region for animals that fly, where would it be?

There are other ways to organize zoos. Here is another map of a zoo:

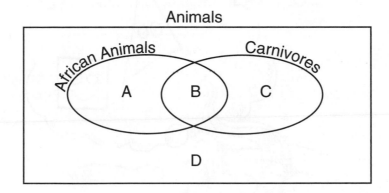

11. In which location (A, B, C, or D) does each animal belong?

   A. buffalo

   B. ostrich

   C. coyote

   D. African lion

The Flatville Zoo

Professor Peabody had a dream that he lived in a two-dimensional town called Flatville. There were two-dimensional creatures in the town, all shaped like polygons.

Help Professor Peabody design a zoo for the creatures. Use the shapes on the *Shapes Zoo Pieces* Activity Page in the *Discovery Assignment Book*.

12. Decide on a way to classify the shapes on the *Shapes Zoo Pieces* Activity Page. Work with your class or your group to design and make a map of the Flatville Zoo.

13. Label each section of your zoo with the type of shape in that section.

14. Write a definition for each type of shape in your zoo.

15. Write a paragraph explaining the organization of your zoo.

These are parallelograms:

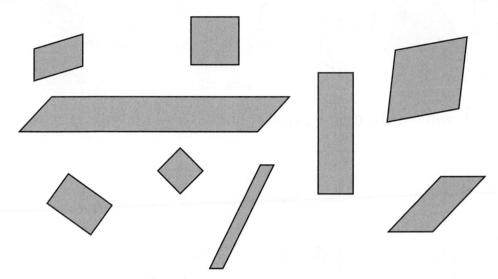

These are not parallelograms:

1. Which of the following is a parallelogram? Explain why.

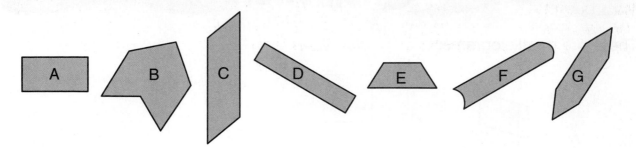

2. In your own words, define parallelogram.

These shapes are convex:

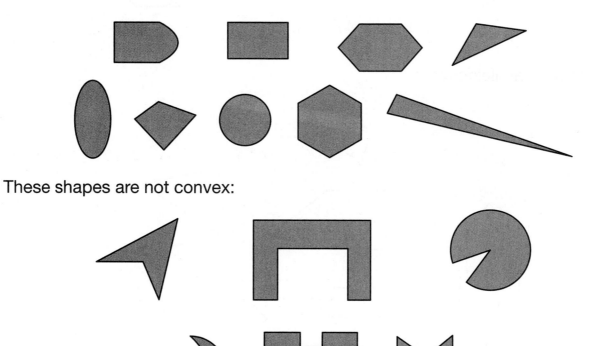

These shapes are not convex:

3. Which of the following are convex? Explain why.

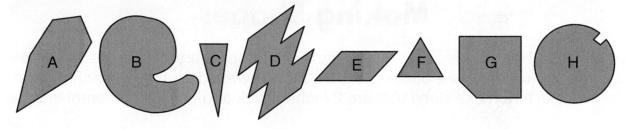

4. Define convex in your own words.

Making Shapes

Simon is the head stonecutter for Pharaoh Akhnaton. Every day, he gets orders from the workers who are building a giant stone pyramid for the Pharaoh. Simon and his assistant make slabs that are 2 inches thick and of many different shapes.

Look at each of the following orders, and draw a scale model of the top of the slab.

- **For each of the orders, draw the shape that is wanted.**
  (*Hint:* The measurements might not be given in the most convenient order.)
- **Some of the orders might have mistakes in them and will be impossible to fill. You might be able to fill other orders in more than one way. For each order, tell if it has many ways to be filled, one way to be filled, or no way to be filled. Show at least two solutions if an order can be filled in more than one way.**
- **Describe the process you used to complete each order.**

The slabs are the same on both sides, so you can turn them over if you like.

1.

ORDER NUMBER: 1

Shape: triangle

Measurements: length of side AB = 12 cm
angle ABC = 45 degrees
length of side BC = 14 cm

2.

ORDER NUMBER: 2

Shape: quadrilateral

Measurements: length of side BC = 10 cm
angle ABC = 45 degrees
length of side AB = 5 cm
angle BCD = 135 degrees
length of side CD = 5 cm

3.

ORDER NUMBER: 3

Shape: triangle

Measurements: angle CAB = 90 degrees
angle ABC = 45 degrees
angle BCA = 45 degrees

4.

ORDER NUMBER: 4

Shape: triangle

Measurements: angle CAB = 90 degrees
angle ABC = 60 degrees
angle BCA = 30 degrees
length of side AB = 16 cm

5.

ORDER NUMBER: 5

Shape: triangle

Measurements: length of side AB = 22 cm
length of side BC = 6 cm
length of side CA = 6 cm

6.

ORDER NUMBER: 6

Shape: triangle

Measurements: length of side AB = 10 cm
length of side BC = 12 cm
length of side CA = 17 cm

7. Make up your own order sheets. Try to list as few measurements as possible.

Unit 7

Decimals and Probability

	Student Guide	Discovery Assignment Book	Adventure Book	Unit Resource Guide*
Lesson 1				
Fractions, Decimals, and Percents	●	●		●
Lesson 2				
Decimal Models	●	●		●
Lesson 3				
Comparing and Rounding Decimals	●	●		
Lesson 4				
Adding and Subtracting Decimals	●	●		
Lesson 5				
Multiplying Decimals with Area	●			
Lesson 6				
Paper-and-Pencil Decimal Multiplication	●			●
Lesson 7				
Flipping One Coin	●			
Lesson 8				
Flipping Two Coins	●	●		
Lesson 9				
Families with Two Children	●			
Lesson 10				
Unlikely Heroes			●	

*Unit Resource Guide pages are from the teacher materials.

Fractions, Decimals, and Percents

Using the Centiwheel to Name Equivalent Fractions

We will use centiwheels to model fractions and to learn about decimals and percents. To make a centiwheel, use two centiwheel disks—one white copy and one colored copy.

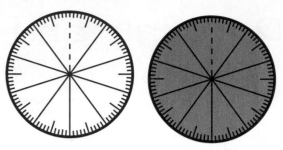

Cut along the dashed line (radius) of each circle to the center. Then fit the two circles together along the slits. Rotate the circles to change the size of the colored area.

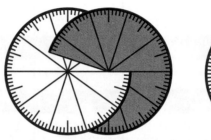

1. Each centiwheel disk is divided into equal sections with long lines.

   A. How many of these sections are on the centiwheel?

   B. What fraction of the centiwheel is each section?

2. Each of these ten sections is divided into smaller sections by tick marks.

   A. How many of these smaller sections are on the centiwheel?

   B. What fraction of the centiwheel is each smaller section?

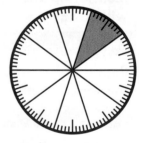

We can use centiwheels to model fractions. Look at the centiwheel below; $\frac{1}{4}$ of the wheel is colored. Edward uses the wheel to find a fraction with a denominator of 100 equivalent to $\frac{1}{4}$.

Look at the large sections first. Count by tens. Two sections of 10 are shown or $\frac{20}{100}$. Then, $\frac{5}{100}$ more. So, $\frac{25}{100}$ is shown.

Since 25 small sections out of 100 are colored, $\frac{25}{100}$ is equivalent to $\frac{1}{4}$.

3. Show another way to find an equivalent fraction for $\frac{1}{4}$: $\frac{1}{4} = \frac{?}{100}$.

4. A. Model $\frac{1}{2}$ with the centiwheel.

   B. Use the centiwheel to name a fraction with a denominator of 100 equivalent to $\frac{1}{2}$.

5. A. Model $\frac{3}{4}$ with the centiwheel.

   B. Use the centiwheel to name a fraction with a denominator of 100 equivalent to $\frac{3}{4}$.

Translations

Using the centiwheel, we can see that $\frac{1}{4}$ is equivalent to $\frac{25}{100}$.

Twenty-five hundredths is a fraction that can be written as 0.25 or $\frac{25}{100}$.

Fractions like 0.25 are called **decimal fractions** or just **decimals.** Fractions like $\frac{25}{100}$ are called **common fractions** or just **fractions.**

Another way to write decimals and fractions is as percents. **Percent** means "per 100" or "out of 100." When we say $\frac{25}{100}$ (or 0.25) of the centiwheel is green, we mean that 25 out of 100 sections are green. We can write this as 25%, which is read "twenty-five percent."

$$\frac{25}{100} = 0.25 = 25\%$$

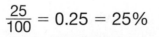 

6. The fraction $\frac{1}{2}$ is equivalent to $\frac{50}{100}$. Write $\frac{1}{2}$ as a decimal and a percent.

7. The fraction $\frac{3}{4}$ is equivalent to $\frac{75}{100}$. Write $\frac{3}{4}$ as a decimal and a percent.

8. **A.** Model the fraction $\frac{1}{10}$ using the centiwheel.

   B. Using the centiwheel, name a fraction with a denominator of 100 equivalent to $\frac{1}{10}$.

   C. Write $\frac{1}{10}$ as a decimal.

   D. Write $\frac{1}{10}$ as a percent.

9. **A.** Model $\frac{1}{20}$ using the centiwheel. $\frac{1}{20} = \frac{?}{100}$

   B. Write $\frac{1}{20}$ as a decimal.

   C. Write $\frac{1}{20}$ as a percent.

10. **A.** Model $\frac{1}{5}$ using the centiwheel. $\frac{1}{5} = \frac{?}{100}$

    B. Write $\frac{1}{5}$ as a decimal.

    C. Write $\frac{1}{5}$ as a percent.

11. Model each fraction with a centiwheel. Then write each fraction as a percent.

    A. $\frac{36}{100}$ **B.** $\frac{1}{2}$ **C.** $\frac{6}{100}$ **D.** $\frac{2}{5}$

12. Model each percent using a centiwheel. Then write each percent as a fraction with a denominator of 100.

    A. 95%   **B.** 70%   **C.** 7%

13. Model each decimal on the centiwheel. Write each decimal as a fraction with a denominator of 100.

    A. 0.80   **B.** 0.08   **C.** 0.85

14. Write each decimal as a percent.

    A. 0.80   **B.** 0.08   **C.** 0.85

Using the Centiwheel to Compare Fractions

15. **A.** Model 43% using the centiwheel.

    B. Is 43% closer to $\frac{1}{4}$, $\frac{1}{2}$, or 1 whole?

16. **A.** Model 0.79 using the centiwheel.

    B. Is 0.79 closer to $\frac{1}{2}$, $\frac{3}{4}$, or 1 whole?

17. **A.** Model $\frac{21}{100}$ using the centiwheel.

    B. Is $\frac{21}{100}$ closer to 0, $\frac{1}{4}$, or $\frac{1}{2}$?

Using the Small Centiwheel

Look at the circle graph at the right. We can use a small centiwheel to translate the fractions $\frac{1}{20}$, $\frac{7}{20}$, and $\frac{3}{5}$ to fractions with a denominator of 100.

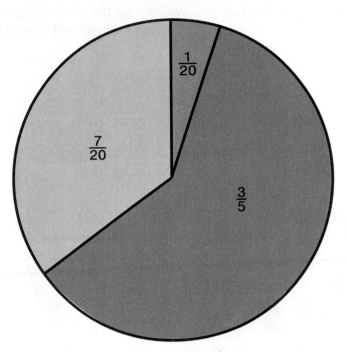

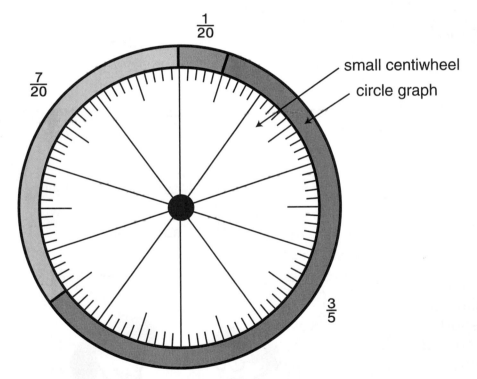

Place the small centiwheel on top of the circle graph as shown at left. Match the center of the centiwheel to the center of the pie graph.

small centiwheel

circle graph

18. Find the part of 100 represented by each fraction below. You can use the centiwheel to count the number of intervals around the edge.

A. $\frac{1}{20} = \frac{?}{100}$ **B.** $\frac{7}{20} = \frac{?}{100}$ **C.** $\frac{3}{5} = \frac{?}{100}$

19. Use the small centiwheel. Find fractions with denominators of 100 that are close or equivalent to the fractions in the two circle graphs below. If the lines on the centiwheel do not match lines on the circle graphs exactly, use the closest lines.

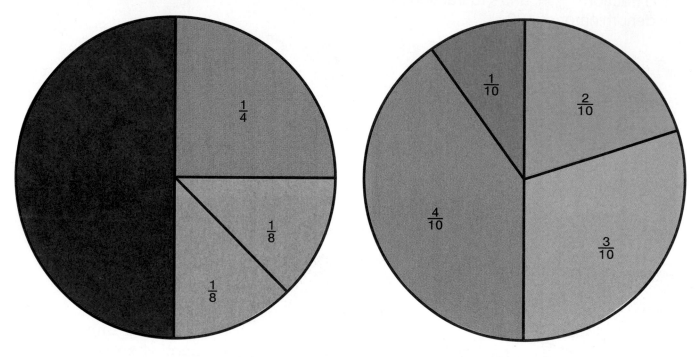

Good Sports

Janet and her cousin Lee Yah are in fifth grade in two different schools. They like the same kind of books and clothes. However, they disagree about one topic—sports.

They argued about soccer and volleyball. Aunt Carol suggested that they each take a survey of their classmates' favorite sports. Later, Aunt Carol found an article which said that baseball, basketball, football, soccer, and volleyball are the 5 most popular sports in high school. The girls agreed to use these sports for their survey.

I love volleyball, and all the kids in my class like volleyball more than soccer.

I love soccer, and all the kids that I know agree that soccer is the best sport.

When Lee Yah's survey was done, she was disappointed to find that basketball was more popular than volleyball. But she was happy that volleyball was selected more often than soccer. She was anxious to show Janet the circle graph that she made on the computer.

Janet was disappointed that her class selected baseball as their favorite sport. She was really disappointed that volleyball and soccer were equally liked by her classmates. But she thought it showed that she was fair when she conducted her survey. Janet made a circle graph on the computer so they could compare results.

The girls found it difficult to compare the data. They still didn't know if soccer was more popular in Lee Yah's class than Janet's. Since there are 22 kids in Lee Yah's class and 37 kids in Janet's class, it is difficult to compare fractions such as $\frac{4}{22}$ and $\frac{7}{37}$. They decided that comparing fractions with unlike denominators requires some thought.

Lee Yah's Data: 22 kids

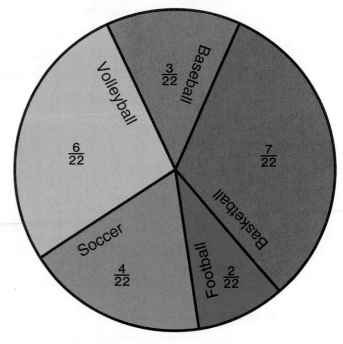

Janet's Data: 37 kids

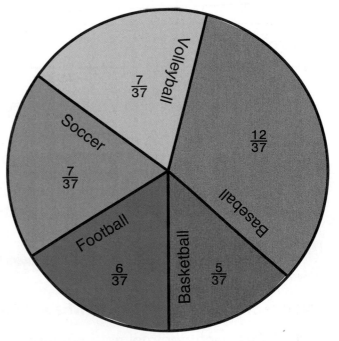

20. Use a *Three-trial Data Table*. Set up the table like the one below.

- First record in your table each sport and the fraction of students that selected that sport in Lee Yah's survey.
- Then, use your small centiwheel to find fractions with denominators of 100 that are close to the fractions in the circle graph. Record these fractions in the column labeled "nearest $\frac{N}{100}$."
- Record these new fractions as decimals and percents. The first one is done for you as an example.

Team Sport	Lee Yah's Data			
	Fraction on Circle Graph	Nearest $\frac{N}{100}$	Decimal (to the nearest hundredth)	Percent (to the nearest percent)
Baseball	$\frac{3}{22}$	$\frac{14}{100}$	0.14	14%
Basketball				
Football				
Soccer				
Volleyball				

21. Complete a second table for Janet's data.

22. Check your work by adding up the numbers in the percent column in both your tables. Are your totals equal to 100% or close to 100%?

23. Write a summary report comparing the data collected from the two classes. Use percents to compare the results of the two surveys.

You may wish to use the centiwheel for some of these translations.

1. Write each decimal as a percent.

    A. 0.04   **B.** 0.26   **C.** 0.40

2. Write each percent as a fraction with a denominator of 100.

    A. 59%   **B.** 8%   **C.** 30%

3. Write each decimal as a fraction with a denominator of 100.

    A. 0.50   **B.** 0.07   **C.** 0.68

4. Write each fraction as a percent.

    A. $\frac{27}{100}$ **B.** $\frac{4}{100}$ **C.** $\frac{1}{2}$ **D.** $\frac{3}{20}$

5. Write each fraction as a fraction with a denominator of 100.

    A. $\frac{1}{4}$ **B.** $\frac{1}{2}$ **C.** $\frac{3}{5}$ **D.** $\frac{3}{10}$ **E.** $\frac{9}{20}$

Quilt Designs

Mr. Moreno's classroom is making a quilt for a class project. They plan to make the quilt with 100 squares of material. They have 50 blue squares, 30 red squares, 25 yellow squares, 25 orange squares, and 9 green squares to choose from. After each student designs a quilt, the class will vote to choose one pattern for the class. Here are Lin's and John's designs.

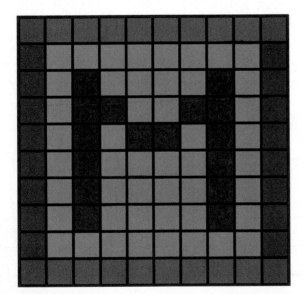
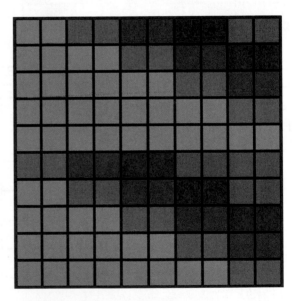

Use the *Designing Quilts* Activity Page in the *Discovery Assignment Book* to design a quilt. You will use your quilt design in the next lesson.

- You must use all five colors: blue, red, yellow, orange, and green.
- You may use no more than 50 blue, 30 red, 25 yellow, 25 orange, and 9 green squares.

Decimal Models

David's Homework

Here are David's quilt design and his homework data table.

Color	Number of Squares
Green	2
Red	26
Yellow	24
Blue	28
Orange	20

He used the information from his homework table to fill in the table at the right.

Fractions, Decimals, and Percents

Color	Common Fraction	Decimal	Percent
Green	$\frac{2}{100}$	0.02	2%
Red	$\frac{26}{100}$	0.26	26%
Yellow	$\frac{24}{100}$	0.24	24%
Blue	$\frac{28}{100}$	0.28	28%
Orange	$\frac{20}{100}$	0.20	20%

Discuss

1. Say each decimal in David's table out loud. For example, for 0.26 say, "twenty-six hundredths."

2. List the decimals in David's table in order from smallest to largest.

3. Make a Fractions, Decimals, and Percents table like David's for the quilt design you made on the *Designing Quilts* Homework Page. Fill in the fractions, decimals, and percents for each color in your design.

4. Write the fractions in order from smallest to largest.

5. Write the decimals in order from smallest to largest.

Decimal Models: Hundredths

In this unit you will use grids to model decimals. The large square on the left will represent one whole.

one whole

.01

6. **A.** How many small squares are there on a 10 × 10 grid?

   B. What fraction does each small square represent?

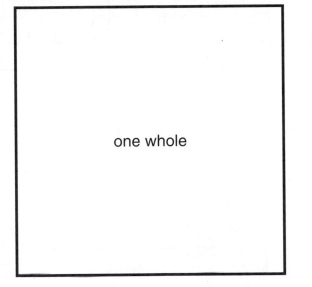

1st Place

---

7. **A.** On Grid 1, what fraction of the small squares are blue?

　　B. Write a decimal and a percent modeled by Grid 1.

8. Write a fraction, decimal, and percent modeled by Grid 2.

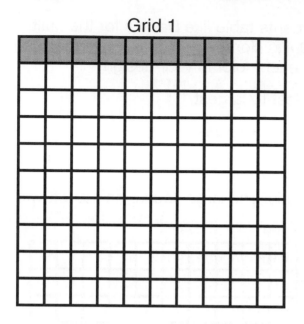

Grid 1　　　　　　　　　　　　Grid 2

Decimal Models: Tenths

9. **A.** How many long, thin rectangles are there on the grids shown below?

　　B. What fraction does each rectangle represent?

10. Give a fraction, decimal, and percent modeled by the grid on the right.

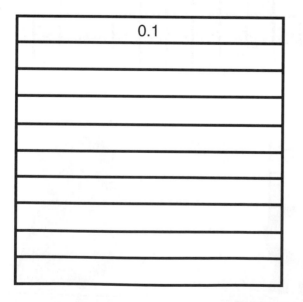

0.1

Decimal Models: Thousandths

11. A. In each small square, like this, how many tiny rectangles are there?

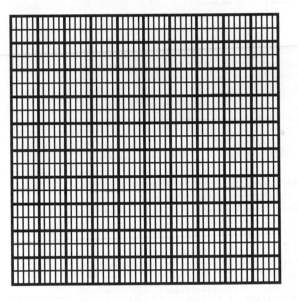

B. How many tiny rectangles are there in a row of small squares?

C. How many tiny rectangles are there in one whole?

Each tiny rectangle represents one-thousandth ($\frac{1}{1000}$) of the whole. This is written 0.001 as a decimal. Grids like these can be used to model thousandths.

The grid shown below models 0.357 (three hundred fifty-seven thousandths).

12. **A.** How many tiny rectangles are green on the grid below?

   B. What fraction of the grid is green? What are other names for this fraction?

   C. How many tiny rectangles are blue?

   D. What fraction of the grid is blue?

   E. How many tiny rectangles are red?

   F. What fraction of the grid is red?

   G. How many of the tiny rectangles are colored in?

   H. Write 0.357 as a common fraction.

0.357

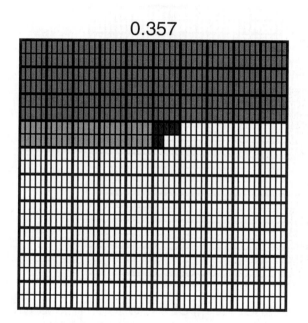

13. **A.** How many tiny rectangles are colored yellow on this grid?

   B. Write 0.087 (eighty-seven thousandths) as a common fraction.

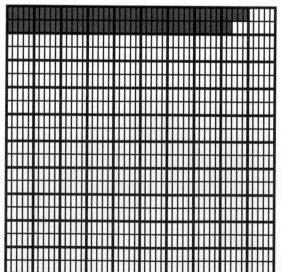

14. Give a fraction and a decimal modeled by each grid.

A.　　　　　　　　　　　　　　　　**B.**

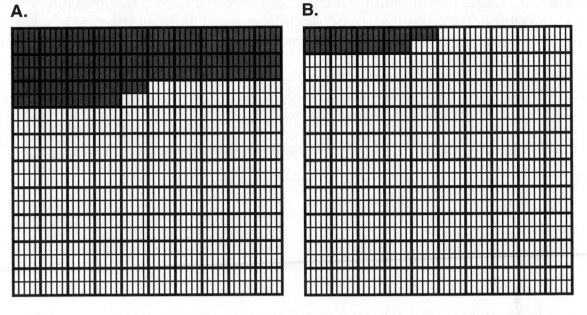

Decimal Place Value

A place value chart can be helpful when reading or comparing decimals.

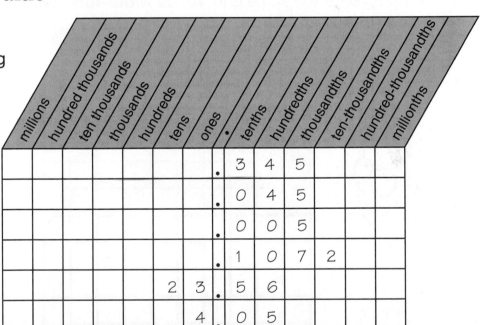

millions	hundred thousands	ten thousands	thousands	hundreds	tens	ones	.	tenths	hundredths	thousandths	ten-thousandths	hundred-thousandths	millionths
							.	3	4	5			
							.	0	4	5			
							.	0	0	5			
							.	1	0	7	2		
					2	3	.	5	6				
						4	.	0	5				

Discuss

15. Study the places in the place value chart. Describe any patterns you see.

16. If each tiny rectangle on a thousandths grid were divided into ten parts, what fractional part of the whole would one of these parts represent?

The first four numbers written in the place value chart are less than one, since there are no digits to the left of the decimal place. To read a decimal less than one, read the number as if there were no decimal point. Then say the place value name of the last digit. For example, 0.345 is read "three hundred forty-five thousandths."

To read a decimal that is greater than one, read the whole number part. Then say "and" for the decimal point and read the decimal part. For example, 23.56 is read "twenty-three and fifty-six hundredths."

17. Read each number in the place value chart out loud.

18. Read these numbers out loud, then write them in word form.

    A. 1.5

    B. 23.567

    C. 2.06

    D. 0.432

19. Shannon wrote 0.4 for the decimal modeled by the grid below. Lee Yah wrote 0.40 for the same grid. Alexis wrote 40%. Who is correct? Explain your thinking.

20. Model the numbers in the place value chart below on the *Decimal Grids* Activity Page that your teacher will give you. Label each model with the decimal it represents.

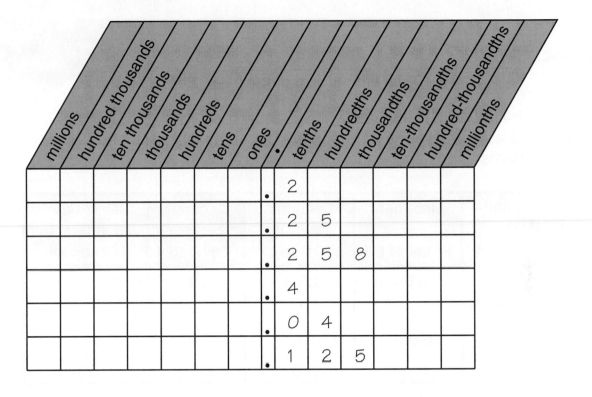

millions	hundred thousands	ten thousands	thousands	hundreds	tens	ones	.	tenths	hundredths	thousandths	ten-thousandths	hundred-thousandths	millionths
							.	2					
							.	2	5				
							.	2	5	8			
							.	4					
							.	0	4				
							.	1	2	5			

Homework

1. Show these numbers on a *Decimal Grids* Activity Page that your teacher will give you. Label each model with the decimal it represents.

   A. 0.6   **B.** 0.65   **C.** 0.653

   D. 0.8   **E.** 0.09   **F.** 0.075

2. List the decimals in order from smallest to largest.

3. Write each decimal in word form.

4. Write each decimal as a common fraction.

5. Write each of these numbers in word form.

   A. 32.76   **B.** 2.7

   C. 3.08   **D.** 3.085

Comparing and Rounding Decimals

Discuss

In the table below, 0, 0.1, 0.5, and 1 are used as benchmarks to sort decimals.
Benchmarks are convenient numbers for comparing and rounding numbers.
Look for patterns within each column.

Decimals Near or Equal to 0	Decimals Near or Equal to 0.1	Decimals Near or Equal to 0.5	Decimals Near or Equal to 1	Decimals Much Greater Than 1
0.0	0.09	0.500	0.9	3
0.0099	0.10	.48	1.0	5.26
.01	0.081	0.6	.819	30.5
0.003	0.21	0.607	1.05	7.9

1. Use a table like the one above to sort these decimals. Modeling the decimals on grids or using a centiwheel may help you.

    0.61   0.007   0.100   4.005   0.981   0.50

2. **A.** How are the decimals near 0 alike?

    B. How are the decimals near 0.1 alike?

    C. How are the decimals near 0.5 alike? What is another name for 0.5?

    D. How are the decimals near 1 alike?

    E. How can you tell if a decimal is greater than 1?

3. Put these decimals in your table:

    0.89   0.11

    23.56   1.075

    0.0089   0.452

    1.000   0.008

.48 is close to .5 while .048 is close to 0.

4. List each of the following sets of decimals in order from smallest to largest. Use your table and benchmarks of 0, 0.1, 0.5, and 1 to help you. Follow the example:

Example: 0.6

0.0099

7.9

.10

$$0.0099 < .10 < 0.6 < 7.9$$

A. 0.452	**B.** 0.92	**C.** 1.125
1.000	0.005	0.009
0.0089	.625	0.47
0.89	3	0.100

A place value chart is another tool that can help you compare decimals.

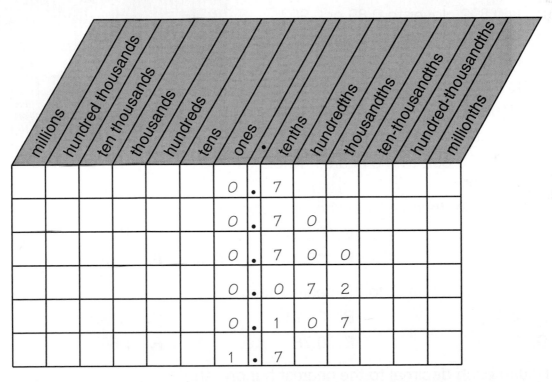

millions	hundred thousands	ten thousands	thousands	hundreds	tens	ones	•	tenths	hundredths	thousandths	ten-thousandths	hundred-thousandths	millionths
						0	•	7					
						0	•	7	0				
						0	•	7	0	0			
						0	•	0	7	2			
						0	•	1	0	7			
						1	•	7					

5. Use $<$, $>$, or $=$ to write a true number sentence using each pair of decimals.

   A. 0.7 and 0.70   **B.** 0.072 and 0.70   **C.** 0.70 and 0.700

   D. 0.072 and 0.107   **E.** 1.7 and 0.107   **F.** 0.5 and 0.072

For Questions 6–7 you may use benchmarks, decimal grids, fractions, or a place value chart to help you. Explain how you found each answer.

6. Write the following sets of decimals in order from smallest to largest:
   A. 0.729   12   1.25   0.099
   B. 0.8   8.0   0.888   0.08
   C. 0.48   1.5   0.525   0.5

7. Use <, >, or = to write a true number sentence using each pair of decimals.
   A. 0.9 and 0.900
   B. 0.55 and 0.155
   C. 0.23 and 0.234

Rounding Decimals

The grid at the right shows 0.892

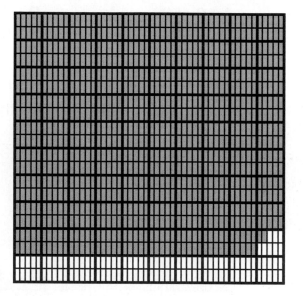

8. A. Is 0.892 closer to 0.89 or 0.90?
   B. Round 0.892 to the nearest hundredth.
   C. Is 0.892 closer to 0.8 or 0.9?
   D. Round 0.892 to the nearest tenth.
   E. Is 0.892 closer to 0 or 1?
   F. Round 0.892 to the nearest whole number.

9. Round each decimal to the nearest whole number.
   A. 4.32   B. 0.891   C. 19.9
   D. 1.09   E. 35.9   F. 2.58

10. Round each decimal to the nearest tenth.
    A. 4.32   B. 0.891   C. 0.199
    D. 0.109   E. 0.78   F. 1.657

11. Round each decimal to the nearest hundredth.
    A. 0.487   B. 0.531   C. 1.019
    D. 0.899   E. 3.154   F. 0.607

12. Complete the table. The first one is done for you.

	Fraction	Decimal	Decimal (to the Nearest Hundredth)	Percent (to the Nearest Percent)
A.	$\frac{254}{1000}$	0.254	.25	25%
B.	$\frac{327}{1000}$			
C.	$\frac{43}{1000}$			
D.	$\frac{789}{1000}$			
E.	$\frac{799}{1000}$			

Homework

Use a copy of the *Decimal Grids* Activity Page to answer Questions 1–8.

1. Shade each of the following decimals. Label each one clearly.
   - **A.** 0.5
   - **B.** 0.87
   - **C.** 0.067
   - **D.** 0.2
   - **E.** 0.20
   - **F.** 0.427

2. Write each of the decimals in Question 1 as a common fraction.

3. **A.** Write 0.5 as a percent.
   B. Write 0.2 as a percent.
   C. Write 0.20 as a percent.
   D. Write 0.87 as a percent.

4. **A.** Round 0.87 to the nearest tenth.
   B. Round 0.067 to the nearest tenth.
   C. Round 0.427 to the nearest tenth.

5. **A.** Round 0.067 to the nearest hundredth.
   B. Write 0.067 as a percent to the nearest percent.

6. **A.** Round 0.427 to the nearest hundredth.
   B. Write 0.427 as a percent to the nearest percent.

7. **A.** Is 0.427 closer to 0.1, 0.5, or 1?

  B. Is 0.067 closer to 0.1, 0.5, or 1?

  C. Is 0.87 closer to 0.1, 0.5, or 1?

  D. Is 0.20 closer to 0.1, 0.5, or 1?

8. Use <, >, or = to write a true number sentence using each pair of decimals. Explain how you found each answer.

  A. 0.5 and 0.427   **B.** 0.2 and 0.20   **C.** 0.87 and 0.427

9. Place the following set of decimals in order from smallest to largest:

A. 0.201	1.03	10	0.023	0.63
B. 6.01	6.10	6.4	0.6	0.06
C. 11	1.01	0.101	1.1	0.11
D. 0.487	0.88	1.08	0.098	0.5

10. Look at the decimals on the blackboard in the picture. Explain how Roberto knows that 0.327 is less than 0.37.

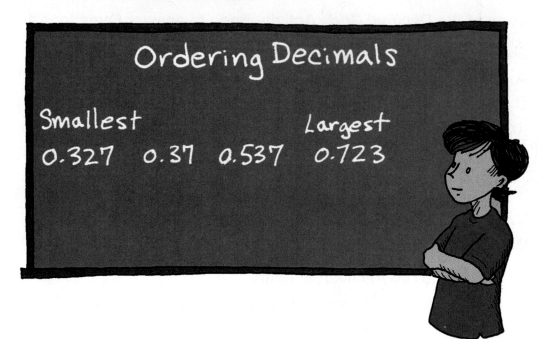

Adding and Subtracting Decimals

Mr. Moreno's class is learning about decimals at the grocery store. Most food and cleaning products give the weight or volume of the contents in both standard and metric units. Roberto and Jessie are shopping for juice to make punch.

Roberto, we need 0.5 liter of orange juice and 0.25 liter of lemon juice for our recipe.

That means we need 0.30 liter of juice in all, Jessie.

0.30 liter? That can't be right. We should need more than $\frac{1}{2}$ a liter since 0.5 is the same as $\frac{1}{2}$.

Psst, you're all out of line.

"Let's use the grid to help us add the liters," said Jessie.

"Using the grid, I see that we need 0.75 liter of juice for our recipe," said Roberto.

"Now, let's try adding the liters using just paper and pencil," said Jessie. "Mr. Moreno told us that it's very important to line up the numbers by their place value when adding decimals."

$$
\begin{array}{r}
0.5 \ \text{liter} \\
+ \ 0.25 \ \text{liter} \\
\hline
0.75 \ \text{liter}
\end{array}
$$

0.5 + 0.25

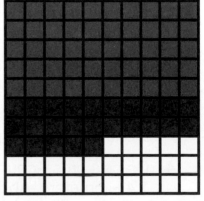

Shannon found some decimals on orange juice labels. "I found two cans of frozen orange juice," said Shannon. "One can makes 0.345 liter and the other can makes 1.38 liters of juice. I found out how much more orange juice the larger can makes using paper and pencil."

$$\begin{array}{r} 1.38 \ \text{liters} \\ -\ 0.345 \ \text{liter} \\ \hline \end{array}$$

"I wrote 1.38 liters as 1.380 liters to make it easier to subtract," said Shannon.

$$\begin{array}{r} 1.380 \ \text{liters} \\ -\ 0.345 \ \text{liter} \\ \hline 1.035 \ \text{liters} \end{array}$$

Explore

Solve the following problems. Show your work. Estimate to see if your answers are reasonable.

1. **A.** $4.35 + 12.7 =$

   B. $16.2 + 3.8 =$

2. There is 0.47 liter in a bottle of a popular pancake syrup. About how many bottles would it take to make 1 liter of syrup?

3. Grace bought a notebook for $1.25 and a pencil for $0.10. How much money did Grace spend?

4. Grace's cross-country race course is 3.25 kilometers long. She has run 1.4 kilometers. About how much farther does she need to go?

5. Do you see something wrong with the way the problem at the right is written? Explain.

$$\begin{array}{r} 51.07 \\ +\ 6.394 \\ \hline \end{array}$$

Jessie solved the following problems. Use estimates to tell if each answer is reasonable. Explain your reasoning.

6. .8 + .7 = .15

7. 12.8 + 6.7 = 73.8

8. 15.002 + 2.5 = 17.117

9. 3.706 − 1.597 = .2289

Solve.

10. 0.124
     + 2.33

11. 1.49
     − 1.08

12. 3.1
     + 0.13

13. 0.379
     + 0.375

Homework

Use paper and pencil to solve the problems. For some problems you will need an exact answer. For other problems, an estimate will do.

1. There are 15.1 servings in a box of a popular cereal. How many servings are in two boxes?

2. If we use the serving information on the label of a bottle of barbecue sauce, there are 25.6 servings per bottle. About how many servings are in three bottles?

3. One serving of a very well-known tortilla chip has 27.6 grams. How many grams are in two servings?

4. The same bag of tortilla chips has a total of 382.7 grams. About how many grams will be left after the two servings from Question 3 are eaten?

5. A portion of whole wheat flour contains 30.2 grams. A recipe calls for 2 portions. How many grams are in two portions?

6. A small bag of whole wheat flour contains 907 grams. How much is left after the two portions from Question 5 are used?

7. Use estimates to tell which of the following solutions are reasonable.
   A. 0.6 + 0.06 = 0.12
   B. 1.78 − .99 = .79
   C. 0.07 + 0.004 = 0.074

8. Solve. Estimate to check if your answers are reasonable.
   A. 80.23 + 22.58 =
   B. 13.89 − 5.53 =
   C. 17.7 + 8.62 =
   D. 0.64 + 0.9 =
   E. 1.3 + 0.687 =
   F. 42.34 + 87.9 =

9. Tanya wanted to buy a $5.00 binder for her notes. She has saved $3.60 so far. How much more money does Tanya need to save?

10. Linda and Jackie pooled their money to buy some snacks. They had $9.57 altogether. If Jackie gave $4.65, how much money did Linda give?

Multiplying Decimals with Area

Discuss

Mr. Moreno decided to carpet his front hall. His front hall measures 8.5 feet by 7.5 feet. Mr. Moreno challenged his students to find out how many square feet of carpet he needs to buy.

"I can estimate the area for you, Mr. Moreno," said Jacob. "8.5 feet is about 9 feet and 7.5 feet is about 8 feet. 9 feet × 8 feet = 72 square feet of carpet."

"Jacob, you estimated too high. You'll have too much carpet," said Jackie. "I think a better estimate is 8 feet × 7 feet = 56 square feet of carpet."

"Jackie, you estimated too low. You won't have enough carpet," said Jerome. "I think the best estimate is to round 8.5 feet down to 8 feet and 7.5 feet up to 8 feet. 8 feet × 8 feet = 64 square feet of carpet."

"Those estimates are useful, but I need a more exact answer to buy carpet," said Mr. Moreno.

"I've got it," said John. "I can use grid paper to find the answer."

John drew an 8.5 by 7.5 rectangle on grid paper. He counted whole squares and parts of squares.

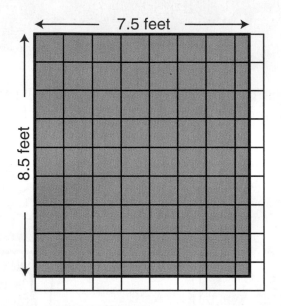

1. Find the area of Mr. Moreno's front hall by counting whole squares and parts of squares.

2. Mr. Moreno decided to carpet other rooms in his house. John helped him find the area of a closet floor. He drew this rectangle on grid paper. Use the rectangle to find the area of the closet floor.

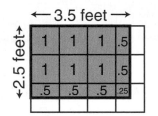

"Let's multiply to find out," suggested Jessie. She used paper and pencil to multiply.

$$
\begin{array}{r}
2.5 \\
\times\,3.5 \\
\hline
25 \\
100 \\
150 \\
600 \\
\hline
875
\end{array}
$$

"Your answer is 875 square feet! That can't be right!" exclaimed Jackie. "I'll estimate to check. First, round 2.5 ft down to 2 ft and 3.5 ft up to 4 ft. Then 2 times 4 is 8. The answer should be close to 8 sq ft, so John got the right answer using a rectangle. The area is 8.75 sq ft."

"Jessie forgot to put the decimal point in her answer," said Mr. Moreno. "The decimal point should go between the 8 and the 7 to make 8.75 square feet of carpet in my closet."

Find the areas of the floors of each of the following rooms in two ways:

- First, draw a rectangle on *Centimeter Grid Paper* to represent the floor of each room or closet. Find the area by counting squares and parts of squares. Show the areas of parts of squares by using decimals.
- Then, find the areas by multiplying using a paper-and-pencil method. Be sure both answers are the same.

3. Coat closet is 5 ft × 2.5 ft.

4. Upstairs hall is 3.5 ft by 12 ft.

5. Bedroom is 9.25 ft by 10 ft.

6. Bedroom closet is 4 ft by 2.1 ft.

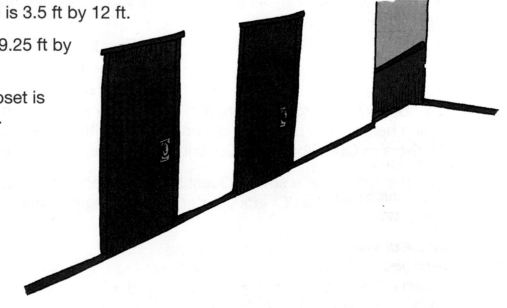

You can usually estimate to find where to put the decimal point when you multiply decimals. Multiply 3.4 by 4.3 using paper and pencil as if there were no decimal points. Then, estimate to place the decimal.

Jerome multiplied 3.4 by 4.3 this way. He used convenient numbers to estimate: $3 \times 4 = 12$. Since he knew the answer should be close to 12, he placed the decimal point between the 4 and 6. That way his answer is between 14 and 15.

$$
\begin{array}{r}
3.4 \\
\times\,4.3 \\
\hline
12 \\
90 \\
160 \\
1200 \\
\hline
14.62
\end{array}
$$

7. Multiply the following using paper and pencil. Then estimate to place the decimal point accurately.

A. $\begin{array}{r} 24.1 \\ \times\,0.5 \\ \hline \end{array}$
 B. $\begin{array}{r} 4.7 \\ \times\,6.2 \\ \hline \end{array}$
 C. $\begin{array}{r} 2.13 \\ \times\,0.9 \\ \hline \end{array}$
 D. $\begin{array}{r} 8.03 \\ \times\,0.47 \\ \hline \end{array}$

8. Jacob, Jackie, Jerome, John, and Jessie saw a pattern in the problems, which helps them place the decimal points. Study the problems and your answers in Questions 3–7. Describe the pattern the students saw.

9. Use the pattern you saw in Question 8 and paper and pencil to solve the following problems. Check your answers using grid paper.

A. 11.5×2.5

B. 8×3.5

Homework

Estimate the answers to the following problems. Then use paper and pencil to multiply. Use your estimates to place the decimal point in the answer.

1. 4.21 × 5.0	**2.** 42.1 × 0.9	**3.** 4.21 × 0.5	**4.** 23.9 × 1.0
5. 2.39 × 0.5	**6.** 2.39 × 0.7	**7.** 53 × 1.6	**8.** 0.53 × 0.8
9. 0.53 × 1.6	**10.** 25 × 2.4	**11.** 2.5 × 0.2	**12.** 0.25 × 0.4

13. Mr. Moreno is buying sports equipment for the school. He bought three basketballs and paid $19.79 for each one. How much money did he spend on basketballs?

14. The school owns 3 ping-pong tables, but the paddles and balls are lost. He can buy a set of six balls, four paddles, and one net for $29.29. How much will it cost for Mr. Moreno to buy one set for each table?

15. Mr. Moreno wants to help his class become physically fit. He decides to buy 4 jump ropes. The ropes are $15.65 each. How much do 4 ropes cost?

16. In order for his class to play softball, he needs 3 bats, 2 balls, and a set of bases. Each set of bases includes first, second, third, home plate, and a pitcher's mound. The bats are $14.55 each. The balls are $4.55 each. Each of the bases costs $2.59. How much money will he spend on softball equipment?

Paper-and-Pencil Decimal Multiplication

Lee Yah's dad sends her to the grocery store to buy bleach. She finds two sizes of bleach containers. One size holds 3.7 liters, and the other size is $1\frac{1}{2}$ times larger. Lee Yah wonders how much bleach the larger container holds.

I can estimate the amount of bleach. Since 3.7 liters is close to 4 liters and 1.5 is close to 2, then 4 liters × 2 = 8 liters.

But, how much bleach actually is in the container?

Lee Yah uses paper and pencil to find out:

$$
\begin{array}{r}
3.7 \\
\times\,1.5 \\
\hline
35 \\
150 \\
70 \\
300 \\
\hline
5.55
\end{array}
$$

She knows to place the decimal point between the first two fives because 5.55 is closer to her estimate than 0.555 or 55.5. There are 5.55 liters in the larger container.

In Lesson 5, you solved multiplication problems with decimals. You looked for a pattern in the problems to help you place the decimal point in the answer. Lee Yah thinks of the rule this way: the sum of the number of digits after the decimal points in the factors should equal the number of digits after the decimal point in the product.

"In my problem, there is one digit after the decimal point in 3.7 and one digit after the decimal point in 1.5. That's a total of two digits after the decimal points in the factors, so there should be two digits after the decimal point in the product, 5.55," said Lee Yah.

1. **A.** Use your own words to tell how to place the decimal point in the answer to a multiplication problem with decimals. Use this problem as an example:

$$
\begin{array}{r}
2.34 \\
\times\,0.6 \\
\hline
24 \\
180 \\
1200 \\
\hline
1404
\end{array}
$$

   B. Does your answer make sense? Estimate the answer to 2.34 × 0.6.

Use a paper-and-pencil method to solve the problems below. Use the rule or estimation to place the decimal point in the product.

2. $\begin{array}{r} 3.4 \\ \times\,0.4 \\ \hline \end{array}$

3. $\begin{array}{r} .47 \\ \times\,7.9 \\ \hline \end{array}$

4. $\begin{array}{r} .003 \\ \times\,0.8 \\ \hline \end{array}$

5. $\begin{array}{r} 5.42 \\ \times\,.5 \\ \hline \end{array}$

Solve the following problems. Estimate to check and see if your answers are reasonable.

1. A cheeseburger from a popular fast-food restaurant has 5.7 grams of saturated fat. If you eat $2\frac{1}{2}$ cheeseburgers, how much saturated fat will you eat?

2. A bottle of liquid soap holds 2.4 liters. How many liters of soap are in 4.5 bottles?

3. A small order of onion rings can have as much as 67.5 milligrams of sodium (salt). How many milligrams of sodium can be in $\frac{1}{2}$ serving?

4. One teaspoon of strawberry topping has 46.33 calories. How many calories are there in 3 teaspoons?

5. One order of french fries from a well-known fast-food restaurant contains 17.7 grams of fat. If you eat 3 orders, how much fat will you eat?

6. One serving of potato chips has 10.1 grams of fat. The whole bag of chips holds 12 servings. If you eat the whole bag, how many grams of fat have you eaten?

7. Three breadsticks have 1.5 grams of fat. How much fat do 5 breadsticks have?

Explain your estimation strategies for Questions 8–12. Then find exact answers.

8. 21.7×4.2

9. 1.2×0.54

10. 4.5×4.5

11. 0.4×6.07

12. 0.98×1.02

Flipping One Coin

1. Predict how many times heads will show and how many times tails will show if you flip a coin 40 times. Write your prediction in a data table like the one below. Explain how you made your prediction.

Outcome	Predicted Number of Flips	Actual Number of Flips
H		
T		

2. Now flip a coin 40 times. Make a list of your outcomes by writing H each time heads shows and T each time tails shows.

3. Count the number of heads and the number of tails you flipped. Record your results in your table in the Actual Number of Flips column.

Flipping One Coin

4. Discuss what happened. Compare your prediction with your actual number of flips. Explain any differences.

5. What do you think will happen if you flip the coin 100 times? 1000 times?

Probability Discussions

Probability is a measure of how likely an event is to happen. Probabilities can be expressed as fractions, decimals, or percents. Events that are **certain** to happen have probability 1 or 100% (since 100% means <u>one</u> whole). Events that are **impossible** have probability 0 or 0%. All other events have probabilities between 0 and 1, or between 0% and 100%.

The closer the probability of an event is to one, or 100%, the more likely the event is to happen. When the weather forecaster reports a 95% or 0.95 probability of rain, we can be pretty sure it will rain. However, if the probability of rain is 5%, or 0.05, you probably won't need an umbrella.

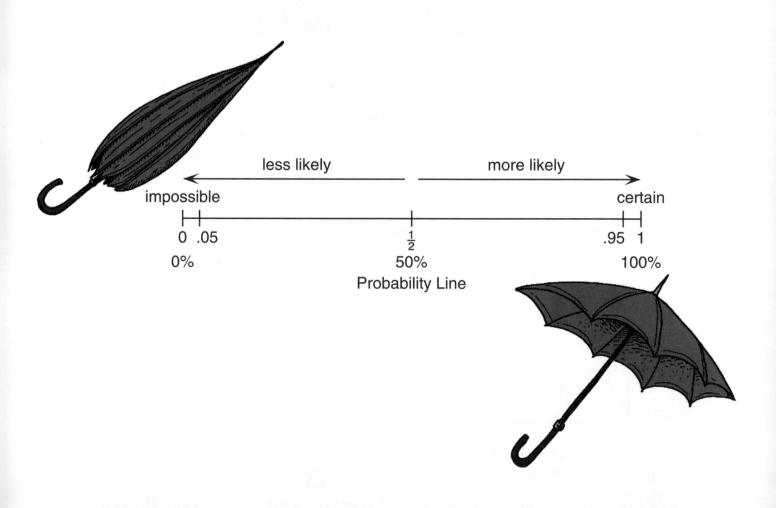

Probability Line

Since flipping heads is just as likely as flipping tails, we expect that heads will show about half the time when a coin is flipped many times. The probability of flipping heads is $\frac{1}{2}$.

6. Did you get heads about half the time when you flipped your coin?

With coin flipping, there are two possible outcomes—heads or tails—and each has a probability of $\frac{1}{2}$. We say that flipping heads and flipping tails are **equally likely** since the probability that each will happen is the same. However, there are other situations with two possible outcomes, which are not equally likely. Consider some of the examples below.

7. **A.** <u>Right- or left-handed</u>. How many of the students in your class are right-handed, and how many are left-handed? Based on your class's data, do you think the probability of being right-handed is more or less than one-half?

B. <u>Right or left thumb</u>. Clasp your hands together in front of you. Is your right thumb on top, as in the picture, or is your left thumb on top? Most people clasp their hands the same way each time they do this. Based on your class's data, do you think the probability of being a person who places the right thumb on top is more or less than $\frac{1}{2}$?

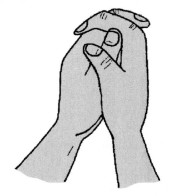

C. <u>Boy or girl baby</u>. Was the firstborn child in your family a girl or a boy? Based on data from the families of all the students in your class, do you think the probability of having a girl firstborn is more than, less than, or about equal to $\frac{1}{2}$?

Flipping Two Coins

Game: How Many Heads?

Players

This is a game for 3 players.
One person is the 0-Heads Player,
the second is the 1-Head Player,
and the third is the 2-Heads Player.

Materials

- 2 coins
- How Many Heads? table

Rules

Flip 2 coins.
If 0 heads show, then the 0-Heads Player gets a point.
If 1 head shows, then the 1-Head Player gets a point.
If 2 heads show, then the 2-Heads Player gets a point.

The first player to score 10 points wins.

1. Play several games. For each game, keep score in a table like this.

How Many Heads?

Player	Points	
	Tallies	Total
0-Heads Player		
1-Head Player		
2-Heads Player		

2. If you could play again, which player would you choose to be and why?

3. Mathematicians say that a game is **fair** if all players have an equal chance of winning. Tell whether this is a mathematically fair game and why.

Lab: Flipping Two Coins

In this lab, you will flip two coins, a penny and a nickel, 100 times. For each trial, or time you flip two coins, you will count how many heads show.

4. Before the lab, predict how many times each number of heads will show in your 100 trials. Make a table like this to record your prediction. Explain how you made your prediction.

Prediction Data Table

Number of Heads	Predicted Number of Trials
0	
1	
2	

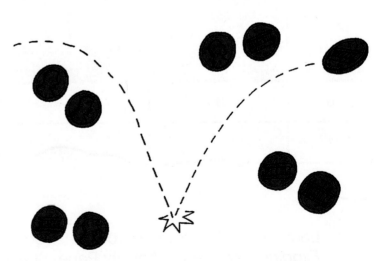

Data Tables

5. Now flip the penny and the nickel 100 times. Record your trials in the table on the *100 Two-Coin Flips* Activity Page in the *Discovery Assignment Book.* Write the outcome of the penny first and the nickel second. For example, if the penny shows heads and the nickel shows tails, then record HT in the outcome column.

100 Two-Coin Flips

Trial	Outcome	Number of Heads
1.	HT	1
2.	HH	2
3.	TH	1
4.	TT	0
5.	TH	1

6. Look at the data for your first 10 trials only. Complete the 10-Trial Table on the *Coin Flipping Data Tables* Activity Page in the *Discovery Assignment Book* to show the number, fraction, and percent of the first 10 trials that have 0, 1, and 2 heads. The first row shows an example. Write your data in your table.

10-Trial Table

Number of Heads	N Number of Trials Out of 10	$\frac{N}{10}$ Fraction of Trials Out of 10	Equivalent Fraction with Denominator of 100	Percent of 10 Trials
0	3	$\frac{3}{10}$	$\frac{30}{100}$	30%
1				
2				

7. Look at the data from all 100 trials. Complete the 100-Trial Table on the *Coin Flipping Data Tables* Activity Page. Show the number, fraction, and percent of your 100 trials that have 0, 1, and 2 heads.

    Flipping Two Coins

8. Now collect data from 10 groups to get a total of 1000 trials. Complete the 1000-Trial Table on the *Coin Flipping Data Tables* Activity Page. Show the number, fraction, and percent of 1000 trials that have 0, 1, and 2 heads.

9. Make 3 graphs—one for each of your data tables in Questions 6, 7, and 8.
   - Plot the Number of Heads on the horizontal axis and the Percent of Trials on the vertical axis.
   - Think about whether bar graphs or point graphs make more sense here.

10. Describe your graphs.
   A. How are they alike? How are they different?
   B. Which bar is the tallest?
   C. In the 1000-Trial Graph, how many times taller is the tallest bar than the other two bars?

11. A. What are the possible outcomes when you flip 2 coins? List them.
   B. How many ways can 0 heads come up? List the way(s).
   C. How many ways can 1 head come up? List the way(s).
   D. How many ways can 2 heads come up? List the way(s).

12. How does knowing the number of ways the coins can land help you to understand why the experiment (and your graphs) turned out the way they did?

Probability

The **probability** of 2 heads (HH) when two coins are flipped is the number of ways 2 heads can show, divided by the total number of ways the coins can land.

$$\text{Probability of 2 heads showing} = 1 \div 4 = \tfrac{1}{4}$$

The probability tells us about how often we can expect an event to occur when an experiment is repeated many times.

13. Since the probability of 2 heads is one-fourth, we can expect 2 heads to show about one-fourth of the time, when we flip the coin many times. Did that happen in your experiment?

14. Use your answers to Question 11 to compute the probabilities of getting 0 heads and 1 head. Enter the probabilities in a probability table like the one below. Your copy is on the *Comparing Probability with Results* Activity Page in the *Discovery Assignment Book*.

Probabilities of Coin Flipping

Number of Heads	Ways Heads Can Come Up	Probability (as a fraction)	Probability (as a percent)
0			
1			
2	HH	$\frac{1}{4}$	25%

15. Use the Results of Coin Flipping table from the *Comparing Probability with Results* Activity Page. Enter the percents of the trials in your experiment that had 0, 1, and 2 heads. (Use the data from the last column of the tables in Questions 6, 7, and 8.)

Results of Coin Flipping

Number of Heads	Percent of 10 Trials	Percent of 100 Trials	Percent of 1000 Trials
0			
1			
2			

16. Compare your tables from Questions 14 and 15. What pattern do you see? Explain what is happening as more trials are made.

17. Do the results of your experiment match your predictions in Question 4? Why or why not?

1. For each centiwheel, write a fraction, decimal, and percent that show the part of the wheel that is shaded.

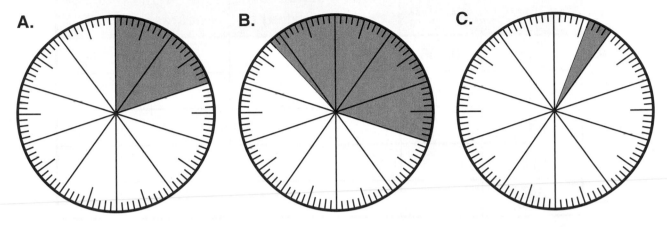

A.   B.   C.

2. For each grid, write a fraction, decimal, and percent that show the part of the grid that is shaded.

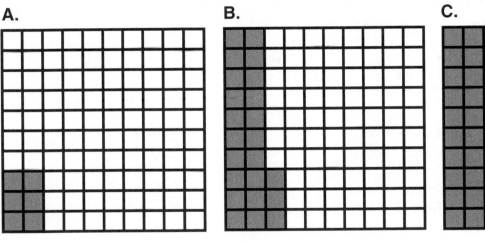
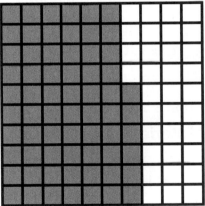

A.   B.   C.

3. Write the following fractions as decimals and percents.

A. $\frac{7}{10}$ B. $\frac{12}{100}$

C. $\frac{3}{10}$ D. $\frac{28}{100}$

E. $\frac{5}{10}$ F. $\frac{5}{100}$

G. $\frac{4}{10}$ H. $\frac{40}{100}$

4. Complete the following table to help you write the following fractions as percents. Give your answers to the nearest percent. The first one is done for you.

	Fraction	Decimal	Decimal (to the nearest hundredth)	Percent (to the nearest percent)
A.	$\frac{256}{1000}$	0.256	.26	26%
B.	$\frac{492}{1000}$			
C.	$\frac{36}{1000}$			
D.	$\frac{40}{1000}$			
E.	$\frac{487}{1000}$			

5. The first game of the lesson *How Many Heads?* was not a fair game because the players did not have an equal chance of winning. Below are the directions for another game, *Matching Two Pennies*. Answer Questions A–D to decide whether this game is fair.

Game: Matching 2 Pennies

Players

This is a game for 2 players.

Materials

- 2 pennies
- How Many Heads? table

Rules

Flip two pennies.
If the pennies match—both heads or both tails—then Player 1 gets a point.
If the pennies don't match, then Player 2 gets a point.
The first player to score 10 points is the winner.

A. Play several games with a family member. Keep track of the final scores of each game.

B. List the possible outcomes of flipping 2 coins.

C. For which of the outcomes you listed in B will Player 1 get a point? For which outcomes will Player 2 score a point?

D. Is this a fair game (do the players have an equal chance of winning)? Explain your answer.

Families with Two Children

Romesh would like to have two children
when he grows up, a boy and a girl.
Some families with two children do have
a boy and a girl, but some have only boys
or only girls.

1. Make a list of the different types of two-children families that are possible.

Types of Two-Children Families

First Child (Boy or Girl)	Second Child (Boy or Girl)

2. What are the different possible numbers of boys a family with two children might have?

3. From your list in Question 1, how many different types of two-children families have:

    A. 0 boys? List them.

    B. 1 boy? List them.

    C. 2 boys? List them.

4. If a family has two children:

   A. What is the probability of having 0 boys? Express as a fraction and as a percent. *Hint:* The probability of 0 boys is

   $$\frac{\text{the number of types of families with 0 boys}}{\text{the number of types of families with 2 children}}$$

   B. What is the probability of having 1 boy? Express as a fraction and as a percent.

   C. What is the probability of having 2 boys? Express as a fraction and as a percent.

5. If you sampled 100 families that have two children, about how many of them would you expect to have:

   A. 0 boys?

   B. 1 boy?

   C. 2 boys?

Testing Your Predictions

Compare the two-children families that you and your classmates know with the predictions you made in Question 5.

6. Think of some families you know that have two children—perhaps your family or the families of your neighbors or relatives. Don't include families of other students in the class. List them in a table like the table below.

Boys Per Family

Family Name	Children	Number of Boys
Jones	BB	2
Young	BG	1
Jackson	GG	0
Clinton	BB	2
Martinez	GB	1

7. Combine your list of families with your classmates' lists until you have a list of 100 families that have two children. (Be sure not to list the same families more than once.) Make a table like the one below.

Two-Children Families We Know

Number of Boys	Number of Families (out of 100)	Percent of Families
0		
1		
2		

8. How do your results compare with your predictions from Question 5?

Unit 8

Applications:
An Assessment Unit

	Student Guide	Discovery Assignment Book	Adventure Book	Unit Resource Guide*
Lesson 1				
Experiment Review	●	●		
Lesson 2				
Three in a Row		●		
Lesson 3				
Florence Kelley	●		●	
Lesson 4				
Florence Kelley's Report				●
Lesson 5				
Life Spans	●	●		
Lesson 6				
Comparing Lives of Animals and Soap Bubbles	●	●		
Lesson 7				
Review Problems	●			
Lesson 8				
Midyear Test				●
Lesson 9				
Portfolio Review	●			

Unit Resource Guide pages are from the teacher materials.

Experiment Review

Professor Peabody volunteered to be a timer at the Bessie Coleman Elementary School field day. He timed students as they ran the 50-yard dash. For each student, he recorded the time it took them to run the distance. As he timed each student, he remembered a lab he had worked on some months ago.

Discuss

1. Which lab does Professor Peabody remember?

2. Answer the following questions about the lab. You may use your *Student Guide* or your portfolio to help you.

   A. What variables did you study in the lab?

   B. Did you have to keep any variables the same so that the experiment would be fair? If so, which ones?

   C. Did you measure anything? If so, what did you measure? What units did you use?

   D. How many trials did you do? If you did more than one trial, tell why.

   E. Describe your graph.

   F. What were the most important problems you solved using your data and your graph?

3. Use your *Student Guide* and your portfolio to make a list of the labs you completed. One or more labs will be assigned to your group. Answer each part of Question 2 for these labs. Use the *Experiment Review Chart* Activity Pages in the *Discovery Assignment Book* to organize your work.

Florence Kelley

Florence Kelley was Chief Inspector of Factories in Illinois. She wrote a report with all the facts she collected during the year. Here is the data table for her third report.

Third Annual Report of the Factory Inspectors of Illinois

Increase in Work Done

Year	Places inspected	Men employed	Women employed	Children employed	Total employed
1895..........................	4,540	151,075	30,670	8,624	190,369
1894..........................	3,440	97,600	24,335	8,130	130,065
Increase.................	1,100	53,475	6,335	494	60,304
1895..........................	4,540	151,075	30,670	8,624	190,369
1893..........................	2,362	52,480	17,288	6,456	76,224
Increase.................	2,178	98,595	13,382	2,168	114,145

Discuss

1. Study the data table.
   A. How many children were employed in 1895?
   B. Where did you find this information?
   C. How many children were employed in 1894? 1893?
   D. Was there an increase or decrease in the number of children employed from 1894 to 1895?
   E. Was the number of children employed in 1894 more or less than the number employed in 1893? How many more or less?

2. What do the other columns in the data table tell you?

3. **A.** How many places were inspected in 1895? 1894? 1893?

   B. Was there an increase or decrease in the number of places inspected from 1894 to 1895?

   C. Was the number of places inspected in 1894 more or less than the number inspected in 1893? How many more or less?

4. In the story, Florence Kelley studies the Third Annual Report and says,

   " . . . I think these numbers show a trend, . . . a trend toward a reduction in the number of children employed. And I predict that because of the new law that this trend will continue."

   A. Do the numbers in the table show a trend toward fewer numbers of children employed? Why or why not?

   B. Was her prediction a good one? Use the data in the table to support your thinking.

Life Spans

The students in Mr. Moreno's classroom are studying the history of the United States. They learned that the United States changed rapidly during the 1900s. During this time, many people began working in factories instead of on farms. Living conditions and sanitation improved for most people. At the same time, the discovery of antibiotics and other improvements in medical care changed the way doctors treated diseases.

The students wondered if these changes had any effect on the length of time people lived. Mr. Moreno suggested that they collect information on the life spans of people before these changes occurred. They could then compare them with the life spans of people after these changes occurred. The students decided to compare the life spans of a set of people who lived during the 1800s to the life spans of a set of people who lived during the 1900s.

Brandon and David went to the library to collect data. Brandon looked for obituaries in old newspapers. He looked through newspapers from the year 1858 and found 25 death notices that listed the names of the people who died and their age at death. He wrote down the age of each person: 56 yr, 1 yr 3 mo, 54 yr, 9 mo, 27 yr, 42 yr, $2\frac{1}{2}$ mo, 5 yr, 38 yr, 34 yr, 79 yr, 59 yr, 76 yr, infant, 21 yr, 25 yr, 24 yr, 19 yr, 30 yr, 62 yr, 51 yr, 43 yr, 20 yr, 1 yr, and 5 yr.

David looked in more recent newspapers. He found 50 obituaries that gave the age at death. He wrote down these ages, which were all given in years: 75, 88, 84, 79, 85, 86, 51, 77, 85, 88, 88, 71, 84, 85, 89, 92, 77, 97, 80, 60, 95, 62, 85, 64, 44, 74, 62, 87, 81, 73, 89, 15, 96, 84, 72, 89, 84, 90, 88, 50, 68, 72, 75, 63, 90, 65, 38, 77, 79, and 73. All the people in David's data set died in February of 2007.

Discuss

David and Brandon shared their data with the class.

1. Compare the two sets of life spans. What do you notice about the length of the life spans in the 1858 data and in the 2007 data?

---

2. The students in Mr. Moreno's class found it difficult to compare the two sets of data as David and Brandon reported it. They decided to make two graphs to display the data. How can you set up the graphs to tell the story of the data?

Mr. Moreno suggested that the students **bin** their data. He explained that when you bin data, you look at how data falls within equal intervals. For example, if you measure the height of each person in the class, you can group the data into bins: For example, heights of 120–129 centimeters, 130–139 centimeters, 140–149 centimeters, 150–159 centimeters, and 160–169 centimeters. The number of heights in each bin is recorded.

3. A. What intervals can you use to bin the life span data? (*Hint:* Listing the ages on a separate sheet of paper may help you choose your bins.)

    B. What are some reasons to bin data?

4. The students binned the data and recorded the number of life spans in each interval. They knew they had a different number of people in each data set.

    A. How many life spans are in the 1858 data?

    B. How many life spans are in the 1997 data?

    C. What strategies can the students use to compare the data in the two sets?

5. Use the 1858 data to complete a data table like the one shown below. You may use the *Life Spans Data Tables* Activity Page in the *Discovery Assignment Book.* (*Hint:* To tally the data, list the ages on a separate sheet of paper. Then you can check off each number as you tally.)

A Age (in years)	*N* Number of Deaths		Fraction of Deaths	Percent of Deaths (to the Nearest Percent)
	Tallies	Number		

6. For this type of data, mathematicians usually use a bar graph.

    • Make a bar graph of this data.

- Plot the Percent of Deaths on the vertical axis.
- Plot the Age in Years on the horizontal axis.
- Draw the bars between the lines to show that most of the ages fall between the numbers on the horizontal axis.
- When you start graphing the data, your graph might look like the graph to the right.

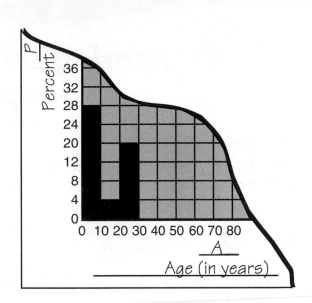

7. Describe the shape of your graph. The shape of the graph tells the story of the data. Use these questions to help you.
- Are all the bars about the same height, or are some bars much taller than others?
- Where are the tallest bars—at the beginning, middle, or end of the graph?
- What do the heights of the bars tell you about life spans in this set of data?

8. **A.** Use your graph to estimate the median life span for the 1858 data.
   B. Use your data to find the median life span.

9. Use the 2007 data to complete a data table like the one in Question 5.

10. Make a bar graph of the 2007 data.
- Plot the Age in Years on the horizontal axis and the Percent of Deaths on the vertical axis.
- Use the same scales you used for the graph in Question 6.

11. Describe the shape of this graph. Use the questions in Question 7 to help you tell the story of the data.

12. **A.** Use your graph to estimate the median life span for the 2007 data.
   B. Use your data to find the median life span.

13. Use the graphs to help you compare the two sets of data. What do the graphs tell you about the length of the life spans in the two data sets?

14. What do you think caused the changes in life spans?

Comparing Lives of Animals and Soap Bubbles

Lives of Animals

The shape of a graph can give important information. In Lesson 5 you graphed data on the life spans of people in the United States. You compared the shapes of two graphs. Biologists also gather similar information about animals. They collect data on the age at death of many animals of the same species. Once graphed, these data give important information to the scientist about that species.

The following are brief descriptions of the lives of three different kinds of animals:

Humans. Humans nurture their young until they are old enough to care for themselves. However, babies are at greater risk of illness and disease because their immune systems are still developing. Humans die from disease and accidents as they age, but modern medicine has controlled many diseases, so the majority of people live a long time.

American robins. Robins care for their young until they are old enough to fly and gather food for themselves. From the time they leave the nest, robins of all ages are equally likely to be eaten by predators or to die from accidents. Chance has a much greater effect on how long robins live than it does for other kinds of organisms.

Oysters. Early in life, oysters are very small and have thin shells. Most are eaten by predators when they are very young. As adults with thick shells, surviving oysters live for a very long time.

1. The following three graphs show the age at which these animals are most likely to die. Find the graph that matches the description for each animal: humans, American robins, and oysters.

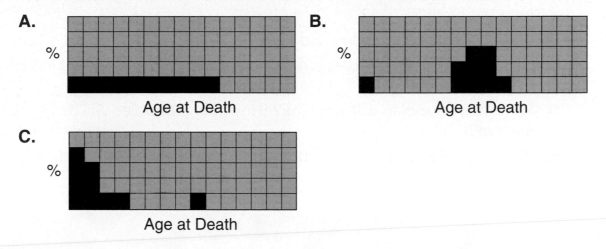

A.

% | Age at Death

B.

% | Age at Death

C.

% | Age at Death

Experimenting with Soap Bubbles

Often, scientific experiments are limited by the conditions in a laboratory. As scientists in a classroom, you cannot collect data on the life spans of many kinds of animals. Biologists have found that the shape of a graph showing the "age at death" of soap bubbles resembles the shape of similar graphs for some animals.

In this experiment, you will collect data on the life spans or "age at death" of soap bubbles. Using these data, you will make graphs similar to those you made of the life spans of people in Lesson 5. Then the graphs from your soap bubble data will be compared to the three graphs shown in Question 1.

To collect the data for this experiment, measure the time that each bubble lives. Then find the percentage of the bubbles that live for a given time.

Discuss

2. Try out your bubble solution. Observe the bubbles. Catch some with your wand, and observe them until they pop. What variables are involved in the experiment? What variables do you think affect the life span of a soap bubble?

3. Develop a plan for collecting reliable data on the life spans of soap bubbles. Consider the following:

   A. When does a bubble's "life" begin and end? (When will you start and stop the timer?)

   B. What variables should be held fixed?

   C. Sometimes, many bubbles are made at once. Which bubbles will be part of your sample?

   D. How many bubbles will you time? (How many bubbles will be in your sample?)

   E. What will each member of your group do to help collect the data?

4. Draw a picture of the experiment. Label the important variables. Show your procedure.

5. Time a few bubbles. Will you need to bin your data?

6. You will make a bar graph of the life spans of soap bubbles. Use what you have learned from Question 5 to predict what the shape of your bar graph will look like. Make a sketch, or write a description for your prediction. Use these questions to help you:

   • Will all the bars be about the same height, or will some bars be much taller than others?

   • Where will the tallest bars be—at the beginning, middle, or end of the graph?

   • Will your graph look like one of those shown for humans, robins, or oysters?

7. Draw a data table like the one that follows, or use a copy of the *Soap Bubbles Data Table* Activity Page from the *Discovery Assignment Book*. Choose time intervals such as 5 or 10 seconds to bin the data. Fill in the first column of the data table with the intervals. Be sure the intervals do not overlap and are the same size.

Life Spans of Soap Bubbles

t Time in Seconds	Tallies	*N* Number of Bubbles	*P* Percent of Bubbles

8. Collect your data. Fill in your data table.

9. Make a bar graph of your data. Graph time on the horizontal axis and the percent of bubbles on the vertical axis. Number the lines on the horizontal axis with the first value of each interval.

10. Describe the shape of your graph. What does it tell you about the life spans of bubbles? Consider the following:

   • Did most of the bubbles burst immediately with only a few lasting for a long time?

   • Were the bubbles as likely to last 10 seconds as 15, 25, or 50 seconds?

   • Did most of the bubbles live for a long time and burst after about the same amount of time?

11. Compare the shape of your graph to the shape you predicted in Question 6. Was your prediction correct? Why or why not?

12. Compare your graph to the graphs of the life spans of humans, American robins, and oysters in the *Student Guide*. Which of these three graphs is most like your graph? Explain.

Review Problems

Answer the following questions. You may use any tools that you use in class. For example, you may need to use a ruler, a calculator, or a small centiwheel. You will need graph paper to complete Question 6. Show all your work.

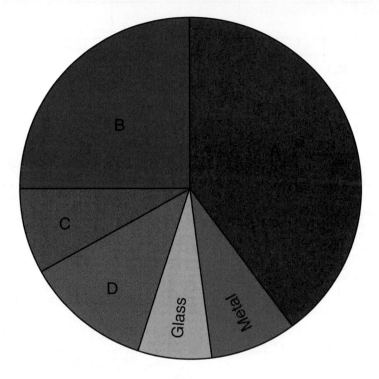

Lin, Irma, Romesh, and John presented this circle graph to their class during a unit on the environment. This graph shows one way experts divide the categories of trash thrown into landfills.

Use this graph to answer Questions 1–5.

1. Organic waste makes up 25% of our trash. What part of the circle graph represents organic waste?

2. We throw away about the same amount of plastic as we do metal. What part of the circle graph represents plastic?

3. Paper makes up between one-third and one-half of our garbage. What part of the circle graph represents paper?

4. There are some things that we throw away that do not fit any of the categories we have listed so far. Examples might include an old telephone or a worn-out chair. This category is labeled miscellaneous. About $\frac{1}{8}$ of the garbage we throw out is considered miscellaneous. What part of the circle graph represents the category miscellaneous?

5. About what percent of our trash comes from each category? Use a small centiwheel to help you.

6. Brandon and Roberto discovered an interesting fact while studying recycling: the energy saved from recycling one glass bottle will light a 100-watt bulb for four hours.

    A. Use this fact to complete the data table below. Copy the completed data table on your paper.

N Number of Recycled Glass Bottles	t Time (in hours) a 100-Watt Bulb Can Burn
1	4
3	
	20
7	

    B. Make a graph using your data table.

    C. Use your graph to find how many hours you can light a 100-watt bulb from the energy saved from 4 recycled glass bottles. Show your work on your graph.

    D. If you recycled 10 glass bottles, how many hours can a 100-watt bulb burn with the energy saved? Show your work.

    E. Write a ratio of time to number of glass bottles as a fraction.

    F. Write 2 ratios equivalent to the ratio in Part E.

7. Today, about $\frac{1}{5}$ of our paper is recycled. About what percent of our paper is recycled?

8. Alexis, Felicia, and Ana found that you can compost most organic waste. They learned that 1 pound of red worms will eat 0.5 pound of organic waste each day. The students in Mr. Moreno's class built a worm bin to compost the organic waste from their lunches. The students produce an average of 3.25 pounds of organic waste each week. How many pounds of red worms will they need in their bin if they expect the waste to be fully composted weekly?

Portfolio Review

Since the start of the school year, the students in Mr. Moreno's class have collected work for their portfolios. They have saved work that shows what they know, how they solve problems, and how well they can explain their work. Today, the students are updating their portfolios.

"Look through the work in your collection folders," said Mr. Moreno. "Find the activities and labs that best show how you use what you know to solve problems. These are the pieces that you should put in your portfolio. You can compare the work you did earlier this year to the work you are doing now. And don't forget to update your table of contents."

1. If you have not done so recently, choose items from your collection folder to add to your portfolio. Examples of items you might choose are:
    *   *Distance vs. Time* from Unit 3
    *   *A Day at the Races* from Unit 5
    *   *Making Shapes* from Unit 6
    *   Work with paper-and-pencil multiplication and division

2. Put your *Experiment Review Chart* from Lesson 1 in your portfolio.

3. Choose one or two other pieces of work from this unit to include in your portfolio. Select pieces that are like other work that you put in your portfolio earlier in the year. For example, if you already have a lab in your portfolio, put *Comparing Lives of Animals and Soap Bubbles* in your portfolio, too. Or, if you included a written solution to a problem like *Stack Up*, then also include your writing and graph for *Florence Kelley's Report* in Lesson 4.

4. Add to your Table of Contents. The Table of Contents should include the name of each piece of work, a short description of the work, and the date it was finished.

5. Write a paragraph comparing two pieces of work in your portfolio that are alike in some way. For example, you can compare two labs or your solutions to two problems you have solved. One piece should be new, and one should be from earlier in the year. Here are some questions for you to think about as you write your paragraph:

   • Which two pieces did you choose to compare?

   • How are they alike? How are they different?

   • Do you see any improvement in the newest piece of work as compared to the older work? Explain.

   • If you could redo the older piece of work, how would you improve it?

   • How could you improve the newer piece of work?

6. Write about your favorite piece of work in your portfolio. Tell why you like it. Explain what you learned from it.

My favorite piece is my work on *Florence Kelley.*

When I compare my work on *Stack Up* to my work on the slab maker problems, I can really see a difference.

Unit 9

Connections to Division

	Student Guide	Discovery Assignment Book	Adventure Book	Unit Resource Guide*
Lesson 1				
Fractions and Division	●	●		
Lesson 2				
Division	●	●		
Lesson 3				
Multiplication Methods	●	●		
Lesson 4				
Understanding Remainders	●			●
Lesson 5				
Calculator Strategies: Division	●			
Lesson 6				
Grass Act	●			●

Unit Resource Guide pages are from the teacher materials.

Fractions and Division

Edward and Brandon walk into the lunch room. Edward says, "My mom packed 2 brownies in my lunch today. I'll share them with you if you want."

"Sure," Brandon replies. "We can each have one brownie then."

As the boys sit down, Romesh walks over and joins them. "Those brownies look great. How about sharing them with me, please?"

"Okay, but how can we share them equally?" Edward asks.

1. Think about how the three boys can share the two brownies equally. One solution is to divide each brownie into three equal pieces. You can show this using rectangles on dot paper.

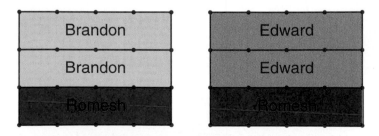

A. How many pieces will each boy get?

B. What fraction of 1 whole brownie does this represent?

2. **A.** Nicholas joins the boys at their table. They decide to split the 2 brownies among the four boys. Draw rectangles to show how you can divide 2 brownies among the four boys.

   B. If they divide each brownie into four equal pieces, how many pieces will each boy get?

   C. What fraction of one whole brownie does this represent?

   D. Using rectangles, find another way to divide the two brownies among 4 boys.

A fraction is also a way to show division. The fraction line, or bar, means you divide the numerator by the denominator. For example, $\frac{2}{3}$ means 2 divided by 3. We can write this as a division number sentence:

$$\frac{2}{3} = 2 \div 3$$

Explore

The following chart shows what happens when 2 brownies are shared with more and more people.

Sharing Brownies

Number of Brownies	Number of Boys	Number of Brownies Each Boy Will Get	Division Number Sentence
2	1	$\frac{2\text{ brownies}}{1\text{ boy}}$ = 2 brownies per boy	$2 \div 1 = 2$
2	2	$\frac{2\text{ brownies}}{2\text{ boys}}$ = 1 brownie per boy	$2 \div 2 = 1$
2	3	$\frac{2\text{ brownies}}{3\text{ boys}}$ = $\frac{2}{3}$ of a brownie per boy	$2 \div 3 = \frac{2}{3}$
2	4	$\frac{2\text{ brownies}}{4\text{ boys}}$ = $\frac{2}{4}$ of a brownie per boy	$2 \div 4 = \frac{2}{4}$
2	5	?	?

Fractions and Division

3. **A.** If Edward divides his 2 brownies among 5 people, what fraction of a brownie will each person get?

   B. Write the division number sentence that this fraction represents. Use the boxes as a guide.

   $$\frac{\square}{\square} = \square \div \square$$

4. **A.** Brandon's mother packed 6 cookies in his lunch. How can Brandon share his six cookies with Edward, Romesh, and Nicholas? (*Note:* The 6 cookies will be divided among 4 boys.)

   B. 6 cookies ÷ 4 boys = ? Draw circles to represent the 6 cookies. Show how Brandon can divide the cookies fairly among the 4 boys. How many will each of the four boys get?

   C. What are other names for this number?

Decimals

We can use a calculator to change fractions to decimals.

5. Jackie shares her apple with Nila. If they share it fairly, how much apple will each girl get?

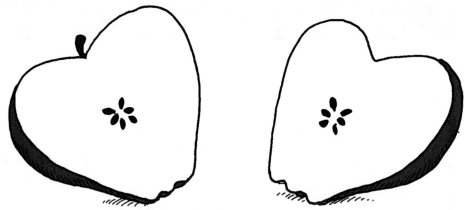

Each girl will get $\frac{1}{2}$ of the apple. This fraction means 1 apple divided between 2 girls or 1 ÷ 2. Use your calculator to find a decimal equivalent to $\frac{1}{2}$ by pressing $\boxed{1}$ $\boxed{\div}$ $\boxed{2}$ $\boxed{=}$. You should see 0.5 on your calculator. This tells you that 0.5 is equal to $\frac{1}{2}$. Notice that $\frac{1}{2} + \frac{1}{2} = 1$ just as 0.5 + 0.5 = 1.

6. **A.** Felicia has 4 granola bars to share among 5 children. Use rectangles to show how Felicia can divide the four granola bars among 5 people.

   B. What fraction of one granola bar will each child get?

   C. Use your calculator to find the decimal equivalent. What are other names for this number?

   D. Complete this number sentence: $0.8 = \frac{?}{5}$

7. **A.** Frank, Roberto, Michael, and Manny share one pizza. What fraction of the pizza will each boy get?

   B. Use your calculator to find the decimal equivalent.

   C. What are other names for this number?

8. **A.** Shannon's mother baked a pie. She cut the pie into 8 equal pieces. Each piece is what fraction of the pie?

   B. Use your calculator to find a decimal for this fraction.

   C. What are other names for this number?

   D. Complete the following number sentence: $\frac{1}{8} = \frac{?}{1000}$

9. Draw this table on your paper. Use your calculator to change each fraction into a decimal. Write the decimal exactly as it is shown in your calculator's window. Complete the table.

Fraction	Decimal on Calculator
$\frac{1}{10}$	
$\frac{1}{8}$	
$\frac{1}{4}$	
$\frac{1}{3}$	
$\frac{2}{4}$	
$\frac{1}{2}$	0.5
$\frac{2}{3}$	
$\frac{3}{4}$	
1	1.0
$\frac{9}{8}$	
$\frac{5}{4}$	
$\frac{14}{10}$	

10. **A.** Look at the decimal for $\frac{1}{3}$. What do you notice about this decimal?

  B. $\frac{1}{2}$ and 0.5 are equal. Are $\frac{1}{3}$ and 0.3333333 equal?

  If your calculator had more space in the window, the 3s would continue to repeat. Decimals that have digits that repeat are called **repeating decimals.** Your calculator cannot give an exact decimal equivalent for $\frac{1}{3}$, but 0.333333333 is a very close approximation. We use the symbol ≈ to show that 0.333333333 is approximately equal to $\frac{1}{3}$.

$$\frac{1}{3} \approx 0.333333333$$

  C. Use the fraction circle that is divided into thirds and your small centiwheel to find a decimal for $\frac{1}{3}$ (to the nearest hundredth).

11. **A.** Look at the decimal for $\frac{2}{3}$ in the table you completed for Question 9. What number continues to repeat?

  B. What is the last digit in the decimal for $\frac{2}{3}$ shown on your calculator?

  C. Complete this number sentence: $\frac{2}{3} \approx$?

  D. Place your centiwheel on top of the circle. Use your centiwheel and the circle divided into thirds to find a decimal for $\frac{2}{3}$ (to the nearest hundredth).

12. A. Use your calculator to change $\frac{1}{6}$ to a decimal. Write the decimal exactly as it appears on your calculator.

B. Use your centiwheel and the fraction circle divided into sixths to find a decimal for $\frac{1}{6}$ (to the nearest hundredth).

C. Look at the decimals for $\frac{1}{6}$ you found with a calculator and with a centiwheel. Is $\frac{1}{6}$ exactly equal to or approximately equal to these decimals?

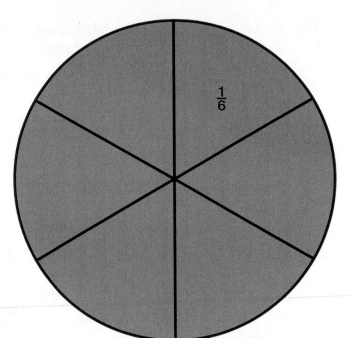

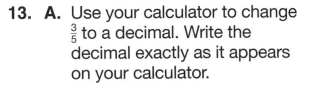

13. A. Use your calculator to change $\frac{3}{5}$ to a decimal. Write the decimal exactly as it appears on your calculator.

B. Use your centiwheel and the fraction circle to the right to find a decimal for $\frac{3}{5}$ (to the nearest hundredth).

C. Look at the decimals for $\frac{3}{5}$ you found with a calculator and with a centiwheel. Is $\frac{3}{5}$ exactly equal to or approximately equal to these decimals?

14. A. Use your calculator to change $\frac{3}{8}$ to a decimal. Write the decimal exactly as it appears on your calculator.

   B. Use your centiwheel and the fraction circle below to find a decimal for $\frac{3}{8}$ (to the nearest hundredth).

   C. Is $\frac{3}{8}$ exactly equal to or approximately equal to the decimal in Part A? How do you know?

   D. Is $\frac{3}{8}$ exactly equal to or approximately equal to the decimal in Part B? How do you know?

15. A. Use your calculator to find the decimal equivalent for $\frac{5}{8}$.

   B. Use your calculator to find the decimal equivalent for $\frac{10}{16}$.

   C. Is $\frac{5}{8} = \frac{10}{16}$? How do you know?

   D. Is $\frac{16}{20} = \frac{5}{8}$? Use your calculator to help you decide.

   E. How can you use your calculator to help you decide if two fractions are equivalent?

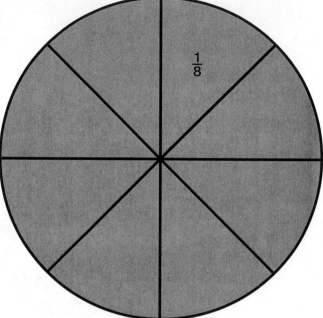

16. Use your calculator to help you decide which of the following fractions are equivalent to $\frac{3}{4}$.

   A. $\frac{15}{20}$ **B.** $\frac{8}{12}$

   C. $\frac{75}{100}$ **D.** $\frac{12}{16}$

17. Use your calculator to help you decide which fractions are equivalent to $\frac{2}{3}$.

   A. $\frac{6}{9}$ **B.** $\frac{7}{11}$

   C. $\frac{666}{1000}$ **D.** $\frac{44}{66}$

18. Use your calculator to help you decide which fractions are equivalent to $\frac{7}{8}$.

   A. $\frac{140}{160}$ **B.** $\frac{87}{100}$

   C. $\frac{875}{1000}$ **D.** $\frac{22}{25}$

You will need a calculator and a small centiwheel to complete the homework.

1. **A.** Use your calculator to change $\frac{5}{12}$ to a decimal. Write the decimal exactly as it appears on your calculator.

   B. Use your centiwheel and the fraction circle divided into twelfths to find a decimal for $\frac{5}{12}$ (to the nearest hundredth).

   C. Is $\frac{5}{12}$ exactly equal to or approximately equal to the decimals in Parts A and B? How do you know?

2. **A.** Use your calculator to change $\frac{9}{12}$ to a decimal. Write the decimal exactly as it appears on your calculator.

   B. Use your centiwheel and the fraction circle above to find a decimal for $\frac{9}{12}$ (to the nearest hundredth).

   C. Is $\frac{9}{12}$ equal to or approximately equal to the decimals in Parts A and B? How do you know?

$\frac{1}{12}$

3. Use your calculator to help you decide which of the following fractions are equivalent to $\frac{2}{9}$.

   A. $\frac{6}{27}$ **B.** $\frac{10}{49}$ **C.** $\frac{5}{18}$ **D.** $\frac{22}{99}$

4. Use your calculator to help you decide which of the following fractions are equivalent to $\frac{15}{6}$.

   A. $\frac{12}{5}$ **B.** $\frac{76}{32}$ **C.** $2\frac{1}{2}$ **D.** $\frac{25}{10}$

5. Change each fraction to a decimal. Try different strategies and tools including calculators, centiwheels, or paper and pencil. Be prepared to share your strategies. Round decimals to the nearest hundredth when appropriate.

   A. $\frac{1}{5}$ **B.** $\frac{6}{8}$ **C.** $\frac{7}{10}$

   D. $\frac{7}{9}$ **E.** $\frac{7}{100}$

Division

Planning Ahead

The fifth-grade classes at Bessie Coleman Elementary School are planning a dinner for their parents. Brandon, Arti, and Manny are on the food committee. They are meeting with Mr. Cline, one of the school's cooks. He is helping them plan a menu that includes an enchilada casserole, a salad, and a dessert.

"Each casserole pan will serve an average of 32 people," said Mr. Cline. "If you know how many people you expect to serve, you can figure out how many pans of the enchilada casserole you will need to prepare."

"Three hundred eighty-nine people said that they will come," said Arti.

"This sounds like a division problem," said Manny. "To figure out the number of pans we need to prepare, we need to divide the total number of people we expect by the number of servings each pan will make."

"I know how to do this," Brandon exclaimed. "First we need to decide how many groups of 32 there are in 389. I think a good way to do this is to estimate with multiples of 10."

1. **A.** If Mr. Cline prepares 10 pans of enchilada casserole, how many people can the fifth grade serve?

    B. Are 10 pans too much or too little?

    C. How many people can they serve if Mr. Cline prepares 20 pans of enchilada casserole?

    D. Are 20 pans too much or too little?

Brandon decided to start the division problem by estimating that they would need at least 10 pans of enchilada casserole. He recorded his work.

$$
\begin{array}{r}
32\,\overline{\smash{\big)}\,389} \\
-\,320 \quad | \, 10 \\
\hline
69
\end{array}
$$

    E. If Mr. Cline made only 10 pans of casserole, how many people would not get served?

    F. How did Brandon record this?

"I think that we will need to make at least two more pans of enchilada casserole in order to feed everyone," said Arti. Arti recorded her work.

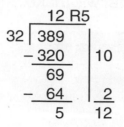

$$
\begin{array}{r}
12\ \text{R5} \\
32\ \overline{\smash{)}389} \\
-\ 320 \quad\ \ \big|\ 10 \\
\hline
69 \\
-\ 64 \quad\ \ \big|\ \underline{\ 2} \\
\hline
5 \quad\ \ \ \ 12
\end{array}
$$

2. **A.** If Mr. Cline makes two more pans of casserole, how many more people can be served?

    B. How many people will not be served?

"This shows that we need to make 10 + 2 or 12 pans of enchilada casserole to serve 320 + 64 or 384 people," said Manny. "We still have 5 people who will be without food. 5 is the remainder. Since we don't want anyone to be without food, Mr. Cline needs to make 1 more pan of casserole, or a total of 13 pans."

Arti remembered that she could check her division by multiplying the **quotient** by the **divisor** and adding the **remainder**: $12 \times 32 + 5 = 389$. Arti's computation gave her the **dividend** 389, so she knew her division was correct.

Ordering Clay

The art teacher at Ontario School, Mrs. Sorenson, is ordering clay for the school.

Clay comes in 24-pound blocks. She knows that each student uses an average of 1 pound of clay each year. This year there are 531 art students. Mrs. Sorenson knows that she needs to divide 531 by 24 to find out how many blocks of clay she needs to order.

$$24\ \overline{\smash{)}531}$$

3. **A.** What does the number 24 tell us in this problem?

    B. What does the number 531 tell us in this problem?

Mrs. Sorenson knows that 24 is close to 25 and that there are four 25s in 100. So she decides to use multiples of 25 to estimate how many blocks of clay she should order. Mrs. Sorenson estimates that she should order at least 20 blocks of clay, since there are twenty 25s in 500.

C. If she orders only 20 blocks of clay, how many students will not get clay this year?

$$\begin{array}{r} 24\overline{)531} \\ -480 \quad |20 \\ \hline 51 \end{array}$$

D. Mrs. Sorenson sees that she needs to order at least two more blocks of clay. She records her second estimate. Is this enough clay to make sure that each student will get clay? Explain your answer.

$$\begin{array}{r} 22 \text{ R3} \\ 24\overline{)531} \\ -480 \quad |20 \\ \hline 51 \\ -48 \quad |\underline{2} \\ \hline 3 \quad 22 \end{array}$$

E. Write a number sentence to check the division.

F. How much clay should Mrs. Sorenson order so that every child will get clay? Explain your answer.

Explore

Complete the following problems. Use estimation to help you divide. Record your work using a paper-and-pencil method. Write a number sentence to check your work.

4. The students at Bessie Coleman School are setting up tables for their parent dinner. Students can use either the rectangular tables or the round tables.

   A. Each of the rectangular tables will seat 12 people. How many rectangular tables will they need to seat all 389 people?

   B. Each of the round tables will seat 10 people. How many round tables will they need to seat all 389 people?

5. Alexis, Edward, and Irma are making centerpieces for each table. Each centerpiece will use 24 inches of ribbon. They have a spool with 864 inches of ribbon.

   A. How many centerpieces can they make?

   B. Will they have enough centerpieces to place one on each of the rectangular tables if they use only rectangular tables? Explain your answer.

   C. Will they have enough centerpieces to place one on each of the round tables if they use only round tables? Explain your answer.

6. The plates that the students will use come in packages of 48.

   A. How many packages will they need to serve all 389 people?

   B. How many plates will be left over?

7. A. $39 \overline{\smash{\big)}873}$ **B.** $12 \overline{\smash{\big)}3706}$

   C. $26 \overline{\smash{\big)}785}$ **D.** $50 \overline{\smash{\big)}900}$

Homework

For Questions 1–6:

   A. Use a paper-and-pencil method or mental math to solve each division problem. Record all your work on your paper.

   B. Check your answer using a different method. Write a number sentence to show how you checked your work.

   1. $20 \overline{\smash{\big)}163}$ **2.** $36 \overline{\smash{\big)}952}$ **3.** $40 \overline{\smash{\big)}8000}$

   4. $56 \overline{\smash{\big)}598}$ **5.** $45 \overline{\smash{\big)}3607}$ **6.** $23 \overline{\smash{\big)}4594}$

7. Jackie has chosen a 364-page book from the library. She wants to finish reading it in two weeks. How many pages should she plan to read each day?

8. Mr. Moreno asked Edward and Roberto to help him divide 943 marbles evenly among 15 bags.

   A. How many marbles will be in each bag?

   B. Will there be any marbles left over? If so, how many?

9. Mr. Moreno wanted to know the average number of miles he traveled each day. He kept track of the miles he traveled and found that in a two-week period he traveled 882 miles. What is the average number of miles he traveled each day?

10. Mr. Cline is making rolls for the school lunch. He needs 465 rolls. Each package contains 12 rolls. How many packages should he prepare?

11. Mrs. Sorenson is cutting ribbon for an art project. She has 650 cm of ribbon. Each student needs a strip 15 cm long. How many strips can she cut?

Multiplication Methods

Multiplying with Pencil and Paper

Mr. Moreno's class decided to make a book of the best short stories that they wrote. They decided to call this book *Life in Fifth Grade*. Mr. Moreno made copies of the book on the school copy machine. He used 9568 sheets of paper. He knows that he used 26 sheets of paper to make each book.

1. How many copies of *Life in Fifth Grade* did Mr. Moreno make?

2. Ana divided the 9568 sheets of paper by 26 and got the answer 368 copies. Is Ana correct? Show how you would check Ana's answer.

Romesh checked Ana's calculation by multiplying. He used the all-partials method to multiply 26 by 368.

```
    368
×    26
     48
    360
   1800
    160
   1200
   6000
   9568
```

3. How did Romesh get the partial product 48?

4. How did Romesh get the partial product 1200?

5. How did Romesh get the partial product 6000?

6. What color is the ones' column shaded?

7. What color is the tens' column shaded?

8. Which column is shaded green and which column is shaded yellow?

Lattice Multiplication

Blanca said she knew another way to multiply 368 × 26. She called it **lattice multiplication.** To start the problem, she drew this diagram with 368 across the top and 26 down the right side.

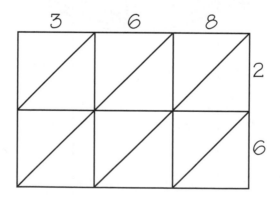

She multiplied 8 × 2 and filled in 16.

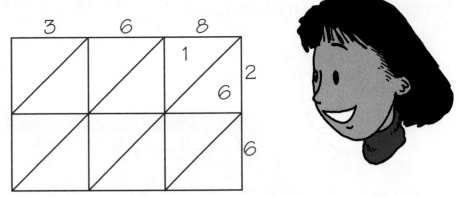

Blanca then filled in all the partial products in the lattice, like this:

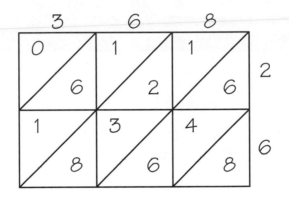

Finally, she added along the diagonals. If a diagonal totaled more than 9, she "carried" a digit to the next diagonal to the left. This is what the problem looked like when she was done.

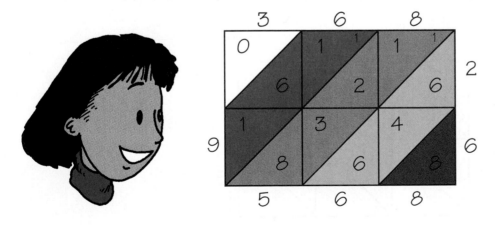

Compare Blanca's method with Romesh's method. The diagonals have been colored to help you think about this.

9. Where do you see the answer to 26 × 368 in Blanca's method?

10. Compare the digits shaded orange in Blanca's method to the digits shaded orange in Romesh's method. What is similar?

11. Compare the digits shaded blue in Blanca's method to the digits shaded blue in Romesh's method. What is similar?

12. What color are the thousands shaded in both methods?

"The lattice is like a place value chart. The diagonals have different place values," said Blanca.

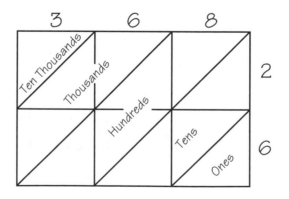

Many Ways to Multiply

Five of the students worked on the problem 37 × 499. They each used a different method.

"I didn't realize there were so many methods for multiplying," said Romesh.

"Yes," said Jessie. "I learned the compact method from my Dad."

"There are a lot more methods than the ones we have talked about. In some countries children learn even different methods," replied Mr. Moreno. "Most methods are based on the idea that multiplication problems with big numbers can be broken into many multiplications."

Find the following products in at least two different ways. Discuss with your classmates which methods were most efficient. Which were most reliable?

13. 36 × 502

14. 499 × 6

15. 53 × 123

16. 76 × 804

Estimate the answers to the following problems. Then show how to find an exact answer using as many methods as you can.

1. 4598 × 5

2. 45 × 36

3. 201 × 35

4. 399 × 32

5. 3002 × 50

6. Which method of solving these problems do you like the most? Do you think the same method is best for all problems?

Understanding Remainders

The remainder in a division problem is used in different ways, depending on the problem that you are solving.

1. There are 358 children going on a weekend camping trip. The children will ride buses to the camp. Each bus seats 63 children. How many buses are needed?

   A. Write a division problem for this question. Use paper and pencil to find an answer.

   B. What does the remainder mean in this problem?

   C. How did you use the remainder to decide how many buses are needed?

2. Some of the children want to sleep in tents. They need 8 stakes to set up each tent. They have 102 stakes. How many tents can they set up?

   A. Write a division problem for this question. Use paper and pencil to find an answer.

   B. What does the remainder mean in this problem?

   C. How did you use the remainder to decide how many tents can be set up?

3. The camp cook has 1282 cookies to divide into boxes. Each cabin will receive one box of cookies. There are 30 cabins in all. The cook promised all of the leftover cookies to the camp office staff. How many cookies will the camp staff get to share?

   A. Write a division problem for this question. Use paper and pencil to find an answer.

   B. What does the remainder mean in this problem?

C. How should you use the remainder to decide how many cookies the camp office staff will get to share?

D. If there are 4 members of the camp office staff, how many cookies will each person get?

Explore

Solve each of the following problems using paper and pencil. Explain how the remainder is used in each answer.

4. The Ontario School is hosting a sports day. Mrs. Sorenson is making medals for awards. Each medal uses 18 inches of ribbon. Mrs. Sorenson has 1450 inches of ribbon. How many medals can she make?

5. Award certificates come in packages of 25. Mrs. Lange, the principal, plans to give a certificate to each student in an event. There are 962 children competing in the events. How many packages of certificates should be ordered?

6. **A.** There are 92 children playing volleyball. Teams of 6 players are preferred but teams of 7 will be accepted. How many teams can be formed?

   B. How many teams will have a seventh player?

   C. How can you use multiplication to check your answer?

7. **A.** Jessie's mom is baking oatmeal bars for the refreshment table. She bought 4 dozen eggs. She already had 5 eggs at home. She uses 3 eggs for each pan she makes. How many pans can she make?

   B. After making the bars, Jessie's mom decided to bake a cake. The recipe calls for 4 eggs. Can she bake the cake using the leftover eggs?

8. The 160 fifth graders made teams for soccer of 11 players each. The extra students will be officials. How many students will be officials?

9. **A.** At the end of the sports day, 1697 ice cream treats were served to the children and their families. The treats came in boxes of 36. How many boxes of ice cream treats were opened?

   B. The leftover ice cream treats were given to the volunteers. How many ice cream treats did they get to share?

More Remainders

The answer to a division problem can be written as a whole number and a remainder, or, as a mixed number. A mixed number is a whole number plus a fraction. Depending on the problem, one way may be more useful than another.

Lin and David have 18 graham crackers to split among 8 children. To find out how many graham crackers to give each child, Lin wrote this problem: $\frac{18}{8}$. David wrote this problem: $8\overline{)18}$.

10. How are these two problems the same?

Lin found that $\frac{18}{8}$ equals $2\frac{2}{8}$, or $2\frac{1}{4}$. Each child will receive 2 whole crackers. The two leftover crackers will be divided into 8 equal pieces.

Lin's Solution

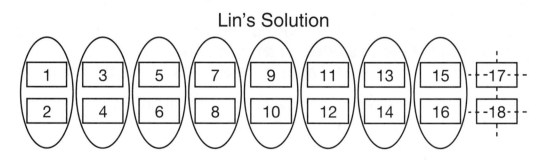

When David solved his problem, he found that 18 divided by 8 is 2 with a remainder of 2 crackers. He wrote his answer as a mixed number: $2\frac{2}{8}$. The fraction $\frac{2}{8}$ in the mixed number $2\frac{2}{8}$ shows that he took the two crackers that were left over and divided them among the eight children.

$$
\begin{array}{r}
2\ R2 \\
8\overline{)18} \\
-\underline{16} \quad | 2 \\
2
\end{array}
\qquad 2\frac{2}{8}
$$

David's Solution

11. **A.** Where did David get the numbers in this fraction?

    B. What information does the numerator give in this fraction?

    C. What information does the denominator give in this fraction?

    D. Rename $\frac{2}{8}$ using smaller numbers in the numerator and denominator.

    E. How many crackers will each child receive?

12. Mrs. Sorenson has large rolls of paper for bulletin boards and murals. She has 690 yards. There are 24 classrooms in the school. If she divides the paper evenly among the 24 classrooms, how many yards of paper can each class have this year?

Mrs. Sorenson used the forgiving division method. She found that each class can have 28 yards of paper, but she will still have a remainder of 18 yards. Mrs. Sorenson wants to divide this 18 yards among the 24 classes.

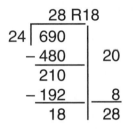

$$
\begin{array}{r}
28 \text{ R}18 \\
\hline
24\,|\,690 \\
-480 \quad 20\\
\hline
210 \\
-192 \quad 8\\
\hline
18 \quad 28
\end{array}
$$

A. What fraction should Mrs. Sorenson write to show 18 divided among 24 classes?

B. What is another name for this fraction using smaller numbers?

C. How much more paper can she give to each classroom?

D. What is the total amount of paper that each classroom can have?

13. Mr. Moreno filled his gas tank before leaving on a weekend trip. He drove 351 miles before stopping to refill his tank. When he refilled his gas tank, he found that he had used 15 gallons of gas. What is the average number of miles Mr. Moreno traveled on each gallon of gas? Write the answer as a mixed number.

Understanding Remainders

14. The Simply Shirts Company used 608 yards of fabric to make 64 shirts. How much fabric is used in each shirt? Write the answer as a mixed number.

15. Nila is helping her father lay a walkway. They will lay bricks in rows that are each 8 feet 6 inches long. Each brick is 8 inches long. How many bricks will they need for each row in the walkway? Write the answer as a mixed number.

For each of the problems write the answer as a mixed number.

1. Frank and his mother made wooden trains to sell at the yearly craft sale. Over a two-month period, they worked a total of 63 hours and made 18 trains. How many hours did it take to make each train?

2. On a pizza day at Bessie Coleman School, 78 pizzas were divided equally among 24 classrooms. How much pizza did each class receive?

3. The TIMS Candy Company made 60 pounds of Chocos. They put these candies in 24 gift boxes. How many pounds of candy are in each gift box?

4. Romesh is helping his mother build a fence. The fence will be 62 feet 3 inches long. Each fence board is 6 inches wide. How many boards will they need?

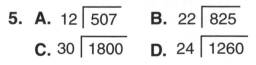

5. **A.** 12 | 507   **B.** 22 | 825

   C. 30 | 1800   **D.** 24 | 1260

Solve each of the problems in Questions 6–10 using paper and pencil.

6. Jackie is working at Billy's Fruit Stand after school. Jackie has to put 2600 apples into bags. Each bag holds three dozen apples. How many bags can she fill?

7. Mrs. Colligan is buying enough lemons so that her third grade class can sell lemonade during lunchtime. The recipe they will use calls for 8 lemons for a pitcher of lemonade. Each pitcher serves 10 people.

   A. If they plan to make enough lemonade to serve 480 students and teachers, how many pitchers do they have to make?

   B. Eighteen lemons come in a bag. How many bags of lemons should she buy?

8. Billy divides 60 pounds of cherries evenly into 24 boxes. How many pounds of cherries are in each box?

9. Jackie's last job for the day is to divide 725 oranges evenly and put them into 45 bags. Billy told her that she may take any extras home. How many oranges can Jackie take home?

Write any remainders in Question 10 as whole numbers.

10. **A.** 41$\overline{)8945}$ **B.** 60$\overline{)4800}$ **C.** 68$\overline{)4912}$

Calculator Strategies: Division

Think about this division problem: 29 $\overline{\smash{)}\,42{,}601}$

1. **A.** Why is using a calculator a good method for finding the answer to this problem?

   B. Use estimation to decide if the quotient is in the 100s, the 1000s, or the 10,000s.

   C. Here is a set of keystrokes you can use on your calculator to find an answer to this division problem: 42601 $\div$ 29 = . Use your calculator to solve this problem. Is your answer reasonable based on your estimate?

Money

2. The Parent Teacher Organization gave Mrs. Sorenson $1140 to share among the 24 classrooms for extra art supplies. First, she used a paper-and-pencil method to divide the money. She found that she could give each classroom $47.00, but that would leave a remainder of $12.00.

```
        47 R12
   24 | 1140
      - 960  | 40
        180
      - 168  | 7
         12  | 47
```

Next, she used her calculator to divide the money among the classrooms.

   A. What keystrokes can she use to find an answer to this division problem?

   B. Use your calculator to decide how much money each classroom should receive.

   C. What do the numbers to the left of the decimal point mean?

   D. What do the numbers to the right of the decimal point mean?

   E. Why is a calculator a good tool for dividing money?

Use a calculator to solve these problems. List your keystrokes, and tell what the numbers to the left and to the right of the decimal point mean.

3. A school spent $2489 to replace 76 science books. What was the cost of each book?

4. The Tasty Pizzeria served 52 large cheese pizzas in one evening. They calculated a total of $650 on the sale of these pizzas. How much did each pizza cost?

5. Three students earned a total of $5.00 washing cars. If they split the money evenly, how much will each student receive?

Whole Number Remainders

6. **A.** Jackie and Jessie are dividing cookies into boxes for a bake sale. They have 231 cookies, and they are putting 12 into each box. Use your calculator to divide 231 by 12.

   B. What does the number to the left of the decimal point tell you?

   C. What does the number to the right of the decimal point tell you?

   D. Jessie and Jackie fill 19 boxes with cookies. How many cookies have they put in boxes?

To find the number of leftover cookies, Jackie first found 12 × 19 = 228. This means 228 cookies have been packed. To find the number of cookies remaining, Jackie computed 231 − 228 = 3 cookies.

Use a calculator to solve these problems. Show your operations with number sentences. Tell what the numbers to the left and to the right of the decimal point mean. Give whole number remainders with your answer.

7. The Happy Day Bakery made 542 muffins on Monday.

   A. If they package 2 dozen (24) muffins per box, how many full boxes of muffins did they package?

   B. How many muffins did not get packaged?

8. Penny and Pete's Pencil Company made 38,664 pencils. They packaged them in boxes of 144 pencils.

   A. How many full boxes can they package?

   B. How many pencils will be left over?

For Questions 1–4, estimate the size of each quotient. Use your calculator to find the answer to each division problem. Write each remainder as a whole number.

Example:
$$264.5 = 264 \text{ R}19$$
$$38 \overline{)10{,}051}$$

1. $44 \overline{)23{,}375}$ 2. $52 \overline{)150{,}000}$ 3. $39 \overline{)164{,}754}$ 4. $15 \overline{)8925}$

Use your calculator to solve the following problems. Write your remainder as a whole number.

5. David has collected 1385 different stamps. He wants to organize them in a book.

   A. If he puts 20 stamps on each page, how many full pages will he use?

   B. How many stamps will be left?

Calculator Strategies: Division

6. Irma is cutting ribbon for a craft project. Each piece must be 16 inches long. She has 508 inches of ribbon.

   A. How many 16-inch pieces can she cut?

   B. How many inches of ribbon will be left?

Use your calculator to solve these problems. Explain any remainders.

7. Mrs. Morgan is a civil engineer. Her job is to plan a bike path around the new park. She needs to decide how many lights she will need along the path. Mrs. Morgan knows that there must be a light every 120 feet. How many lights will she need if the path is 12 miles long? (*Hint:* There are 5280 feet in 1 mile.)

8. Crystal Clear window washers washed some large windows on a skyscraper for $3500. If they washed 56 windows on the skyscraper, how much did the company charge to wash each window?

9. Perky's Plentiful Peanuts purchased 28 pounds of peanuts from a proprietor for $46.76. How much did Perky's Plentiful Peanuts pay per pound of peanuts?

10. Perky's Plentiful Peanuts puts 24 peanuts in a package. Pat, the packer, packaged 1375 peanuts. She ate the leftover peanuts. How many peanuts did she eat?

Grass Act

Manny: I can't believe how long it took me to cut the grass in our yard Saturday. There must be a zillion blades of grass there.

Felicia: There's no such thing as a zillion.

Manny: I know. It's just a way of saying there's a whole lot. Still, I wonder how many blades of grass are in my yard? It would be really interesting to find out. I wonder how we can.

1. Think about how Manny and Felicia can estimate the number of blades of grass in the yard. Work with your group to develop a plan to solve this problem.

2. Record your group's plan. Use the Student Rubric: *Solving* to help you as you write your plan.

Unit 10

Maps and Coordinates

	Student Guide	Discovery Assignment Book	Adventure Book	Unit Resource Guide*
Lesson 1				
Negative Numbers	●			
Lesson 2				
Introducing Cartesian Coordinates	●			
Lesson 3				
Wherefore Art Thou, Romeo?			●	
Lesson 4				
Mr. Origin	●	●		●
Lesson 5				
Plotting Shapes	●			
Lesson 6				
These Boots Are Made for Sliding	●	●		
Lesson 7				
These Boots Are Made for Flipping	●	●		●
Lesson 8				
Reading a Map	●			●
Lesson 9				
Escher Drawings	●			

Unit Resource Guide pages are from the teacher materials.

Negative Numbers

Brrr, It's Cold Out There!

International Falls, Minnesota, is one of the coldest places in the country. On a winter night, the temperature might fall as quickly as one degree every 5 minutes. The thermometers shown begin to chart the falling temperature on such a night.

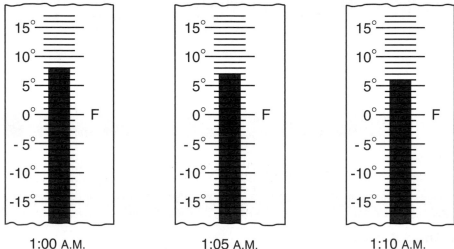

1:00 A.M.   1:05 A.M.   1:10 A.M.

Note: The F on the thermometer shows the temperature is measured using the Fahrenheit scale. That is the system usually used in the United States.

Discuss

1. What is the temperature at 1:00 A.M.?

2. What is the temperature at 1:05 A.M.?

3. If the temperature keeps falling one degree every 5 minutes, what will the temperature be at 1:15 A.M.?

As the temperature continues to fall, it will go below zero. Numbers less than zero are called **negative numbers.** To report a temperature two degrees below zero, we can say "two degrees below zero," or "negative two degrees," or "minus two degrees." We write this as "-2°F." Numbers greater than zero are called **positive numbers.** Two degrees above zero is a positive temperature. We write this as "2°F" or "+2°F." For our work with positive numbers, we will leave off the + sign.

4. Look at the thermometers above Question 1. Which numbers are positive? Which numbers are negative?

5. Make a table like the one below on your own paper. Record the temperature for five minute intervals, beginning at 1:00 A.M. and ending at 3:00 A.M.

International Falls

Time	Temperature
1:00 A.M.	8°F
1:05 A.M.	7°F
1:10 A.M.	6°F
1:15 A.M.	

6. How many degrees did the temperature fall between 1:00 A.M. and 3:00 A.M.?

7. How many degrees did the temperature fall between 1:45 A.M. and 2:15 A.M.?

8. If the temperature keeps falling at the same rate, what will the temperature be at 4:00 A.M.? How do you know?

9. By 10:00 A.M., the temperature had risen to 15°F. How much warmer is the temperature compared to 2:45 A.M.?

10. How much colder is it at 2:30 A.M. than it was at 1:30 A.M.?

11. The dog needed to be let outside at 1:10 A.M. He stayed outside until 1:50 A.M. How much did the temperature fall while the dog was outside?

12. If it is 10°F during the day and it falls to -10°F at night, how many degrees did it fall? (*Hint:* Use the picture of the thermometer.)

1. Professor Peabody visited International Falls during the winter. He took a plane from California to Minnesota. The temperature in California was 67°F when Professor Peabody left. The temperature in Minnesota was -12°F when he arrived. What is the difference in the temperatures?

2. Professor Peabody was at an altitude of 100 feet below sea level (-100 feet) in California. His altitude in Minnesota was 600 feet above sea level. How much did his altitude change?

3. Professor Peabody recorded the high and the low temperature each day while visiting International Falls. He recorded his data in a table.

	Monday	Tuesday	Wednesday	Thursday	Friday
High	11°F	4°F	1°F	8°F	14°F
Low	-5°F	-23°F	-14°F	-16°F	3°F

A. Find the difference between the high and the low temperature for each of the days.

B. Which day had the greatest change in temperature?

C. What was the highest and the lowest temperature during the week?

D. What was the change in temperature between the highest and the lowest temperature for the week?

4. Professor Peabody had $213.25 in his checking account when he went to Minnesota. He wrote checks for $45.50 for a tour, $122.75 for lodging, and $42.00 for food.

A. How much money did Professor Peabody have left in his account?

B. Professor Peabody wants to buy a souvenir to take home. The souvenir costs $9.00. Can he pay for the souvenir by check? Why or why not? What would his balance be if he wrote a check for $9.00?

5. When Professor Peabody left International Falls the temperature was -17°F. When he arrived in California, the temperature was 73°F. What was the change in temperature?

Introducing Cartesian Coordinates

The Great Barrier Reef

The Great Barrier Reef stretches along the eastern coast of Australia for 1240 miles. A **reef** is a ridge of rocks, sand, or coral in an ocean. Sometimes the reef is covered by water, and sometimes the top of the reef is above the surface and forms islands. The Great Barrier Reef covers an area about half the size of Texas. It is considered the world's largest living structure. For many thousands of years, 400 kinds of reef-building corals have added to the size of the reef. It is home to fish, worms, sea urchins, sea cucumbers, clams, snails, and many other animals.

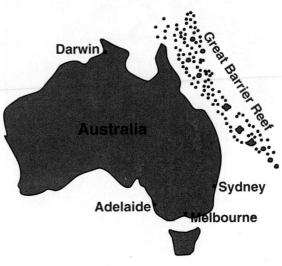

The Great Barrier Reef is not a solid wall. It is comprised of more than 2600 separate reefs and over 300 islands. Scientists from around the world come to Australia to study the Great Barrier Reef and the animals that make the reef their home. The people of Australia are very proud of their reef and take great care to protect it.

Exploring the Great Barrier Reef Using Cartesian Coordinates

The map on the next page shows one section of the reef. It is covered by a grid system known as **Cartesian coordinates.** This method of mapping was invented by the French philosopher and mathematician René Descartes in the 17th century. It is a very effective method of mapping. To identify the location of an object on a flat surface, we need a reference point, called the **origin,** and two straight lines that pass through the origin at right angles to each other. The lines are called the **axes.** The axes divide the surface into 4 parts called **quadrants.**

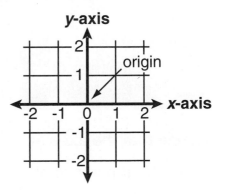

The map below shows one quadrant of the Cartesian coordinate system placed on top of a map.

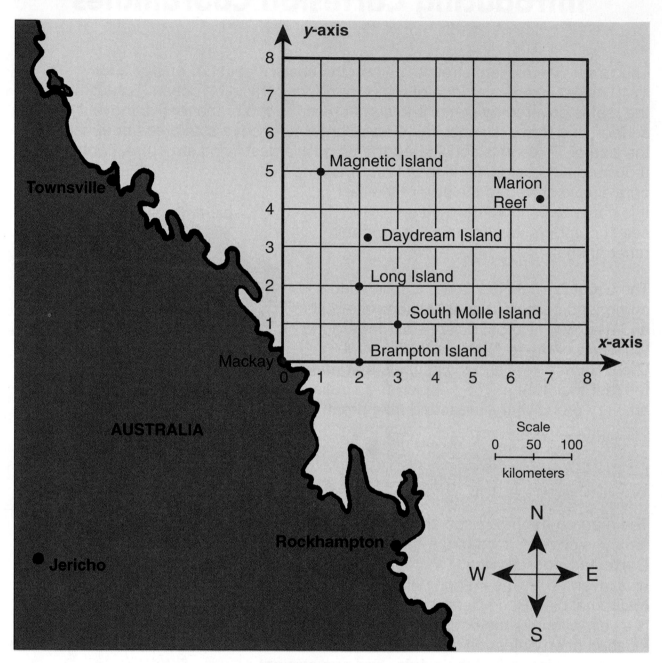

Notice that the axes are named using letters of the alphabet.

1. What name is given to the horizontal axis?

2. What name is given to the vertical axis?

Introducing Cartesian Coordinates

The letters *x* and *y* are used the world over to identify the axes of the Cartesian coordinates. On this map, the *x*-axis corresponds to east/west and the *y*-axis to north/south.

3. What is the point of **origin** on the map? In other words, what are the coordinates of the point where the horizontal and vertical axes meet?

4. What do the arrows at the end of the lines mean?

(1, 5) is an example of a location using the Cartesian coordinate system. The 1 tells you to move 1 space to the right (east). The 5 then tells you to move up 5 spaces (north).

5. What island is at location (1, 5) on the map?

Coordinates are always given by saying the *x*-coordinate first, then the *y*-coordinate. For the point (1, 5), the 1 is the *x*-coordinate and the 5 is the *y*-coordinate. (1, 5) is also called an **ordered pair.**

6. What are the coordinates for Long Island?

7. What is located near (2, 3)?

8. What is located at (0, 0)?

9. What are the coordinates for Brampton Island?

10. What is located near (7, 4)?

Find Mackay on the map. Mackay is a city on the eastern coast of Australia. Rockhampton is another city on the coast of Australia. How would you describe Rockhampton's location to someone?

We can expand our coordinate system to include Rockhampton by extending the *x*- and *y*-axes in both directions from (0, 0). By using negative as well as positive numbers, any point can be named in relation to the origin.

The first coordinate of an ordered pair tells us how much to move horizontally (right or left) starting at the origin. The second coordinate tells us how to move vertically (up or down).

Some examples of ordered pairs and their locations are given here.

The ♥ is at (2, 3).

The ★ is at (4, -2).

Point A is at (-3, 5).

Point B is at (-2, -5).

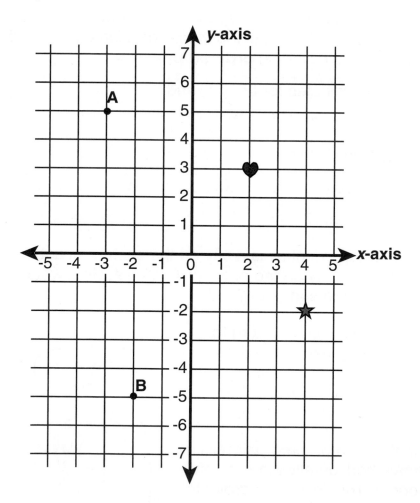

Name the point at the given coordinates on the following grid.

11. (4, 1)

12. (-2, 0)

13. (-3, -4)

14. (0, -2)

Give the coordinates of the following points.

15. E

16. B

17. C

18. H

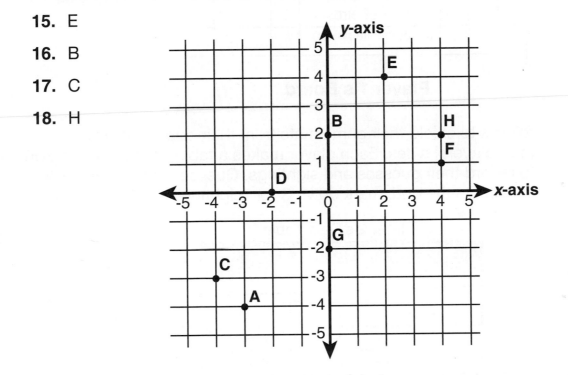

The *Barrier Reef* Game

Players

This is a game for 2 players and a moderator.

Materials

- a sheet of *Four-Quadrant Grid Paper*
- paper for making table

Rules

On a sheet of *Four-Quadrant Grid Paper*, each player "hides" a pod of whales, a shipwreck, migrating turtles, and a flock of birds. An example of the ways to place them on a grid is shown on the following page. Each can be placed either horizontally or vertically.

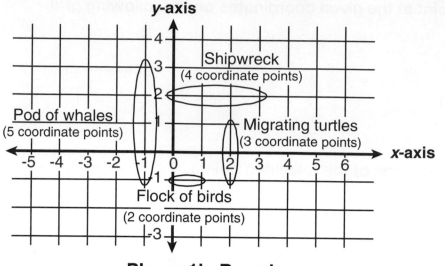

Player 1's Board

Players can use folders to shield their game mats from their opponent. The moderator sits at the players' sides. Each player makes a table like the one shown below on which to record their guesses and sightings. Guesses are also recorded on the game mat itself. On the grid, mark down S for "sighting" and M for "miss."

Player 2's Data Table

X	Y	Sighting?
-1	0	whales
-1	1	whales
-1	-1	whales
-1	2	whales
-1	3	whales
4	-1	miss

The first player begins by naming an ordered pair and recording it in his or her data table. The second player says either "sighting" and the type of object that has been sighted (if there is an object at those coordinates) or "miss" (if there is no object). For example, say the game board shown here belongs to Player 1. If Player 2 guesses (-1, 0), then Player 1 must say "sighting, a pod of whales." Player 2 should record the coordinates in the table and write "whales" in the sighting column. If the first player records a sighting, his or her turn continues. If not, it becomes the second player's turn. The moderator keeps the game fair. The first player to correctly identify all the coordinates of all of the opponent's objects wins the game.

Historical Note—The Invention of Coordinates

The notion of using coordinates to locate objects was invented by the French philosopher and mathematician, René Descartes. Here is a story that has been told about how he got that idea. Historians are not sure that this story is true, but parts of it are.

Descartes was in the habit of lying in bed in the morning and thinking.

He was working on a problem about how to say where an object is located. The ceiling of his room was covered with square tiles, and a fly was walking around on the ceiling.

He suddenly realized that he could say where the fly was at any time by choosing an origin, and telling how many ceiling tiles the fly was to the right or left and above or below the origin.

On your own paper, make a table like the one shown. Give the coordinates of the objects listed. Then write the coordinates as an ordered pair.

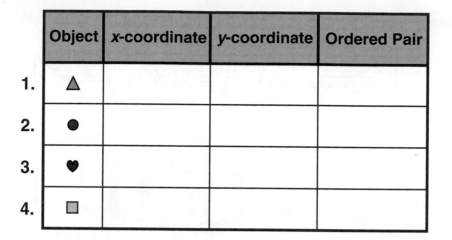

	Object	x-coordinate	y-coordinate	Ordered Pair
1.	△			
2.	●			
3.	♥			
4.	▢			

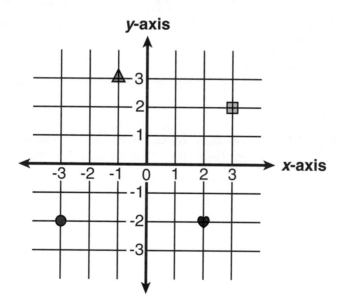

Use *Four-Quadrant Grid Paper*, or draw the *x*- and *y*-axes on *Centimeter Grid Paper*. Mark the following points on the coordinate system.

5. A at (1, 3)

6. B at (-5, 2)

7. C at (0, -1)

8. D at (-1, -1)

9. E at (4, 0)

10. F at (-3, -2)

11. G at (4, -2)

12. H at (0, 0)

Mr. Origin

Mr. Moreno's class uses the plastic figure **Mr. Origin** to help make coordinate maps. The **origin** is another name for the point (0, 0) on a coordinate graph. Mr. Origin helps keep track of directions when making a map.

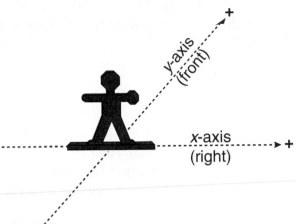

The imaginary line running from left to right through Mr. Origin is called the *x*-axis or the left-right axis. Mr. Origin's right hand is shown with an octagon. It points to the positive part of the *x*-axis. The line running from back to front through Mr. Origin is called the *y*-axis or the front-back axis. The positive *y*-axis is always in front of Mr. Origin. His front is the side with the button. In this picture, Mr. Origin's back is to us.

One way to describe the location of an object relative to Mr. Origin is to use directions (left or right, front or back) and distances. For example, Shannon placed Mr. Origin in the center of her class. She said that the center of the teacher's desk was 200 centimeters to the left and 150 centimeters behind Mr. Origin.

Instead of using directions like left and right, mathematicians and scientists use positive and negative numbers. They have agreed that on the *x*-axis, right is positive and left is negative. On the *y*-axis front (or forward) is positive and back is negative.

Shannon translated her work into scientific language. She said that the *x*-coordinate of the teacher's desk was -200 centimeters and the *y*-coordinate was -150 centimeters.

Finding Coordinates Relative to Mr. Origin

- You and your classmates will use Mr. Origin to help make a map of your classroom or your playground. First, place Mr. Origin somewhere in the area to be mapped. Your teacher may have placed Mr. Origin for you.
- The class or your teacher will choose some objects in the classroom to be mapped. Each object should be labeled with a letter of the alphabet.

1. Work with your group to find the coordinates of each object. Measure to the center of each object. Record your data in a table like the one at the right. Measure to the nearest centimeter.

Object	*x*-coordinate in cm	*y*-coordinate in cm
A.		
B.		
C.		
D.		
E.		
F.		

Making a Map

- You will need a sheet of *Centimeter Grid Paper* to make your map. Look at your data points. Decide where you need to draw the coordinate axes so that all the points will fit. Label the *x*-axis and the *y*-axis. Look at your data points and decide what scale you should use.
- Discuss with your group how to number the axes on your map.
- Decide on the scale for your map.

2. Plot the points from your data table on your map.

Explore

3. Use the map and the scale to predict the distance from object A to object B in your classroom. Record your predicted distance. Explain how you found your answer.

4. **A.** Measure the distance from object A to object B in your classroom and record the distance.

   B. Find the difference between your predicted distance and the distance you measured. This is called the error.

   C. Was your prediction close?

   D. Is the error less than 10% of the measured distance?

5. Here is a map of a playground:

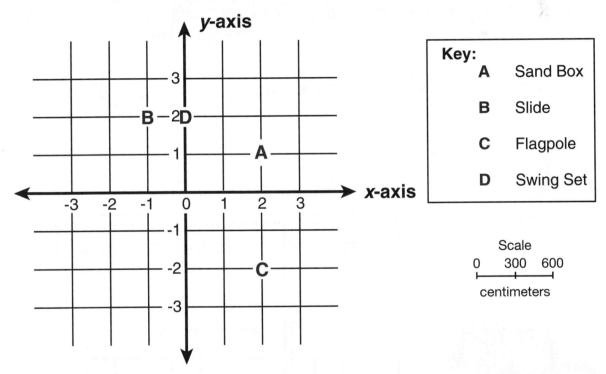

One centimeter on the map represents 300 cm in the classroom.

   A. Estimate the distance from the flagpole to the slide (in centimeters) on the map.

   B. Using your ruler, find the distance from the flagpole to the slide on the map.

   C. Predict the distance from the flagpole to the slide in the playground. Explain your strategy.

Plotting Shapes

Just give us your coordinates and we'll do the rest!

José likes to help out at The Great Shapes Factory. When José receives an order, he uses his computer to plot the points listed on the order. He then connects the dots in the order listed to make a shape.

Here is an order José filled:

Shape Order

(3, 2)

(4, 5)

(6, -2)

José marked the points.

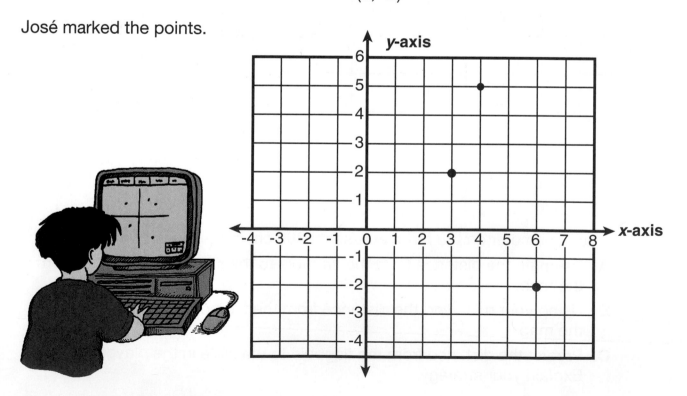

Then José connected the points in the order in which they were given. He connected the last point to the first point.

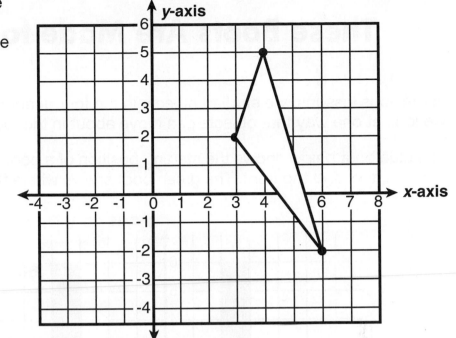

On *Four-Quadrant Grid Paper,* fill the following shape orders. Make sure you connect the points in order. Connect the last dot to the first dot. Then describe the shape you made.

1. (1, 2), (3, 5), (7, 1)   **2.** (-2, -3), (-2, 2), (5, 4), (5, -1)

3. (-1, 6), (4, 3), (1, -3), (-6, -2), (-5, 3)

José was given the title of Master Shape Maker. José gets many difficult projects. See if you can make the shape for this problem and become José's assistant. Use a sheet of *Half-Centimeter Graph Paper* as the first quadrant. Place (0, 0) in the lower left corner and label the axes.

4. A. (7, 11), (7, 18), (8, 20), (8, 23), (10, 26), (14, 23), (20, 22), (23, 24), (24, 22), (24, 19), (25, 18), (25, 14), (24, 9), (22, 7), (12, 7)

Draw the decorations on the shape you made in Part A separately:

B. Decoration 1: (10, 20), (12, 18), (14, 20)

C. Decoration 2: (17, 20), (19, 19), (21, 20)

D. Decoration 3: (16, 17), (15, 16), (16, 14)

5. Draw a shape on *Half-Centimeter Graph Paper* whose vertices are ordered pairs. Label the points with the ordered pairs. Then write down the ordered pairs in order on another sheet of paper. Give the coordinates to a friend, and see if he or she can graph your shape.

These Boots Are Made for Sliding

Sliding Along

In previous lessons, we studied objects in the four quadrants. In this lesson, we look at one way that objects can move about in the four quadrants.

The blue boot below shows the starting position of a boot. There are dots drawn on the heel, toe, and top front. The green boot shows where the boot is after one slide.

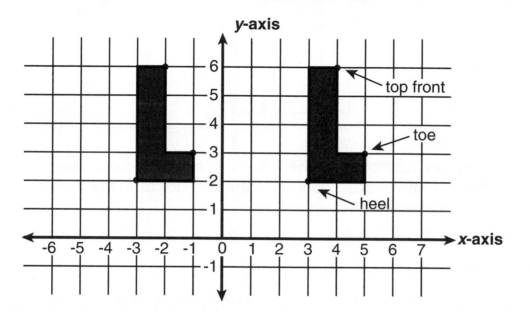

1. What are the coordinates of the old heel?

2. What are the coordinates of the new heel?

3. How did the coordinates of the heel change?

4. What are the coordinates of the old toe?

5. What are the coordinates of the new toe?

6. How did the coordinates of the toe change?

7. How do you think the coordinates of the top front changed? Check your idea by finding the new and old coordinates of the top front.

The purple triangle shows where the triangle starts. The red triangle shows where the triangle is after one slide.

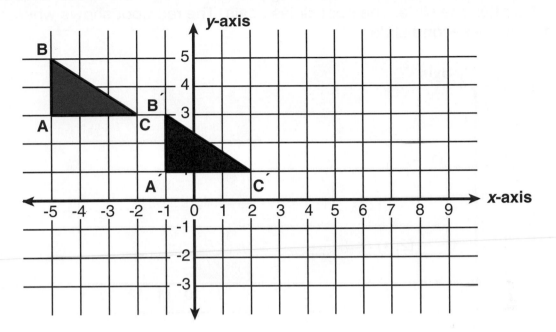

8. Describe how the triangle moved.

9. How did the *x*-coordinates change?

10. How did the *y*-coordinates change?

When all the points of an object move the same distance in the same direction, the movement is called a **slide.** Triangle A′B′C′ (read A prime, B prime, C prime), the new shape, is called the **image** of triangle ABC. Matching parts of the shape such as Sides AB and A′B′ are **corresponding parts.** Vertex A and Vertex A′ are corresponding parts too.

11. Name four more pairs of corresponding parts (sides or vertices).

Patterns with Slides

The orange boot below shows the starting position. The yellow boot shows where the boot is after one slide. The boot slides again. The red boot shows where the boot is after the second slide.

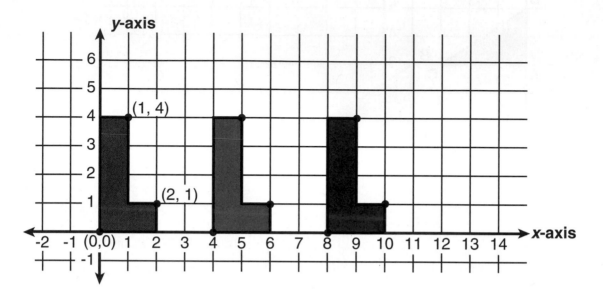

12. Describe how this boot moved.

13. Imagine that the boot follows the same pattern for each slide. Use a *Four-column Data Table* to complete the table.

Slide	Heel Coordinates	Toe Coordinates	Top Front Coordinates
0	(0, 0)	(2, 1)	(1, 4)
1	?	?	(5, 4)
2	?	(10, 1)	?
3	(12, 0)	?	?
4	?	(18, 1)	?
10	?	?	(41, 4)

14. Explain what you did to find the answers in the table.

15. If the heel is at (64, 0), then how many slides has the boot made?

16. In this question, we will study a different boot and a different slide. Use the first row (Slide 0) of the chart to draw the boot on a piece of *Four-Quadrant Grid Paper.* Shade this boot.

Slide	Heel Coordinates	Toe Coordinates	Top Front Coordinates
0	(5, 3)	(7, 4)	(6, 7)
1	(2, 1)	(4, 2)	(3, 5)
2	?	?	?
3	?	?	?
4	?	?	?
5	?	?	?
10	?	?	?

17. Use the second row of the chart in Question 16 to draw the new boot.

18. Fill in the rest of the chart in Question 16.

19. Explain how the boot in Question 16 slides.

Homework

For each shape on the following grid, describe the slide needed to move the purple figure onto its image, the pink figure. How many units to the right or left and up or down is the slide?

1. Parallelogram
2. Triangle
3. Pentagon
4. Rectangle

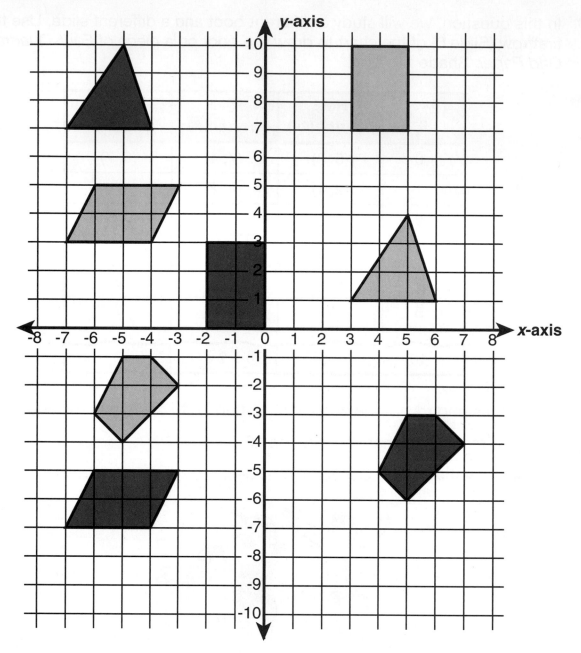

Do Questions 5–7 on *Four-Quadrant Grid Paper*.

5. Draw the triangle that has vertices at (1, 2), (-3, 2), and (0, 4). Slide the triangle four units to the right. Draw the new triangle and label the vertices.

6. Draw the rectangle with vertices at (4, -2), (7, -2), (7, 3), and (4, 3). Slide the rectangle up (forward) 5 units. Draw the new rectangle and label the vertices.

7. Draw the square with vertices at (-4, -5), (-2, -5), (-2, -3), and (-4, -3). Slide the square 4 units up (forward) and 3 units right. Draw the new square and label the vertices.

These Boots Are Made for Flipping

1. Trace and cut out a boot from graph paper that is like the blue boot. Shade in the boot and place it on top of the blue boot here.

2. Can you slide your boot, without lifting the boot off the paper, onto the green boot? Why or why not?

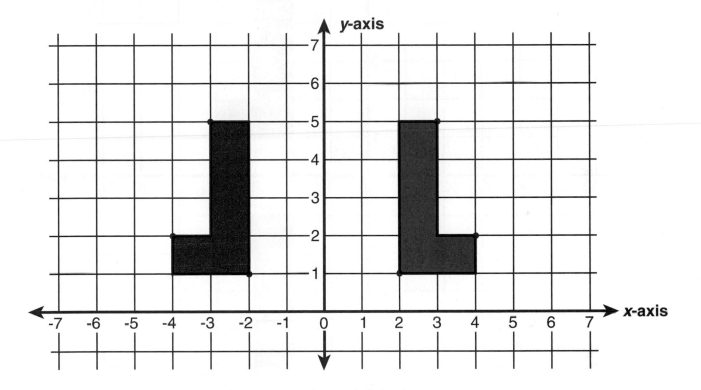

To move the blue boot onto the green boot in one move, we have to **flip** the blue boot over a line. That line is called the **line of reflection.**

3. Where is the line of reflection in the picture?

4. Make a table like the one below and complete it.

Boot	Heel Coordinates	Toe Coordinates	Top Front Coordinates
Blue Boot	?	?	?
Green Boot	?	?	?

5. Explain how the x-coordinates changed in Question 4.

6. Explain how the y-coordinates changed in Question 4.

Here is another flip.

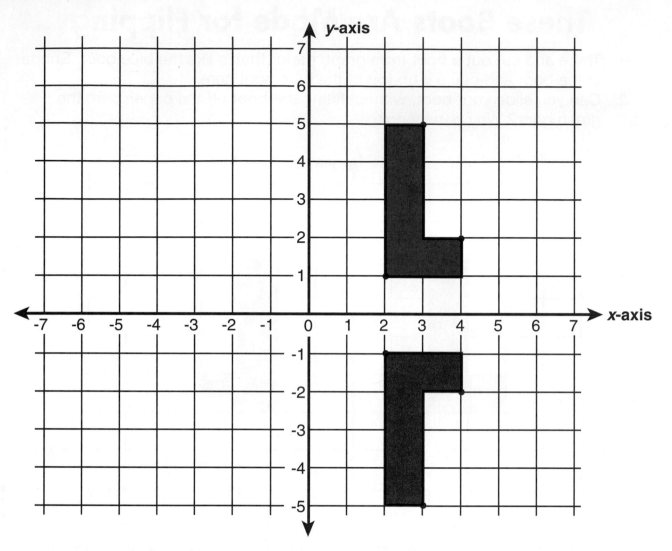

7. Where is the line of reflection in the picture?

8. Make a table like the one below and complete it.

Boot	Heel Coordinates	Toe Coordinates	Top Front Coordinates
Blue Boot	?	?	?
Green Boot	?	?	?

9. Explain how the *x*-coordinates changed in Question 8.

10. Explain how the *y*-coordinates changed in Question 8.

11. Which of the following pairs are flips over the *y*-axis?

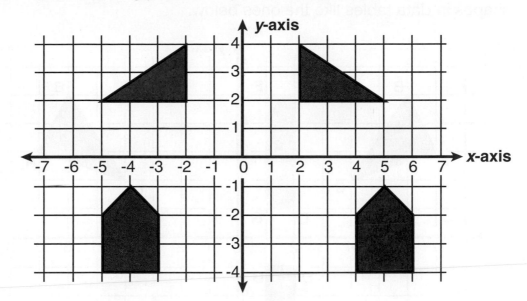

12. Which of the following are flips over the *x*-axis?

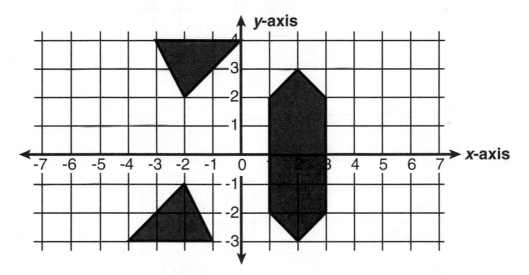

13. There are two pairs of flips shown. Record the coordinates of each of the shapes in data tables like the ones below.

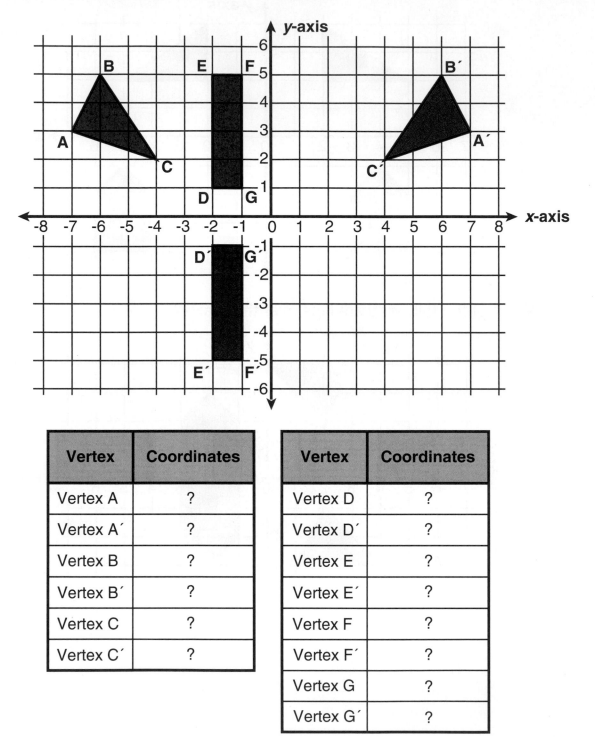

Vertex	Coordinates
Vertex A	?
Vertex A´	?
Vertex B	?
Vertex B´	?
Vertex C	?
Vertex C´	?

Vertex	Coordinates
Vertex D	?
Vertex D´	?
Vertex E	?
Vertex E´	?
Vertex F	?
Vertex F´	?
Vertex G	?
Vertex G´	?

14. What happens to the coordinates when a shape is flipped over the x-axis?

15. What happens to the coordinates when a shape is flipped over the y-axis?

For each matching shape on the next page, tell how you need to move the purple shape to lie exactly on its image, the pink figure. Some shapes need slides. Other shapes need flips.

Example: Triangle ABC to triangle A′B′C′. A slide, 4 units up.

1. Triangle DEF to triangle D′E′F′.

2. Quadrilateral GHIJ to quadrilateral G′H′I′J′.

3. Triangle KLM to triangle K′L′M′.

4. Quadrilateral NOPQ to N′O′P′Q′.

5. The purple arrow to the pink arrow.

6. The purple house to the pink house.

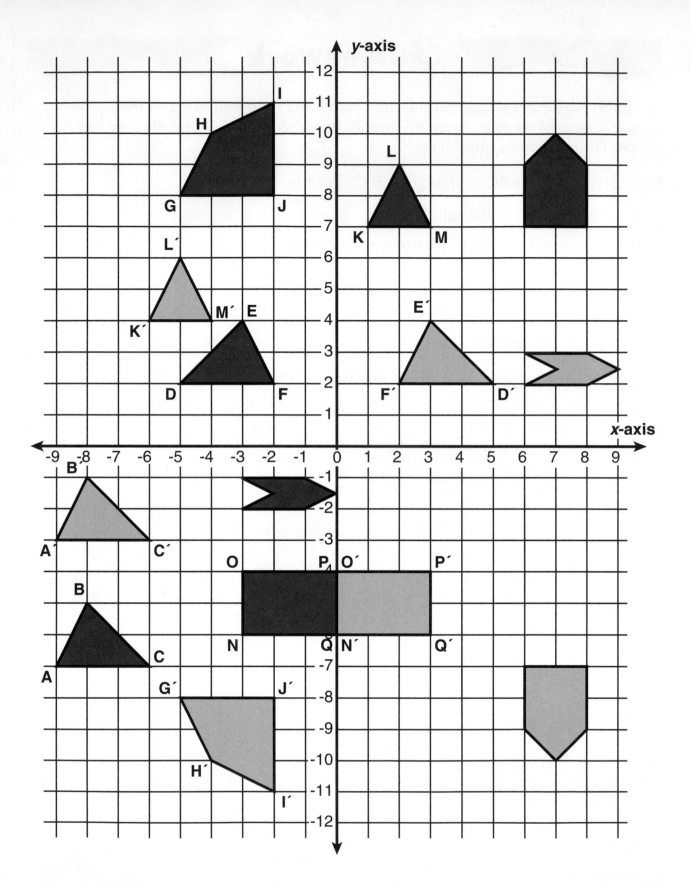

These Boots Are Made for Flipping

Reading a Map

Suzanne is a big fan of Carlton Fisk, the great catcher who played with both the Boston Red Sox and the Chicago White Sox. When she traveled with her family, she looked for places that might have "Fisk" in the name. One summer, her family was planning a trip to Alabama. She looked in an atlas at a list of the names of towns and found that there was indeed a Fisk, Alabama. Next, she looked at a map.

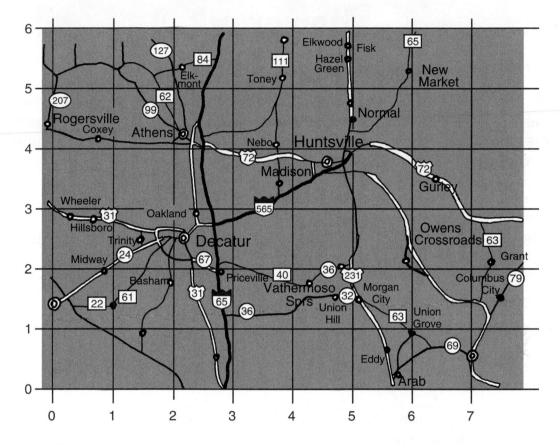

Suzanne had a very difficult time locating Fisk. If you were with her, how might you help her? What do you know about the way maps and atlases work that would aid in finding Fisk?

Suzanne's mother pointed out that it is possible to use the numbers on the map in the same way Suzanne had used a coordinate system in school. When Suzanne looked up Fisk again in the atlas, she paid attention to the ordered pairs following the name. She found (5, 6). Suzanne also learned that a lot of maps use a combination of letters and numbers as a coordinate system. On another map, for example, Fisk might be named as (E, 6).

1. Use this information to find Fisk on the map. Is Fisk at exactly (5, 6)? What are the coordinates designed to do?

Use the map to answer the following questions.

2. What town is located at about (3, 2)?

3. Look at the four ordered pairs (1, 2), (1, 3), (2, 2), and (2, 3). What town is located almost in the center of all the points?

Using a Map to Find Distances

The map of north central Alabama on the previous page has a scale in which 1 centimeter represents 10 miles. Use the ordered pairs below to help you locate the towns and solve the distance problems. You will need your ruler. Measure distances "as the crow flies."

Athens (2, 4)   Elkmont (2, 5)   Grant (7, 2)
New Market (6, 5)   Owens Crossroads (6, 2)   Priceville (3, 2)
Toney (4, 5)   Union Grove (6, 1)   Morgan City (5, 1)

1. About how far is it from Morgan City to Grant?

2. About how far is it from Union Grove to Toney?

3. About how far is it from Priceville to New Market?

4. Suppose you traveled from Grant to New Market to Elkmont. How many miles would you have gone?

5. If you wanted to travel to all the towns listed above without zig-zagging across the region, in what order might you travel? How many miles would you cover? Think about the shortest route possible. Plan to share your proposed route with the class.

Escher Drawings

M.C. Escher was a Dutch artist who used many mathematical ideas to create his works. Escher was born in 1898 and died in 1972. Escher often began with a tessellating shape, such as a square or a hexagon. He changed these shapes so that they looked like other objects, such as animals. The changes were made so that the final shape also tessellated. Escher then used slides and turns, along with interesting details on the shapes, to create his art.

This picture at the right is called *Symmetry Drawing with Pegasus.*

1. Describe the horses you see in the picture.

2. Describe the slides you see in the picture.

Below is another Escher drawing called *Symmetry Drawing with Fish.*

M.C. Escher's Symmetry Drawings © 1996 Cordon Art-Baarn-Holland.

3. Describe the fish you see in the picture.

4. Describe the slides you see in the picture.

5. Look at the direction the pink fish are swimming and the direction the red fish are swimming. Do you see a difference?

6. Compare the two pictures. What is the same about them? What is different about them?

M.C. Escher's Symmetry Drawings © 1996 Cordon Art-Baarn-Holland.

Unit 11

Number Patterns, Primes, and Fractions

	Student Guide	Discovery Assignment Book	Adventure Book	Unit Resource Guide*
Lesson 1				
Factor 40	●	●		
Lesson 2				
Sifting for Primes	●	●		
Lesson 3				
Patterns with Square Numbers	●			
Lesson 4				
Finding Prime Factors	●	●		
Lesson 5				
Comparing Fractions	●			
Lesson 6				
Reducing Fractions	●			●
Lesson 7				
A Further Look at Patterns and Primes				●
Lesson 8				
From Factors to Fractions	●			

Unit Resource Guide pages are from the teacher materials.

Factor 40

This is a game about factors. Remember, the **factors** of a number are the whole numbers that can be multiplied together to get the number. For example, 3 and 4 are factors of 12 since $3 \times 4 = 12$. All the factors of 12 are 1, 2, 3, 4, 6, and 12.

Players

This is a game for two players. (Manny and Brandon in this example.)

Materials

one *Factor 40 Game Board* from the *Discovery Assignment Book*

Rules

Each player selects either an X or an O as a symbol to record his or her moves on the game board. The object of the game is to earn points by marking factors of numbers.

- Player A (Brandon) chooses a number on the *Factor 40 Game Board* and marks the square containing that number with his or her symbol (X or O). Player A records this number as his or her score for this turn.

I marked 14 with an X so 14 is my score for this turn.

- Player B (Manny) finds and circles all of the remaining factors of Player A's number. Then Player B selects another number as his or her turn. Player B adds up all of the numbers he or she has marked and records a score. (Note: Each player gets points two ways—points for the factors of the other player's number and points for the number he or she chooses.)

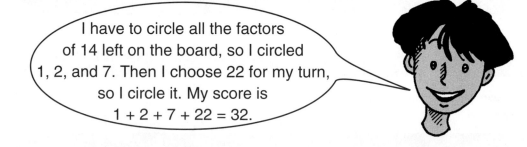

I have to circle all the factors of 14 left on the board, so I circled 1, 2, and 7. Then I choose 22 for my turn, so I circle it. My score is $1 + 2 + 7 + 22 = 32$.

- A number can be used only once.
- If a player chooses a number that has no available factors, this is considered an illegal move. He or she earns no points. The game resumes with the opponent choosing a number.
- Play continues until there are no more legal moves. Players add up their points. The player with the most points wins the game.

Here is what Brandon's and Manny's game board looks like so far. Remember, Brandon is Player A and Manny is Player B.

Play the game twice with a partner.

Discuss

1. While playing the game a second time, think about the moves you and your partner make. Were you more successful in the second game? Describe any strategies you used or things you learned while playing the second time around.

After Manny and Brandon finished their second game of *Factor 40,* Brandon began thinking about the moves that he made during the game. He realized that sometimes when he chose a number to mark, Manny actually got more points on his next turn. This was because the sum of the factors was sometimes greater than the number chosen. For example, in the second game Brandon marked 24 for his first move. Manny was then able to circle 1, 2, 3, 4, 6, 8, and 12. Brandon only got 24 points, while Manny scored 36 before he chose his own number!

①	②	③	④	5	⑥	7	⑧
9	10	11	⑫	13	14	15	16
17	18	19	20	21	22	23	⨉24

Brandon decided to make a chart showing all of the factors for the numbers 1 through 40. He wanted to use the chart to find the best first move for the game.

Factor Chart

Possible First Choice for Player A	Factors	Points from Factors for Player B (first move)
1	1	0
2	1, 2	1
3	1, 3	1
4	1, 2, 4	$1 + 2 = 3$
5	1, 5	1
6	1, 2, 3, 6	$1 + 2 + 3 = 6$
7	1, 7	
8		

2. **A.** Copy Brandon's chart on your paper. Fill in the first column with the numbers 1 to 40.

   B. Complete the second column of the chart for all the numbers from 1 to 40. Be prepared to describe the strategies you used.

   C. Complete the third column of the chart. Find how many points Player B will get for each number Player A might choose on the first move.

3. **A.** Look at your chart. Make a list of all the first moves that give Player A more points than Player B. (Remember, Player B's score will also be determined by the number he or she chooses. We are comparing Player A's points with Player B's points *before* Player B chooses his or her number.)

   B. Make a list of all of the moves that will give Player B more points than Player A (if Player B marks all of the factors of Player A's number left on the board).

C. Make a list of all of the moves that will give Player A the same number of points as Player B (if he marks them all).

4. **A.** No matter which number Player A chooses on his or her first move, which factor will Player B definitely mark on his or her first turn?

   B. It is illegal to mark a number that does not have any available factors. After Player B's first turn, which numbers are illegal moves?

5. A **prime number** is defined as a number with exactly two factors—1 and itself. Make a list of all of the prime numbers from 1 to 40. Compare this list with the list you made in Question 4B. What do you notice about the two lists?

6. A **composite number** is a number with more than 2 distinct (or different) factors. Which are the composite numbers on your chart?

> Since the number 1 doesn't have 2 distinct factors, it is not considered prime or composite.

7. Use your lists and what you have learned as you play another game of *Factor 40.* See if your lists help you as you choose your moves.

Complete the following questions. You can use a calculator to help you find factors.

1. Irma and Jackie are playing *Factor 40* in class. Jackie is the first player. She chooses 27 as her first number.

   A. What are the factors of 27 that Irma can mark?

   B. How many points will Irma earn for these factors?

2. Felicia and Jessie designed a *Factor 100* game board. *Factor 100* has the same rules as *Factor 40*. It includes the numbers 1 to 100. Felicia is the first player. She chooses 40 as her first number.

   A. What are the factors of 40 that Jessie can mark?

   B. How many points will Jessie earn for these factors?

3. Romesh and David are playing *Factor 100*. David is the first player. He chooses 76 as his first move.

   A. What factors of 76 can Romesh mark?

   B. How many points will Romesh earn for these factors?

4. Nicholas and Michael are playing *Factor 100*. Nicholas is the first player. He wants to choose either 84 or 92 as his first move.

   A. Find the factors of both 84 and 92.

   B. Which number is a better move for Nicholas?

   C. Explain your answer.

5. Edward and Nila are playing *Factor 100*. Nila is the first player. She chooses 72 as her first move. Edward marks 1, 2, 3, 8, 9, and 24. He recorded 47 points.

   A. Did Edward mark all the possible factors of 72? If not, what other numbers could he mark?

   B. If Edward marks all the factors he can, how many points will he earn?

6. List all the factors of the following numbers.

   A. 31

   B. 56

   C. 63

   D. 67

   E. 100

7. Which of the numbers in Question 6 are prime? How do you know?

8. Which of the numbers in Question 6 are composite? How do you know?

Sifting for Primes

Discuss

"Okay, it's time to get started on your reports for mathematics class. Get into your groups. If you need any help getting started, let me know," said Mr. Moreno, as he cleared the center table in the classroom.

Michael, Ana, Nila, Lin, and John pulled out their notes and got right to work on their topic, prime numbers. Ana said, "I found some great information on a famous Greek mathematician named Eratosthenes."

"Era . . . who?" asked Lin.

"You pronounce his name 'Air - uh - tahs - thuh - neez,' " replied Mr. Moreno.

Ana continued, "He was a librarian in Alexandria, Egypt. In about 240 BCE, he found a way to determine prime numbers. They call his process The Sieve of Eratosthenes."

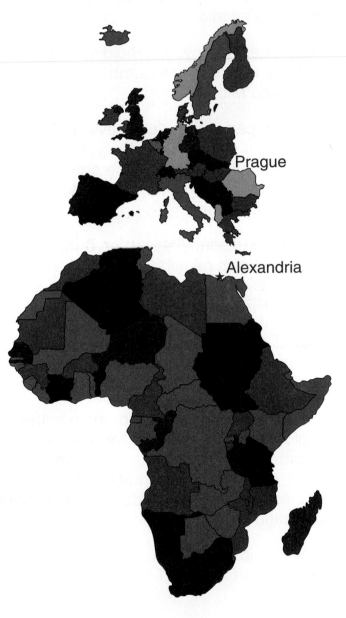

Prague

Alexandria

"This book says that Eratosthenes had etched a list of consecutive numbers on a table made on a metal plate. He considered each number one by one and marked each of its multiples with a small hole. The numbers that were not marked in this way were the prime numbers. In the end, it resembled a sieve. Since it was used to separate prime numbers from nonprime numbers, it got the name **The Sieve of Eratosthenes.** He presented this table to a king in Egypt."

Nila added to the discussion. "I found out that in the mid-1800s, an astronomer named J.P. Kulik used the Sieve of Eratosthenes to find the prime numbers up to 100,000,000. He spent 20 years of his life doing this."

"I can't believe anyone would spend 20 years finding prime numbers!" exclaimed Michael.

"The sad part is that Kulik gave his manuscript to a library in Prague. They lost the sections that had the prime numbers from 12,642,000 to 22,852,800," added Mr. Moreno.

"I also found some interesting data," said John. "I found out that in 1742 a Russian mathematician named Christian Goldbach made a conjecture that every even number except 2 can be written as a sum of two prime numbers. For example, $10 = 3 + 7$."

"Right," said Mr. Moreno, "and it is called a **conjecture** because up to now no one has been able to prove or disprove it. Who knows, maybe someday one of you will be the person to do this!"

"I found a modern use for prime numbers," said Lin. "Prime numbers are used in cryptography. **Cryptography** is the study of secret codes. Some codes are based on factoring numbers with 100 or more digits into prime factors. One use of these codes is to protect information stored on computers. Many banks and other businesses use these codes to make sure that nobody can change or steal the information from their computers."

"Wow," said Michael, "with all of this information we should be able to write a great report for class. Let's get started."

You can use the Sieve of Eratosthenes to find all of the prime numbers between 1 and 100. Use the *200 Chart* Activity Page in the *Discovery Assignment Book*.

1. Begin by crossing out the number 1. (Remember, 1 is not a prime.)

2. **A.** The next number is 2. This is the first prime number. Circle the number 2. Cross out all of the multiples of 2 up to 100.

   B. Why can't any of the numbers you crossed out be prime?

3. **A.** Find the next number that is not circled or crossed out. What number is it?

   B. Is this a prime number?

   C. Circle this number. Cross out all of the multiples of this number up to 100.

   D. Why can't these numbers be prime?

4. Continue the steps in Question 3 until you have only prime numbers left on your chart. List all the prime numbers from 1 to 100.

5. **A.** As you made your chart, what patterns did you see?

   B. What digits do prime numbers end in?

   C. Are prime numbers ever next to each other?

   D. **Twin primes** are pairs of prime numbers that are separated by only one number. For example, 5 and 7 are twin primes. Can you find any other twin primes?

Continue your investigation of prime numbers by finding all the prime numbers between 1 and 200.

Patterns with Square Numbers

1. Use tiles to build squares of different sizes, as shown, up to at least a 10 × 10 square. As you build each square, record the data in a table like the one shown below.

1 × 1 square

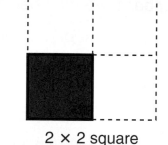

2 × 2 square

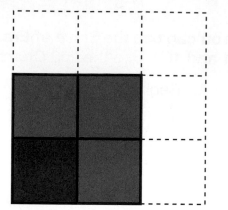

3 × 3 square

N Number of Tiles on Each Side of Square	A Number of Tiles Added	T Total Number of Tiles
1	1	1
2	3	4
3	5	
4		
5		

2. Graph your data. Write N, the number of tiles on each side of a square, on the horizontal axis. Write T, the total number of tiles, on the vertical axis.
   - If your points lie on a straight line, draw the line.
   - If your points do not lie on a straight line, draw a curve that goes through all the points.

3. Look at your data table. Describe any patterns you see.
   - Look down the columns.
   - Look across the rows. Look from one row to the next.
   - Try to find patterns that use addition, subtraction, multiplication, or division.

4. How can you get the next value of *T* without counting all the tiles? Give more than one way. Use your patterns from Question 3 to help you.

5. Write a number sentence using *N* and *T* that tells how to find the total number of tiles without counting. This kind of number sentence is called a **formula.**

6. A. To build a 5 × 5 square from a 4 × 4 square, you added a band of 5 + 5 − 1 = 9 new tiles, as in the picture. Five tiles were along the top and five were along the side. The corner tile is counted twice this way, so we subtract 1 to get 5 + 5 − 1 = 9 tiles in the band. Using the same pattern, how big is the band of new tiles you need to add to a 10 × 10 square to build an 11 × 11 square? Draw a picture to go with your answer.

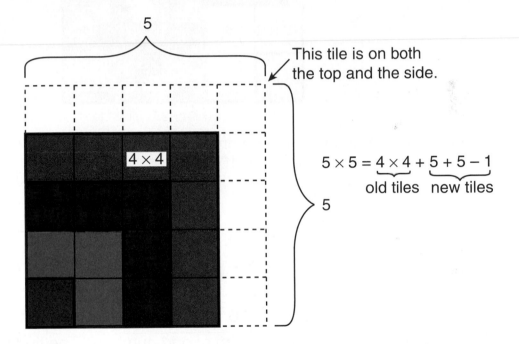

This tile is on both the top and the side.

$5 \times 5 = \underbrace{4 \times 4}_{\text{old tiles}} + \underbrace{5 + 5 - 1}_{\text{new tiles}}$

B. Write a formula that tells how to find the number of tiles added using *A* and *N*.

C. Use your answer to Part A and the fact that 10 × 10 = 100 to find 11 × 11.

D. Use the fact that 15 × 15 = 225 to find 16 × 16. Draw a picture to go with your answer.

E. Use the fact that 25 × 25 = 625 to find 26 × 26.

F. How much is 30 × 30? Use this to compute 31 × 31.

Challenge Questions

7. **A.** On a piece of grid paper, draw a picture like this—up to at least 10 × 10. Write the size of the square inside before drawing the next larger one, as shown here.

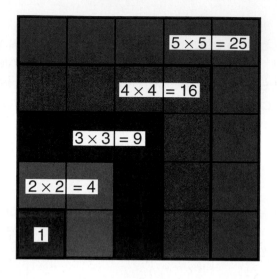

$5 \times 5 = 25$

$4 \times 4 = 16$

$3 \times 3 = 9$

$2 \times 2 = 4$

1

B. Look back at the picture you drew in Question 7A. Use it to help you complete the following up to 10 × 10:

$$1^2 = 1 \times 1 = 1 = 1$$
$$2^2 = 2 \times 2 = 1 + 3 = 4$$
$$3^2 = 3 \times 3 = 1 + 3 + 5 = 9$$
$$4^2 = 4 \times 4 = 1 + 3 + 5 + 7 = 16$$
$$5^2 = 5 \times 5 = 1 + 3 + 5 + 7 + 9 = 25$$
$$6^2 = 6 \times 6 = 1 + 3 + 5 + 7 + 9 + 11 = ?$$

C. Every square number is the sum of odd numbers. The first number in the sum is 1. Do you see a pattern that lets you know what the last number in the sum is? Describe the pattern.

D. Use the pattern from Part C to write 14^2 as the sum of odd numbers.

E. Use this pattern to write 50^2 as the sum of odd numbers. What is the last number in the sum?

8. If you add odd numbers in order, starting with 1, you will always get a square number. Look for a pattern in your list from Question 7B. Describe that pattern, then use it to:

   A. Find the sum of the odd numbers from 1 to 19.

   B. Find the sum of the odd numbers from 1 to 25.

   C. Find the sum of the odd numbers from 1 to 99.

Patterns with Square Numbers

Finding Prime Factors

Mr. Moreno challenged his class to find different ways to name 144 as a product of smaller numbers.

Find different ways to write 144 as a product of smaller numbers.

"I found that one way to factor 144 is to use two factors such as 2×72 or 4×36," shared Romesh.

1. Write 144 as a product of two factors in as many ways as you can.

"You can also write 144 as the product of more than two factors, such as $2 \times 2 \times 36$ or $2 \times 3 \times 4 \times 6$," added Alexis.

2. Find at least two other ways to write 144 as the product of three or more factors.

"In fourth grade, you learned to write numbers as a product of primes. Can you write 144 as the product of prime factors?" asked Mr. Moreno. "This is called **prime factorization.** A **factor tree** is one way to organize your work."

3. Brandon made a factor tree for 144. Look at his factor tree and read the explanation.

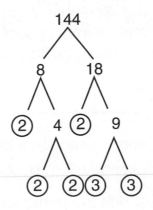

Begin by writing 144 as a product of two factors, for example 8 × 18. Next, write 8 as 2 × 4 and 18 as 2 × 9. Since 2 is a prime number, circle both 2s. Write 4 as 2 × 2 and circle both 2s as prime numbers. Write 9 as 3 × 3. 3 is a prime number so circle both 3s. You have now identified the prime factors of 144. These can be written as a prime factorization: 2 × 2 × 2 × 2 × 3 × 3 = 144.

A. Make a different factor tree for 144.

B. What prime factors were identified using your factor tree from Part A?

Brandon rewrote his prime factorization using **exponents.**

2 × 2 × 2 × 2 × 3 × 3 = 144 can also be written as: $2^4 \times 3^2 = 144$.

4. A. Make a factor tree for 180.

B. Write the prime factorization for 180 without exponents.

C. Use exponents to write the prime factorization for 180.

Brandon wanted to check that he used exponents correctly to write 144. He decided to use his calculator. Scientific calculators have an exponent key. They are shown with different symbols such as $\boxed{\wedge}$, $\boxed{y^x}$, and $\boxed{x^y}$. Find the exponent key on your calculator. To calculate $2^4 \times 3^2$, Brandon recorded his keystrokes as follows:

$\boxed{2}\ \boxed{\wedge}\ \boxed{4}\ \boxed{\times}\ \boxed{3}\ \boxed{\wedge}\ \boxed{2}\ \boxed{=}$

5. Use your calculator to check Brandon's keystrokes.

   A. What does your display read?   **B.** Are Brandon's keystrokes correct?

6. Use your calculator to check the prime factorization you wrote for 180 in Question 4C. Record your keystrokes.

Homework

1. Find the prime factorization of each number. Organize your work using a factor tree. Write a number sentence showing each number as a product of its prime factors using exponents.

   A. 84   **B.** 385   **C.** 297

   D. 120   **E.** 441   **F.** 182

2. The following numbers have been factored correctly. However, these are not the prime factorizations. Rewrite each number using only prime factors. Then rewrite the number as a product of its prime factors using exponents.

   A. $7 \times 12 \times 13 = 1092$

   B. $2 \times 4 \times 7 \times 27 = 1512$

   C. $2 \times 2 \times 9 \times 15 \times 11 = 5940$

3. **A.** Use your calculator to find the value of 2^3. Write your keystrokes.

   B. Use your calculator to find the number factored as $2^4 \times 3^3$. Write your keystrokes.

4. Use your calculator to find each number that has been written as a product of its primes. Then check your answer by multiplying without using the exponent key.

   A. $2^5 \times 3^3 \times 5 =$ **B.** $3 \times 5^2 \times 11 =$

   C. $2 \times 3^4 \times 7^2 =$ **D.** $2^3 \times 5 \times 13^2 =$

Comparing Fractions

Finding Equivalent Fractions

We learned in Unit 3 that when we multiply both the numerator and denominator of a fraction by the same number, we get a fraction that is equivalent to the first. For example, if we multiply both the numerator and denominator of $\frac{2}{3}$ by 5, we get the equivalent fraction $\frac{10}{15}$.

$$\frac{2}{3} = \frac{2 \times 5}{3 \times 5} = \frac{10}{15}$$

Sometimes it is helpful to find equivalent fractions when we want to compare fractions. Can you find three other fractions that are equivalent to $\frac{2}{3}$?

Comparing Fractions

John and his mother were shopping for ingredients to make cookies and fudge for the school bake sale.

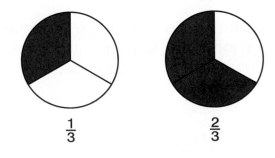

"The cookie recipe calls for $\frac{1}{3}$ can of evaporated milk," said John. "After we make the cookies, we'll have $\frac{2}{3}$ of a can left over. I wonder whether that will be enough to make the fudge."

"The fudge recipe calls for $\frac{3}{4}$ can of evaporated milk," said his mother. "If $\frac{2}{3}$ is more than $\frac{3}{4}$, we'll have enough. Otherwise, we'll have to buy another can. Which do you think is larger, $\frac{2}{3}$ or $\frac{3}{4}$?"

Before solving John's problem, think about some other fractions:

Which is larger, $\frac{1}{3}$ or $\frac{2}{3}$?

It is easy to compare fractions that have the same denominator. Two-thirds is more than one-third, since two is more than one.

Which is larger, $\frac{1}{2}$ or $\frac{1}{3}$?

$\frac{1}{3}$ $\frac{2}{3}$

One-half is larger than one-third. Remember that when the numerators are equal, as they are here, the fraction with the smaller denominator is larger. When we cut the whole into 2 pieces, each piece is larger than when we cut the whole into 3 pieces.

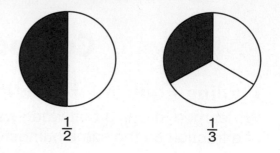

$$\frac{1}{2} \qquad \frac{1}{3}$$

Which is larger, $\frac{2}{3}$ or $\frac{3}{4}$?

This was John's problem. One way to compare fractions with different denominators is to find equivalent fractions with the same denominator.

To compare $\frac{2}{3}$ and $\frac{3}{4}$, John chose 12 as the denominator because it is a multiple of both 3 and 4. To compare $\frac{2}{3}$ and $\frac{3}{4}$, John renamed them so they had the same denominator (12).

$$\frac{2}{3} = \frac{2 \times 4}{3 \times 4} = \frac{8}{12} \qquad \frac{3}{4} = \frac{3 \times 3}{4 \times 3} = \frac{9}{12}$$

Since $\frac{8}{12} < \frac{9}{12}$, then $\frac{2}{3} < \frac{3}{4}$.

"I guess $\frac{2}{3}$ of a can isn't enough milk for the recipe that calls for $\frac{3}{4}$ can," said John. "We'll have to buy another can."

When fractions have the same denominator, we say they have **common denominators.** Twelve is a common denominator for $\frac{2}{3}$ and $\frac{3}{4}$. To find a common denominator for two fractions, we need to find a number that is a multiple of both denominators.

1. Write each pair of fractions with a common denominator. Then compare the fractions. Use the symbols < or >.

   A. $\frac{1}{2}$ $\frac{3}{8}$

   B. $\frac{5}{6}$ $\frac{7}{12}$

   C. $\frac{17}{20}$ $\frac{3}{4}$

   D. $\frac{2}{3}$ $\frac{7}{9}$

One way to find a common denominator for two fractions is to multiply both denominators together. For example, a common denominator for $\frac{2}{3}$ and $\frac{4}{5}$ is 15. Since $3 \times 5 = 15$, we know that 15 is a multiple of both 3 and 5.

2. Which is larger? To answer, find common denominators and compare.

   A. $\frac{4}{5}$ or $\frac{2}{3}$

   B. $\frac{3}{4}$ or $\frac{4}{5}$

   C. $\frac{7}{12}$ or $\frac{3}{5}$

   D. $\frac{3}{8}$ or $\frac{4}{9}$

One way to find a common denominator for two fractions is to multiply the two denominators. Often, you can find a smaller common denominator. For example, $96 = 8 \times 12$. So 96 is a common denominator for $\frac{3}{8}$ and $\frac{5}{12}$. But 24 is also a multiple of 8 and 12. And 24 is easier to work with than 96. To compare $\frac{3}{8}$ and $\frac{5}{12}$, we write:

$$\frac{3 \times 3}{8 \times 3} = \frac{9}{24} \qquad \frac{5 \times 2}{12 \times 2} = \frac{10}{24}$$

Since $\frac{9}{24} < \frac{10}{24}$, we know that $\frac{3}{8} < \frac{5}{12}$.

3. Compare the following pairs of fractions. For each pair of fractions, find a common denominator that is smaller than the product of the denominators.

   A. $\frac{5}{12}$ $\frac{3}{9}$

   B. $\frac{3}{10}$ $\frac{5}{15}$

   C. $\frac{8}{15}$ $\frac{5}{9}$

   D. $\frac{5}{6}$ $\frac{7}{9}$

4. A survey said that $\frac{2}{3}$ of the households in Popperville read the *Daily Gazette* and that $\frac{3}{5}$ of the households read the *Daily News*. Which paper do more households read?

5. John helped his mother put shelves in his closet. He used a drill. He had 3 drill bits in sizes $\frac{3}{8}$ inch, $\frac{1}{2}$ inch, and $\frac{5}{16}$ inch. List the drill bit sizes in order, from smallest to largest.

6. Compare each pair of fractions. You may use any method you wish. Show the strategies you use.

   A. $\frac{6}{7}$ $\frac{1}{7}$ **B.** $\frac{5}{6}$ $\frac{3}{4}$ **C.** $\frac{2}{5}$ $\frac{2}{7}$

   D. $\frac{6}{11}$ $\frac{4}{9}$ **E.** $\frac{2}{3}$ $\frac{3}{5}$ **F.** $\frac{1}{9}$ $\frac{7}{8}$

Homework

1. Find equivalent fractions:

   A. $\frac{3}{5} = \frac{?}{10}$ **B.** $\frac{5}{4} = \frac{15}{?}$

   C. $\frac{5}{9} = \frac{?}{36}$ **D.** $\frac{7}{10} = \frac{70}{?}$

2. Write each of the following pairs of fractions with a common denominator. Then compare the fractions. Use the symbols =, <, or > to write a number sentence involving each pair.

   A. $\frac{2}{3}$ $\frac{4}{6}$ **B.** $\frac{7}{12}$ $\frac{15}{24}$

   C. $\frac{3}{4}$ $\frac{8}{12}$ **D.** $\frac{4}{5}$ $\frac{20}{25}$

   E. $\frac{1}{5}$ $\frac{3}{8}$ **F.** $\frac{7}{8}$ $\frac{2}{3}$

   G. $\frac{3}{5}$ $\frac{6}{15}$ **H.** $\frac{3}{4}$ $\frac{5}{6}$

3. Compare each pair of fractions. You may use any method you wish. Show the strategies you use.

   A. $\frac{1}{4}$ $\frac{11}{12}$

   B. $\frac{5}{6}$ $\frac{7}{8}$

   C. $\frac{3}{5}$ $\frac{3}{11}$

   D. $\frac{1}{10}$ $\frac{10}{13}$

4. Compare the following. Write each pair of fractions with a common denominator that is smaller than the product of the denominators. For example, for Part A, find a denominator that is smaller than 12×8.

   A. $\frac{5}{12}$ $\frac{3}{8}$

   B. $\frac{5}{6}$ $\frac{3}{4}$

   C. $\frac{11}{18}$ $\frac{7}{12}$

5. John was hiking when he came to this sign on the trail. Which was closer, the overlook or the waterfall?

6. John ordered a small pizza. It was cut into 6 equal pieces. His brother also ordered a small pizza from the same restaurant. It was cut into 4 equal pieces. John ate 4 of his 6 pieces, and his brother ate 3 of his 4 pieces. Who ate more pizza? Explain your answer.

Reducing Fractions

"I know that multiplying the numerator and denominator of a fraction by the same number gives me a fraction that is equivalent to the first," Jackie said. "I remember that the rule is the same for division as for multiplication: dividing both the numerator and denominator by the same number gives a fraction that is equivalent to the first."

"Show me an example," said Mr. Moreno. "Try $\frac{4}{8}$."

"Okay," said Jackie. "I can divide both 4 and 8 by 4." She wrote:

$$\frac{4}{8} = \frac{4 \div 4}{8 \div 4} = \frac{1}{2}$$

"I remember that $\frac{4}{8}$ and $\frac{1}{2}$ are equivalent. We showed that before with pattern blocks. Dividing the numerator and denominator of $\frac{4}{8}$ by 4 gave me an equivalent fraction, $\frac{1}{2}$."

"You're right, Jackie, we can multiply the numerator and denominator of $\frac{1}{2}$ by 4 and get $\frac{4}{8}$ back," said Mr. Moreno.

$$\frac{1}{2} \times \frac{4}{4} = \frac{4}{8}$$

"Let's try some more. How about $\frac{12}{30}$?"

Jackie wrote:

$$\frac{12}{30} = \frac{12 \div 3}{30 \div 3} = \frac{4}{10}$$

"So $\frac{12}{30}$ is equivalent to $\frac{4}{10}$," she decided.

Renaming a fraction with another fraction that has a smaller denominator is called **reducing** the fraction. To be able to reduce a fraction, the numerator and denominator need to have a common factor. In the example, Jackie divided 12 and 30 by their common factor, 3. Can she divide again? That is, can she find another common factor of the numerator and denominator and use it to reduce $\frac{4}{10}$?

The numerator and denominator of $\frac{4}{10}$ have the common factor 2. Divide the numerator and denominator by 2.

$$\frac{4}{10} = \frac{4 \div 2}{10 \div 2} = \frac{2}{5}$$

So $\frac{4}{10}$ is equivalent to $\frac{2}{5}$. When there are no other common factors other than 1, the fraction cannot be reduced anymore. We say it is in **lowest terms.** Reducing $\frac{12}{30}$ to lowest terms gives $\frac{2}{5}$.

Here is another example. Write $\frac{30}{36}$ in lowest terms. To do this, we can begin by dividing 30 and 36 by 2.

$$\frac{30 \div 2}{36 \div 2} = \frac{15}{18}$$

This fraction is not in lowest terms, because 15 and 18 have the common factor 3. So we'll reduce $\frac{15}{18}$.

$$\frac{15 \div 3}{18 \div 3} = \frac{5}{6}$$

Since 5 and 6 have no common factors other than one, $\frac{5}{6}$ is in lowest terms.

Discuss

1. Reduce the following fractions to lowest terms. If the fraction is already in lowest terms, say so.

   A. $\frac{12}{16}$ B. $\frac{20}{30}$ C. $\frac{15}{45}$

   D. $\frac{48}{60}$ E. $\frac{9}{26}$ F. $\frac{75}{100}$

2. Can you think of another way to reduce $\frac{30}{36}$ instead of dividing first by 2? If so, how?

3. Solve the following. Reduce your answers to lowest terms.

   A. $\frac{2}{15} + \frac{7}{15} =$ B. $\frac{11}{12} - \frac{5}{12} =$ C. $\frac{7}{16} + \frac{5}{16} =$

4. Solve the following. Reduce your answers to lowest terms.

   A. $\frac{1}{4} + \frac{2}{3} =$

   B. $\frac{5}{12} + \frac{1}{3} =$

   C. $\frac{4}{5} - \frac{3}{10} =$

5. Jenny buys material to make doll clothes. She needs $\frac{1}{6}$ yard for the pants and $\frac{1}{3}$ yard for the shirts. How many yards does she need in all?

6. When Peter's family went camping, they brought a gallon of fuel to use in their camp stove and lantern. The stove held $\frac{1}{3}$ gallon of fuel, and the lantern held $\frac{1}{4}$ gallon.

   A. How much of the gallon was left after they filled the stove and the lantern?

   B. After filling the stove and the lantern, did they have enough fuel left in the tank to fill the lantern a second time? Explain your answer.

   C. Did they have enough fuel left to fill both the stove and the lantern a second time? Explain your answer.

7. Divide. Write each quotient as a mixed number. Reduce all fractions to lowest terms.

   A. $219 \div 9 =$

   B. $5230 \div 8 =$

   C. $7728 \div 36 =$

8. **A.** How many hours are there in 1180 minutes? Express your answer as a mixed number. Reduce.

   B. How many feet are there in 188 inches? Express your answer as a mixed number. Reduce.

9. Rename each decimal as a fraction and reduce to lowest terms.

   A. 0.8   **B.** 0.45   **C.** 0.250

1. Reduce the following fractions to lowest terms. If a fraction is already in lowest terms, say so.

   A. $\frac{4}{10}$　　　　　　　　**B.** $\frac{8}{24}$

   C. $\frac{18}{48}$　　　　　　　　**D.** $\frac{12}{36}$

   E. $\frac{16}{64}$　　　　　　　　**F.** $\frac{27}{81}$

   G. $\frac{7}{15}$　　　　　　　　**H.** $\frac{60}{100}$

2. Solve the following. Reduce your answers to lowest terms.

   A. $\frac{5}{8} - \frac{3}{8} =$　　　　**B.** $\frac{11}{24} + \frac{5}{24} =$　　　　**C.** $\frac{7}{20} - \frac{3}{20} =$

3. Solve the following. Reduce your answers to lowest terms.

   A. $\frac{1}{2} + \frac{3}{10} =$　　　　**B.** $\frac{5}{6} - \frac{1}{3} =$　　　　**C.** $\frac{4}{5} + \frac{1}{10} =$

4. Rename each decimal as a fraction and reduce to lowest terms.

   A. 0.15　　　　　　**B.** 0.4　　　　　　**C.** 0.375

5. Abby's mother is making her a costume for the skating show. She needs to buy $\frac{1}{4}$ yard of sequins to go around the wrists, $\frac{5}{6}$ yard of sequins to trim her cape, and $\frac{2}{3}$ yard of sequins to go around the waist. The sequins are expensive, so she does not want to buy any more than she needs. How many yards of sequins should she buy? Express your answer as a mixed number, then reduce.

6. Tim's family went for a walk around the 1-mile nature loop. They first walked $\frac{1}{3}$ mile to the waterfall. They continued $\frac{1}{4}$ mile farther along the trail until they came to a picnic area. While they were having their picnic, it started to rain. They wanted to return to their car the shortest way. Was it shorter for them to return along the trail the way they had come, or to continue around the loop until they came back to the parking lot? Give reasons for your answer.

7. Here is a data table showing the number of minutes Danny practiced violin each day last week. How many hours did he practice in all? Express your answer as a mixed number, then reduce.

Day	Minutes Practiced
Sunday	30
Monday	25
Tuesday	45
Wednesday	40
Thursday	20
Friday	0
Saturday	40

8. Divide. Write each quotient as a mixed number. Reduce all fractions.

A. $472 \div 6 =$

B. $3894 \div 4 =$

C. $6970 \div 15 =$

From Factors to Fractions

Complete each of the following problems. Show how you found each solution.

1. Romesh and John were playing *Factor 40* after school. John made the first move. He chose to circle 29.

    A. Was this a good first move? Explain the reasons for your answer.

    B. Was there a better first move? Explain your thinking.

2. Arti's family drove for $\frac{2}{3}$ of an hour to visit her aunt and uncle. They then drove $\frac{1}{4}$ of an hour to attend a concert. What fraction of an hour did Arti's family spend in the car?

3. Remember that a number is divisible by 3 if the sum of its digits equals a multiple of three. Use this strategy to decide which of the following numbers are divisible by 3:

    A. 1083

    B. 748

    C. 1536

4. Edward lives $\frac{5}{8}$ of a mile from school, Brandon lives $\frac{7}{10}$ of a mile from school, and John lives $\frac{2}{5}$ of a mile from school.

    A. Which boy lives the farthest from school?

    B. Which boy lives the closest to school?

    C. Explain the strategies you used to answer Parts A and B.

5. Marcus likes to help his family with their work at the Good For You Bakery. He often packages cookies into dozens. Marcus had 6738 cookies to package into dozens on Saturday.

    A. How many dozens could Marcus package?

    B. What fraction of a dozen cookies did Marcus have left over?

    C. Write a reduced fraction for the fraction of a dozen left over.

Unit 12

Using Fractions

	Student Guide	Discovery Assignment Book	Adventure Book	Unit Resource Guide*
Lesson 1				
Hexagon Duets	●	●		
Lesson 2				
Adding Mixed Numbers	●			
Lesson 3				
Fractions of Groups	●			
Lesson 4				
Multiplication of Fractions	●	●		
Lesson 5				
Using Patterns to Multiply Fractions	●			
Lesson 6				
Peanut Soup			●	
Lesson 7				
Party Problems	●			
Lesson 8				
Midterm Test				●

Unit Resource Guide pages are from the teacher materials.

Hexagon Duets

Players

This game is played by four players, two players on each team.

Materials

Each group of four players needs:

- pattern blocks
- paper and pencil
- *Hexagon Duets Spinner* Game Page from the *Discovery Assignment Book,* four copies
- a clear, plastic spinner (or a paper clip and a pencil)

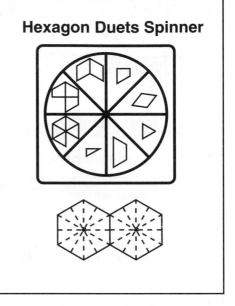

Hexagon Duets Spinner

Rules

1. One yellow hexagon is one whole.
2. Each player takes a turn. On your turn, spin the spinner twice. Each time you spin, place the pattern blocks on the outline of the two hexagons on your *Hexagon Duets Spinner* Game Page. Follow Jackie and Lin's example in Questions 1–3.
3. Add the two fractions together. You may need to trade your pattern blocks for other pattern blocks to find the sum.
4. Write a number sentence for the sum of your two fractions.
5. Add your sum to your partner's sum to find a grand total. Write a number sentence for the grand total.
6. The team with the largest total wins the round and earns $\frac{1}{3}$ of a point.
7. Continue to play more rounds. The first team to earn one whole point is the winner.

one whole

Jackie and Lin are a team in a game of *Hexagon Duets.* In the first round of the game, Jackie spins $\frac{5}{6}$ and $\frac{1}{2}$. She adds her fractions together with pattern blocks. Then she writes a number sentence.

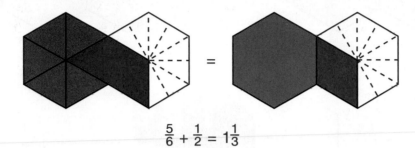

$$\frac{5}{6} + \frac{1}{2} = 1\frac{1}{3}$$

1. What pattern blocks did Jackie trade?

Lin spins $\frac{1}{6}$ and $\frac{2}{3}$. Here is her work.

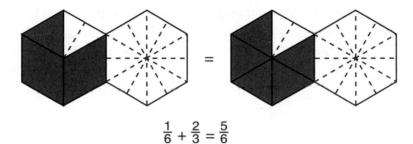

$$\frac{1}{6} + \frac{2}{3} = \frac{5}{6}$$

2. What pattern blocks did Lin trade?

To complete the round, the girls put their pieces together to find the grand total of their two sums.

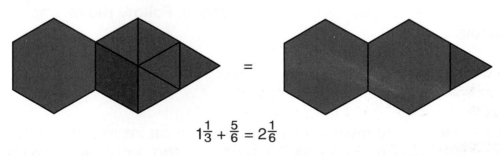

$$1\frac{1}{3} + \frac{5}{6} = 2\frac{1}{6}$$

3. The two players on the other team take their turns. Their grand total is $2\frac{1}{12}$. Did Jackie and Lin win the round? Why or why not?

Many Names for Mixed Numbers

When using mixed numbers and fractions, you often need to use different names for the same mixed number. For example, $2\frac{1}{3}$, $2\frac{2}{6}$, and $1\frac{8}{6}$ are all equal.

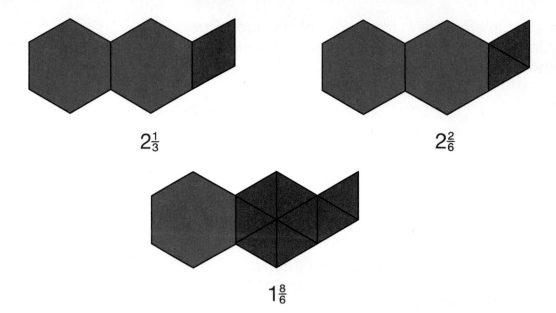

$2\frac{1}{3}$ $\qquad\qquad\qquad\qquad$ $2\frac{2}{6}$

$1\frac{8}{6}$

4. Find as many fractions and mixed numbers as you can that are equivalent to $2\frac{1}{3}$ that can be shown using pattern blocks. For this lesson, one yellow hexagon is one whole. You may use the yellow, red, blue, green, brown, and purple blocks, but you may use no more than two colors of blocks. For any number, be prepared to show the class your solutions using pattern blocks and number sentences.

Work with your group to answer Questions 5–6. Share pattern blocks. Follow these directions:

- **Find as many mixed numbers and improper fractions as you can that are equivalent to the number in the problem. You must be able to show the mixed number or fraction with no more than two colors of pattern blocks.**
- **Write number sentences for your solutions. Follow the example for $2\frac{1}{3}$ above.**

5. $3\frac{1}{4}$

6. 2

In Questions 7–9 you are given a mixed number or an improper fraction. Show this number with pattern blocks as it is written in the problem. Then show it using only two colors and the fewest pieces possible. Write the mixed number represented by the pattern blocks when you use the fewest pieces.

Example: $1\frac{6}{4}$

Solution:

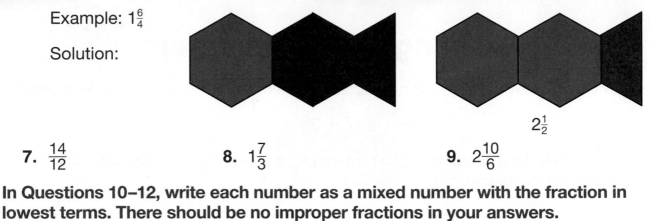

$2\frac{1}{2}$

7. $\frac{14}{12}$　　　　　**8.** $1\frac{7}{3}$　　　　　**9.** $2\frac{10}{6}$

In Questions 10–12, write each number as a mixed number with the fraction in lowest terms. There should be no improper fractions in your answers.

10. $\frac{15}{10}$　　　　　　**11.** $1\frac{17}{8}$　　　　　　**12.** $3\frac{14}{6}$

Homework

1. Write each number as a mixed number with the fraction in lowest terms. There should be no improper fractions in your answers.

   A. $\frac{15}{12}$　　　　　**B.** $2\frac{15}{20}$　　　　　**C.** $1\frac{10}{3}$

   D. $3\frac{12}{8}$　　　　　**E.** $5\frac{16}{6}$　　　　　**F.** $2\frac{18}{15}$

2. David is filling boxes with candy. One box holds $\frac{3}{8}$ pound and the other holds $\frac{1}{2}$ pound. He has 1 pound of candy. Does he have enough candy to completely fill both boxes? How do you know?

3. Jackie is sewing a skirt. The instructions call for $\frac{5}{8}$ yard of material. She bought $\frac{3}{4}$ yard. How much material will she have left over after she makes the skirt?

4. Nicholas lives $1\frac{3}{4}$ miles from school. Alexis lives $1\frac{7}{10}$ miles from school. Who lives farther from school? Justify your answer.

5. Jessie found a piece of wood that is 7 inches long. She needs a piece $6\frac{3}{8}$ inches long. How much wood will be left if she cuts off $6\frac{3}{8}$ inches?

6. Write all answers in lowest terms.

   A. $\frac{7}{8} + \frac{7}{8} =$　　　　　**B.** $\frac{5}{6} - \frac{1}{4} =$

   C. $\frac{4}{5} + \frac{7}{10} =$　　　　　**D.** $\frac{11}{12} + \frac{2}{3} =$

Hexagon Duets

Adding Mixed Numbers

Mr. Moreno's class is working on fraction problems. Here is one of the problems:

$$1\frac{1}{2} + 2\frac{3}{4} =$$

Frank modeled the problem using pattern blocks. First he represented each fraction with the blocks.

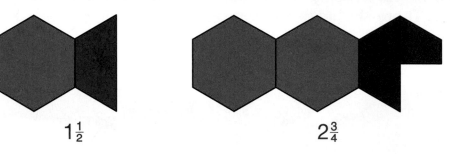

$$1\frac{1}{2} \qquad\qquad 2\frac{3}{4}$$

Then he moved the blocks together. The sum is $4\frac{1}{4}$.

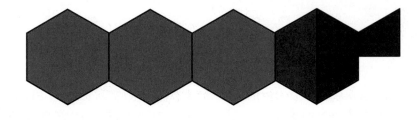

Ana solved the problem using pencil and paper. First, she wrote the following:

$$\begin{array}{r} 1\frac{1}{2} \\ + 2\frac{3}{4} \\ \hline \end{array}$$

Then she found a common denominator:

$$\begin{array}{r} 1\frac{2}{4} \\ + 2\frac{3}{4} \\ \hline \end{array}$$

She added the whole numbers and then added the fractions.

$$\begin{array}{r} 1\frac{2}{4} \\ + 2\frac{3}{4} \\ \hline 3\frac{5}{4} = 4\frac{1}{4} \end{array}$$

She changed $\frac{5}{4}$ to $1\frac{1}{4}$ because $\frac{5}{4}$ is an improper fraction.

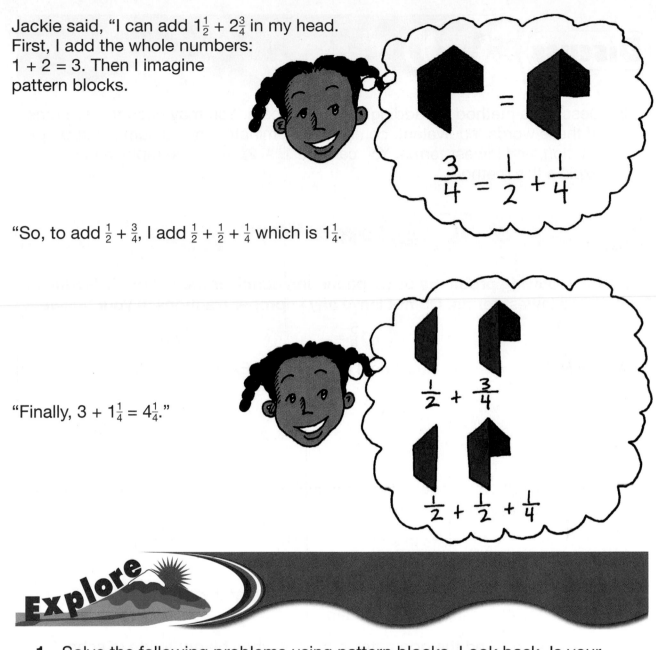

Jackie said, "I can add $1\frac{1}{2} + 2\frac{3}{4}$ in my head. First, I add the whole numbers: $1 + 2 = 3$. Then I imagine pattern blocks.

$$\frac{3}{4} = \frac{1}{2} + \frac{1}{4}$$

"So, to add $\frac{1}{2} + \frac{3}{4}$, I add $\frac{1}{2} + \frac{1}{2} + \frac{1}{4}$ which is $1\frac{1}{4}$.

"Finally, $3 + 1\frac{1}{4} = 4\frac{1}{4}$."

$$\frac{1}{2} + \frac{3}{4}$$

$$\frac{1}{2} + \frac{1}{2} + \frac{1}{4}$$

Explore

1. Solve the following problems using pattern blocks. Look back. Is your answer reasonable?

   A. $1\frac{5}{6} + \frac{5}{6} =$ **B.** $1\frac{1}{4} + 2\frac{1}{6} =$ **C.** $2\frac{1}{3} + 1\frac{5}{6} =$ **D.** $\begin{array}{r} 1\frac{2}{3} \\ + 1\frac{3}{4} \\ \hline \end{array}$

2. Solve the following problems using pencil and paper. Show each step. Check to see if your answers are reasonable.

   A. $2\frac{4}{9} + 3\frac{7}{9} =$ **B.** $3\frac{3}{8} + 2\frac{7}{8} =$ **C.** $4\frac{3}{5} + 2\frac{9}{10} =$ **D.** $\begin{array}{r} 5\frac{3}{4} \\ + 1\frac{7}{8} \\ \hline \end{array}$

Discuss

3. Describe a method for adding mixed numbers. You may need to use some of these words: equivalent, common denominator, mixed number, improper fraction, and lowest terms. You can use $1\frac{1}{2} + 2\frac{5}{6}$ as an example to help explain this method.

Homework

Solve the following problems using paper and pencil or mental math. Reduce all fractions to lowest terms. Do not leave any improper fractions in your answers.

1. $2 + 4\frac{3}{5} =$

2. $4\frac{3}{4} + 1\frac{5}{6} =$

3. $1\frac{7}{10} + 3\frac{1}{2} =$

4. Solve the problem in Question 3 another way. Explain both of your strategies.

5. $5\frac{2}{3} + 3\frac{1}{12} =$

6. $3\frac{4}{5} + 2\frac{1}{5} =$

7. $\begin{array}{r} 7\frac{1}{5} \\ + 2\frac{1}{10} \\ \hline \end{array}$

8. $\begin{array}{r} 4\frac{3}{5} \\ + 5\frac{3}{4} \\ \hline \end{array}$

9. Look back at your answer to Question 8. Is it reasonable? Should it be more than 10 or less than 10? Explain.

10. Lee Yah spent $6\frac{1}{2}$ hours in school and $1\frac{3}{4}$ hours doing her homework. What is the total time she spent at school and on her homework?

11. A recipe calls for $1\frac{1}{3}$ cups of whole wheat flour and $2\frac{3}{4}$ cups of white flour. How many cups of flour are needed?

12. Nicholas checked the odometer in the car when he got a ride to school. His route to school is 1.3 miles. His soccer coach told him that it is a mile and a half from school to the practice field. How far does Nicholas have to walk to get from home to school to soccer practice?

13. **A.** A customer bought $2\frac{1}{3}$ yards of print material and $2\frac{3}{4}$ yards of solid color material. How many yards did the customer buy?

    B. Both kinds of material cost $3.00 a yard. The customer has $15. Is this enough money to buy the material? Explain.

14. Jessie is making a bird house. She needs 2 boards that measure $1\frac{3}{4}$ feet each and a board that measures $1\frac{1}{2}$ feet long. She has one board that is 4 feet long. Can she cut the 3 shorter boards from the longer one? Why or why not?

Fractions of Groups

Johnny Appleseed Apple Company sells gift boxes. The small gift boxes have 12 apples, and the large gift boxes have 24 apples.

 **Discuss**

1. If one-fourth of the apples in each gift box are yellow,

   A. How many apples in the small gift box are yellow?

   B. How many apples in the large gift box are yellow?

2. **A.** In the fraction $\frac{1}{4}$, what information does the denominator give you?

   B. What information does the numerator give you?

   C. What other information do you need in order to know the number of apples in $\frac{1}{4}$ of a box?

   D. What is the difference between $\frac{1}{4}$ and $\frac{4}{1}$?

3. Write number sentences for the following:

   A. Four groups of three apples make 12 apples in all.

   B. Four groups of six apples make 24 apples in all.

   C. What operation did you use in your number sentences?

Lin used the diagram and number sentence shown here to represent one-fourth of the apples in the large box. Both her diagram and number sentence represent one-fourth of a group of 24 apples. We write this as: $\frac{1}{4} \times 24 = 6$ apples.

$\frac{1}{4} \times 24 = 6$ apples

```
╭─────────────╮
( X X X X X X )
│ X X X X X X │
│ X X X X X X │
│ X X X X X X │
╰─────────────╯
```

4. Draw a diagram similar to Lin's. Show the following using your diagram and write a number sentence for each:

   A. One-fourth of a group of 24 apples.

   B. Two-fourths of a group of 24 apples.

   C. Three-fourths of a group of 24 apples.

   D. Four-fourths of a group of 24 apples.

5. **A.** What patterns do you see in the number sentences?

   B. What is another name for $\frac{4}{4}$? Write another number sentence for Question 4D using this name.

John used this diagram to show one-third of a small box of apples.

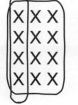

$\frac{1}{3} \times 12 = 4$ apples

He used this diagram to show four-thirds of a small box of apples.

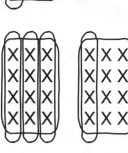

$\frac{4}{3} \times 12 = 16$ apples

6. Copy the following chart on your paper. Complete the chart following the example in the first row. (Remember, the answer to a multiplication problem is a **product.** For example, 4 is the product of $\frac{1}{3} \times 12$.)

Multiplication Number Sentences
$\frac{1}{3} \times 12 = 4$
$\frac{2}{3} \times 12 =$
$\frac{3}{3} \times 12 =$
$\frac{4}{3} \times 12 = 16$
$\frac{5}{3} \times 12 =$
$\frac{6}{3} \times 12 =$

7. **A.** Describe the patterns you see in the table.

   B. When is the product less than 12? Why?

   C. When is the product equal to 12? Why?

   D. When is the product greater than 12? Why?

8. Draw a diagram and write a number sentence for each problem.

    A. $\frac{1}{4} \times 12$ **B.** $\frac{2}{4} \times 12$ **C.** $\frac{3}{4} \times 12$

    D. $\frac{4}{4} \times 12$ **E.** $\frac{5}{4} \times 12$ **F.** $\frac{6}{4} \times 12$

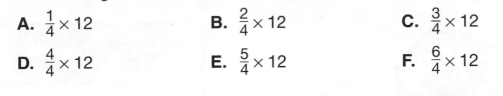

Solve the following problems. Draw a diagram and write a number sentence for each problem. Follow the example.

Example: Edward gave $\frac{2}{3}$ of a small box of apples to his grandmother. How many apples did he give her?

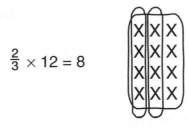

$$\frac{2}{3} \times 12 = 8$$

Remember, there are 12 apples in a small box and 24 apples in a large box.

1. **A.** One-half of the apples in the small box of apples are red. How many are red?

    B. One-fourth of the apples in the small box are green. How many are green?

2. Nila's family received a large box of apples.

    A. Nila ate $\frac{1}{6}$ of the apples. How many apples did Nila eat?

    B. Nila's father took $\frac{5}{6}$ of the apples to work to share with his co-workers. How many apples did he take to work?

3. For each problem, decide how many apples each person ate.

    A. Manny ate $\frac{1}{3}$ of a large box of apples.

    B. Blanca ate $\frac{1}{8}$ of the apples in a large box.

    C. Michael ate $\frac{3}{4}$ of the apples in a small box.

    D. Romesh ate $\frac{5}{6}$ of the apples in a small box.

4. Muffy's Muffins are sold in packages of eight. Complete the following table:

Multiplication Number Sentences
$\frac{1}{4} \times 8 = 2$
$\frac{2}{4} \times 8 =$
$\frac{3}{4} \times 8 =$
$\frac{4}{4} \times 8 =$
$\frac{5}{4} \times 8 =$
$\frac{6}{4} \times 8 =$

5. **A.** Describe the patterns you see in the table.

B. When is the product equal to the number of muffins in the whole package? Why?

C. When is the product less than the number of muffins in the whole package? Why?

D. When is the product more than the number of muffins in the whole package? Why?

E. What is another name for $\frac{2}{4}$? Rewrite a number sentence from your chart using this name.

6. Lee Yah's friends ate $1\frac{1}{2}$ packages of Muffy's Muffins. How many muffins did they eat?

7. Solve the following problems.

A. $\frac{1}{10} \times 20 =$ **B.** $\frac{1}{5} \times 20 =$

C. $\frac{1}{4} \times 20 =$ **D.** $\frac{1}{2} \times 20 =$

E. $\frac{3}{5} \times 20 =$ **F.** $\frac{3}{4} \times 20 =$

G. $\frac{9}{10} \times 20 =$ **H.** $1\frac{1}{2} \times 20 =$

Multiplication of Fractions

Multiplication of Fractions and Whole Numbers

For this lesson, the yellow hexagon is one whole. Mr. Moreno's class uses diagrams and pattern blocks to show multiplication of fractions. Here are several ways to show $\frac{1}{2} \times 4$ and $4 \times \frac{1}{2}$:

Here is Frank's diagram:

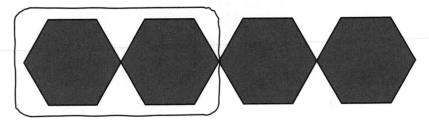

$\frac{1}{2} \times 4 = 2$

Brandon uses pattern blocks to show that $\frac{1}{2}$ of 4 = 2. Here is one way.

Here is another way Brandon shows that $\frac{1}{2}$ of 4 = 2.

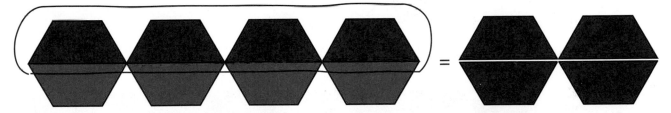

Arti thinks that $\frac{1}{2} \times 4$ is the same as $4 \times \frac{1}{2}$. Here is her diagram for $4 \times \frac{1}{2}$. Is she correct?

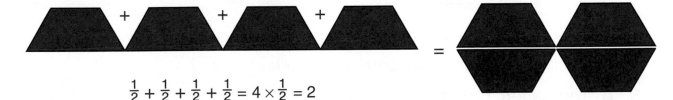

$$\frac{1}{2} + \frac{1}{2} + \frac{1}{2} + \frac{1}{2} = 4 \times \frac{1}{2} = 2$$

1. **A.** Use pattern blocks to show $3 \times \frac{1}{2}$.

   B. Use pattern blocks to show $\frac{1}{2}$ of 3.

   C. Is the product of $\frac{1}{2}$ and 3 larger or smaller than 3?

2. **A.** Use pattern blocks to show 2 groups of $\frac{3}{4}$.

   B. Use pattern blocks to show $\frac{3}{4}$ of 2.

   C. Is the product of $\frac{3}{4}$ and 2 larger or smaller than 2?

3. Write number sentences for the following problems.
   A. Use pattern blocks to show $7 \times \frac{1}{6}$.
   B. Use pattern blocks to show $\frac{2}{3} \times 4$.

Multiplication of Two Fractions

Here is how Nicholas showed $\frac{2}{3} \times \frac{1}{2}$: First, he showed $\frac{1}{2}$. Then he showed $\frac{2}{3}$ of $\frac{1}{2}$ by covering $\frac{2}{3}$ of a red trapezoid with green triangles.

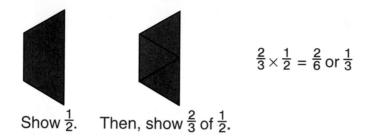

$$\frac{2}{3} \times \frac{1}{2} = \frac{2}{6} \text{ or } \frac{1}{3}$$

Show $\frac{1}{2}$.   Then, show $\frac{2}{3}$ of $\frac{1}{2}$.

Then he recorded his work on a *Pattern Block Record Sheet.*

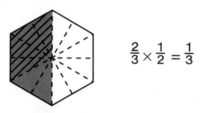

$$\frac{2}{3} \times \frac{1}{2} = \frac{1}{3}$$

Using pattern blocks, he saw that $\frac{2}{3}$ of $\frac{1}{2}$ is $\frac{1}{3}$ of the whole.

Discuss

4. A. Is the product of $\frac{2}{3}$ and $\frac{1}{2}$ greater than or less than $\frac{1}{2}$?
   B. Is the product of $\frac{2}{3}$ and $\frac{1}{2}$ greater than or less than $\frac{2}{3}$?

5. A. Use pattern blocks to show $\frac{1}{6}$ of $\frac{1}{2}$.
   B. Is the product more or less than $\frac{1}{6}$?
   C. Is the product more or less than $\frac{1}{2}$?

6. A. Use pattern blocks to show $\frac{2}{3} \times \frac{3}{4}$.
   B. Is the product more or less than $\frac{2}{3}$?
   C. Is the product more or less than $\frac{3}{4}$?

7. Use pattern blocks to show each of the following products.

- First, estimate the size of the product.
- Solve the problem and write a number sentence.
- Reduce fractions to lowest terms, but do not change improper fractions to mixed numbers.
- Record your work on a *Pattern Block Record Sheet.*

A. $3 \times \frac{1}{12}$ **B.** $\frac{1}{3} \times \frac{1}{4}$ **C.** $\frac{5}{6} \times \frac{1}{2}$ **D.** $8 \times \frac{1}{6}$

Use the *Pattern Block Record Sheet* Activity Pages to show each of the following products.

- **First, estimate the size of the product.**
- **Solve the problem and write a number sentence.**
- **Reduce answers to lowest terms, but do not change improper fractions to mixed numbers.**
- **Record your work on a *Pattern Block Record Sheet.***

    Follow the example: $6 \times \frac{1}{4}$

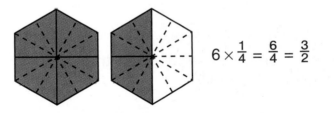

$$6 \times \frac{1}{4} = \frac{6}{4} = \frac{3}{2}$$

1. $3 \times \frac{1}{4} =$ **2.** $10 \times \frac{1}{6} =$

3. $2 \times \frac{1}{12} =$ **4.** $4 \times \frac{1}{12} =$

5. $2 \times \frac{5}{12} =$ **6.** $\frac{1}{2} \times \frac{1}{2} =$

7. $\frac{1}{3} \times \frac{3}{4} =$ **8.** $\frac{2}{3} \times \frac{1}{4} =$

9. $\frac{1}{2} \times \frac{1}{3} =$

Using Patterns to Multiply Fractions

Mr. Moreno's class used paper folding to investigate multiplication of fractions. After solving several problems this way, they looked for a pattern to help them multiply fractions with pencil and paper. Shannon explained her group's strategy, using $\frac{3}{4} \times \frac{2}{3}$ as an example:

"To multiply $\frac{3}{4} \times \frac{2}{3}$, we folded a sheet of paper into thirds the long way, traced the folds, and colored $\frac{2}{3}$ yellow.

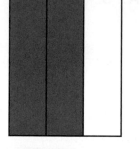

$\frac{2}{3}$

"Then we folded the paper into fourths the other way, traced the folds, and colored $\frac{3}{4}$ of the $\frac{2}{3}$ with blue.

"We saw that we had divided the paper into 4×3, or 12 parts. We colored 3×2, or 6 of the 12 parts blue. So, $\frac{6}{12}$ of the parts are colored blue. That's the same as $\frac{1}{2}$, so we wrote:

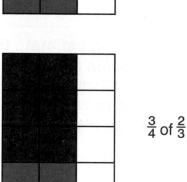

$\frac{3}{4}$ of $\frac{2}{3}$

$$\frac{3}{4} \times \frac{2}{3} = \frac{3 \times 2}{4 \times 3} = \frac{6}{12} = \frac{1}{2}$$

"Our answer makes sense because we know that the answer should be less than $\frac{2}{3}$, since we were finding a part of $\frac{2}{3}$."

Discuss

1. **A.** Multiply $\frac{2}{5} \times \frac{3}{4}$ using paper and pencil. Reduce your answer to lowest terms.

   B. Is your answer reasonable? Why?

2. Felicia and Edward solved the problem $\frac{1}{2} \times \frac{4}{5}$ in two different ways. Felicia used paper and pencil and wrote the following:

$$\frac{1}{2} \times \frac{4}{5} = \frac{1 \times 4}{2 \times 5} = \frac{4}{10}$$

Edward reasoned that since $\frac{1}{2}$ of 4 is 2, then $\frac{1}{2}$ of $\frac{4}{5} = \frac{2}{5}$. Who is correct? Explain.

3. Multiply $\frac{3}{5} \times 2$. (*Hint:* You can write 2 as $\frac{2}{1}$.)

    A. Should the answer be more or less than 2?

    B. Should the answer be more or less than 1?

    C. Solve the problem another way. Explain your strategy.

4. Solve. Reduce your answers to lowest terms. Is your answer reasonable?

    A. $\frac{2}{3} \times \frac{3}{5} =$ **B.** $\frac{1}{3} \times \frac{3}{10} =$ **C.** $\frac{3}{4} \times 6 =$ **D.** $\frac{2}{5} \times \frac{5}{8} =$

Homework

Find the following products. Write your answers in lowest terms.

1. $\frac{5}{8} \times \frac{1}{2} =$ 2. $\frac{1}{3} \times \frac{3}{4} =$ 3. $\frac{3}{10} \times \frac{1}{2} =$

4. $\frac{3}{5} \times \frac{3}{4} =$ 5. $\frac{3}{8} \times 4 =$ 6. $\frac{2}{3} \times \frac{2}{3} =$

7. $3 \times \frac{5}{6} =$ 8. $\frac{7}{10} \times \frac{1}{2} =$ 9. $10 \times \frac{4}{5} =$

10. $\frac{4}{5} \times \frac{3}{4} =$ 11. $8 \times \frac{2}{3} =$ 12. $\frac{2}{3} \times \frac{7}{8} =$

13. Brandon made a cheese pizza. He put pepperoni on $\frac{1}{2}$ of the pizza. He put onions on $\frac{3}{4}$ of the half with pepperoni. Draw a picture showing the toppings on the pizza.

    A. How much of the whole pizza has pepperoni and onions?

    B. How much of the whole pizza has only cheese?

    C. How much of the whole pizza has only pepperoni, but no onions?

14. **A.** Frank's guests ate $\frac{2}{3}$ of a cake at his party. How much cake was left over?

    B. The next day Frank ate $\frac{1}{4}$ of the leftover cake. How much of the whole cake did he eat the day after the party?

Party Problems

Solve the following problems. Show how you solved each problem.

1. Jeff's sister made a HAPPY BIRTHDAY sign for Jeff. Since Jeff is 10 years old, his sister drew 10 flowers. She colored $\frac{2}{5}$ of the flowers yellow and the rest she colored red. What fraction of the flowers are red?

2. At the beginning of the party, Jeff set 18 cups of lemonade on the table. After the party was over, $\frac{1}{6}$ of the cups of lemonade were left. How many cups of lemonade did Jeff's guests drink?

3. Jeff's mother bought 2 bags of balloons. Each bag contained 8 balloons. She used $1\frac{1}{4}$ bags of balloons to decorate the room. How many balloons did she use?

4. For the party, Jeff's mother bought sandwich trays from the Servin' Sandwiches Shop. Each tray contained 9 sandwiches. The party guests left $\frac{2}{3}$ of a tray of sandwiches. How many sandwiches did they leave?

5. To make a pitcher of lemonade, Jeff needed 8 cups of water. He could only find a $\frac{1}{3}$-cup measuring cup. How many times did Jeff fill the $\frac{1}{3}$-cup when he made the lemonade?

6. One-half of Jeff's guests were relatives. Three-fifths of the relatives were cousins.

   A. What fraction of his guests were cousins?

   B. Jeff had 20 guests at his party. How many of the guests were cousins?

7. Jeff's family spent $77.50 on the party. If there were 20 guests at the party, about how much money did they spend on each guest?

8. It was very cold when the guests arrived at the party. The temperature was -5°F. When the guests left, the temperature was -17°F. What was the difference between the two temperatures?

9. Jeff had a total of 43 favors to give to his guests. If each guest got the same number of favors, how many favors did each guest take home? How many favors were left over?

10. Jeff's mother created a riddle for the guests to solve:

   Today is also Jeff's uncle's birthday. His age has 2 and 5 as some of its factors; 3 is not a factor. His age is more than the square of 7 but less than the square of 8.

   A. Is Jeff's uncle's age prime or composite?

   B. What is the square of 7? of 8?

   C. What is Jeff's uncle's age?

Ratio and Proportion

	Student Guide	Discovery Assignment Book	Adventure Book	Unit Resource Guide*
Lesson 1				
Ratios, Recipes, and Proportions	●			
Lesson 2				
Variables in Proportion	●			
Lesson 3				
Sink and Float	●	●		●
Lesson 4				
Mass vs. Volume: Proportions and Density	●			
Lesson 5				
Problems of Scale	●			●

*Unit Resource Guide pages are from the teacher materials.

Ratios, Recipes, and Proportions

Peanut Brittle

Mr. Moreno's class is reviewing ratios using recipes. They are using two recipes for peanut brittle they found in a publication written by George Washington Carver at Tuskegee Institute in 1925.

No. 83, Peanut Brittle Number One
3 cups granulated sugar
1 cup roasted peanuts
1 scant cup boiling water
1/4 teaspoon soda

Melt all together over a slow fire; cook gently without stirring until a little hardens when dropped in cold water; add the nuts; turn the mixture in well buttered pans and cut while hot. Stirring will cause the syrup to sugar.

No. 84, Peanut Brittle Number Two
2 cups granulated sugar
1 cup freshly roasted peanuts

Shell and clean the peanuts; put in the stove to heat; put sugar in frying pan, and heat over a hot fire until it changes to caramel; put the peanuts in a well buttered tin; pour the sugar over them at once; when cold turn the pan upside down, and tap bottom until the candy falls out; break into small pieces.

Remember, a **ratio** is a way to compare two quantities or numbers. Ratios are often written as fractions. The ratio of peanuts to sugar in the recipe for Peanut Brittle Number One is 1 cup peanuts to 3 cups sugar. We can write this ratio as a fraction: $\frac{1\,c}{3\,c}$.

We also write:

$$\frac{P}{S} = \frac{1\,c}{3\,c},$$

where P stands for cups of peanuts and S stands for cups of sugar.

The ratio of peanuts to sugar can also be written with a colon between the quantities:

$$1:3$$

We can choose to compare the quantities in a different order. For example, we can compare the amount of sugar to the amount of peanuts. In words we say, "The ratio of sugar to peanuts is 3 cups to 1 cup." Using a fraction, we write this as $\frac{S}{P} = \frac{3c}{1c}$. Using a colon, we write the ratio of sugar to peanuts as $3:1$.

Discuss

1. Write the ratio of peanuts to sugar in the recipe for Peanut Brittle Number Two.
   A. Write this ratio as a fraction.
   B. Write this ratio with a colon.

2. Write the ratio of sugar to peanuts in the recipe for Peanut Brittle Number Two.
   A. Write this ratio as a fraction.
   B. Write this ratio with a colon.

3. David and Edward will make Peanut Brittle Number Two for the whole class. They will use 4 cups of peanuts. How much sugar do they need? Explain how you solved this problem.

4. Felicia and Arti will make Peanut Brittle Number One. They will use 4 cups of peanuts. How much sugar do they need? Explain how you solved this problem.

Mr. Moreno asks the students to show their solutions using equal ratios.

Felicia writes: $\dfrac{1 \text{ cup peanuts}}{3 \text{ cups sugar}} = \dfrac{4 \text{ cups peanuts}}{12 \text{ cups sugar}}$

John writes: $\dfrac{P}{S} = \dfrac{1c}{3c} = \dfrac{4c}{12c}$

A **proportion** is a statement that two ratios are equal. So, Felicia's and John's number sentences are proportions.

5. If Felicia and Arti use 6 cups of sugar to make Peanut Brittle Number One, how many cups of peanuts do they need? Show your solution using a proportion: $\dfrac{P}{S} = \dfrac{1c}{3c} = \dfrac{?}{6c}$.

6. If David and Edward use 5 cups of peanuts to make Peanut Brittle Number Two, how much sugar do they need? Show your solution using a proportion. (*Hint:* Remember what you know about equivalent fractions.)

Orange Punch

Shannon plans to make punch using a family recipe. She mixes 5 parts orange juice with 2 parts lime soda. For example, if she uses 5 cups of orange juice, she uses 2 cups of lime soda. Shannon makes a chart so that the other members of the class can help her make different amounts of punch.

S Lime Soda (in cups)	J Orange Juice (in cups)
2	5
4	10
8	20

7. **A.** Write the ratio of orange juice to lime soda with a colon.

   B. Write this ratio as a fraction.

8. Describe any patterns you see in the table.

9. **A.** If Shannon uses 4 cups of lime soda, how many cups of orange juice does she use? Write your solution as a proportion: $\frac{J}{S} = \frac{5c}{2c} = \frac{?c}{4c}$.

   B. If Shannon uses 20 cups of orange juice, how many cups of lime soda does she use? Write your solution as a proportion.

10. Shannon can also use a graph to help her make different amounts of punch. Make a graph of the data in the table.

    • Plot the amount of lime soda on the horizontal axis. Scale the horizontal axis from 0 to at least 30.

    • Plot the amount of orange juice on the vertical axis. Scale the vertical axis from 0 to at least 40.

    • Will you use a point graph or a bar graph? (*Hint:* You will want to find points in between the data.)

    • If you graph points that form a line, use your ruler to fit a line to the points. Extend your line in both directions.

11. Describe your graph. (Where does it meet the vertical axis? Is it a straight line or a curve? Does it go up or down as you read from left to right?)

12. A. Use your graph to find the number of cups of orange juice to mix with 6 cups of lime soda.

   B. Use your graph to find the number of cups of lime soda to mix with 35 cups of orange juice.

Using the graph to find an amount of soda or juice that lies *between* two data points you plotted on the graph is called **interpolation.** "Inter" means between points.

Using the graph to find an amount of soda or juice that lies *beyond* the points you plotted is called **extrapolation.** "Extra" means beyond or outside.

13. A. Did you use interpolation or extrapolation to answer Question 12A?

   B. Did you use interpolation or extrapolation to answer Question 12B?

14. A. Choose a point on the line and circle it. Use this point to write a ratio of the amount of orange juice to the amount of lime soda.

   B. Circle two more points on the line. Use them to write ratios of the amount of orange juice to the amount of lime soda.

   C. Are the three ratios equal? How do you know?

15. A. Find the number of cups of lime soda to mix with 25 cups of orange juice. How did you solve this problem?

   B. One way to solve this problem is to use a proportion. Find ? so that the number sentence is true. $\frac{J}{S} = \frac{5\ c}{2\ c} = \frac{25\ c}{?}$

16. A. Use a proportion to find the number of cups of orange juice to mix with 18 cups of lime soda.

   B. Use a proportion to find the number of cups of lime soda to mix with 55 cups of orange juice.

Unit Ratios

17. Find the number of cups of orange juice to mix with 1 cup of lime soda.

A **unit ratio** is a ratio in which the denominator is one. For example, $\frac{J}{S} = \frac{2.5\ c}{1\ c}$ is a unit ratio. You can use unit ratios to help you solve problems. To find the number of cups of orange juice to mix with 3 cups of lime soda, multiply 2.5×3 to get 7.5 cups of orange juice.

18. Find the number of cups of orange juice to mix with 7 cups of lime soda. Show how you solved this problem.

19. Shannon's little sister mixed 4 cups of orange juice with 10 cups of lime soda. When Shannon drank the punch, she thought it tasted funny.

   A. Why did the punch taste different from the usual recipe?

   B. Plot a point for 10 cups of lime soda and 4 cups of orange juice on your graph. Does the point lie on the line?

20. **A.** If Shannon follows the recipe and uses 5 cups of orange juice, how many total cups of punch will she make?

   B. Write a ratio comparing the number of cups of orange juice to the total number of cups of punch.

Peanut Cake

Jessie and Jackie will make peanut cakes for the whole class:

21. **A.** Write the ratio of the amount of flour in the Peanut Cake to the amount of butter using a colon.

   B. Write the ratio of the amount of flour to the amount of butter as a fraction.

22. If the girls use 18 ounces of flour, how many ounces of butter should they use? Write a proportion to help you solve this problem.

> No. 30, Peanut Cake Number Two
> 9 ounces flour   1 teaspoon vanilla
> 4 ounces butter   1/4 teaspoon salt
> 4 eggs   1 teaspoon baking powder
> 1 cup sugar   4 ounces of chopped peanuts
>
> Sift flour, salt, and baking powder together; cream the butter and sugar; add the vanilla, chopped nuts, yolks of eggs, well beaten; add flour, then whipped whites, and beat well; bake in a shallow pan in medium oven.

23. If they use 12 ounces of butter, how much flour should they use? Write a proportion to help you solve this problem.

Homework

Edward decided to use ratios to compare some of the things in his life.

- The ratio of guppies to the total number of fish in his fish tank is 3 to 5. (guppies : fish = 3 : 5)
- The ratio of fish to snails is 10 to 1. ($\frac{\text{fish}}{\text{snails}} = \frac{10}{1}$)
- The ratio of the time it takes to feed the fish compared to the time it takes them to eat is 15 seconds to 65 seconds. ($\frac{\text{feeding time}}{\text{eating time}} = \frac{15 \text{ sec}}{65 \text{ sec}}$)

1. Think of some examples in your own life that you can use for making comparisons using ratios. Here are some ideas to get you started, but be as creative as you can.

   - your socks (ratio of new to old, white to colors)
   - your games (board to video, one player to several players)
   - your baseball team (pitchers to fielders, infielders to outfielders, rookies to veterans)

   Choose one of your favorite topics, and use ratios to write as many comparisons as you can for that topic. Be sure to use labels so others can tell what is being compared.

2. Explain to your family some of the ratios you have written. With your family, write at least three ratios comparing the members of your family. For example, you can write a ratio comparing the number of people in your family who like chocolate ice cream to the number of people who do not, or the number of males compared to the number of females.

Fruit Salad

3. Brandon has a fruit salad recipe that calls for 2 cups of strawberries, 3 cups of blueberries, and 5 cups of watermelon cut in small cubes.

   A. Using words, write a ratio comparing the amount of strawberries to the amount of blueberries in the fruit salad.

   B. Using a colon, write a ratio comparing the amount of blueberries to the amount of watermelon in the fruit salad.

   C. Using a fraction, write a ratio comparing the amount of strawberries to the amount of watermelon in the fruit salad.

   D. Write a ratio using a fraction that compares the amount of strawberries to the total amount of fruit salad. (*Hint:* How many cups of fruit salad will this recipe make?)

4. Brandon needs to change the recipe so that it will feed the whole class. He plans to use 9 cups of blueberries to make a larger fruit salad. How much of each of the other ingredients does he need?

Variables in Proportion

When scientists do experiments, they compare variables. They look for simple patterns that will help them better understand the variables and the way they are related. One especially useful pattern is the relationship of proportion. If the ratio of two variables in an experiment is always the same (or equivalent), the **variables are in proportion.**

For example, in the lab *Distance vs. Time* in Unit 3, we investigated the variables distance and time. A student walked at a steady pace. Other members of the group measured the time it took the student to travel different distances.

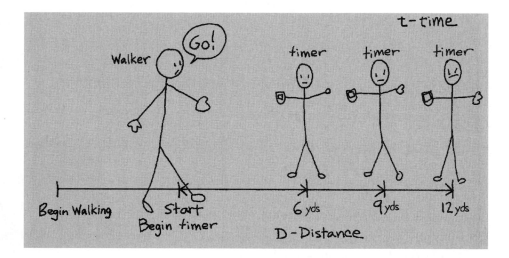

If you walk at a steady pace, then the ratio $\frac{distance}{time}$ is always the same. For example, if a student walks 3 yards every 2 seconds, then this data table shows the distance traveled (*D*) for several different times (*t*):

Distance vs. Time

Time in Seconds	Distance in Yards	$\frac{D}{t}$ Ratio in yd/sec
2	3	$\frac{3 \text{ yd}}{2 \text{ sec}}$
4	6	$\frac{6 \text{ yd}}{4 \text{ sec}}$
6	9	$\frac{9 \text{ yd}}{6 \text{ sec}}$

The ratio *D/t* is called the speed. It is usually written as a unit ratio. In the example, the student is walking at a speed of $\frac{1.5 \text{ yd}}{1 \text{ s}}$. We also write this as 1.5 yd/sec and say "1.5 yards per second."

Since the student walks at the same speed, the ratios in the table are all equal to one another.

Since the ratio *D/t* is always the same (even though *D* and *t* can be different), the variables distance and time are in proportion. We can write proportions using the ratios in the table. For example, $\frac{D}{t} = \frac{3 \text{ yd}}{2 \text{ sec}} = \frac{6 \text{ yd}}{4 \text{ sec}}$.

Answer the following questions about the variables in the lab *Distance vs. Time* if the ratio of distance to time is 3 yards to 2 seconds.

1. Show how you know that all the ratios in the table are equal to one another.

2. **A.** Graph the variables in the data table. Write time (*t*) on the horizontal axis and distance (*D*) on the vertical axis.

   B. Describe your graph. Tell where it meets the vertical axis. Is it a straight line or a curve? Does it go up or down as you read from left to right?

3. Choose two points from your graph that lie on grid lines. Write the ratio of distance to time for each point. Are the two ratios equal?

4. **A.** If you double the time (*t*), what happens to the distance (*D*)? Give an example.

   B. If you triple the time (*t*), what happens to the distance (*D*)? Give an example.

   C. If you multiply the time by any number, what happens to the distance traveled? For example, if a student walks 3 yards in 2 seconds, how far will the student walk in 8 sec (4 × 2 sec)?

5. If you know the time, how can you find the distance? (*Hint:* How far does the walker travel on average in 1 second?)

Here are some examples of variables we have studied this year that are in proportion. Choose <u>one</u> of these pairs of variables to explore in this lesson. Answer Questions 6–10 <u>for that example</u>. Then report your answers to the class. (Your teacher will help you choose the variables to investigate.)

Example 1: A Day at the Races (Distance/Time)

In the lab *A Day at the Races* (Unit 5), we explored the relationship between distance and time for different methods of traveling: running, crawling, walking backwards, etc. If you choose this example, use a crawling speed of 6 feet every 3 seconds to find values for *D* and *t*.

A Day at the Races

t Time in Seconds	D Distance in Feet	$\frac{D}{t}$ Ratio in $\frac{F}{S}$
3	6	$\frac{6}{3}$
6		
9		

Example 2: Quarters and Dimes (Quarters/Dimes)

In a problem in Unit 3, we compared the number of dimes to the number of quarters for equal amounts of money. If you choose this example, use what you know about dimes and quarters to complete the table.

Quarters and Dimes

Dimes	Quarters	$\frac{Q}{D}$ Ratio
5	2	$\frac{2}{5}$
10		

Example 3: Spreading Out (Area/Number of Drops)

In the lab *Spreading Out* (Unit 4), we made spots on paper towels by dropping different numbers of drops on a towel. Then we measured the area of the spots. As the number of drops increased, the area of the spots got larger. Alexis found that the ratio of the Area of the Spot to the Number of Drops was $\frac{11 \text{ sq cm}}{2 \text{ drops}}$. Use Alexis's ratio to complete the table.

Spreading Out

N Number of Drops	A Area in cm	$\frac{A}{N}$ Ratio
2	11	$\frac{11}{2}$
4		
6		

Example 4: Peanut Brittle (Peanuts/Sugar)

In Lesson 1 of this unit, we investigated a recipe for peanut brittle in which the ratio of the amount of peanuts to the amount of sugar was 1 c : 3 c. If you choose this example, use this ratio to complete the table.

Peanut Brittle

S Sugar (in cups)	P Peanuts (in cups)	$\frac{P}{S}$ Ratio
3	1	$\frac{1}{3}$
6		
9		

Answer Questions 6–10 for <u>one</u> of the four examples.

6. **A.** Complete the data table for your variables. Show at least 3 different values of your variables.

   B. Are the ratios in your table equal to one another? If so, tell how you know.

7. **A.** Graph the variables in the data table. Write the variable in the first column on the horizontal axis and the variable in the second column on the vertical axis. Choose the scale on each axis before you plot the points.

   B. Describe your graph. Tell where it meets the vertical axis. Is it a straight line or a curve? Does it go up or down as you read from left to right?

8. Choose two points from your graph. Write ratios for these two points. (Write the ratio of the variable on the vertical axis to the variable on the horizontal axis.) Are the two ratios equal?

9. **A.** If you double the value of one of your variables, what happens to the value of the other variable? Give an example.

   B. If you triple the value of one of your variables, what happens to the value of the other variable? Give an example.

   C. If you multiply the value of one of your variables by any number, what happens to the value of the other variable? Give an example.

10. If you know the value of one of your variables, how can you find the value of the other variable? Give an example.

Exploring Variables That Are Not in Proportion

11. For each graph below, check whether the variables are in proportion: choose 2 points on the graph and check whether the ratios of their coordinates are equivalent. If they are, write a proportion involving the variables.

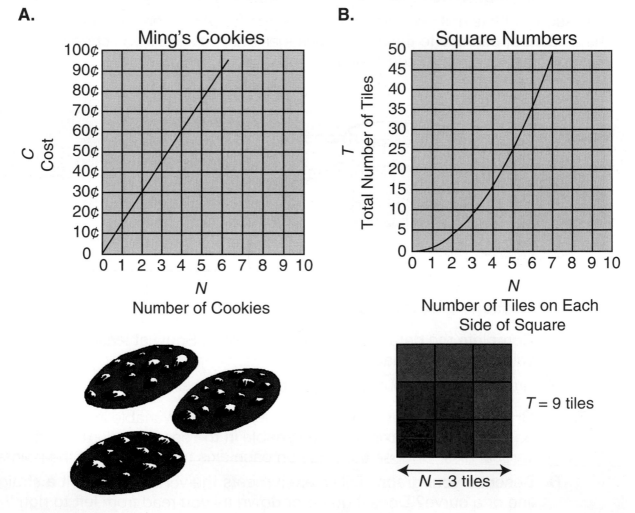

A.

Ming's Cookies

C Cost — *N* Number of Cookies

B.

Square Numbers

T Total Number of Tiles — *N* Number of Tiles on Each Side of Square

T = 9 tiles

N = 3 tiles

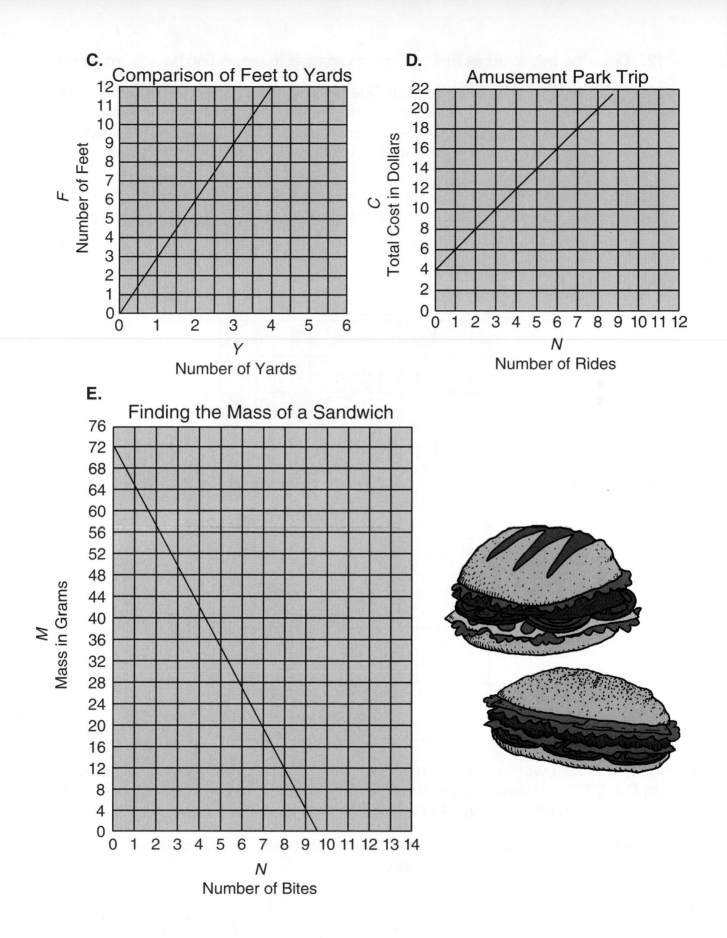

C. Comparison of Feet to Yards

F
Number of Feet

Y
Number of Yards

D. Amusement Park Trip

C
Total Cost in Dollars

N
Number of Rides

E. Finding the Mass of a Sandwich

M
Mass in Grams

N
Number of Bites

12. Describe two features that graphs of variables in proportion have in common.

13. Choose one of the graphs from Question 11 that represents variables that are not in proportion. Choose a value of one of the variables and double it. Does the corresponding value of the other variable double? Show your example. How is this different from variables that are in proportion?

Solving Problems Using Graphs of Variables in Proportion

John dropped a tennis ball from three different drop heights (*D*): 40 cm, 80 cm, and 120 cm. He measured how high it bounced (*B*). He made the following graph of his data.

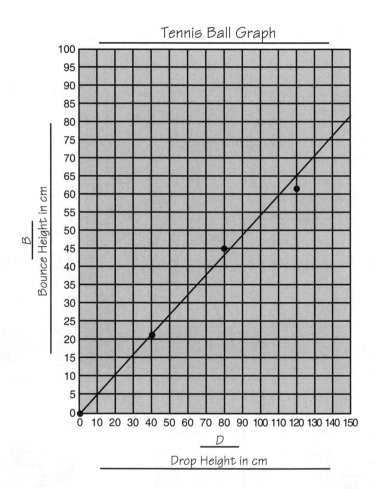

John and Felicia wondered how high the ball would bounce if it were dropped from *D* = 200 cm. However, the numbers they wanted are not on the graph. They thought of two different ways to solve this problem:

Method 1. John used his graph to set up a proportion involving the variables *B* and *D*. Then he solved the proportion.

John saw that the point $D = 100$ cm, $B = 54$ cm is on his line. Using this information, he wrote the proportion:

$$\frac{B}{D} = \frac{54 \text{ cm}}{100 \text{ cm}}$$

Since the graph is a straight line through (0, 0), John knew that the ratio $\frac{B}{D}$ would be equivalent for all points on the line, including the point he wondered about: $D = 200$ cm. So, John wrote the proportion:

$$\frac{B}{200 \text{ cm}} = \frac{54 \text{ cm}}{100 \text{ cm}}$$

14. A. Solve John's proportion to find how high the ball would bounce if it were dropped from 200 cm.

   B. Write and solve a proportion to find the height from which John would have to drop the ball for it to bounce 162 cm.

Method 2. Felicia thought of another method to find how high a ball would bounce if it were dropped from 200 cm. She read on the graph that $B = 54$ cm when $D = 100$ cm. Since the variables are in proportion, she knew that doubling D would cause B to double too. Therefore, the bounce height would be $B = 2 \times 54$ cm $= 108$ cm.

15. Use Felicia's Method 2 to find how high the ball would bounce if it were dropped 400 cm.

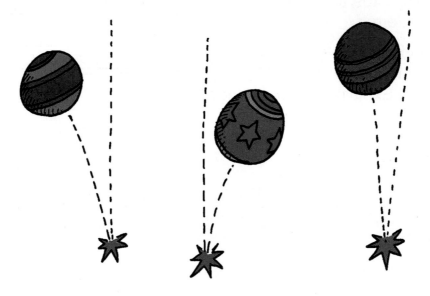

John's Super Ball Experiment

John repeated his experiment using a super ball. Below is a graph of his data.

1. Predict how high the super ball would bounce if it is dropped from a height of 60 cm.

2. From what height should John drop the ball if he wants the ball to bounce 75 cm?

3. Are the variables drop height (*D*) and bounce height (*B*) in proportion? How do you know?

4. Predict how high the ball will bounce if it is dropped from a height of *D* = 240 cm.

   A. Use John's Method 1 from page 408 to solve the problem. (*Hint:* $\frac{B}{D} = \frac{?}{?}$)

   B. Use Felicia's Method 2 from page 409 to solve the problem.

5. Predict how high the ball will bounce if it is dropped from *D* = 150 cm. Explain your reasoning.

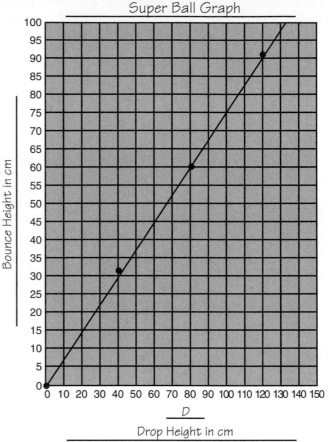

Sink and Float

Mr. Moreno put some objects in a pan of water. Some of them sank to the bottom. Others floated. "What makes an object sink or float?" asked Mr. Moreno.

"I think heavy things sink and light things float. So, I think an object's mass is the reason things sink or float," said Nicholas.

"I think big things sink and little things float. So, I think volume is the reason things sink or float," said Jackie.

"But ships are big and heavy. Why do they float?" wondered Luis.

In this activity, you will explore the reasons why things sink or float. Before you begin, discuss what properties of an object you think determine whether it will sink or float.

Mass

1. Find the mass of several objects your teacher has provided. Record your results in the data table on the *Sink and Float Tables* Activity Page like the one shown here.

2. Put each object into a pan of water. Record in the table whether it sinks or floats.

Sink and Float Data Table

Object	V Volume in cc	M Mass in g	Sink or Float?
water			——

3. Do each of the objects that sink have more mass than the objects that float? If not, give an example.

4. Does whether an object sinks or floats depend only upon its mass? Explain.

Volume

5. Find the volume of the objects your teacher has provided. Record your results in the same table you used for mass.

6. Are each of the objects that sink larger in volume than the objects that float? If not, give an example.

7. Does whether an object sinks or floats depend only upon its volume? Explain.

Now that you have collected and thought about your data, discuss again what properties of an object you think determine whether it will sink or float.

Density

Sinking or floating has something to do with both mass and volume. If something is heavy for its size, it will sink. If it is light for its size, it will float. We can measure heaviness by mass and size by volume. To help predict whether an object will sink or float, scientists compare an object's mass to its volume. To compare, they find the ratio of the object's mass to its volume. This ratio is called **density.**

$$\text{Density} = \frac{\text{Mass}}{\text{Volume}} = \text{Mass} \div \text{Volume}$$

Since density involves both mass and volume, the unit of measure involves both as well.

For example, if a rock has a mass of $M = 65$ g and a volume of $V = 23$ cc, its density is:

$$\frac{M}{V} = \frac{65 \text{ g}}{23 \text{ cc}}$$

Sometimes, densities are expressed as unit ratios using decimals. This makes them easier to compare. We can find the density of the rock as a decimal by dividing; $65 \div 23$ is about 2.8, so:

$$\frac{65 \text{ g}}{23 \text{ cc}} \approx \frac{2.8 \text{ g}}{1 \text{ cc}}$$

This means that 1 cc of rock has a mass of 2.8 g.

A common unit of density is grams per cubic centimeter ($\frac{g}{cc}$). Scientists usually write 2.8 g/cc as shorthand for $\frac{2.8 \text{ g}}{1 \text{ cc}}$.

Sinking and floating have something to do with density. Let's explore this more. We'll find the density of some objects and look for patterns in the data.

8. **A.** Complete data tables like the ones below on the *Sink and Float Tables* Activity Page. Write the density of each object as a ratio of its mass to volume.

   B. Compute the density of each object to the nearest tenth, and record it in tables like the ones below.

Sinks in Water

Object	Density as Ratio $\frac{M}{V}$	Density as Decimal
		$\frac{? \text{ g}}{1 \text{ cc}}$

Floats in Water

Object	Density as Ratio $\frac{M}{V}$	Density as Decimal
		$\frac{? \text{ g}}{1 \text{ cc}}$

9. **A.** Find the mass and the volume of an easy to measure amount of water. (*Hint:* Be sure to subtract the mass of the cylinder.) Record your data in the Sink and Float Data Table.

   B. What is the density of the water? Write your answer as a ratio and as a decimal in the space provided on the *Sink and Float Tables* Activity Page. Is it greater than one, less than one, close to one, or equal to one?

Finding Patterns

10. Look at your tables. What patterns do you see about objects that sink and those that float in water? Write your conclusions in sentences.

11. An object has a mass of 30 g and a volume of 40 cc. Will it sink or float in water?

12. Will an object with a mass of 500 g sink or float in water?

13. **A.** Which is heavier, a pound of feathers or a pound of lead?

    B. Which is denser, a pound of feathers or a pound of lead?

Challenge:

14. A boat in the shape of a box is shown here.

    The mass of the empty boat is 150 g. How much extra mass can the boat hold before it sinks? Show your work.

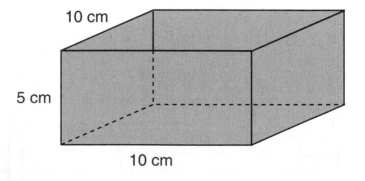

10 cm

5 cm

10 cm

Mass vs. Volume: Proportions and Density

Mr. Moreno's class is experimenting with things that sink and float.

"This piece of clay sinks in water," observed Romesh. "I'll try a smaller piece. That will be lighter, so maybe it will float."

"I'm not sure," said Ana. "A smaller piece would have less mass, but wouldn't it have less volume too? Maybe its density wouldn't be different."

"We can do an experiment to find out whether a different amount of the same material has a different density," said Mr. Moreno.

The students measured the mass and volume of 3 different amounts of clay, recorded their data in a data table, and graphed their data. Then they did the same thing for different amounts of steel to see whether they got similar results for different materials. In the lab that follows, you will do the same.

You will find the mass and volume of 3 steel balls your teacher gives you and 3 lumps of clay you make about the same size as the steel balls.

1. Discuss with your group how you will do the experiment. Then draw a picture that shows what you will do. Be sure to label the variables and include all the equipment you will use.

2. Find the mass and volume of 3 different-sized steel balls. Record your data in a table like this. (To get accurate measurements for the small steel ball, measure the mass and volume of 5 identical small steel balls and divide by 5.)

Material 1: Steel

Size of Object	V Volume (in cc)	M Mass (in g)
Small ($\frac{1}{2}$-inch diameter)		
Medium (1-inch diameter)		
Large ($1\frac{1}{4}$-inch diameter)		

3. Find the mass and volume of 3 different-sized clay balls. Make your lumps of clay about the same size as the steel balls, so your data will fit on the same graph. Record your data in a table like this.

Material 2: Clay

Size of Object	V Volume (in cc)	M Mass (in g)
Small		
Medium		
Large		

4. Plot the data for each material on the same graph. Scientists usually put Mass (M) on the vertical axis and Volume (V) on the horizontal axis. Scale your axes so that M goes up to at least 180 g and V goes up to at least 24 cc.

5. What is the value of M when V is 0 cc? Plot this point on your graph.

6. If there is a pattern to your points, draw a best-fit line or curve to show the pattern. Draw one for steel and a separate one for clay. Label each line or curve with the name of the material it represents.

7. Use your graph to do the following:

   A. Find the mass of a steel ball whose volume is 12 cc. Did you interpolate or extrapolate?

   B. Find the volume of a steel ball whose mass is 180 g. Did you interpolate or extrapolate?

   C. Find the mass of a piece of clay whose volume is 5 cc. Did you interpolate or extrapolate?

   D. Find the volume of a piece of clay whose mass is 60 g. Did you interpolate or extrapolate?

8. **A.** Choose a point on your line for clay. Use it to write the ratio of the mass of clay to the volume of clay as a fraction.

   B. Choose two more points on the line for clay. Use them to write ratios of mass to volume. Are the three ratios from the line for clay equal (or approximately equal)?

9. **A.** Choose a point on your line for steel. Use it to write the ratio of the mass of steel to the volume of steel as a fraction.

   B. Choose two more points on the line for steel. Use them to write ratios of mass to volume. Are the three ratios from the line for steel equal (or approximately equal)?

10. Answer Romesh's and Ana's original questions:

    A. Do different amounts of the same material have the same density?

    B. Will a smaller piece of clay float? Why or why not?

11. **A.** Using your data, give the density of clay.

    B. Using your data, give the density of steel.

12. Suppose you wanted to find the volume of a lump of clay that was too big to fit in your graduated cylinder. How can you use your two-pan balance to help find its volume?

13. **A.** How is your graph for steel the same as your graph for clay?

   B. How is your graph for steel different from your graph for clay?

Explore

14. Maria put a mystery object in a box. She told the class it had a mass of 30 g and a volume of 6 cc. Was it steel, clay, or a third material? Explain your answer.

MYSTERY BOX

mass= 30g   V=6cc

? ? ? ? ? ? ?

15. A piece of clay has a volume of 100 cc. Find its mass. (Since the numbers are too big to be on the graph, the problem can't be solved by reading the graph directly.)

16. A piece of steel has a mass of 1500 g. Find its volume.

Patterns with Graphs: Sink and Float

Graph

17. Use your data from the *Sink and Float* lesson to graph the mass vs. volume line for each of the materials in that lesson. Be sure to include the line for water. The line for each material will go through the point (0, 0) and that material's data point from the *Sink and Float* lesson. Romesh's line for a rock is shown at the right.

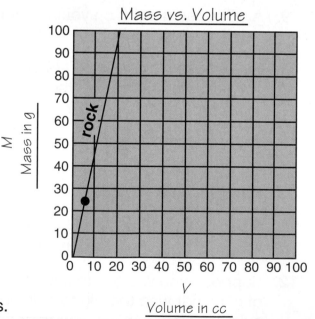

Mass vs. Volume

* Graph all the lines (one line for each material) on one sheet of graph paper.

* Label each line with the name of the material that the line represents.

* Indicate whether the material sinks or floats by labeling its line with (S) or (F).

18. What pattern do you see in your graph? Explain how to tell from your graph whether an object will sink or float.

19. On your graph, plot the data point for a mystery object with a mass of 50 g and a volume of 80 cc. Draw the line through this point and the point $M = 0$, $V = 0$, representing the mass vs. volume line for this material. (Label it "Question 19.")

    A. Based on the pattern you observed in your graph, would you expect the object to sink or float in water? Explain.

    B. Find the object's density. Based on its density, would you expect the object to sink or float in water? Explain.

20. **A.** Explain how to use the mass and volume data table to compare densities.

    B. Explain how to use the graph to compare densities.

21. The final product from a steel mill should not have air pockets trapped inside. You are given a piece of steel with a volume of 20 cc. Explain how you would go about determining whether the piece was solid steel or had air trapped inside.

22. Two rocks are thought to be made of the same material. Explain how you could investigate whether this is true.

23. An object has a density of $\frac{4\,g}{1\,cc}$ or 4 g/cc.

    A. If its volume is 80 cc, what is its mass? Show your work.

    B. If its mass is 100 g, what is its volume? Show your work.

Archimedes and the King's Gold Crown

About 2000 years ago, King Hieron of Syracuse asked his goldsmith to make a crown out of a lump of pure gold. When the beautiful new crown arrived, King Hieron admired it, but he was also suspicious. Did the goldsmith keep some of the gold for himself and replace it with less valuable silver? King Hieron turned to his good friend Archimedes, the most famous mathematician and inventor of his day, and asked him to find out.

Archimedes found that the mass of the crown was the same as the mass of the lump of gold, but the king was still suspicious. Archimedes knew that 1 pound of silver had a smaller volume than 1 pound of gold. He reasoned that if the goldsmith had substituted some silver, then the volume would be different. But he needed to find a way to measure the volume without melting down the crown.

Puzzling over the problem, Archimedes chanced to come to one of the city's bathhouses. As he eased himself into the full tub, he noticed that the water rose and spilled over the side. Archimedes immediately realized that he had found a method for solving the puzzle. He could put the crown in water. The amount of water that spilled out would be equal to the volume of the crown! If it were different from the volume of the same mass of gold, he would know that the crown was not pure gold.

Archimedes was so excited about his discovery that in his joy he leaped out of the tub, and, rushing towards his home, he cried out, "Eureka! I have found it." What Archimedes had discovered over 2000 years ago was a way to find the volume of an object. This enabled him to compare the density of materials. If two different objects have different densities, then they must be made from different materials. Unfortunately for the goldsmith, the crown was not pure gold, and the goldsmith lost more than his stolen gold.

Mass vs. Volume: Proportions and Density

1. An object has a mass of 48 g and a volume of 8 cc.

   A. Express its density as a ratio of mass to volume.

   B. An object made of the same material has a volume of 16 cc. What is its mass?

   C. An object made of the same material has a mass of 300 g. What is its volume?

2. A material has a density of $\frac{4 \text{ g}}{3 \text{ cc}}$. Balls of different sizes are made from this material. The masses of the balls are listed below. Find the volumes.

   A. 20 g   **B.** 36 g   **C.** 8 g

   D. 2 g   **E.** 100 g   **F.** 60 g

3. Here is the mass vs. volume graph of an unknown material.

   A. What is the mass of 28 cc of this material? Did you interpolate or extrapolate to find your answer?

   B. What is the volume of 40 g of this material? Did you interpolate or extrapolate to find your answer?

4. A piece of the unknown material represented in the graph has a mass of $M = 200$ g. Find its volume. (Since the numbers are too big to be on the graph, the problem can't be solved by reading the graph directly.)

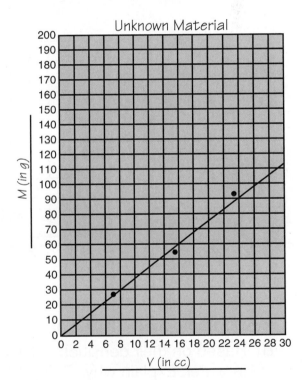

Unknown Material

M (in g)

V (in cc)

5. Copy the following table. Then find the density of the objects in the table. Which object has greatest density?

Object	Volume of Object (in cc)	Mass of Object (in g)	Density in g/cc
A	24	11.0	
B	9	11.0	
C	4	5.5	
D	11	5.5	

6. Here is a graph of the mass vs. volume of several materials. Using the graph, tell which of the materials will sink and which will float in water. Explain why.

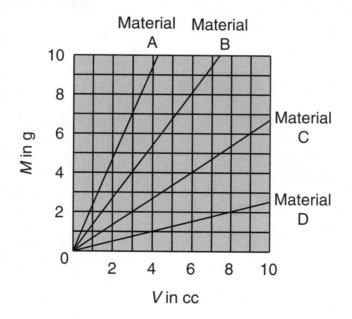

7. A. Compute the densities of the materials in the graph.

B. Based on their densities, tell which materials will sink and which will float in water. Explain why.

SG • Grade 5 • Unit 13 • Lesson 4   Mass vs. Volume: Proportions and Density

Problems of Scale

Each of these problems describes a scale model, a scale drawing, or a map scale. Each scale can be written as a ratio. We write *M* to stand for the distance on the map and *A* to stand for the actual distance. For example, if 1 cm represents 9 miles on a map, we can write:

$$\frac{M}{A} = \frac{1 \text{ cm}}{9 \text{ mi}} \quad \text{or} \quad \frac{A}{M} = \frac{9 \text{ mi}}{1 \text{ cm}}$$

1. On an architect's drawing, one inch represents one foot on the actual house. If the windows are two inches wide on the drawing, how wide are they on the actual house?

2. On a map of Florida, 1 cm represents 9 miles. On the same map, it is about 6 cm from Disney World to the Atlantic Ocean. Write a proportion showing the actual distance to the ocean.

3. Jessie and Manny are building a model airplane. It is an accurate scale model of an actual airplane. The wing of their plane is 12 cm long. The wing of the actual airplane is 6 meters long. If the actual airplane body is 18 meters long, how long should the model airplane body be?

4. On another architect's drawing, one inch represents two feet on the actual house. If the door on the house will be seven feet tall, how high will it be on the drawing?

5. A banana that is 6 cm long on a picture is 3 cm long on a reduced-size copy of the picture. If a pineapple on the same picture is 12 cm long on the original, how long is it on the reduced-size copy?

6. A line that is 6 cm long on a blueprint is 15 m long on the actual building. If another line on the same blueprint is 9 cm, how long is it on the building?

Unit 14

Using Circles

	Student Guide	Discovery Assignment Book	Adventure Book	Unit Resource Guide*
Lesson 1				
Exploring Circumference and Diameter	●	●		
Lesson 2				
Circumference vs. Diameter	●			●
Lesson 3				
Constructing Circles with Terry	●	●		
Lesson 4				
Complex Constructions	●			●
Lesson 5				
Circle Graphs	●	●		
Lesson 6				
Practice and Problems	●			

*Unit Resource Guide pages are from the teacher materials.

Exploring Circumference and Diameter

Mr. Moreno took his fifth-grade class on a field trip to Navy Pier in Chicago. The highlight of the trip was a ride on the Ferris wheel. While waiting in line, Nila and David starting talking.

That Ferris wheel is like a giant circle.

I wonder how tall it is?

It says in the brochure that the Ferris wheel is about 150 feet tall.

I wonder how far we are going to travel when we go around.

Nila and David decided to investigate circles. A **circle** is a curve that is made up of all the points that are the same distance from one point, called the **center.**

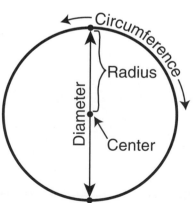

The **circumference** is the distance around the circle. The circumference of the Ferris wheel is the distance that Nila and David will travel when they make a trip around it. A **diameter** is a line segment (with a length) that connects two points on a circle and passes through the center. The phrase "the diameter of a circle" means the length of any diameter.

The circumference and the diameter of a circle can be measured in many ways.

1. Tell some ways that you might measure the circumference and the diameter of a circle. For example, how can you measure the circumference and diameter of a clock face or a can lid?

2. Use two pieces of string to measure the diameter and circumference of objects shaped like circles, such as lids or cans. Explore the relationship between the circumference and the diameter of a circle.

3. Estimate the number of diameters that will fit around the same circle.

4. Estimate the circumference of the Ferris wheel at Navy Pier. (*Hint:* Remember the diameter is 150 feet.)

Circumference vs. Diameter

In Lesson 1 *Exploring Circumference and Diameter,* Manny and Alexis discovered a relationship between the circumference and diameter of a circle.

We found that the circumference was about three times longer than the diameter.

But, is it exactly three times longer? It could be a little more or a little less than three.

In this laboratory investigation, you will investigate the relationship between the circumference and the diameter of circles by measuring more precisely than you did in Lesson 1. You will measure the circumference and diameter of at least three different-sized circles.

Discuss

1. How can you accurately measure the circumference and diameter of a can or a lid? Choose a method to use in the lab.

2. Draw a picture that shows your experiment. Your picture should show the method you chose to measure the circumference and the diameter. Label the circumference *C* and the diameter *D*.

Take your measurements from at least three different-sized cans or lids.

3. A. Measure the diameter for each circle to the nearest tenth of a centimeter. Compare your measurements to your partner's measurements. Agree on the length of the diameter for each circle. Then record the value in a table similar to the one shown below.

B. Measure the circumference of each circle to the nearest tenth of a centimeter three times. Record each of your measurements in a table similar to the one shown below.

Circle	*D* in _____	*C* in _____			
		Trial 1	Trial 2	Trial 3	Mean
Small					
Medium					
Large					

4. Use a calculator to find the mean circumference for each size can or lid and record it in your data table. Find the mean to the nearest tenth of a cm.

5. Why is it a good idea to do more than one trial and find a mean value for the circumference of each can or lid?

6. Make a graph of your data.

   • Decide whether to make a bar graph or a point graph.

   • Plot the diameter on the horizontal axis and the circumference on the vertical axis.

   • Scale your graph to at least 100 centimeters for the circumference and 25 centimeters for the diameter.

Use your graph to answer the following questions. Show your work on your graph.

7. **A.** Describe your graph.

   B. If the points on your graph suggest a line, use a ruler to draw a best-fit line.

8. **A.** If a circle has a diameter of 5 centimeters, what is its circumference?

   B. Did you use interpolation or extrapolation?

9. **A.** If a circle has a circumference of 70 centimeters, what is its diameter?

   B. Did you use interpolation or extrapolation?

10. Use points on your line to find three ratios. Complete a table like the one shown here. The first row in the table shows an example. (Do not include this example in your data table.)

Diameter	Circumference	$\dfrac{C}{D}$	$C \div D$
4 cm	12.5 cm	$\dfrac{12.5}{4}$	3.1

11. Is the ratio about the same for each diameter?

The ratio of the circumference to the diameter of a circle is a special number in mathematics. It is called *pi* (pronounced "pie"). The symbol for *pi* is the Greek letter π.

Historical Note

π is a nonrepeating decimal that goes on and on forever. One of the earliest good estimates for π was made by a famous Greek mathematician named Archimedes in about 240 BCE. Archimedes's estimate for π was correct to two decimal places (3.14). Today, mathematicians, with the help of computers, have accurately calculated π to billions of decimal places.

---

12. Press the π key on your calculator. Compare the number in the window of your calculator to the numbers in the last column of the data table in Question 10. They should be close.

13. A. Copy the table at the right and find the missing values. Use the π key on your calculator, and round your answers to the nearest hundredth.

Diameter	Circumference	$\frac{C}{D}$	$C \div D$
8 cm	25.13 cm		
10 cm			3.14
26 cm			3.14
	12 cm		3.14
	6 cm		3.14

B. Write a number sentence using *C* and *D* that tells how to find the diameter of a circle if the circumference is known. Remember, this kind of number sentence is called a **formula.**

C. Write a formula using *C* and *D* that tells how to find the circumference of a circle if the diameter is known.

14. The diameter of a circle is 20 cm.

A. Estimate the circumference using "3" for π.

B. Use paper and pencil and "3.14" for π to get a better estimate of the circumference.

C. Use your calculator and the π key. Compare your answers.

15. A. Use your formula to find the circumference of a circle with a diameter of 24.5 cm. Give your answer to the nearest tenth of a centimeter.

B. Use your formula to find the diameter of a circle with a circumference of 48 cm. Give your answer to the nearest tenth of a centimeter.

There is a definite relationship between the circumference and the diameter of a circle.

- The circumference of a circle is equal to the diameter of the same circle times π. This means that $C = \pi \times D$.
- The diameter of a circle is equal to the circumference of the same circle divided by π. This means that $D = C \div \pi$.

Use the formulas for finding the circumference or the diameter of a circle to solve the following problems. Use the π key on your calculator.

16. Nila measured the circumference of a circle as $9\frac{1}{4}$ inches. Find the diameter. Round your answer to the nearest inch.

17. Brandon measured the diameter of a circle as 87 cm. Find the circumference. Round your answer to the nearest tenth of a centimeter.

18. Copy the table at the right. Then find the missing values of D (diameter) and C (circumference). Round answers to the nearest tenth of a centimeter.

D	C
15 cm	
30 cm	
	14 cm
	60 cm

In Questions 19–21, round all answers to the nearest centimeter. Estimate to see if your answers are reasonable.

19. A tire on a car has an inside diameter of 43 centimeters and an outside diameter of 71 centimeters.

    A. What is the inner circumference?

    B. What is the outer circumference?

    C. How far will the tire roll in one turn?

20. One wheel on Frank's chair has a diameter of 64 centimeters. If he goes to the store and back, a distance of 3000 meters, how many turns does the wheel make?

21. It takes 30 fifth graders, arms outstretched, to surround a Giant Sequoia tree. Estimate the tree's diameter. (*Hint:* An average fifth grader's arm span is about 140 cm.)

22. A bicycle wheel rolls 75 inches with one turn of the wheel. What is the diameter of the wheel to the nearest inch?

1. Use your calculator to find the circumference of a circle that has a diameter of 3367 inches. Round your answer to the nearest inch.

2. Use your calculator to find the diameter of a circle that has a circumference of 82,771 inches. Round your answer to the nearest inch.

Professor Peabody was having fun exploring different numbers for the circumference and the diameter of circles on his calculator.

First, estimate in your head. Then use your calculator to find a better estimate of the diameter for the circles with circumferences listed in Questions 3 and 4. Round your answer to the nearest tenth of a unit.

3. $C = 942$ units

4. $C = 8075$ units

First, estimate in your head. Then use your calculator to find a better estimate of the circumference for the diameters listed in Questions 5 and 6. Round your answer to the nearest tenth of a unit.

5. $D = 9460$ units

6. $D = 5977.6$ units

7. A trundle wheel is a disk that rolls along the ground and clicks once every time it makes a complete turn. It is often used for surveying land. What is the diameter of a trundle wheel that clicks once every meter? Round your answer to the nearest hundredth of a meter.

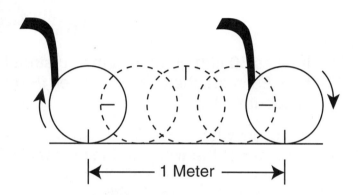

1 Meter

Constructing Circles with Terry

Terry is a furniture designer. Her specialty is circular tables. She makes many different tables. Terry needs to know a lot about circles to make her tables. Here are some of the terms Terry uses every day.

Central angle: An angle whose vertex is at the center of a circle.

Center: The point such that every point on a circle is the same distance from it.

Chord: Any line segment that connects two points on a circle.

Circumference: The distance around a circle.

Diameter: A segment connecting two points on a circle and going through the center of the circle. The word can also mean the length of the segment.

Radius: A line segment connecting the center of a circle to any point on the circle. The word can also mean the length of this segment.

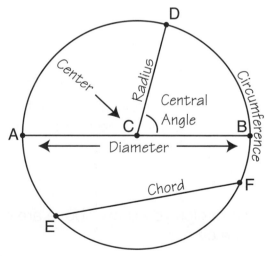

Remember, we write $\overline{AB}$ for line segment AB. In the circle, $\overline{AB}$ is a diameter and a chord.

Constructing Circles with Terry

Answer the questions about the circle drawn on the previous page. You will need a ruler and a protractor.

1. What is the length of the diameter of circle C?

2. What is the length of the radius of circle C?

3. What is the length of chord EF?

4. Estimate the circumference of circle C.

5. What is the measure of central angle DCB? You may need to trace the angle on a separate sheet of paper and extend a side.

Terry always makes scale drawings of the tabletops that she is going to build. Make the following drawings for Terry using a compass, ruler, and protractor.

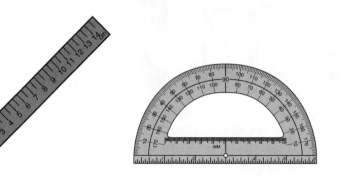 

Table 1

Table 1 is a circular table with a circular border made of a dark wood. The inside is light wood.

Directions:

    A. Draw a circle with radius 6 cm.

    B. Draw a circle with radius 4 cm using the same center point as the 6 cm circle.

The two circles you drew above are concentric circles. **Concentric circles** have the same center.

6. What is the distance between the two circles?

Table 2

Table 2 is a circular table with a square inlay.

Directions:

  A. Draw a circle with radius 2 inches.

  B. Lightly draw a diameter.

  C. Lightly draw another diameter, perpendicular to the first diameter. (**Perpendicular lines** are lines that meet at right angles.)

  D. Make a quadrilateral by connecting the endpoints of the diameters.

  E. Erase the diameters.

7. How can you check that the quadrilateral is a square?

Table 3

Table 3 is a table for a hallway. It is a circle with a piece cut off.

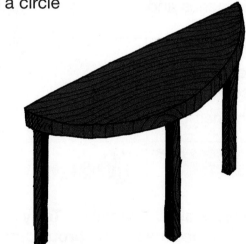

Directions:

  A. Draw a circle with radius 4.5 cm.

  B. Draw a chord with length 8 cm.

  C. Erase the larger part of the circle cut off by the chord.

Table 4

Table 4 is a wedge-shaped coffee table.

Directions:

A. Lightly draw a circle of radius 5 cm.

B. Draw two radii that make a central angle of 115°.

8. What is the measure of the other central angle? Erase the part of the circle not included in the wedge.

Table 5

Table 5 is a countertop. It looks like a rectangle with half a circle attached.

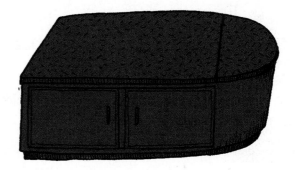

Directions:

A. Draw a rectangle with sides $3\frac{3}{4}$ inches and $2\frac{1}{4}$ inches.

B. Mark the midpoint of a $2\frac{1}{4}$-inch side. This is the center of the half-circle.

C. Draw the half-circle.

Homework

Make the following scale drawings for Terry's tables and answer the questions. You will need a ruler, compass, and protractor. If the problem is impossible, say so.

1. Terry is building a circular hall table with a piece cut off.

A. Draw a circular table with radius 2.5 cm.

B. What is the diameter of the table?

C. Draw a chord of length 4 cm.

D. Erase the larger part of the table cut off by the chord.

2. Terry is building a different circular hall table with a piece cut off.

    A. Draw a circular table with diameter 5 cm.

    B. What is the radius of the table?

    C. Draw a chord of length 6 cm.

    D. What is the length of the longest chord possible for this circle?

3. Terry is building a triangular-shaped coffee table. Terry drew a circle with a radius of $1\frac{1}{2}$ inches. She then drew two radii so that the central angle between them measured 78°.

    A. Follow Terry's directions.

    B. What is the measure of the other central angle?

    C. Draw the chord that connects the endpoints of the radii.

    D. Erase the circle.

    E. What are the lengths of the sides of the triangle?

4. Terry drew a circle with circumference 10 cm.

    A. What is the approximate radius of this circle?

    B. Draw the circle.

5. Terry is building a table from light wood with a border made of dark wood.

Draw two concentric circles. Make the radius of the inner circle 6 cm. Make the radius of the outer circle 3 cm more than the radius of the inner circle.

6. Terry is building a circular table with leaves that fold down to form a square.

To see what the table will look like, she drew a circle with diameter 7 cm.

    A. Draw the circle.

    B. Draw a square inside the circle. (*Hint:* Draw 2 diameters.)

    C. Erase the diameters.

    D. What is the approximate length of a side of the square?

7. Design your own table. Make a drawing, and write instructions to tell someone else how to make your table.

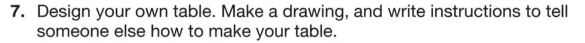

Complex Constructions

For centuries, Arabic architects, decorators, and craftsmen created complex designs using just a compass and a straightedge. A straightedge is like a ruler with the ruler markings left off. These designs were used to decorate their walls, floors, and ceilings. They often used a simple pattern to start complex designs.

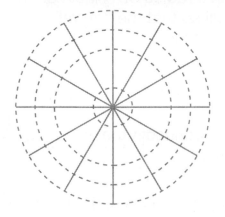

The design above can be used to create these designs:

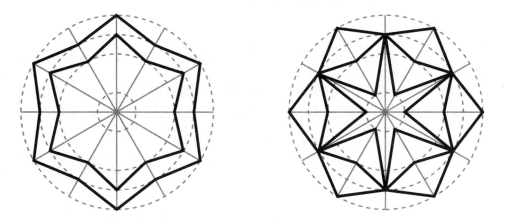

Terry uses a compass, just like the ancient designers, to make scale drawings of her tables.

Terry received an order to build a triangular coffee table. The table is to have sides with lengths of 4 feet, 6 feet, and 7 feet. Terry explained that she can use a compass to draw a picture of the table top. She decided to use the scale 1 cm represents 1 foot.

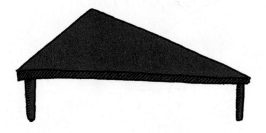

To construct a triangle with sides 4 cm, 6 cm, and 7 cm, Terry started by measuring a length of 7 cm and naming the endpoints A and B.

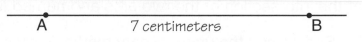

A   7 centimeters   B

She measured 4 cm with her compass. She drew a 4-cm arc with the center at point A as shown below. An **arc** is a part of a circle. The distance from point A to any point on the arc is 4 centimeters.

A   7 centimeters   B

Terry then measured 6 cm with her compass. She drew a 6-cm arc with the center of the circle at point B.

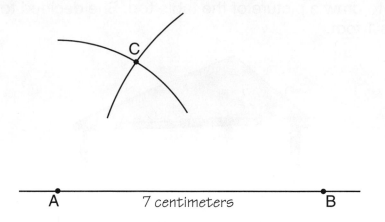

A   7 centimeters   B

Terry drew a point at the intersection of the two arcs and named it C.

She drew $\overline{AC}$ and $\overline{BC}$. She erased the unnecessary marks. Terry now has a picture of the table top.

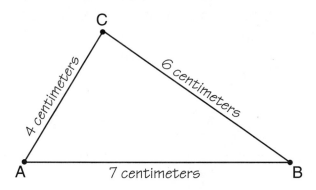

1. Draw a triangle DEF with sides 2.5 inches, 3 inches, and 4 inches using the same method Terry used.

2. Find the measures of the angles of the triangle you drew in Question 1.

Terry was asked to build a triangular table. Her scale drawing has sides 6 cm and 4 cm. The angle between these two sides is 110°.

To construct the triangle, Terry drew the 6 cm length on her working line and labeled it AB. She then used her protractor to make the 110° angle using point A as the vertex.

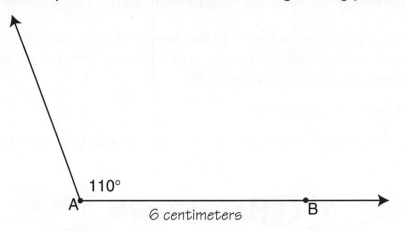

Terry marked off 4 cm on the new ray and labeled the new endpoint C.

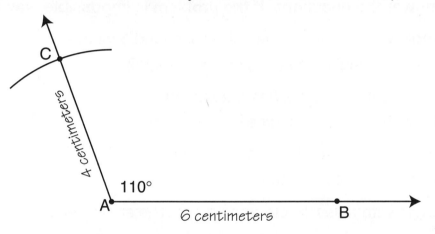

Terry knew that point C is the third vertex of her triangle. She connected points B and C to make her triangle.

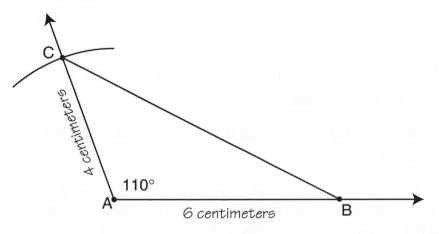

3. Construct the triangle Terry made on your own paper.

4. What is the length of the third side of triangle ABC?

Terry was asked to make a table that is in the shape of a quadrilateral. Her scale drawing has sides 1 inch, 2 inches, 1 inch, and 2 inches. The 1-inch sides are opposite each other and the angles are all 90°.

5. Construct Terry's quadrilateral.

6. What is another name for the type of quadrilateral you constructed in Question 5?

Make the following scale drawings for Terry using a compass, a protractor, and a ruler. Then answer the questions. If the problem is impossible, say so.

1. **A.** A triangle with sides 3 inches, 4 inches, and 5 inches.

   B. What are the angle measures of the triangle?

2. **A.** A triangle with all three sides measuring 2 inches.

   B. What are the angle measures of the triangle?

3. **A.** A triangle with sides 15 cm, 10 cm, and 3 cm.

   B. What are the angle measures of the triangle?

4. **A.** A triangle with sides 10 cm and 18 cm. The angle between the two sides is 45°.

   B. What is the length of the third side?

5. **A.** Quadrilateral ABCD with sides 10 cm, 5 cm, 10 cm, and 5 cm. Make the 10-cm sides opposite each other; $\angle A = 50°$ and $\angle B = 130°$.

   B. What are the measures of $\angle C$ and $\angle D$?

6. **A.** Quadrilateral EFGH with sides all 10 cm and $\angle E = 60°$, $\angle F = 120°$.

   B. What type of quadrilateral is this?

7. **A.** Quadrilateral JKLM with sides 8 cm, 8 cm, 8 cm, and 6 cm, and $\angle J = 90°$.

   B. What is the sum of the angles of the quadrilateral?

8. The only instructions Terry was given for her last order was to build a triangular coffee table with angles 30, 60, and 90 degrees. Construct a drawing for Terry.

Circle Graphs

Alexis and Frank researched endangered animals for an article they wrote for the school newspaper. They found that the United States Department of the Interior identified 607 different species of vertebrates as endangered in 1990. A vertebrate is an animal with a hard, internal skeleton including a backbone (vertebral column) and a brain enclosed in a skull. Alexis and Frank found a circle graph that showed the percentage of endangered species belonging to each of these groups of vertebrates: mammals, birds, reptiles, amphibians, and fish.

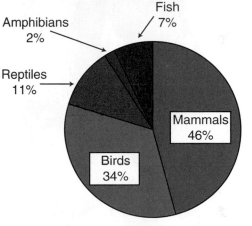

Endangered Species of Vertebrates

- Fish 7%
- Amphibians 2%
- Reptiles 11%
- Mammals 46%
- Birds 34%

1. What questions can Alexis and Frank answer using this graph?

2. Use the circle graph to answer the following questions:

   A. What percent of the endangered species represented in this graph are mammals?

   B. What percent of endangered species are reptiles?

   C. What percent of these species are neither reptile nor mammal?

Circle Graphs

Alexis wants to report the number of species of birds that are endangered. She used the circle graph to help her find this number. First, she looked at the graph and found that 34 percent of all endangered vertebrate species are birds. She knows that 34 percent is about $\frac{1}{3}$ of the species. Then she looked back and saw that there are 607 total species of vertebrates listed as endangered. Alexis rounded 607 to 600. Finally, she found that $\frac{1}{3}$ of 600 is 200. So, she reported that about 200 species of birds are endangered.

3. **A.** What group of animals has about $\frac{1}{2}$ of all endangered vertebrate species?

   B. Estimate the number of species in this group that are endangered.

Explore

Use the Endangered Species circle graph to answer the following questions:

4. Estimate the number of species of reptiles that are endangered.

5. Which two groups of vertebrates together have about the same number of endangered species as reptiles?

6. **A.** What three groups make up about $\frac{1}{5}$ of all endangered vertebrate species?

   B. Estimate the number of species represented by these three groups.

Making a Circle Graph

Nila and Arti wanted to find out what types of television shows the fifth-grade students in their school preferred. They surveyed a total of 60 students.

After organizing their data in a table, Arti suggested that they make a circle graph to display their data for the class.

Type of Show	Tally	Number of Students
Comedy	~~JHT~~ ~~JHT~~ ~~JHT~~ ~~JHT~~ ~~JHT~~ ~~JHT~~	30
News	~~JHT~~ I	6
Drama	~~JHT~~ IIII	9
Sports	~~JHT~~ ~~JHT~~ ~~JHT~~	15

7. How must Arti and Nila express their data in order to make a circle graph?

8. Copy the following data table on your paper. Use what you know about fractions, decimals, and percents to fill in the missing information.

Type of Show	Number of Students	Fraction of Students	Decimal	Percent
Comedy	30	$\frac{30}{60}$	0.5	
News	6			10%
Drama	9		0.15	
Sports	15			

After expressing their data as percents, Nila and Arti are ready to make their circle graph.

"We can use the small centiwheels that we used in Unit 7 to help us make our circle graph," Nila said.

9. How will the small centiwheels be helpful to Nila and Arti as they make their circle graph?

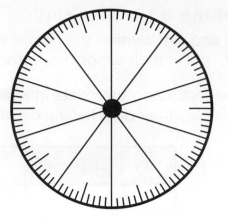

10. Follow Nila's and Arti's steps to create a circle graph.

   A. Nila and Arti used a compass to draw a circle slightly larger than their centiwheel.

   B. They began their graph by placing their small centiwheel inside the circle, making sure to match the center of the wheel with the center of their circle.

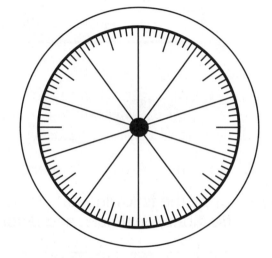

   C. Nila and Arti then used the lines of the small centiwheel to measure and mark each part of the circle graph. After they finished marking their lines, they carefully labeled their graph and added a title. Complete your circle graph of Nila and Arti's data.

Fifth Graders' Favorite Television Shows

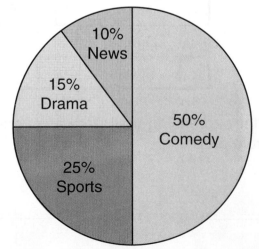

10%
News

15%
Drama

50%
Comedy

25%
Sports

Manny and Jessie found that people in the United States use about 338 billion gallons of water each day. They found the following circle graph that shows how the water is used.

Use this circle graph to answer the following questions.

1. What percent of fresh water in the United States is used for:

   A. farming?

   B. homes?

2. What percentage of fresh water in the United States is used by farms and factories and businesses?

3. **A.** If 338 billion gallons of fresh water are used every day, estimate the number of gallons of fresh water used each day by factories and businesses.

   B. Estimate the number of gallons of fresh water used each day for the production of electricity. Explain your strategy.

   C. Estimate the number of gallons of fresh water used each day for farming. Explain your strategy.

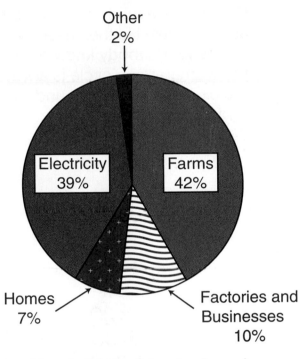

Fresh Water Use in America

4. What percentage of fresh water is used for something other than the production of electricity?

5. What percentage of fresh water is not used in factories and businesses?

6. **A.** Which three ways that water is used make up about $\frac{1}{5}$ of the total water used each day?

   B. Estimate the number of gallons used daily by these three.

Practice and Problems

1. The circumference of a circle is 28 inches. Estimate the diameter.

2. The diameter of a circle is 70 centimeters. Use paper and pencil and 3.14 for π to find the circumference.

3. Use your calculator to find the circumference of a circle that has a diameter of 12,998 inches to the nearest hundredth of an inch.

4. Professor Peabody measured the diameter of a circle and recorded it as 20 inches. He then used paper and pencil to find the circumference. Professor Peabody knew he made a mistake because he knows that the diameter of a circle is always smaller than the circumference. But, the circumference he found was smaller than the diameter. Explain Professor Peabody's error.

$$
\begin{array}{r}
3.14 \\
\times\ 20 \\
\hline
6280 \\
\hline
6.280
\end{array}
$$

5. The diameter of a large soup can is 4 inches. Its height is 5 inches.

   A. What shape did the label have before it was put on the can?

   B. What are the lengths of the sides of the label?

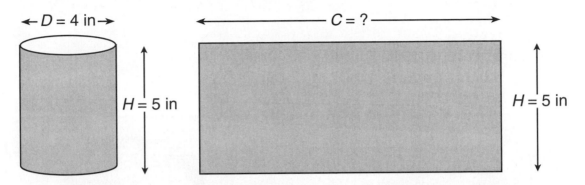

6. Lin measured the diameter of a trash can lid. It was 60.5 centimeters. Arti measured the diameter of another trash can lid. Its diameter was 5 centimeters more than Lin's trash can lid. How much longer is the circumference of Arti's trash can lid than Lin's (to the nearest tenth of a centimeter)?

7. Alexis measured the diameter of a pie tin. It was 8 inches. Manny measured the diameter of another pie tin. Its diameter was 10 inches. What is the difference in the circumferences of the two pie tins (to the nearest inch)?

8. How many people can sit at a round banquet table that is 8 feet across? (Allow 3 feet per person.)

9. How far across should a circular running track be if the distance around is to be 800 meters (about $\frac{1}{2}$ mile)? Give your answer to the nearest meter.

Unit 15

Developing Formulas with Geometry

	Student Guide	Discovery Assignment Book	Adventure Book	Unit Resource Guide*
Lesson 1				
Finding Area—Rectangles	●	●		
Lesson 2				
Rectangle Riddles	●			
Lesson 3				
Finding Area— Right Triangles	●			
Lesson 4				
More Triangles	●			
Lesson 5				
Perimeter	●			●
Lesson 6				
A Variety of Problems	●			

Unit Resource Guide pages are from the teacher materials.

Finding Area—Rectangles

Discuss

Brandon's father is laying square tiles in their kitchen. The length of one side of each tile is 1 foot. Brandon's kitchen is 10 feet by 12 feet. How many tiles will Brandon's father use?

"Brandon's kitchen is in the shape of a rectangle," said Mr. Moreno. "When we find the number of square tiles needed to cover the kitchen floor, we are finding the area in square feet. Each tile is one square foot. What strategies can you use to find the area?"

1. Find the area of Brandon's kitchen floor in square feet.

2. When you multiply to find the area of a rectangle, which pair of sides of the rectangle should you use—opposite sides or adjacent sides?

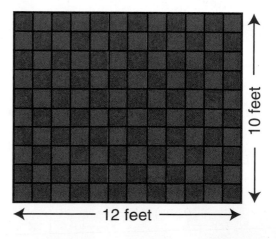

One way to find the area of a rectangle is to multiply the length of the two adjacent sides. We often call one side of a rectangle the **length** and an adjacent side the **width.** Then area = length × width. We write the area of a rectangle in symbols as:

$$A = L \times W$$

3. Alexis is planting a garden. The garden will be 9 feet long by 6.5 feet wide. What is the area of the garden? Solve the problem two ways: use the formula; draw a picture of the rectangle on *Centimeter Grid Paper* and count.

4. Nicholas's bedroom is 12.5 feet long and 11.5 feet wide. Use the formula to find the area of his bedroom. Estimate to make sure that your answer makes sense. Then find the area by drawing a picture on *Centimeter Grid Paper* using a ruler.

Finding Area—Rectangles

5. For each rectangle:
- Use your ruler to find the lengths of the sides of the rectangle to the nearest tenth of a centimeter.
- Find the area of the rectangle. Include units.

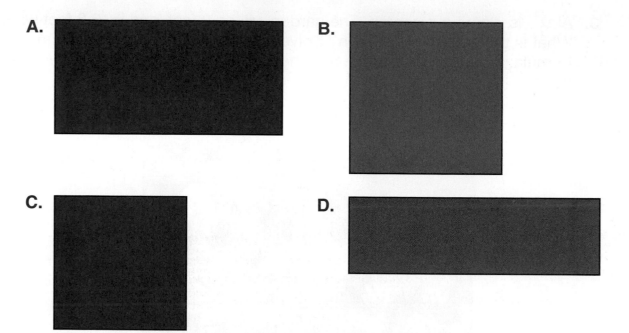

A.

B.

C.

D.

6. A. Look at the rectangles in Question 5. What do you notice about the dimensions of rectangles B and C?

    B. What name do you give to these special rectangles?

7. Shannon wants to buy a square rug for her room. She found a square rug that has a side length of 4.5 feet. What is the area that the rug will cover?

8. A. Draw a rectangle in which each side is 8 cm long.

    B. What is the area of the rectangle?

9. Find the areas of these shapes.

A.

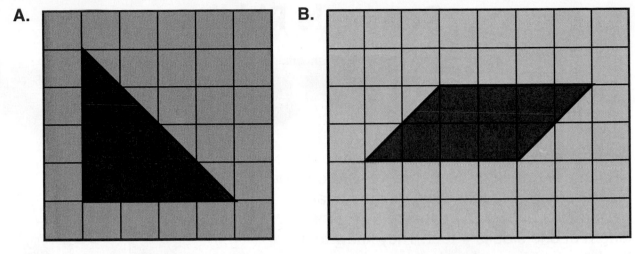

B.

Homework

You will need a calculator and a ruler to solve these problems. Remember to include units in your answers.

1. Find the area of the following rectangles. Explain the strategies you used.

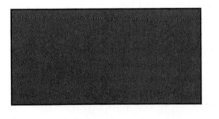

2. A. Draw a rectangle. The length of one side is 9 cm, and the length of another side is 3 cm.

B. What is the area of the rectangle?

3. Roberto is making a banner to announce the school play. The banner is 5 feet long and 8.5 inches wide. What is the area of the banner in square inches? (Remember: there are 12 inches in a foot.)

Rectangle Riddles

Mr. Moreno asked Frank and Lee Yah to make a sign to cover the announcement board outside his classroom. He told them that the board has an area of 36 square feet and that the length of one side is 4 feet. They knew that the board was a rectangle.

1. **A.** What are the lengths of the sides of the announcement board?

   B. What strategy did you use to find the lengths of the sides?

2. Frank's mother asked him to cut fabric squares for a quilt. She told him that each square should have an area of 64 square inches.

   A. Does Frank have enough information to cut the squares?

   B. What is the length of each side of the fabric squares?

Roberto wrote the following rectangle riddle and gave it to Nila to solve:

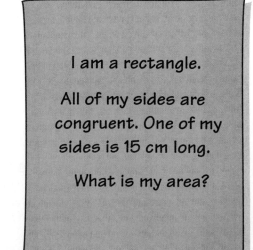

I am a rectangle.

All of my sides are congruent. One of my sides is 15 cm long.

What is my area?

3. Nila knew that she can find the area of this rectangle by solving this number sentence: Area = 15 cm × 15 cm. What is another way to write 15 × 15?

Mr. Moreno pointed out the $\boxed{x^2}$ key on the calculator. To find 15 × 15 on the calculator, Nila pressed: $\boxed{15}$ $\boxed{x^2}$ $\boxed{=}$.

The calculator window showed: $\boxed{\begin{array}{ll} 15^2 & \\ & 225. \end{array}}$

4. Use your calculator to find the solution to Roberto's riddle. Show how to find the solution using two different keystroke paths.

5. Use the $\boxed{x^2}$ key on your calculator to find the following products.

A. 7 × 7   **B.** 5 × 5   **C.** 3 × 4 × 4

D. 2 × 2 × 3 × 3   **E.** 5 × 5 × 2 × 3 × 3

Follow the rules for the order of operations; exponents are done before multiplication and division. For example:

$$6 \times 5^2 = 6 \times 25$$
$$= 150$$

$$14 + 3^2 = 14 + 9$$
$$= 23$$

$$2^2 + 3^2 = 4 + 9$$
$$= 13$$

6. Use the $\boxed{x^2}$ key on your calculator to compute the following.

A. $3 + 4^2 =$ **B.** $5^2 \times 4 =$ **C.** $21 + 7^2 =$ **D.** $3^2 + 4^2 =$

E. $15^2 + 81 =$ **F.** $18^2 \times 2 =$ **G.** $1000 - 21^2 =$ **H.** $17^2 \times 18^2 =$

Use your calculator to solve the following rectangle riddles. Record the calculator keystrokes that you used to solve each riddle for Questions 7–10. Remember to include the proper units in all your answers.

7. I am a rectangle. Two of my sides are each 12 centimeters long. My other two sides are each twice as long. What is my area?

8. I am a square. My sides are each 7.5 inches long. What is my area?

9. I am a rectangle with an area of 129.5 square cm. One of my sides is 9.25 cm. What are the lengths of my sides?

10. I am a rectangle. My area is 49 square inches. One of my sides is 7 inches. How long is each of my sides? What kind of special rectangle am I?

11. I am a rectangle. My area is 36 square centimeters. Find all the possible rectangles with whole number sides.

12. What is the missing length of this rectangle?

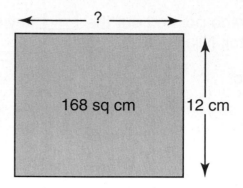

13. Professor Peabody completed a chart with information about some rectangles. He accidentally spilled coffee on the table. Copy the table and fill in the missing information.

Side One	Side Two	Area	Is It a Square?
9 in	5.5 in	?	?
?	?	36 sq in	Yes
12 in	?	120 sq in	?
7 in	?		Yes
11 in	?	93.5 sq in	?
?	?	100 sq in	Yes

Solve the following rectangle riddles. Estimate to make sure your answers make sense.

1. Two of my sides are each 7.5 feet long. The other two sides are each 5.3 feet long. I am a rectangle. What is my area?

2. I am a rectangle. All of my sides are 25.5 centimeters long. What is my area?

3. I am a rectangle. Two of my sides are each 8.5 centimeters long. The other two sides are each 22.5 centimeters long. What is my area?

4. Draw a square with an area of 81 sq cm. What is the length of each side?

5. Blanca has a roll of blue wrapping paper. There are 22 square feet on a roll. She wants to decorate a wall by making a 3-foot-high rectangle. How wide can the rectangle be? (Express your answer in feet and inches.)

6. John's father is building a deck in their backyard. He is planning to build a square deck with an area of 121 square feet. What are the lengths of the sides of the deck?

7. Irma needs a shade for her window. The window covers 14 square feet and measures 3.5 feet across the top. How long will the shade need to be to cover the window?

8. Jackie was asked to make a rectangular poster for the school carnival. She was given a piece of cardboard that had an area of 750 sq cm. One side of the cardboard was 25 cm long. What are the lengths of the sides of the rectangle?

9. What is the missing length of this rectangle?

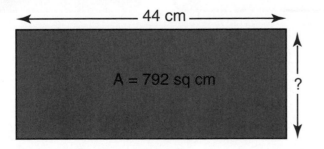

Finding Area—Right Triangles

A **right triangle** is a triangle in which one of the angles is a right angle. The two sides that form the right angle are called the **legs** of the triangle. The third side of a right triangle is called the **hypotenuse.**

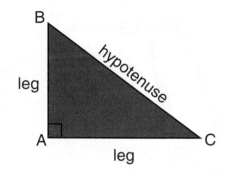

A shortcut way of writing triangle ABC is to write △ABC.

1. Romesh built right triangles on his geoboard. What are the lengths of the legs of each triangle?

2. A. Lee Yah and David both built right triangles on their geoboards with one leg measuring 1 unit in length and the other leg measuring 2 units in length. Compare their work.

B. Are both answers correct?

C. Explain your thinking.

3. Build a right triangle on your geoboard with one leg 2 units long and the other leg 2 units long. What is the area of this triangle?

4. If we cut a rectangle in half on a diagonal, we are left with two right triangles.

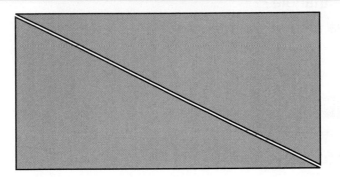

A. Measure the lengths of the sides of the rectangle in centimeters.

B. What is the area of the rectangle?

C. Are the two triangles right triangles? How do you know?

D. What is the area of each of the triangles?

5. A. Build a right triangle on your geoboard with one leg 2 units long and the other leg 4 units long.

B. Use a second rubber band to build the rectangle that surrounds the triangle.

C. Find the area of the rectangle.

D. What do you notice about the length and width of the rectangle and the legs of the triangle?

E. What is the area of the triangle?

Use your geoboard for Questions 6–7.

6. **A.** Build a right triangle with one leg 1 unit long and the other leg 2 units long.

   B. Use a second rubber band to build the rectangle which surrounds the triangle. Find the area of the rectangle.

   C. Compare the length and width of the rectangle with the length of the legs of the triangle.

   D. What is the area of the triangle?

   E. Compare the area of the triangle with the area of the rectangle.

7. **A.** Build a right triangle with one leg 3 units long and the other leg 4 units long.

   B. Use a second rubber band to build the rectangle which surrounds the triangle. Find the area of this rectangle.

   C. Compare the length and width of the rectangle with the length of the legs of the triangle.

   D. What is the area of the triangle?

   E. Compare the area of the triangle with the area of the rectangle.

                    Finding Area—Right Triangles

Use your geoboard or dot paper. Find the area of the right triangles in Questions 8–10 by building a rectangle around the triangle.

8. A right triangle with one leg 2 units long and the other leg 3 units long.

9. A right triangle with one leg 1 unit long and the other leg 4 units long.

10. A right triangle with one leg 4 units long and the other leg 4 units long.

11. Make a chart like the one drawn here. Use the triangles you constructed in Questions 6–10 to fill in the chart.

Length of Legs of Right Triangle (units)	Area of Rectangle around the Triangle (square units)	Area of Right Triangle (square units)
1, 2	2	1
3, 4		
2, 3		

12. Suggest a formula for finding the area of a right triangle.

13. Lee Yah suggested that the formula for the area of a right triangle is the length of leg 1 times the length of leg 2 divided by 2. She wrote:

$$A = \text{leg } 1 \times \text{leg } 2 \div 2$$

   A. Is Lee Yah's formula correct?

   B. How is it different from the formula you suggested in Question 12? How is it the same?

14. David suggested the formula:

$$A = \tfrac{1}{2} \times \text{leg } 1 \times \text{leg } 2$$

   A. Is David's formula correct?

   B. How is it different from your formula or Lee Yah's formula? How is it the same?

For Questions 15–17:

    A. Use *Centimeter Dot Paper* to draw the right triangles.

    B. Find the area by drawing a rectangle around the right triangle.

    C. Find the area by using the formula $A = \frac{1}{2} \times$ leg 1 $\times$ leg 2.

    D. Check that your answers for parts B and C are the same.

15. △DEF is a right triangle whose legs are 5 cm and 8 cm.

16. △GHI is a right triangle whose legs are 6 cm and 4 cm.

17. △KLM is a right triangle whose legs are 7 cm and 7 cm.

Homework

You will need a ruler and dot paper to complete these questions.
Find the area of the triangles in Questions 1–4.

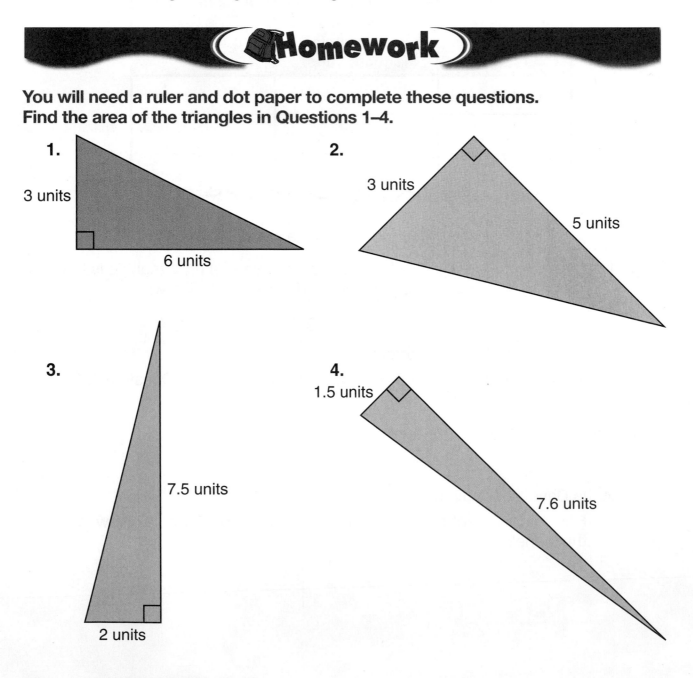

1.
3 units
6 units

2.
3 units
5 units

3.
7.5 units
2 units

4.
1.5 units
7.6 units

Measure the legs of the right triangles in Questions 5–7. Find the area of each triangle to the nearest tenth of a centimeter. Estimate to make sure that your answers make sense.

5.

6.

7.

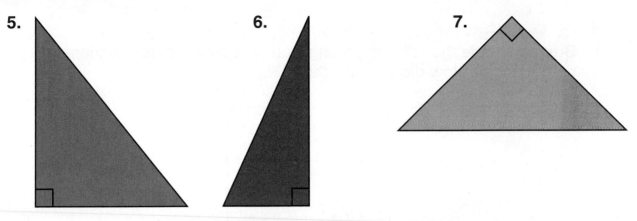

For Questions 8–10, draw the following right triangles on dot paper and find the areas.

8. △ABC with one leg 6 cm long and the other leg 2 times as long as the first.

9. △DEF with one leg 8 cm long and the other leg $\frac{1}{2}$ as long as the first.

10. △GHI with one leg 9 cm long and the other leg $\frac{1}{3}$ as long as the first.

11. The area of a right triangle is 36 square inches. One of the legs is 9 inches. What is the length of the other leg? (*Hint:* Draw a picture.)

12. The area of a right triangle is 50 sq cm. One leg is 20 cm long. What is the length of the other leg? (*Hint:* Draw a picture.)

More Triangles

Acute Triangles

1. Brandon made the following triangle on his geoboard. Is this triangle a right triangle? How did you decide?

2. Are any of the angles in Brandon's triangle greater than 90°?

Brandon's triangle is an acute triangle. Remember, an **acute triangle** is a triangle whose angles all have measures less than 90°.

Brandon wants to find the area of his triangle.

Nila has a strategy for finding the area of Brandon's triangle. She suggests using a rubber band to build a rectangle to surround the triangle and then subtracting.

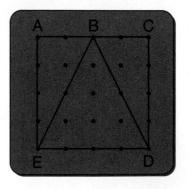

3. **A.** What is the area of the rectangle that surrounds the triangle?

   B. What is the area of each of the two small right triangles, △ABE and △CBD?

   C. What is the area of Brandon's triangle △EBD? Explain how you found the area.

John suggested a different strategy for finding the area. He added a second rubber band to Brandon's geoboard. He stretched his rubber band ($\overline{BF}$) from the top vertex of the triangle to the opposite side of the triangle ($\overline{ED}$), making a right angle at F. Thus, John's rubber band divided Brandon's triangle into two right triangles. He labeled the two triangles △FBE and △FBD.

John knew if he found the area of the two right triangles and then added them together, he would have the area of Brandon's triangle.

4. **A.** Look at the right triangles formed by John's rubber band. What are the lengths of the legs of △EFB?

   B. What is the area of △EFB?

5. **A.** What are the lengths of the legs of △DFB?

   B. What is the area of △DFB?

6. What is the area of △DEB?

A line formed from a vertex of a triangle perpendicular to the opposite side of the triangle is called the **height** of the triangle. Another name for the height is **altitude.** The side of the triangle the line is drawn to is often called the **base** of the triangle.

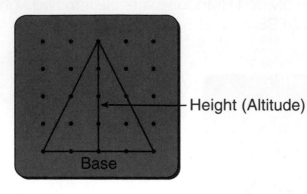

Height (Altitude)

Base

7. For triangles A–F, record the information you find in a table like the one shown below.

- Make the triangle on dot paper. You may also want to make the triangle on your geoboard.
- Find a height of the triangle and draw it. Choose a height that begins and ends on a dot.
- Find a base of the triangle and draw over it with a different color.
- Find the area of the triangle using any method.

Triangle	Base	Height	Area
A			
B			
C			

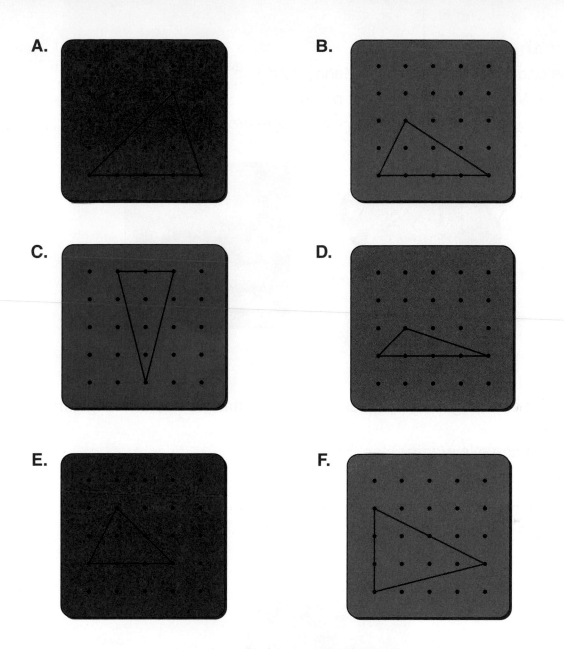

A.

B.

C.

D.

E.

F.

8. Look at the information in your table from Question 7. How are the height and base of an acute triangle like the legs of a right triangle?

9. Think back to the formula you found for finding the area of right triangles. Revise this formula so you can use the same formula to find the area of all the triangles you have looked at.

Obtuse Triangles

10. This is one of the triangles that Manny made on his geoboard.

   A. Draw Manny's triangle on dot paper.

   B. Find the area by constructing a rectangle around the triangle.

△ABC is an obtuse triangle. Remember, an **obtuse triangle** has one angle that is greater than 90°.

   C. Which angle is greater than 90°?

Manny wanted to use $\overline{AC}$ as the base, but he wasn't sure about the height. "Remember, the height has to be perpendicular to the base," said Mr. Moreno. "The height of an obtuse triangle can sometimes be outside of the triangle."

Manny drew the height.

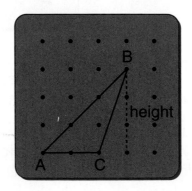

"The area of any triangle is one-half times the base times the height.

A formula for this is: $A = \frac{1}{2} \times b \times h$."

11. What is the measure of the height of Manny's triangle?

12. What is the length of the base?

13. Compute $\frac{1}{2} \times b \times h$ for Manny's triangle. Compare this with the area you found in Question 10B.

For Questions 14–15:

   A. Make the triangle on dot paper.

   B. Find a height of the triangle and draw it. Choose a height that begins and ends on a dot.

   C. Find a base of the triangle and draw it.

   D. Find the area by constructing a rectangle around the triangle.

   E. Compute $\frac{1}{2} \times b \times h$.

14.   **15.**

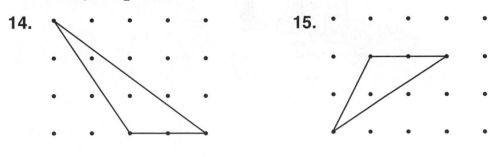

Complete each of the following questions. Record your answers on dot paper. You will need to use your colored pencils.

1. **A.** Draw this triangle on dot paper.

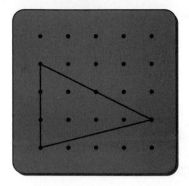

   B. Use a different colored pencil to draw a rectangle around the triangle.

   C. What is the area of the rectangle?

   D. What is the area of the triangle?

2. A. Draw this triangle on dot paper.

   B. Use a different colored pencil to draw a rectangle around the triangle.

   C. What is the area of the rectangle?

   D. What is the area of the triangle?

For Questions 3–8:

   A. Draw the triangle on dot paper.

   B. Use a different colored pencil to draw in a height of the triangle. Choose a height that begins and ends on a dot.

   C. What is the area of the triangle?

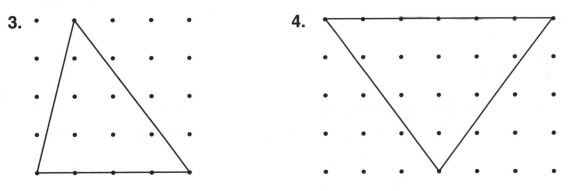

3.

4.

5. **6.**

7. **8.**

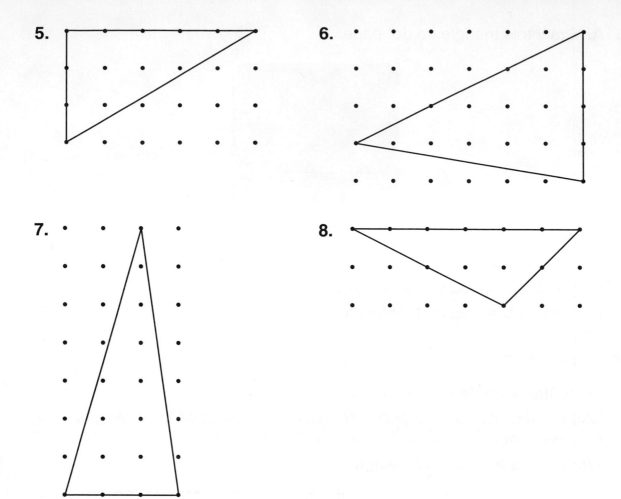

For Questions 9–10:

    A. Draw the triangle on dot paper.

    B. Use a different colored pencil to draw a rectangle around the triangle.

    C. What is the area of the rectangle?

    D. What is the area of the triangle?

    E. Use a different colored pencil to draw a height of the triangle. Choose a height that begins and ends on a dot. Remember that the height of an obtuse triangle can sometimes be outside the triangle.

    F. Use the formula $A = \frac{1}{2} \times b \times h$ to compute the area of the triangle.

    G. Check that your answers for Part D and Part F are the same.

9. 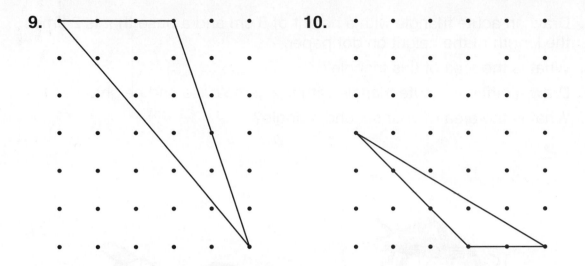 **10.**

11. **A.** Draw an acute triangle with a base of 4 cm and a height of 3 cm on dot paper.

  B. What is the area of this triangle?

  C. Draw a different acute triangle with a base of 4 cm and a height of 3 cm.

  D. What is the area of this triangle?

  E. Draw a right triangle with one leg measuring 4 cm and one leg measuring 3 cm.

  F. What is the area of this triangle?

  G. What do all three of your triangles have in common?

12. **A.** Draw an acute triangle with a height of 5 cm and a base that is 2 times the length of the height on dot paper.

B. What is the area of this triangle?

C. Draw a different acute triangle with the same base and height.

D. What is the area of your second triangle?

Perimeter

Felicia and her mother are putting up a wallpaper border in her room. They want to put the border all around the room near the ceiling. Felicia measured and found that her room is 12 feet long and 10.5 feet wide.

Here is a sketch of Felicia's room.

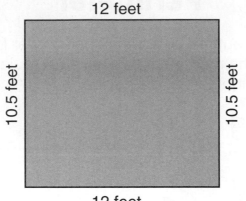

12 feet

10.5 feet

10.5 feet

12 feet

1. How can Felicia use the information she has to find out how much wallpaper border she will need for her room?

2. **A.** What is the distance around a two-dimensional shape called?

    B. How many feet of wallpaper border will Felicia need for her room?

Felicia's room is in the shape of a rectangle. Felicia sees that she can find the perimeter of her room by adding the lengths of the sides. Remember, the **perimeter** is the distance around a shape. Felicia said a formula for the perimeter of a rectangle is:

$$P = L + W + L + W$$

Lee Yah said a formula is:

$$P = 2 \times L + 2 \times W$$

3. Are both Felicia's and Lee Yah's formulas for the perimeter of a rectangle correct? Explain your reasoning.

4. **A.** Can you think of another way to write the perimeter of a rectangle?

    B. Write a formula for the perimeter of a square.

5. Roberto wants to use his calculator to compute the perimeter of rectangles. He wonders which method uses the fewest number of keystrokes. Experiment with a rectangle whose sides are 6 units and 8 units.

6. Find the perimeter and area of each of these rectangles. Remember to use the correct units for perimeter and area.

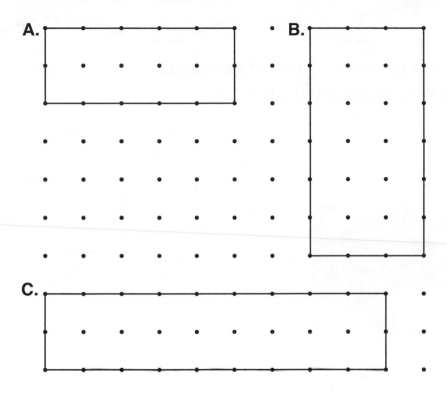

7. Find the perimeter and area of each of these rectangles. Measure to the nearest tenth of a centimeter. Remember to use the correct units for perimeter and area.

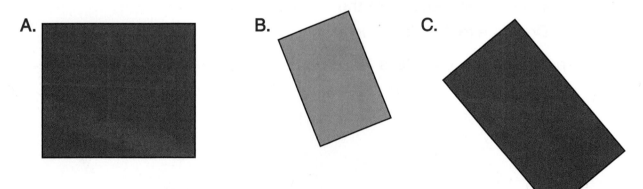

8. Find the perimeter of the following rectangles.

A. A rectangle with length 35 units, width 24 units.

B. A rectangle with length 8.75 units, width 6.5 units.

C. A rectangle with length $5\frac{1}{3}$ units, width $3\frac{5}{6}$ units.

9. **A.** Find the perimeter of each of the shapes.

   B. Find the area of each of the shapes.

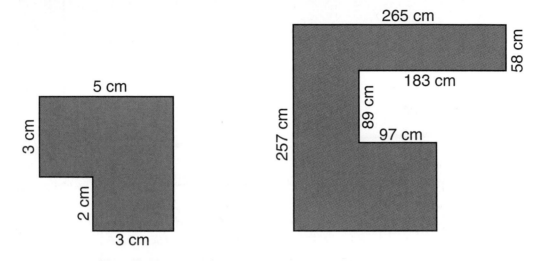

10. One side of a rectangle is 5 cm long. The area of the rectangle is 30 sq cm. Use this information to find the width and the perimeter of the rectangle.

11. The area of a rectangle is 16 sq cm. The perimeter is 20 cm.

    A. What are the lengths of the sides of the rectangle?

    B. Draw the rectangle on dot paper.

12. The area of a rectangle is 16 sq cm. The perimeter is 16 cm.

    A. What are the lengths of the sides of the rectangle?

    B. Draw the rectangle on dot paper.

1. **A.** Find the missing lengths of the sides. Then find the perimeter of each of the following shapes.

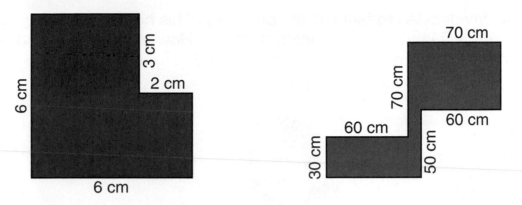

   B. Find the area of each of the above shapes. (*Hint:* Divide the figures into rectangles.)

2. **A.** A square has an area of 81 sq cm. How long is each side of the square?

   B. What is the perimeter of the square?

3. **A.** A rectangle has an area of 30 sq units. The sides all have whole number lengths. What are the lengths of the sides for all the possible rectangles with this area?

   B. One side is 1 unit longer than the other. What are the lengths of each of the rectangle's sides?

   C. What is the perimeter of the rectangle?

4. **A.** A rectangle has an area of 32 sq units. The sides all have whole number lengths. What are the lengths of the sides for all the possible rectangles with this area?

   B. One side is 2 times longer than the other side. What are the lengths of each side of the rectangle?

   C. What is the perimeter of the rectangle?

5. Draw a rectangle with an area of 24 square units and a perimeter of 22 units. What are the lengths of each of the rectangle's sides?

6. Draw a rectangle with an area of 18 square units and a perimeter of 18 units. What are the lengths of each of the rectangle's sides?

A Variety of Problems

1. A rectangle has side lengths of 22 cm and 37 cm. Find the area and the perimeter.

2. **A.** Jay decided to fence in the backyard of his house. His backyard is a square, and one side length is 30 feet. How much fence will Jay need if he only fences in 3 sides of his yard?

   B. What is the area of Jay's backyard?

3. A patio has an area of 72 sq feet and a perimeter of 34 feet. The lengths of the sides of the patio are whole numbers. Find the lengths of the sides of the patio. Show how you found your answer.

4. John's bedroom is shaped like a rectangle that is 10 feet wide and 12 feet long. Jim's bedroom is also shaped like a rectangle. It is 8 feet wide and 14 feet long.

   A. Whose bedroom has the largest area?

   B. John and Jim both decided to put a wallpaper border with sports figures around their room. Who needs more wallpaper border, John or Jim?

5. Find the area and perimeter of this shape. (All angles are right angles.)

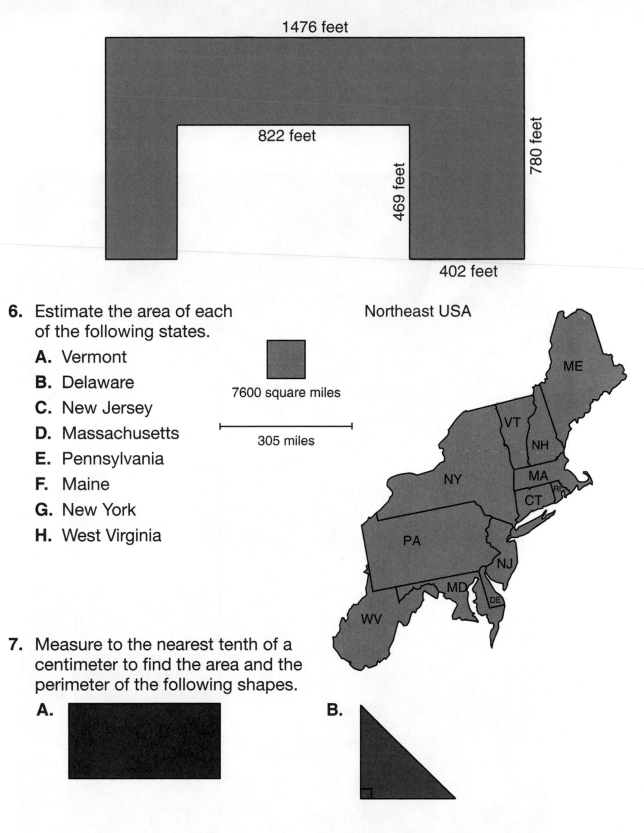

1476 feet

822 feet

780 feet

469 feet

402 feet

6. Estimate the area of each of the following states.

Northeast USA

  A. Vermont
  B. Delaware
  C. New Jersey
  D. Massachusetts
  E. Pennsylvania
  F. Maine
  G. New York
  H. West Virginia

7600 square miles

305 miles

7. Measure to the nearest tenth of a centimeter to find the area and the perimeter of the following shapes.

  A.

  B.

A Variety of Problems

SG • Grade 5 • Unit 15 • Lesson 6   485

Unit 16

Bringing It All Together: An Assessment Unit

	Student Guide	Discovery Assignment Book	Adventure Book	Unit Resource Guide*
Lesson 1				
Experiment Review	●	●		
Lesson 2				
Bats!			●	
Lesson 3				
More Bats!	●			
Lesson 4				
How Many Bats in a Cave?	●			
Lesson 5				
Pattern Block Candy				●
Lesson 6				
End-of-Year Test				●
Lesson 7				
Portfolio Review	●			

Unit Resource Guide pages are from the teacher materials.

Experiment Review

Professor Peabody was in the park one day. He watched children run around and blow bubbles. The bubbles sometimes lasted a long time and sometimes popped right away. As he watched the bubbles children made, he remembered a lab he had worked on some months ago.

Discuss

1. Which lab does Professor Peabody remember?

2. Answer the following questions about the lab. Use your earlier units in the *Student Guide* or your portfolio to help you.

   A. What variables did you study in the lab?

   B. Did you have to keep any variables the same so that the experiment would be fair? If so, which ones?

   C. Did you measure anything? If so, what did you measure? What units did you use?

   D. How many trials did you do? If you did more than one trial, tell why.

   E. Describe your graph.

   F. What were the most important problems you solved using your data and your graph?

3. Use earlier units in the *Student Guide* and your portfolio to make a list of the labs you completed. One or more of the labs will be assigned to your group. Answer each part of Question 2 for these labs. Use the *Experiment Review Chart* Activity Pages in the *Discovery Assignment Book* to organize your work.

More Bats!

John Eagle, Sarah, and Bobby continued to collect data on the bats by helping Joan repeat the capture three more times. Each night, they captured about 100 bats and counted the number of tagged bats in each sample.

They recorded their data in a data table like this:

Bat Capture Data

n Number of Bats Captured	*t* Number of Tagged Bats in the Sample
105	9
110	10
100	11
98	10

"What would happen to the number of tagged bats if we changed the size of our sample?" asked Bobby, after looking at the data.

"Don't you think the number of tagged bats in each sample would get bigger or smaller, depending on the size of the sample?" asked Sarah.

"I wish we could find out for sure," Bobby said.

"Our time here is up, but I think there is still a way to find out what would happen," said John Eagle. "A local park conservation club will help us continue our study. They will capture bats for the next eight nights. For the first four nights, they will try to capture about 50 bats and count the number of tagged bats found in each sample. For the next four nights after that, they will try to capture about 150 bats, counting the tagged bats each time. Then they will send us their data."

"Great!" exclaimed both Bobby and Sarah. "We can't wait to see what happens."

After the eight days had passed, John Eagle received a package from the conservation club. The following data table was included:

Conservation Club Data

n Number of Bats Captured	t Number of Tagged Bats in the Sample
54	6
50	4
53	5
47	6
150	15
149	14
146	13
144	15

1. Make a point graph that shows all the bat data collected by the conservation club.

   - On the horizontal axis, plot the number of bats captured (*n*).
   - On the vertical axis, plot the number of tagged bats in the sample (*t*).

2. Add the points that show the data collected by John Eagle, Sarah, and Bobby to your graph. Use the Bat Capture Data table.

3. **A.** What do you notice about the points on your graph?

   B. If there were no bats in a sample, how many tagged bats would you find? ($n = 0$, $t = ?$) Add this point to your graph.

   C. Draw a best-fit line.

4. **A.** Use your graph to write a ratio for $\frac{t}{n}$ when $n = 80$.

   B. Use your graph to write a ratio for $\frac{t}{n}$ when $n = 160$.

   C. Are these two ratios equal (or approximately equal)?

5. **A.** Choose two other points on your best-fit line. Use those points to write ratios for $\frac{t}{n}$.

   B. Are the ratios equal to (or approximately equal to) the ratios you found in Question 4?

6. **A.** If you take a larger sample, what happens to the numbers of tagged bats in the sample?

   B. If you take a smaller sample, what happens to the numbers of tagged bats in the sample?

7. John Eagle, Bobby, and Sarah used the data they collected. They estimated that 10,000 bats live in the cave. Write a paragraph explaining how they can use the data collected by the conservation club and the graph to support their estimate.

More Bats!

How Many Bats in a Cave?

Bat Ecology: I Didn't Know That!

🦇 *Worldwide, bats are the most important natural enemies of night-flying insects. A single little brown bat can catch 600 mosquitoes in just 1 hour. The 20 million Mexican free-tail bats from Bracken Cave, Texas, eat 250 tons of insects nightly.*

🦇 *Important agricultural plants—from bananas, breadfruit, and mangoes to cashews, dates, and figs—require bats for pollination and seed distribution.*

🦇 *Guano (bat droppings in caves) supports whole ecosystems of unique organisms, including bacteria useful in detoxifying wastes, improving detergents, and producing gasohol and antibiotics.*

Facts provided by Bat Conservation International

Preparing for the Lab

At times, biologists need to estimate animal populations. Sometimes the numbers are so large or the animals are difficult or dangerous to capture that it is not possible to count each animal in the group. One method used to estimate a population of animals is called the capture-recapture technique. The first step is to capture and tag a known number of animals. These tagged animals are released to mix with all the other animals. Samples of the animals are then caught. The number of tagged animals in the sample is recorded along with the total number of animals in the sample.

Using the data from the experiment and proportions, scientists can estimate the total number of animals in the population.

$$\frac{\text{number of tagged animals in a sample } (t)}{\text{total number of animals in a sample } (n)} = \frac{\text{number of tagged animals in the population } (T)}{\text{total number of animals in the population } (N)}$$

We can write this proportion as shown:

$$\frac{t}{n} = \frac{T}{N}$$

In this lab, you will simulate (model) the capture-recapture technique for estimating the number of bats in a cave. Beans will be used to represent the population of bats. A bag will be used to represent the cave. Your job will be to estimate the total number of beans in the bag. The procedure for your experiment will be similar to the experiment described in the Adventure Book *Bats!*

Tagging the Bats. Work with your team to capture and tag exactly 250 bats from your cave. That is, take 250 beans from your bag and tag them by making a mark on both sides of each captured bean with a marker. Then put the tagged beans (bats) back into the bag (cave). Mix the tagged beans with the untagged beans in the bag. Be sure to mix them well.

Sampling the Bat Population. You will collect three different-sized samples of beans: small, medium, and large. For each sample size, you will repeat the following procedure four times:

- Collect a sample of beans from the bag.
- Count the number of tagged beans in the sample (t).
- Count the total number of beans in the sample (n).
- Record the number of tagged beans (t) and the total number of beans in the sample (n) in a data table.
- Return the sample to the bag, and mix the beans with the rest of the beans in the bag. Mix the beans together well.

Note: You will take a total of 12 samples—four samples with a small scoop, four samples with a medium scoop, and four samples with a large scoop.

As you work through this simulation, it is important to keep in mind that you have much more control over the beans than scientists have over bats existing in the wild. For instance, a few beans may drop on the floor as you work, but you should notice that and be able to find them quite easily. In nature, there are many events that cannot be controlled as easily: Some of the bats can leave the cave through openings that the scientist is not aware of. The tagged bats may stay in one part of the cave so that they are not mixed well. Some may be eaten by predators. Some part of the bat colony may move to another cave. Some will die. In lab situations, we can see patterns and trends and make approximations of total populations with greater certainty than we can when we study animals in nature.

Draw

1. Sketch a picture of the lab. Be sure the steps are clear and the variables are labeled.

   - Use t for number of tagged beans in a sample and n for total number of beans in a sample.

   - Use T for number of tagged beans in the bag and N for total number of beans in the bag.

2. What variables are involved in the lab?

3. **A.** What do you know before you start taking samples and collecting data?

   B. What will you be able to find out when you finish the experiment?

4. Why is it important to mix the tagged beans thoroughly with the untagged beans?

Collect

5. Design a table to help you collect the data in an organized way. You will have 3 different sizes of samples (small, medium, and large) and 4 samples for each size.

6. Collect the data. Record the number of tagged beans (t) and the total number of beans (n) for each of the 12 samples.

Graph

7. Graph your data.
   - Plot the total number of beans in the sample (*n*) on the horizontal axis. Plot the number of tagged beans (*t*) in the sample on the vertical axis.
   - If there are no beans in your sample, how many tagged beans will you find? (*n* = 0, *t* = ?) Add this point to your graph.
   - If the points suggest a line, use a ruler to draw a best-fit line.

Explore

8. **A.** If a sample has 100 beans (*n* = 100), how many tagged beans (*t*) would you expect in the sample? Use your graph to find *t*.

   B. If the number of tagged beans in a sample is 50 beans (*t* = 50), use your line to estimate the number of beans in the sample (*n*).

9. Use your best-fit line to find the ratio $(\frac{t}{n})$ of the number of tagged beans in a sample to the total number of beans in the sample. (*Hint:* Choose a point on the line—not a data point—and find the values of *t* and *n*. Write the ratio. For example, you may wish to use *n* = 100 and the value for *t* that you found in Question 8A.)

10. **A.** Choose another point on the line. Find the values for *t* and *n* for this point. Write the ratio of $\frac{t}{n}$ using these values.

    B. Is this ratio equal to (or approximately equal to) the ratio you found in Question 9? How do you know?

    C. Find values for *t* and *n* for another point and write the ratio of $\frac{t}{n}$. Is this ratio equal to (or approximately equal to) the other two ratios?

11. **A.** Use a ratio from the line. Calculate an estimate for the total number of beans in your bag. That is, use equal ratios to find *N*.

$$\frac{\text{number of tagged beans in a sample } (t)}{\text{total number of beans in a sample } (n)} = \frac{\text{number of tagged beans in the bag } (T)}{\text{total number of beans in the bag } (N)}$$

$$\frac{t}{n} = \frac{250}{N}$$

B. Explain how you made your estimate. Use the Student Rubric: *Telling* as a guide.

12. Look at the data in your table.

A. If you had only taken one sample, would the data give you a good estimate for the total number of beans in your bag? Why or why not?

B. You took four samples for each sample size. Do you recommend the same, more, or fewer samples? Why?

Bat Trivia

The world's smallest mammal is the bumblebee bat of Thailand, weighing less than a penny.

Giant flying foxes that live in Indonesia have wingspans of nearly 6 feet.

Facts provided by Bat Conservation International

You will need a piece of graph paper and a ruler to complete the homework.

This is Arti and Lee Yah's data. They captured samples of 100, 200, and 300 bats (pinto beans) from a cave (bag).

Pinto Bat Cave

Number of Beans (Bats) in Sample n	Number of Tagged Beans (Bats) in Sample t
100	7
100	8
100	6
100	5
200	15
200	14
200	13
200	10
300	21
300	20
300	18
300	15

1. Graph Arti and Lee Yah's data. Arti used ordered pairs to plot each point. Plot the number of beans in the sample (n) on the horizontal axis. Plot the number of tagged beans (t) on the vertical axis.

2. **A.** If Arti has no beans in a sample, how many tagged beans will she find? ($n = 0$, $t = ?$) Add this point to your graph.

    B. Fit a line to the points.

3. Use the line to find the number of tagged beans that would be expected in a sample of 150 beans.

4. Use the line to find the number of tagged beans that would be expected if Arti takes a sample of 400 beans.

5. If there are a total of 200 tagged beans in the bag, calculate an estimate for the total number of beans in the Pinto Bat Cave. Show how you made your estimate. Use the Student Rubric: *Telling* as a guide.

Portfolio Review

Romesh, Jackie, and Blanca looked back at the work they collected in their math portfolios since the start of the school year.

Look, here is my work for *Spreading Out*. When I compare it to the work I just did on *How Many Bats in a Cave?*, I can really see how much better I am at using data tables to organize the data I collect.

I can really see how much better I am at writing about math. In the beginning of the year I just put down the answer, and I hardly wrote anything. Now, I use tables and graphs to show my work, and I write a whole paragraph about how I found the answer.

I can't wait to take my portfolio home and show it to my family. They will really like seeing all of the ways I have improved in math this year.

Explore

1. If you have not done so recently, choose items from your collection folder to add to your portfolio. Here are some examples of things you can choose:

   - The solution to a problem you solved. For example, you may choose to include your solutions to *A Further Look at Patterns and Primes* from Unit 11 or *Grass Act* from Unit 12.

   - A lab you have completed. *Mass vs. Volume* from Unit 13 and *Circumference vs. Diameter* from Unit 14 are good examples.

   - Work with area and perimeter from Unit 15

   - Work with paper-and-pencil multiplication and division

2. Put your *Experiment Review Chart* from Lesson 1 in your portfolio.

3. Choose one or two other pieces of work from this unit to include in your portfolio. Select pieces that are similar to the work that is already in your portfolio. For example, if you already have a lab in your portfolio, put *How Many Bats in a Cave?* in your portfolio, too. Or, if you included a written solution to a problem like *Grass Act,* then also include your solution to *Pattern Block Candy* in Lesson 5.

4. Add the name of each new piece to your Table of Contents. Include a short description of the work and the date it was finished.

5. Write a paragraph comparing two pieces of work in your portfolio that are alike in some way. For example, you can compare two labs or your solutions to two problems you solved. One piece should be new and one should be from the beginning of the year. Use these questions to help you write your paragraph:

   - Which two pieces did you choose to compare?

   - How are they alike? How are they different?

   - Do you see any improvement in the newest piece of work as compared to the older work? Explain.

   - If you could redo the older piece of work, how would you improve it?

   - How could you improve the newer piece of work?

6. Write about your favorite piece of work in your portfolio. Tell why you like it. Explain what you learned from it.

Student Rubric: Knowing

In My Best Work in Mathematics:

- I show that I understand the ideas in the problem.

- I show the same mathematical ideas in different ways. I use pictures, tables, graphs, and sentences when they fit the problem.

- I show that I can use tools and rules correctly.

- I show that I can use the mathematical facts that apply to the problem.

Student Rubric: Solving

How does this rubric help you?

It helps me plan strategies, find solutions, and check my work when I solve problems.

In My Best Work in Mathematics:

- I read the problem carefully, make a good plan for solving it, and then carry out that plan.

- I use tools like graphs, pictures, tables, or number sentences to help me.

- I use ideas I know from somewhere else to help me solve a problem.

- I keep working on the problem until I find a good solution.

- I look back at my solution to see if my answer makes sense.

- I look back at my work to see what more I can learn from solving the problem.

Student Rubric: Telling

In My Best Work in Mathematics:

- I show all of the steps that I used to solve the problem. I also tell what each number refers to (such as 15 boys or 6 inches).

- I explain why I solved the problem the way I did so that someone can see why my method makes sense.

- If I use tools like pictures, tables, graphs, or number sentences, I explain how the tools I used fit the problem.

- I use math words and symbols correctly. For example, if I see "6 − 2," I solve the problem "six minus two," not "two minus six."

Index/Glossary

This index provides page references for the *Student Guide.* Definitions or explanations of key terms can be found on the pages listed in bold.

Abacus, 39–45
Acute angle, 185, 468
Acute triangle, 188, 468–471
Adding fractions, 157–159, 171–176, 179–181, 370–371, 376–377
Addition
    decimals, 243–246
    fractions, 157–159, 171–176, 179–181, 370–371, 376–377
    mixed numbers, 376–382
Algebra
    see best-fit line
    see Cartesian coordinates
    see exponent
    see formula
    see negative number
    see order of operations
    see point graph
    see proportion
    see ratio
    see variable
All-partials multiplication method, 53
Altitude (of a triangle), 470
Angle, 184, 468
    acute, **185**
    central, **435**
    degrees, **185**
    measuring, 188, 442
    obtuse, 185–**186**
    in polygons, 192–200
    rays, **184**
    right, **185**
    sides, **184**
    straight, 185–**186, 194**
    triangle, 194–195
    of triangles and polygons, 192–200
    vertex, **184, 207**
Arc, 441
Archimedes, 60, 420, 431
Area, 102–105, 118–122, 131–138, 146, 151, 247–248, 405, **454, 484**–485
    estimating, 131–138
    grids, 102–105
    of irregular shapes, 118
    measurement, 102–105, 484–485
    of polygons, 102–105
    of quadrilaterals, 454–461
    of rectangles, 103–105, 454–461, 481–485
    of triangles, 104–105, 462–478
Average, 12–15, 96, 119, 123–128
    see mean
    see median
    see mode
Axes, 319
    x and *y,* **327**

Bar graph, 6, 8–19, 23, 134, 261, 274–279
    comparing, 134
Base (of an exponent), 60
Base (of a triangle), 470–472
Base-ten pieces (bits, flats, packs, and skinnies), **48**–49
    division, 106–112
    multiplication, 46–55
Base-ten shorthand, 51, 109
Benchmarks, 171, **238**
Best-fit line, 97, 136, 167, 416, 430, 495
Binning data, 274
Bit, 49
    see also base-ten pieces

lines on, 87–93
point, 86–92, 93, 97, 98, 134, 356, 416, 430, 491, 495, 497
see also labs

H

Height (of a triangle), 470–472
Hexagon, 69, 198
Hypotenuse, 462

I

Image, 333
Impossible event, 256
Improper fraction, 74, 75, 377
Integers, 316–318, 322–342
Interpolation, 399

J

K

Kelley, Florence, 271–272
Knowing rubric, 501

L

Labs, see also TIMS Laboratory Method
 Circumference vs. Diameter, 428–434
 Comparing Lives of Animals and Soap Bubbles, 276–279
 A Day at the Races, 164–170
 Distance vs. Time, 94–98
 Eyelets, 2–9
 Flipping Two Coins, 259–262
 How Many Bats in a Cave?, 492–497
 Mass vs. Volume: Proportions and Density, 415–422
 Searching the Forest, 17–23
 Sink and Float, 411–414
 Spreading Out, 131–138
Lattice multiplication, 300–302
Legs (of a right triangle), 462

Length, 103, 455
 measuring, 97, 164–170, 328–329
 of rectangle, 455
Life span, 273–279
Line graph
 see best-fit line
 see point graph
Line segment, 435
 endpoint, **184**
Lowest terms, 369–370

M

Manipulated variable, 133
Map
 reading/making, 343–344
 scale, 329, 344
Mass
 collecting data, 413–422
Math facts
 division, 37–38
 fact families, **36**–37
 Facts I Know, 35–38
  division, 35–38
  multiplication, 35
 multiplication and division facts lesson, 35–38
 Triangle Flash Cards for multiplication and division
  fives, 35–38
  tens, 35–38
Mean, 14, 123–130, **125,** 139
Measurement
 angles, 188, 442
 area, 102–105, 484–485
 area of rectangles and triangles, 103–105, 454–485
 length, 97, 164–170, 328–329
 mass, 411–423
 perimeter, 479–485
 properties of circles, 426–451
 volume, 411–423
 with cylinders, 451
Median, 13–16, 19, 20, 23, 96, 119, 123–130, 139
Meterstick, 95
Miles, 97
Mr. Origin, 327–329
Mixed numbers, 74–76, 150, 376–382
Mode, 6, 9, **12,** 16
Multiple trials, 133
 also see experiment review
Multiplication, 46–63, 299–303
 all-partials method, 53

compact method, 53
decimals, 247–254
estimation with fractions, 388–391
estimation with whole numbers, 56–59, 303
facts, 35
fractions, 383–392
lattice method, 300–302
multiples of ten, 46–55
paper and pencil method, 53, 299–303

Negative numbers, 316–318, 322–331
N-gon, 199
Nonagon, 198
Number lines, 78–84
Numerator, 68, 74, 84, 144, 147
Numerical expression, 128
Numerical variable, 4
   see also variable

Obtuse angle, 185–186
Obtuse triangle, 188, 472–473
Octagon, 198
Ordered pair, 321
Ordering large numbers, 31
Order of operations, 128–129
   parentheses, 128–130
Origin, 319, 321, 327

Pack, 49, 50
   see also base-ten pieces
Parallelogram, 215–216
Partial product, 54
Pattern blocks, 69–72, 152–153, 206–208, 376–382, 387–389
Pentagon, 198
Percent, 223–240, 260–267, 274–280, 286–293, 447–449
Perimeter, 479–485, **480**
Period, 29
Perpendicular lines, 437, 469
Pi (π), 431–432
Pint, 156

Place value, 28, 29, 41–44
   see also base-ten pieces
   abacus, 39–45
   chart, 235, 239
   expanded, standard, and word form, 28–29
   periods, **29**
   reading and writing numerals, 26–34
Plotting points, 330–331
Point graph, 86–92, 93, 97, 98, 134, 356, 416, 430, 491, 495, 497
Polygon, 192, 197–200
   regular, **199**
Populations, 17–23, 26, 31, 34, 492–497
Portfolio, 64–65, 282–283, 498–499
Positive numbers, 316–318
Power, 60
Primes
   factorization, **361**
   numbers, **351,** 352, 353–355
   twin, **355**
Prime factorization, 361
Probability, 21, 23, 256–267, **261**
   certain, **256**
   equally likely, **257**
   impossible, **256**
Problem solving
   coordinates, 329
   division, 297–298, 310–313
   integers, 317–318
   in laboratory experiment, 417, 430–434, 495
   in laboratory investigation, 6–7, 20–23, 97–98, 136–138, 167–170, 261–262, 279
   open ended, 312
   time, 317–318
   in word problems, 24, 45, 57–59, 99, 139–142, 181–182, 218–219, 280–281, 304–309, 310–313, 373, 392–393, 423, 450–451, 458–459, 484
Product, 35
Proper fraction, 74
Proportion, 397–423, 492–497
   variables in, **402**–410
Protractor, 188–189, 436

Quadrant, 319
Quadrilateral, 192, 198, 444
Quart, 92, 156
Quilt, 205–209
Quotient, 37, 108, 296

R

Radius, 426, **435**
Ratio, 85–93, **89,** 97, 98, 138, 141, 165–170, 182,
  280–281, 344, **396**–423, 491, 492–497
  circumference vs. diameter (π), 430–432
Ray, 184
Rectangle, 144, 146, 148, 150, 159, 171–176, 177–181,
  211, 454–457, 458–461
Reflection, see flip
Regular polygon, 199
Remainder, 109–112, **110,** 296, 304–309, 311–312
Repeating decimals, 290
Responding variable, 133
Revolution, 51
Rhombus, 211
Right angle, 185
Right triangle, 188, 462–467
Rotation, 51
Rounding, 32
  decimals, 240–242
  measurements with circles, 428–434
Rubric
  knowing, 501
  solving, 502
  telling, 503

S

Sample, 19, 23, 141
Sampling, 17–23, 141, 489–491, 492–497
Scale drawings, 218–219, **436**–444
Scientific method, see TIMS Laboratory Method
Scientific notation, 61–63
Seconds, 94
Septagon, 198
Shapes, 198, 201–204, 210–219
  circle, **426**–451
    arc, **441**
    center of, **426, 435**
    central angle, **435**
    chord, **435**
    circumference, 426–434, **427, 435**
    concentric circles, **436**
    diameter, 51, 426–434, **427, 435**
    properties of, **427**–451
    radius, 426, **435**
  classification of, 210–217
  congruent, **201**–204

convex, 216–217
decagon, 198
hexagon, 69, 198
parallelogram, 215–216
polygons, **192,** 197–200
  diagonal, 197
  regular, **199**
  triangulating, **197**
quadrilateral, **192,** 198, 444
rectangle, 144, 146, 148, 150, 159, 171–176,
  177–181, **211,** 454–457, 458–461
  length, **455**
  width, **455**
regular polygon, **199**
rhombus, **211**
similar, **201**–204
squares, **211**
triangle, 69, 198, 440–444, 470
  acute, **188, 468**–471
  altitude, **470**
  angles, 194–195
  base, **470**–472
  classification of, 188, 462, 468–473
  height, **470**–472
  hypotenuse, **462**
  legs, **462**
  obtuse, **188, 472**–473
  right, **188, 462**–467
Sides of an angle, 184
Sieve of Eratosthenes, 353, **354**–355
Similar, 201
Similar shapes, 201–204
Skinny, 48, 49
  see also base-ten pieces
Slide, 332–336, **333**
Solar system, 51
Solving rubric, 502
Speed, 94, 97, 98, **165,** 166, 167, 168, 170, 182
Square, 211
Square centimeter, 102
Square numbers, 37, 41, 356–359
Square unit, 146, 147
Standard form, 29, 61
Straight angle, 185–186, **194**
Subtraction
  decimals, 238–246
  fractions, 177–181, 369–371
Surveys, 10, 22
Symmetry
  flip, 337–342

T

Telling rubric, 503
Temperature, 316
Ten percent, 120–122, 136
Tessellation, 205–209, **206**
    Escher drawings, 345
Time, 94–98, 165, 168, 182, 402, 403, 404
TIMS Laboratory Method, 4–7
    see also labs
Transformations
    corresponding parts, **333**
    flip, **337**
    image, **333**
    line of reflection, 337
    reflections, 337–342
    slide, **333**–336
    slides and flips, 345
Translations, see slide
Triangle, 69, 198, 440–444, 470
    acute, **188, 468**–471
    altitude, **470**
    angles, 194–195
    base, **470**–472
    classification of, 188, 462, 468–473
    height, **470**–472
    hypotenuse, **462**
    legs, **462**
    obtuse, **188, 472**–473
    right, **188, 462**–467
Triangle Flash Cards, 35, 37
Triangulating polygons, 197
Twin primes, 355

U

Unit ratio, 165, **399**

V

Values of variables, 3, 22
Variable, 3–7, 18, 22, 48, 54, 96, 135, 164, 168, 199,
    270, 357, 416, 429, 494
    fixed, **96, 133**
    manipulated and responding, **133**
    not proportional, 406–408
    numerical and categorical, **4**
    proportional, **402**–410
Velocity, 165
Vertebrate, 445
Vertex, 184, 207
Volume, 405, 413–422

W

Weight, see mass
Width, 103, 455
    of rectangle, **456**
Word form (of a number), 29–32, 34
Word problem
    sets, 24, 99, 139–141, 182, 265–267, 280–281,
        392–393, 423, 450–451, 484–485

X

Y

Z